GROWING UP

ISSUES FACING
AMERICA'S YOUTH

ISSN 1939-084X

GROWING UP

ISSUES FACING AMERICA'S YOUTH

Barbara Wexler

INFORMATION PLUS® REFERENCE SERIES
Formerly Published by Information Plus, Wylie, Texas

GALE
CENGAGE Learning·

Farmington Hills, Mich • San Francisco • New York • Waterville, Maine
Meriden, Conn • Mason, Ohio • Chicago

GALE
CENGAGE Learning

Growing Up: Issues Affecting America's Youth

Barbara Wexler

Kepos Media, Inc.: Steven Long and Janice Jorgensen, Series Editors

Project Editor: Laura Avery

Rights Acquisition and Management: Ashley Maynard, Carissa Poweleit

Composition: Evi Abou-El-Seoud, Mary Beth Trimper

Manufacturing: Rita Wimberley

Product Design: Kristine Julien

For product information and technology assistance, contact us at **Gale Customer Support, 1-800-877-4253.**
For permission to use material from this text or product, submit all requests online at **www.cengage.com/permissions.**
Further permissions questions can be e-mailed to **permissionrequest@cengage.com**

Cover photograph: © Galina Barskaya/Shutterstock.com.

Gale
27500 Drake Rd.
Farmington Hills, MI 48331-3535

ISBN-13: 978-0-7876-5103-9 (set)
ISBN-13: 978-1-4103-2552-5

ISSN 1939-084X

This title is also available as an e-book.
ISBN-13: 978-1-4103-3268-4 (set)
Contact your Gale sales representative for ordering information.

Printed in the United States of America
1 2 3 4 5   21 20 19 18 17

TABLE OF CONTENTS

PREFACE

Growing Up: Issues Affecting America's Youth is part of the *Information Plus Reference Series*. The purpose of each volume of the series is to present the latest facts on a topic of pressing concern in modern American life. These topics include the most controversial and studied social issues of the 21st century: abortion, animal rights, capital punishment, crime, the environment, health care, immigration, national security, race and ethnicity, water, women, and many more. Although this series is written especially for high school and undergraduate students, it is an excellent resource for anyone in need of factual information on current affairs.

By presenting the facts, it is the intention of Gale, a Cengage Company, to provide its readers with everything they need to reach an informed opinion on current issues. To that end, there is a particular emphasis in this series on the presentation of scientific studies, surveys, and statistics. These data are generally presented in the form of tables, charts, and other graphics placed within the text of each book. Every graphic is directly referred to and carefully explained in the text. The source of each graphic is presented within the graphic itself. The data used in these graphics are drawn from the most reputable and reliable sources, such as from various branches of the U.S. government and from private organizations and associations. Every effort was made to secure the most recent information available. Readers should bear in mind that many major studies take years to conduct and that additional years often pass before the data from these studies are made available to the public. Therefore, in many cases the most recent information available in 2017 is dated from 2014 or 2015. Older statistics are sometimes presented as well, if they are landmark studies or of particular interest and no more-recent information exists.

Although statistics are a major focus of the *Information Plus Reference Series*, they are by no means its only content. Each book also presents the widely held positions and important ideas that shape how the book's subject is discussed in the United States. These positions are explained in detail and, where possible, in the words of their proponents. Some of the other material to be found in these books includes historical background, descriptions of major events related to the subject, relevant laws and court cases, and examples of how these issues play out in American life. Some books also feature primary documents or have pro and con debate sections that provide the words and opinions of prominent Americans on both sides of a controversial topic. All material is presented in an evenhanded and unbiased manner; readers will never be encouraged to accept one view of an issue over another.

HOW TO USE THIS BOOK

Childhood and adolescence are perhaps the most critical periods in any person's life. The education one receives during this time; the environment one is raised in; and the way one is treated by family, friends, and the larger community can have lifelong impacts and consequences. This volume addresses various factors that affect youth, including family income, who cares for children, health and safety issues, educational attainment, and teen sexuality and pregnancy. It also describes crime, violence, and victimization, including gang and school violence, as well as crime prevention and punishment.

Growing Up: Issues Affecting America's Youth consists of 10 chapters and three appendixes. Each chapter is devoted to a particular aspect of youth in the United States. For a summary of the information that is covered in each chapter, please see the synopses that are provided in the Table of Contents. Chapters generally begin with an overview of the basic facts and background information on the chapter's topic, then proceed to examine subtopics of particular interest. For example, Chapter 6: Getting an Education begins with a discussion of education reform principles and the effect of the No Child Left Behind Act and Common Core state standards (CCSS) on academic achievement. It then considers the arguments presented by CCSS supporters and critics. Next, it describes how looking at changes in test scores over time is one way to gauge the performance of the education system. It presents the school voucher controversy and a public-school choice program that enabled parents of students enrolled in failing schools to move their children to better-performing public or charter schools. The chapter also provides enrollment and cost data, and concludes with an examination of the relationship between educational attainment and future earnings. Readers can find their way through a chapter by looking for the section and subsection headings, which are clearly set off from the text. They can also refer to the book's extensive Index, if they already know what they are looking for.

Statistical Information

The tables and figures featured throughout *Growing Up: Issues Affecting America's Youth* will be of particular use to readers in learning about this topic. These tables and figures represent an extensive collection of the most recent and valuable statistics on growing up in the United States, as well as related issues—for example, graphics cover the characteristics of children who are adopted, the cost of raising a child from birth to age 18, the proportion of children who have received vaccinations, and the methods used to advertise e-cigarettes to youth. Gale, a Cengage Company, believes that making this information available to readers is the most important way to fulfill the goal of this book: to help readers understand the issues and controversies surrounding youth in the United States and reach their own conclusions.

Each table or figure has a unique identifier appearing above it for ease of identification and reference. Titles for the tables and figures explain their purpose. At the end of each table or figure, the original source of the data is provided.

To help readers understand these often complicated statistics, all tables and figures are explained in the text. References in the text direct readers to the relevant statistics. Furthermore, the contents of all tables and figures are fully indexed. Please see the opening section of the Index at the back of this volume for a description of how to find tables and figures within it.

Appendixes

Besides the main body text and images, *Growing Up: Issues Affecting America's Youth* has three appendixes. The first is the Important Names and Addresses directory. Here, readers will find contact information for a number of organizations that study children, adolescents, and families. The second appendix is the Resources section, which can also assist readers in conducting their own research. In this section, the author and editors of *Growing Up: Issues Affecting America's Youth* describe some of the sources that were most useful during the compilation of this book. The final appendix is the Index. It has been greatly expanded from previous editions and should make it even easier to find specific topics in this book.

COMMENTS AND SUGGESTIONS

The editors of the *Information Plus Reference Series* welcome your feedback on *Growing Up: Issues Affecting America's Youth*. Please direct all correspondence to:

Editors
Information Plus Reference Series
Gale, a Cengage Company
27500 Drake Rd.
Farmington Hills, MI 48331-3535

CHAPTER 1
CHILDREN AND FAMILIES IN THE UNITED STATES

DEFINING CHILDHOOD AND ADULTHOOD

Exactly when childhood ends and adulthood begins differs among cultures and over time. People in some societies believe adulthood begins with the onset of puberty, arguing that people who are old enough to have children are also old enough to assume adult responsibilities. This stage of life is often solemnized with special celebrations. For example, historically, Native Americans had a rite of passage known as a vision quest, during which older children spent a few days alone in the wilderness to get in touch with the spirit world and envision their paths to adulthood. In the Jewish tradition, bar and bat mitzvah ceremonies for 13-year-old boys and girls commemorate the attainment of adult responsibility for observing Jewish law. Other rites of passage include high school and college graduation, obtaining a driver's license, and marriage.

Modern American society identifies an interim period of life between childhood and adulthood known as adolescence, during which teens reach a series of milestones as they accept increasing amounts of adult responsibility. At age 16 most Americans can be licensed to drive. At age 18 most young people have graduated from high school and are eligible to vote. They can join the military without parental permission and are tried as adults for all crimes in all states (although some states try younger people as adults, and in serious offenses such as murder, rape, or armed robbery, juveniles are sometimes tried as adults). There are contradictions in the rights and privileges conferred, however. In many states teens under the age of 18 years can marry but cannot legally purchase alcohol, gamble, or access pornographic material.

In general, American society recognizes 21 years as the age of full adulthood. At age 21 young people are considered legally independent of their parents and are completely responsible for their own decisions. At 21 years old, they can buy, carry, and consume alcoholic beverages in every state.

According to the Federal Interagency Forum on Child and Family Statistics (known as the Forum), in *America's Children in Brief: Key National Indicators of Well-Being, 2016* (2016, https://www.childstats.gov/americaschildren/tables.asp), in 2016, 73.7 million children younger than the age of 18 years lived in the United States. This number is expected to increase to 79.9 million by 2050. The percentage of children in the population is projected to remain relatively stable, decreasing 2.6 percentage points, from 22.7% in 2016 to 20.1% by 2050.

BIRTH AND FERTILITY RATES

Fertility is measured in several ways. One measure is the birth rate: the number of live births per 1,000 women in the population, regardless of their age, in any given year. In 2014 the birth rate in the United States was 12.5 live births per 1,000 women. Another way to measure the number of births is the fertility rate, which is the number of live births per 1,000 women in the population between the ages of 15 and 44 years in any given year. These are the years generally considered to be a woman's reproductive age range. In "Quarterly Provisional Estimates for Selected Birth Indicators, 2014—Quarter 2, 2016" (*National Vital Statistics Rapid Release: Quarterly Provisional Estimates*, November 22, 2016), Lauren M. Rossen et al. of the Centers for Disease Control and Prevention (CDC) report that the fertility rate for American women during the second quarter of 2016 was 62.3 births per 1,000 women, the lowest rate ever reported in the United States. (See Figure 1.1.)

Projected Birth Trends

The U.S. Census Bureau states in *Methodology and Assumptions for the 2014 National Projections* (December 2014, https://www.census.gov/population/projections/files/methodology/methodstatement14.pdf) that fertility rates among racial and ethnic groups are expected to differ markedly throughout the 21st century. The total

FIGURE 1.1

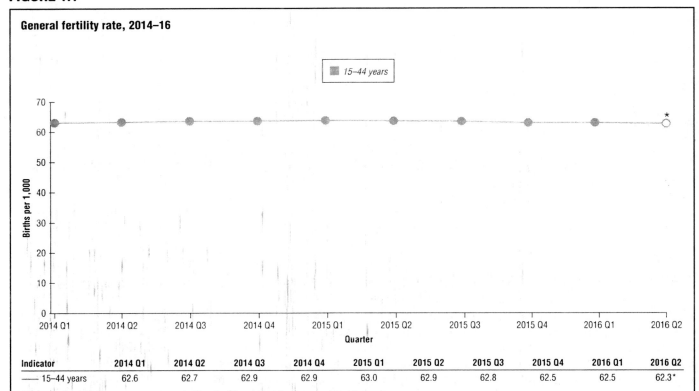

General fertility rate, 2014–16

Births per 1,000

Indicator	2014 Q1	2014 Q2	2014 Q3	2014 Q4	2015 Q1	2015 Q2	2015 Q3	2015 Q4	2016 Q1	2016 Q2
—— 15–44 years	62.6	62.7	62.9	62.9	63.0	62.9	62.8	62.5	62.5	62.3*

*Estimates for the most recent quarter are significantly different from the same quarter of the previous year.
Notes: The general fertility rate refers to the total number of births per 1,000 women aged 15–44. Rates for "12 months ending with quarter" (also called moving average rate) are the average rates for the 12 months that end with the quarter on the horizontal (time) axis. Estimates for the 12-month period ending with a specific quarter include all seasons of the year and, thus, are insensitive to seasonality.

SOURCE: Lauren M. Rossen et al., "12 Month-Ending General Fertility Rate: United States, 2014–Quarter 2, 2016," in *Quarterly Provisional Estimates for Selected Birth Indicators, 2014–Quarter 2, 2016*, National Center for Health Statistics. National Vital Statistics System, Vital Statistics Rapid Release Program, 2016, https://www.cdc.gov/nchs/products/vsrr/natality-dashboard.htm#trends (accessed December 20, 2016)

fertility rate refers to the average number of children a woman will give birth to during her lifetime. The population replacement level (the total fertility rate needed to keep a population stable) is 2.1, or 2,100 births per 1,000 women. In 2014 the total fertility rate (1.9), as well as the rates for foreign- and native-born Asian Americans and Pacific Islanders (1.8 and 1.2, respectively) were below the replacement level. (See Table 1.1.) However, the rate for foreign-born Hispanics (3.1) and foreign-born non-Hispanics (2.5) were well above replacement level. The total fertility rate of non-Hispanic whites is expected to remain steady through 2060. The total fertility rate for native-born Asian Americans and Pacific Islanders is projected to increase from 1.2 in 2014 to 1.6 in 2060. By contrast, the fertility rate for foreign-born Hispanics is projected to decline steadily from 3.1 in 2014 to 2.4 in 2060 but will remain above the replacement level throughout the projected period.

Because of these different fertility rates, the proportion of Americans who are non-Hispanic white is expected to decrease from 62.2% in 2014 to 43.6% in 2060. (See Figure 1.2.) Meanwhile, the proportion of the population that is Hispanic is expected to increase from 17.4% in 2014 to 28.6% in 2060. The percentage of non-Hispanic

African Americans is expected to increase slightly, from 12.4% in 2014 to 13% in 2060. The percentage of non-Hispanic Asian Americans will grow from 5.2% in 2014 to 9.1% in 2060. The proportion of non-Hispanic Native Americans and Alaskan Natives will remain constant as will that of non-Hispanic Native Hawaiians and other Pacific Islanders.

According to the Forum, in *America's Children in Brief*, children made up 22.9% of the population in 2015. This percentage is expected to decrease by 2.8 percentage points by 2050; however, the child population is projected to grow more racially and ethnically diverse. Figure 1.3 compares the racial and ethnic distribution of children in the United States from 1980 to 2015 with the distribution projected from 2016 to 2050. In 2015, 51.5% of all children were non-Hispanic white. By 2020 fewer than half of all children are projected to be non-Hispanic white, and by 2050 the gap between the percentages of Hispanic (31.9%) and non-Hispanic white (38.8%) children will be more narrow.

Evidence also suggests that racial and ethnic lines became less rigid in the United States during the last two

TABLE 1.1

Total fertility rates by race and Hispanic origin, 2014–60

Year	Total	Hispanic	Foreign born			Native born	
			Non-Hispanic API	Non-Hispanic other races		API	Other
2014	1.87	3.11	1.82	2.48		1.19	1.75
2015	1.87	3.09	1.82	2.48		1.20	1.75
2016	1.87	3.08	1.82	2.47		1.20	1.75
2017	1.87	3.06	1.82	2.46		1.21	1.75
2018	1.87	3.05	1.82	2.45		1.22	1.75
2019	1.87	3.04	1.82	2.45		1.23	1.75
2020	1.87	3.02	1.82	2.44		1.24	1.76
2021	1.87	3.01	1.82	2.43		1.24	1.76
2022	1.87	2.99	1.82	2.43		1.25	1.76
2023	1.87	2.98	1.82	2.42		1.26	1.76
2024	1.87	2.96	1.82	2.41		1.27	1.76
2025	1.87	2.95	1.82	2.40		1.27	1.76
2026	1.87	2.93	1.83	2.40		1.28	1.76
2027	1.87	2.92	1.83	2.39		1.29	1.77
2028	1.87	2.90	1.83	2.38		1.30	1.77
2029	1.87	2.89	1.83	2.37		1.31	1.77
2030	1.87	2.88	1.83	2.37		1.31	1.77
2031	1.86	2.86	1.83	2.36		1.32	1.77
2032	1.86	2.85	1.83	2.35		1.33	1.77
2033	1.86	2.83	1.83	2.35		1.34	1.77
2034	1.86	2.82	1.83	2.34		1.34	1.77
2035	1.86	2.80	1.83	2.33		1.35	1.78
2036	1.86	2.79	1.83	2.32		1.36	1.78
2037	1.86	2.77	1.83	2.32		1.37	1.78
2038	1.86	2.76	1.83	2.31		1.38	1.78
2039	1.86	2.74	1.83	2.30		1.38	1.78
2040	1.86	2.73	1.83	2.29		1.39	1.78
2041	1.86	2.72	1.83	2.29		1.40	1.78
2042	1.86	2.70	1.83	2.28		1.41	1.78
2043	1.86	2.69	1.83	2.27		1.41	1.79
2044	1.86	2.67	1.83	2.27		1.42	1.79
2045	1.86	2.66	1.83	2.26		1.43	1.79
2046	1.86	2.64	1.83	2.25		1.44	1.79
2047	1.86	2.63	1.83	2.24		1.45	1.79
2048	1.86	2.61	1.84	2.24		1.45	1.79
2049	1.86	2.60	1.84	2.23		1.46	1.79
2050	1.86	2.59	1.84	2.22		1.47	1.79
2051	1.86	2.57	1.84	2.22		1.48	1.80
2052	1.86	2.56	1.84	2.21		1.48	1.80
2053	1.86	2.54	1.84	2.20		1.49	1.80
2054	1.86	2.53	1.84	2.19		1.50	1.80
2055	1.86	2.51	1.84	2.19		1.51	1.80
2056	1.86	2.50	1.84	2.18		1.52	1.80
2057	1.86	2.48	1.84	2.17		1.52	1.80
2058	1.86	2.47	1.84	2.16		1.53	1.80
2059	1.86	2.45	1.84	2.16		1.54	1.81
2060	1.86	2.44	1.84	2.15		1.55	1.81

API = Asian and Pacific Islander

SOURCE: "Table 1. Total Fertility Rates by Race and Hispanic Origin: 2014 to 2060," in *Methodology, Assumptions, and Inputs for the 2014 National Projections*, U.S. Census Bureau, December 2014, https://www.census.gov/population/projections/files/methodology/methodstatement14.pdf (accessed December 20, 2016)

decades of the 20th century, as people from different ethnic and racial backgrounds parented children together. In *America's Children in Brief*, the Forum finds that growing numbers of children identify with more than one race and/or ethnicity. The percentage of children that identifies with two or more races rose from 2.5% in 2000 to 5.2% in 2015 and is projected to grow to 10% by 2050, so it is not surprising that children identify with more than one race and/or ethnicity more often than adults do.

Birth Rates Decline to Record Low

Madison Park explains in "US Fertility Rate Falls to Lowest on Record" (CNN.com, August 11, 2016) that the record low U.S. birth rate is in part attributable to declining birth rates of teens and women in their early 20s. According to Brady E. Hamilton and T. J. Mathews of the CDC, in *Continued Declines in Teen Births in the United States, 2015* (September 2016, https://www.cdc.gov/nchs/data/databriefs/db259.pdf), births among teens aged 15 to 19 years (22.3 births per 1,000) fell to a record low. Figure 1.4 shows the declining birth rate among teens and the increase in births to women aged 40 to 44 years between 1990 and 2015. The Central Intelligence Agency indicates in *The World Factbook* (2016, https://www.cia.gov/library/publications/the-world-factbook/rankorder/2127rank.html) that the United States has a lower

FIGURE 1.2

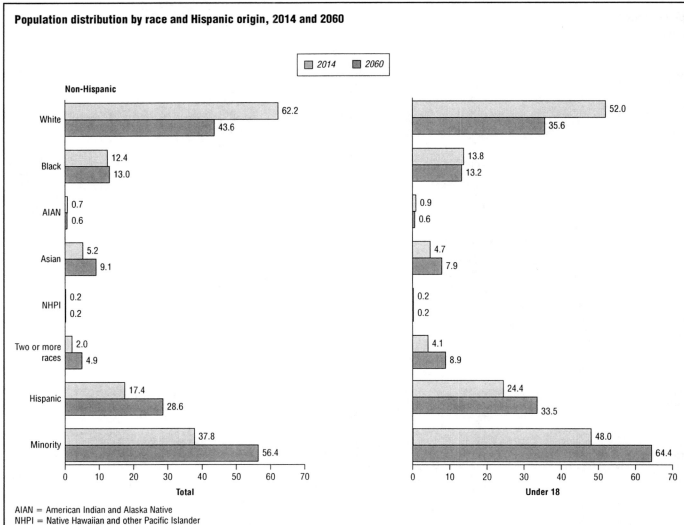

Population distribution by race and Hispanic origin, 2014 and 2060

AIAN = American Indian and Alaska Native
NHPI = Native Hawaiian and other Pacific Islander
Notes: The percentages for the total population or the population under 18 may not add to 100.00 due to rounding. Unless otherwise specified, race categories represent race alone. Minority refers to everyone other than the non-Hispanic white alone population.

SOURCE: Sandra L. Colby and Jennifer M. Ortman, "Figure 8. Distribution of the Population by Race and Hispanic Origin for the Total Population and Population under 18: 2014 and 2060," in *Projections of the Size and Composition of the U.S. Population: 2014 to 2060*, U.S. Census Bureau, March 2015, http://www.census.gov/content/dam/Census/library/publications/2015/demo/p25-1143.pdf (accessed December 20, 2016)

fertility rate (1.9) than France (2.1), Israel (2.7), and New Zealand (2) but has a higher fertility rate than Australia (1.8), China (1.6), Russia (1.6), and Japan (1.4).

In "Why Is the Teen Birth Rate Falling?" (April 29, 2016, http://www.pewresearch.org/fact-tank/2014/04/21/why-is-the-teen-birth-rate-falling/), Eileen Patten and Gretchen Livingston of the Pew Research Center explain that the teen birth rate has declined since its 1990 peak, with the steepest drop during and following the Great Recession (late 2007 to mid-2009). Pew analysis not only attributes this decline to a weak economy but also to the fact that teens are reporting less sexual activity and, among those who are sexually active, increasing use of contraception.

Although the teen birth rate is decreasing, this decline is uneven, and racial and ethnic disparities persist. For

example, the teen birth rates for Hispanic, non-Hispanic African American, and Native American or Alaskan Native teens remain higher than the rates for non-Hispanic white and Asian or Pacific Islander teens. (See Figure 1.5.)

THE CHANGING FAMILY

Family and Household Size

The composition of households in American society changed markedly during the 20th century. Frank Hobbs and Nicole Stoops of the Census Bureau indicate in *Demographic Trends in the 20th Century* (November 2002, https://www.census.gov/prod/2002pubs/censr-4.pdf) that in 1950 families accounted for 89.4% of all households; by 2000 this number had decreased to 68.1%. The proportion of married-couple households that included at

FIGURE 1.3

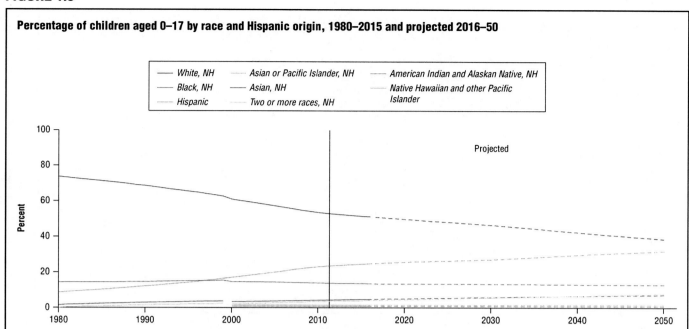

Percentage of children aged 0–17 by race and Hispanic origin, 1980–2015 and projected 2016–50

Note: The abbreviation NH refers to non-Hispanic origin. Each group represents the non-Hispanic population, with the exception of the Hispanic category itself. People of Hispanic origin may be of any race. Data on race and Hispanic origin are collected separately. Race data from 2000 onward are not directly comparable with data from earlier years.

SOURCE: "Figure 1. Percentage of U.S. Children Ages 0–17 by Race and Hispanic Origin, 1980–2015 and Projected 2016–2050," in *America's Children in Brief: Key National Indicators of Well-Being, 2016*, Federal Interagency Forum on Child and Family Statistics, July 2016, http://www.childstats.gov/pdf/ac2016/ac_16.pdf (accessed December 21, 2016)

FIGURE 1.4

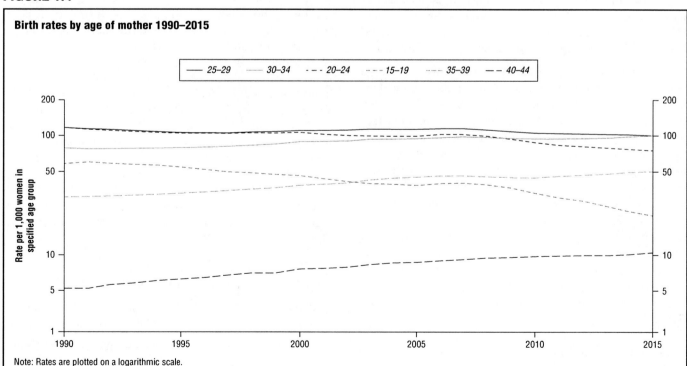

Birth rates by age of mother 1990–2015

Note: Rates are plotted on a logarithmic scale.

SOURCE: Brady E. Hamilton, Joyce A. Martin, and Michelle J. K. Osterman, "Figure 4. Birth Rates, by Selected Age of Mother: United States, Final 1990–2014 and Preliminary 2015," in "Births: Preliminary Data for 2015," *National Vital Statistics Reports*, vol. 65, no. 3, June 2, 2016, https://www.cdc.gov/nchs/data/nvsr/nvsr65/NVSR65_03.pdf (accessed December 21, 2016)

FIGURE 1.5

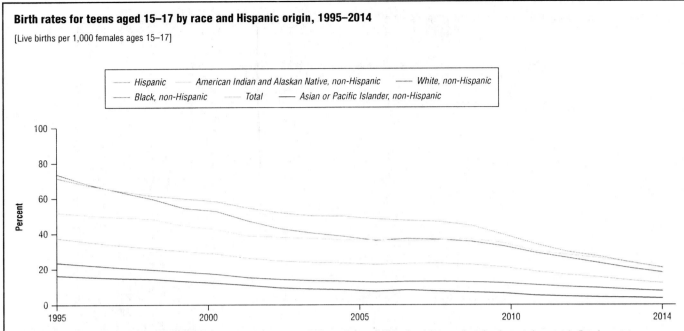

Birth rates for teens aged 15–17 by race and Hispanic origin, 1995–2014

[Live births per 1,000 females ages 15–17]

Note: Race refers to mother's race. Persons of Hispanic origin may be of any race. Data on race and Hispanic origin are collected and reported separately. Data from states reporting multiple races were bridged to the single-race categories of the 1977 Office of Management and Budget Standards on Race and Ethnicity for comparability with other states.

SOURCE: "Figure 3. Birth Rates for Females Ages 15–17 by Race and Hispanic Origin of Mother, 1995–2014," in *America's Children in Brief: Key National Indicators of Well-Being, 2016*, Federal Interagency Forum on Child and Family Statistics, July 2016, http://www.childstats.gov/pdf/ac2016/ac_16.pdf (accessed December 21, 2016)

least one child under the age of 18 years had also decreased from 59.3% in 1960 to 45.6% in 2000. According to the Forum, in *America's Children in Brief*, in 1980, 77% of all children lived in families headed by married couples; this percentage had dropped to 64.7% by 2015.

The American family shrank in size during the 20th century and continued to grow smaller during the first decade of the 21st century. According to Hobbs and Stoops, in 1900, 44.7% of all households contained five or more people, making this the most common type of household. According to the Census Bureau, in *Families and Living Arrangements, Historical Time Series: Households* (2016, http://www.census.gov/hhes/families/data/households.html), by 1960 two-parent households became the most common type and remained so through 2016. The proportion of one-parent households increased between 1960 and 2016, with mother-only households growing to about 22%. (See Figure 1.6.) In 2016 higher percentages of African American and Hispanic children lived with just their mother than did white children. (See Figure 1.7.)

Fewer Traditional Families

One of the significant social changes to occur at the close of the 20th century was a shift away from the traditional family structure of a married couple with their own child or children living in the home. This change continued into the second decade of the 21st century. The Census Bureau divides households into two major categories: family households (defined as groups of two or more people living together related by birth, marriage, or adoption) and nonfamily households (consisting of a person living alone or an individual living with others to whom he or she is not related). As a percentage of all households, family households declined between 2000 and 2016. According to the Census Bureau, in 2000, 71.8 million (68.1%) out of 105.5 million total U.S. households were family households. In *America's Families and Living Arrangements* (2016, https://www.census.gov/hhes/families/data/cps2016.html), the Census Bureau reports that in 2016, 82.2 million (66%) out of the total 125.3 million households were family households. In contrast, the number of nonfamily households increased from 33.7 million (31.9%) in 2000 to 43.6 million (35%) in 2016.

The rise in nonfamily households is the result of many factors, some of the most prominent being:

- People are postponing marriage until later in life and are thus living alone or with nonrelatives for a longer period.

- A rising divorce rate translates into more people living alone or with nonrelatives.

- A rise in the number of people who cohabit before or instead of marriage results in higher numbers of nonfamily households.

FIGURE 1.6

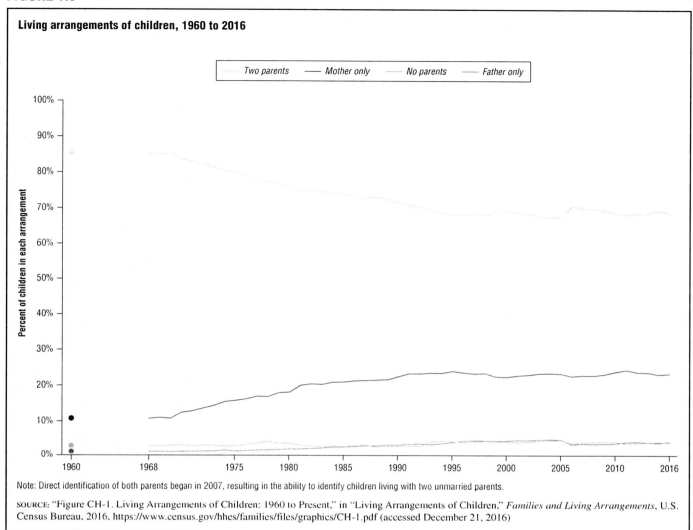

Living arrangements of children, 1960 to 2016

Note: Direct identification of both parents began in 2007, resulting in the ability to identify children living with two unmarried parents.

SOURCE: "Figure CH-1. Living Arrangements of Children: 1960 to Present," in "Living Arrangements of Children," *Families and Living Arrangements*, U.S. Census Bureau, 2016, https://www.census.gov/hhes/families/files/graphics/CH-1.pdf (accessed December 21, 2016)

- The oldest members of the U.S. population are living longer and often live in nonfamily households as widows/widowers.

Although the proportion of family households is shrinking, in 2016 they remained the majority of households. However, in 2016 just half of all households were husband-wife households. The categories of "female householder with other family" and "male householder with other family" include single parents and other types of family households where the head of the household is not married. These two types of families both grew between 1990 and 2016. The two types of nonfamily households tracked by the Census Bureau (people living alone and unrelated people who live together, including unmarried opposite-sex and same-sex couples) also grew during this period.

Children with Stay-at-Home Parents

The Census Bureau compiles in *America's Families and Living Arrangements* data about stay-at-home family groups, which are married-couple families with children in which one parent is in the labor force and the other parent is not in the labor force but is instead "taking care of home and family." The number of families with stay-at-home mothers rose from 4.5 million in 1994 (19.8% of families) to 5.6 million (24.3%) in 2006. From 2007 through 2010 the number of families with stay-at-home mothers declined both in absolute terms and as a share of family groups. The period of decline may have been a response to the Great Recession, which prompted some mothers to enter or reenter the workforce. The number of families with stay-at-home mothers began to rise again in 2011, and by 2016, 5 million (23%) family groups with children had a stay-at-home mother. From 1994 to 2016 the number of families with stay-at-home fathers grew from 76,000 (0.3%) family groups with children in 1994 to 209,000 (1%) in 2016.

In "Most of the Recession's Stay-at-Home Dads Are Going Back to Work" (WSJ.com, April 22, 2016), Ben Leubsdorf reports that although the percentage of stay-at-home fathers rose to 7.4% in 2009 and 2010, by 2015 the

FIGURE 1.7

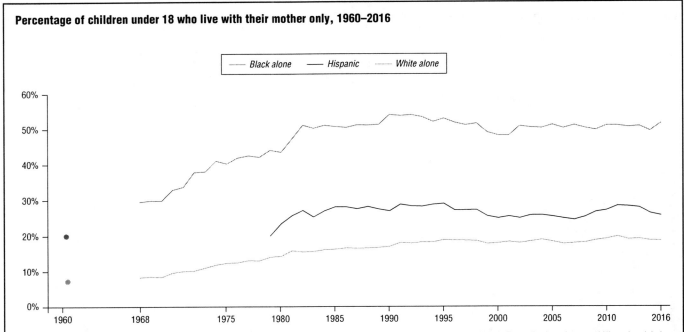

Percentage of children under 18 who live with their mother only, 1960–2016

Note: Direct identification of both parents began in 2007, resulting in the ability to identify children living with two unmarried parents. The collection of race and Hispanic origin has changed over time. Before 2003 respondents had to select a single race. People of Hispanic origin may be of any race.

SOURCE: "Figure CH-2.3.4. Percent of Children under 18 Who Live with Their Mother Only," in "Living Arrangements of Children," *Families and Living Arrangements*, U.S. Census Bureau, 2016, https://www.census.gov/hhes/families/files/graphics/CH-2-3-4.pdf (accessed December 21, 2016)

proportions had returned to its prerecession rate of 5.3%. By contrast, among married couples with children, 31% of mothers did not work outside the home in 2015, a 2% increase from 1995.

One- and Two-Parent Families

In 1990 there were 24.9 million two-parent families, accounting for 72% of all family groups with children under the age of 18 years; in 2016 there were 24.6 million two-parent families with children, but their percentage decreased to 69% of households with children. Although most households with children still had two parents, the decline in the percentage of children being raised in two-parent households has been the subject of much study and attention. Table 1.2 shows the makeup of family groups in the United States as of 2016.

The Census Bureau reports in *America's Families and Living Arrangements* that in 2016, 11.8 million (32%) of the 36.5 million families with children under the age of 18 years were maintained by a single parent. Mothers maintained 9.8 million families with children, whereas fathers alone maintained 2 million; mothers headed families alone nearly five times as often as fathers did. (See Table 1.2.)

The proportion of families headed by a single parent increased between 1990 and 2016 in response to changes in American lifestyles and values. Among these changes is a high divorce rate. The Census Bureau notes that in

2016, 25.5 million (9.9%) out of 257.6 million Americans aged 15 years and older were divorced and had not remarried. The number of divorced individuals in 2016 was nearly six times the number of divorced individuals in 1970. That year only 4.3 million (2.9%) out of 148.3 million Americans aged 15 years and older had divorced and not remarried.

Another reason for the rise in the number of single-parent family households is the dramatic increase in the number of births to unmarried women. In "Births: Final Data for 2014" (December 23, 2015, https://www.cdc.gov/nchs/data/nvsr/nvsr64/nvsr64_12.pdf), Brady E. Hamilton et al. of the CDC report that 40.2% of births in 2014 were to unmarried women. (See Table 1.3.) The rate of births to unmarried women in 2014 was the lowest since 2002.

LIVING ARRANGEMENTS OF CHILDREN
Single-Parent Families

Many children who live in single-parent households face significant challenges that can be exacerbated by racial and ethnic inequalities. According to the Forum, in *America's Children in Brief*, the poverty rate for non-Hispanic African American children in 2014 was 37.3%, and for Hispanic children it was 31.9%, but for non-Hispanic white children it was only 12.3%. (See Table 1.4.)

Children who lived in minority families with a single parent were especially likely to have greatly reduced

TABLE 1.2

Family groups, 2016

[Numbers in thousands, except for percentages]

		Race of family reference person					
	Total	White alone	White alone, non-Hispanic	Black alone	Asian alone	All other single races and combinations	Hispanic (any race)
Total	**87,209**	**68,702**	**55,800**	**10,626**	**5,192**	**2,688**	**14,383**
Number							
Married couples	62,628	52,249	44,185	4,618	4,258	1,504	8,796
With children under 18	24,638	19,899	15,398	1,877	2,103	758	4,964
Without children under 18	37,990	32,349	28,787	2,740	2,155	746	3,831
Unmarried parent couple[a]	1,824	1,373	824	282	56	112	611
Mother only with child(ren) under 18[b]	9,781	6,019	4,090	3,007	217	537	2,321
Father only with child(ren) under 18[b]	2,033	1,588	1,203	301	56	88	423
Householder and other relative(s)[c]	10,942	7,472	5,497	2,419	605	446	2,232
Grandparent householder with grandchild(ren) under 18	1,214	794	552	315	35	70	274
Householder with adult child(ren)	5,959	4,215	3,340	1,329	205	210	982
Householder with young adult child age 18–24	2,350	1,631	1,230	544	82	93	451
Householder with parent	2,750	1,820	1,094	513	290	127	819
Percent	**100.0**	**100.0**	**100.0**	**100.0**	**100.0**	**100.0**	**100.0**
Married couples	71.8	76.1	79.2	43.6	82.0	56.0	61.2
With children under 18	28.3	29.0	27.6	17.7	40.5	28.2	34.5
Without children under 18	43.6	47.1	51.6	25.8	41.5	27.8	26.6
Unmarried parent couple[a]	2.1	2.0	1.5	2.7	1.1	4.2	4.2
Mother only with child(ren) under 18[b]	11.2	8.8	7.3	28.3	4.2	20.0	16.1
Father only with child(ren) under 18[b]	2.3	2.3	2.2	2.8	1.1	3.3	2.9
Householder and other relative(s)[c]	12.5	10.9	9.9	22.8	11.7	16.6	15.5
Grandparent householder with grandchild(ren) under 18	1.4	1.2	1.0	3.0	0.7	2.6	1.9
Householder with adult child(ren)	6.8	6.1	6.0	12.5	3.9	7.8	6.8
Householder with young adult child age 18–24	2.7	2.4	2.2	5.1	1.6	3.5	3.1
Householder with parent	3.2	2.6	2.0	4.8	5.6	4.7	5.7

[a]These couples have at least one joint never married child under 18.
[b]Parent may have a cohabiting partner, but none of their children are also identified as the child of their cohabiting partner.
[c]Sub-categories of "householder and other relative" are not mutually exclusive.

SOURCE: "Table FG10. Family Groups: 2016," in *Families and Living Arrangements*, U.S. Census Bureau, 2016, https://www.census.gov/hhes/families/data/cps2016FG.html (accessed December 27, 2016).

economic, educational, and social opportunities. Single parents were more likely to have a low income and less education and were more likely to be unemployed and to be renting a home or apartment or living in public housing. For children living in female-householder families, the poverty rate was 46.4% in 2014, up more than three percentage points from 2007. (See Table 1.4.) The poverty rate was 6.9 percentage points higher for non-Hispanic African American children in female-householder families (52.9%) and even higher for Hispanic children in female-householder families (53.3%), compared with 35.7% for non-Hispanic white children. By contrast, in 2014 about 11% of children living with married parents lived below the poverty level.

Nontraditional Families

Many single-parent families, however, are not single adult families; some single parents maintain a household with an unmarried partner. In 1990 the Census Bureau sought to reflect changing household composition in the United States by asking for the first time whether unmarried couples maintained households together. In 2000 married couples headed a slight majority (51.7%) of U.S. households; however, nearly 5.5 million unmarried couples (5.2% of all households) also maintained households together. By 2016, 8.1 million unmarried couples cohabited in the United States, as reported by the Census Bureau in *Families and Living Arrangements*, and 3 million lived with at least one biological child of either partner. In 2014, 1.4% of households consisted of an unmarried same-sex couple, and 17.3% of these households had children. Table 1.5 shows the percentages of unmarried opposite- and same-sex couples with biological, step-, or adopted children.

CHARACTERISTICS OF OPPOSITE-SEX UNMARRIED COUPLES. Table 1.6 provides information on families composed of opposite-sex unmarried couples with at least one biological child of either partner in 2016. Most of the members (70.2%) of these couples were aged 39 years or younger. In nearly three out of 10 (27.9%) opposite-sex unmarried couples, the age difference between the male

TABLE 1.3

Births and birth rates for unmarried and married women, 1980, 1985, 1990, 1995, and 2000–14

Year	Births to unmarried women			Birth rate for married women[c]
	Number	Rate[a]	Percent[b]	
2014	1,604,870	43.9	40.2	88.9
2013	1,595,873	44.3	40.6	86.9
2012	1,609,619	45.3	40.7	86.0
2011	1,607,773	46.0	40.7	85.1
2010	1,633,471	47.5	40.8	84.3
2009	1,693,658	49.9	41.0	85.6
2008	1,726,566	51.8	40.6	86.9
2007	1,715,047	51.8	39.7	89.1
2006	1,641,946	50.3	38.5	88.7
2005	1,527,034	47.2	36.9	87.9
2004	1,470,189	46.0	35.8	88.1
2003	1,415,995	44.7	34.6	88.4
2002	1,365,966	43.6	34.0	86.9
2001	1,349,249	43.7	33.5	86.6
2000	1,347,043	44.1	33.2	87.4
1995	1,253,976	44.3	32.2	82.6
1990	1,165,384	43.8	28.0	93.2
1985	828,174	32.8	22.0	93.3
1980	665,747	29.4	18.4	97.0

[a]Births to unmarried women per 1,000 unmarried women aged 15–44.
[b]Percentage of all births to unmarried women.
[c]Births to married women per 1,000 married women aged 15–44.
Note: Rates for 2001–2009 have been revised, using revised intercensal population estimates based on the 2010 census.

SOURCE: Brady E. Hamilton et al., "Table B. Births and Birth Rates for Unmarried and Married Women: United States, 1980, 1985, 1990, 1995, and 2000–2014," in "Births: Final Data for 2014," *National Vital Statistics Reports*, vol. 64, no. 12, December 23, 2015, https://www.cdc.gov/nchs/data/nvsr/nvsr64/nvsr64_12.pdf (accessed December 27, 2016)

and female partners was one year or less; in another 25.2% of couples the age difference was two to three years. In most of the couples in 2016, the partners were of the same race and ethnicity. Both partners were in the labor force and employed in 60% of these couples. More than one-third (37.2%) of the male partners and nearly half (48.6%) of the female partners had attended college or earned a college degree. On average, male partners' earnings outpaced female partners' earnings, with 28.7% of males earning between $10,000 and $29,999 more than their female partner. An additional 12.8% earned between $30,000 and $49,999 more than their partner, and 11.5% of males earned in excess of $50,000 more than their female partner.

Grandparents

Increasingly, grandparents provide housing for, or reside in, the homes of their children and grandchildren. In *Coresident Grandparents and Their Grandchildren: 2012* (October 2014, https://www.census.gov/content/dam/Census/library/publications/2014/demo/p20-576.pdf), the most recent report that was available as of March 2017, Renee R. Ellis and Tavia Simmons analyze census data about the 4.2 million households in which grandparents and children lived together in 2012. Ellis and

Simmons observe that about 10% of all children live with a grandparent. In 1970, 3% of children lived in homes maintained by their grandparents; by 2012 the proportion had doubled to 6%. Between 1970 and 1990 the greatest increases in grandparent-maintained households were among children living with one parent, while between 1990 and 2000 the greatest increases were among children with no parent present. Increases in grandparent-maintained multigenerational households are attributable to a variety of factors, including high rates of divorce, teen pregnancy, substance abuse, incarceration, and economic distress.

Among children living with their grandparents, the percentage with two parents also present in the home was 30% or less during the 1990s. This percentage increased during the first decade of the 21st century, and by 2012 it had reached 34%. Figure 1.8 shows that one out of 10 of the 65 million grandparents in the United States lived with their grandchildren.

Ellis and Simmons observe that the living arrangements of grandparents and grandchildren varied by race and ethnicity. Although the percentage of children living with at least one grandparent rose among people of all races and ethnicities between 1992 and 2012, white children were less likely to live with their grandparents than Hispanic, Asian American, or African American children.

Children living in a grandparent-headed household were more likely to be living below the poverty level and receiving public assistance than were children living with grandparents in a parent-headed household or children without grandparents in their home. A quarter of children living in a grandparent-maintained household were in poverty, compared with 20% of children who lived in a parent-maintained household and 22% of children who did not live with a grandparent.

Foster Care and Adoption

As of March 2017, there was no comprehensive federal registry system for adoptions, which may be arranged by government agencies, by private agencies, or through private arrangements between birth mothers and adoptive parents with the assistance of lawyers. The federally funded National Center for Social Statistics collected information on all finalized adoptions between 1957 and 1975, but with the dissolution of the center, only limited statistical information is now available. With the passage of the Adoption and Safe Families Act of 1997, there was renewed effort to improve the data available about adoption. The U.S. Department of Health and Human Services, through the Adoption and Foster Care Analysis and Reporting System (AFCARS), tracks adoptions that are arranged through the foster care system, but this represents only some of the children who are adopted by American families each year.

TABLE 1.4

Percentage of children under age 18 years living below 100% of the poverty level by selected characteristics, 1980–2014

Characteristic	1980	1981	1982	1983	1984	1985	1986	1987	1988	1989	1990	1991	1992	1993	1994	1995	1996	1997
Below 100% poverty																		
Total	18.3	20.0	21.9	22.3	21.5	20.7	20.5	20.3	19.5	19.6	20.6	21.8	22.3	22.7	21.8	20.8	20.5	19.9
Gender																		
Male	18.1	19.7	21.9	21.8	20.9	20.3	20.5	20.3	19.8	19.5	20.5	21.3	21.9	22.7	21.4	20.4	20.0	19.7
Female	18.6	20.4	21.9	22.8	22.1	21.1	20.4	20.3	19.3	19.8	20.8	22.2	22.8	22.7	22.2	21.2	20.9	20.0
Age																		
Ages 0–5	20.7	22.4	23.8	25.0	24.0	23.0	22.2	22.6	22.3	22.5	23.6	24.6	26.4	26.2	25.1	24.1	23.2	22.0
Ages 6–17	17.3	18.9	20.9	21.0	20.2	19.5	19.6	19.1	18.1	18.1	19.0	20.2	20.1	20.8	20.1	19.1	19.1	18.8
Race and Hispanic origin[c]																		
White, non-Hispanic	11.8	12.9	14.4	14.8	13.7	12.8	13.0	11.8	11.0	11.5	12.3	13.1	13.2	13.6	12.5	11.2	11.1	11.4
Black, non-Hispanic	42.3	45.1	47.6	46.5	46.5	43.3	43.0	45.0	43.6	43.7	44.5	45.7	46.6	45.8	43.7	41.5	39.4	37.0
Hispanic	33.2	35.9	39.5	38.1	39.2	40.3	37.7	39.3	37.6	36.2	38.4	40.4	40.0	40.9	41.5	40.0	40.3	36.8
Region[d]																		
Northeast	16.3	18.2	20.3	20.5	21.0	18.5	16.5	17.3	16.1	16.0	18.4	19.7	20.2	21.3	20.1	19.0	19.2	19.7
South	22.5	24.2	25.5	24.3	23.5	22.8	23.7	23.9	23.6	22.8	23.8	24.0	25.5	25.3	23.8	23.5	22.9	21.6
Midwest	16.3	17.2	19.5	21.2	20.9	20.7	19.6	18.5	16.4	18.2	18.8	19.8	19.7	19.6	19.1	16.9	15.5	15.2
West	16.1	18.5	20.5	22.3	19.4	19.3	19.9	19.0	19.5	19.5	19.8	22.2	22.1	23.2	23.1	22.1	22.9	22.1
Children in married-couple families, total	10.1	11.4	12.8	13.3	12.2	11.4	10.5	10.3	9.5	9.9	10.3	10.6	11.3	11.8	10.9	10.0	10.1	9.5
Ages 0–5	11.6	12.9	13.9	15.1	13.8	12.9	11.4	11.7	11.3	11.3	11.7	12.0	13.4	13.6	12.4	11.1	11.6	10.7
Ages 6–17	9.4	10.7	12.2	12.3	11.3	10.5	10.0	9.6	8.6	9.2	9.5	9.9	10.1	10.9	10.1	9.4	9.3	8.9
White, non-Hispanic	7.5	8.5	9.9	10.1	9.0	8.2	7.7	6.7	6.6	6.6	6.9	7.2	7.4	7.8	6.8	6.0	5.4	5.2
Black, non-Hispanic	19.7	22.7	23.3	23.0	22.6	17.2	14.9	18.1	17.2	18.1	17.8	14.9	18.2	17.7	14.6	12.0	13.3	12.3
Hispanic	23.0	24.3	27.8	26.8	27.5	27.2	26.1	27.4	25.3	25.4	26.6	29.1	28.9	30.5	30.2	28.4	29.4	26.1
Children in female-householder families, no husband present, total	51.4	52.9	56.6	56.0	54.7	54.1	55.2	54.4	53.5	51.9	54.2	55.9	55.4	54.3	53.2	50.7	49.7	49.6
Ages 0–5	65.4	66.2	67.2	67.8	65.7	65.7	65.5	66.0	64.3	63.0	65.9	65.9	66.8	64.2	64.1	61.9	59.3	59.5
Ages 6–17	46.2	47.6	51.9	51.1	49.9	49.1	50.6	49.3	48.4	46.4	48.4	50.9	49.4	49.1	47.7	45.2	45.5	45.4
White, non-Hispanic	38.6	39.3	42.3	43.1	41.4	39.1	42.5	39.6	38.6	38.1	41.4	42.6	41.7	40.8	39.3	34.9	36.6	38.9
Black, non-Hispanic	64.9	67.9	70.5	68.2	66.3	66.7	67.3	67.4	65.4	63.3	65.1	67.9	67.0	65.5	63.3	61.5	57.8	55.3
Hispanic	64.8	67.5	71.8	70.8	71.5	73.0	67.1	69.9	69.7	65.1	68.9	68.8	66.9	66.8	68.1	66.0	66.8	63.3

In *The AFCARS Report* (June 2016, https://www.acf .hhs.gov/sites/default/files/cb/afcarsreport23.pdf), AFCARS states that on September 30, 2015, 427,910 children under the age of 21 years were living with foster parents. Table 1.7 shows the growing number of children in foster care between fiscal years (FYs) 2011 and 2015 as well as the number of children entering and exiting the foster care system.

Foster parents are trained to provide space in their home and care for children who have been neglected, abused, or abandoned, as well as children whose parents have surrendered them to public agencies because they are unable to care for them. Foster parents are supervised by local social service agencies. According to the American Public Welfare Association, foster care is the most common type of substitute care, but children needing substitute care might also live in group homes, emergency shelters, child care facilities, hospitals, correctional institutions, or on their own. It is becoming more difficult to place children in foster care. The number of potential foster care families is down, due in part to the fact that women, the primary providers of foster care, have entered the workforce in greater numbers.

AFCARS reports that in FY 2015, 269,509 children younger than 21 years old entered foster care, with an average age of 7.3 years. Non-Hispanic African American children made up 23% of all children entering foster care in FY 2015, a notably higher percentage than their share of the overall population (13.3%). By contrast, non-Hispanic white children were underrepresented; 45% of those entering foster care were non-Hispanic white children, whereas 77.1% of the population was non-Hispanic white. Hispanics were more proportionally represented, as 20% of children entering foster care were Hispanic, compared with 17.6% of people in the general population. Asian American children were underrepresented in foster care; only 1% of children entering foster care were Asian American, compared with 5.6% of people in the general population.

A child's stay in foster care can vary from just a few days to many years. Among children who left foster care in FY 2015, 11% had been in care for less than a month, 15% had been in care from one to five months, 20% had been in care from six to 11 months, 28% were in care from 12 to 23 months, and 26% had lived in foster care for two years or longer. (See Table 1.8.)

TABLE 1.4

Percentage of children under age 18 years living below 100% of the poverty level by selected characteristics, 1980–2014 [CONTINUED]

Characteristic	1998	1999	2000	2001	2002	2003	2004	2005	2006	2007	2008	2009	2010	2011	2012	2013[a]	2013[b]	2014
Below 100% poverty																		
Total	18.9	17.1	16.2	16.3	16.7	17.6	17.8	17.6	17.4	18.0	19.0	20.7	22.0	21.9	21.8	19.9	21.5	21.1
Gender																		
Male	18.4	16.7	16.0	16.2	16.8	17.7	17.8	17.4	17.2	17.9	18.8	20.4	22.2	21.6	21.3	19.8	21.5	21.2
Female	19.4	17.5	16.3	16.4	16.6	17.6	17.8	17.8	17.6	18.1	19.2	21.0	21.9	22.2	22.3	20.0	21.5	21.1
Age																		
Ages 0–5	21.0	18.7	18.3	18.4	18.8	20.1	20.3	20.2	20.3	21.1	21.7	24.3	25.8	25.0	24.8	22.5	24.1	23.9
Ages 6–17	17.8	16.4	15.2	15.3	15.7	16.4	16.6	16.3	16.0	16.5	17.6	18.9	20.2	20.4	20.4	18.7	20.3	19.8
Race and Hispanic origin[c]																		
White, non-Hispanic	10.6	9.4	9.1	9.5	9.4	9.8	10.5	10.0	10.0	10.1	10.6	11.9	12.3	12.5	12.3	10.7	13.4	12.3
Black, non-Hispanic	36.4	33.1	31.0	29.9	32.3	34.0	33.7	34.5	33.3	34.4	34.7	35.7	39.1	38.8	38.4	39.1	33.4	37.3
Hispanic	34.4	30.3	28.4	28.0	28.6	29.7	28.9	28.3	26.9	28.6	30.6	33.1	34.9	34.1	33.8	30.4	33.0	31.9
Region[d]																		
Northeast	18.5	16.4	14.5	14.7	15.1	15.3	15.7	15.5	15.7	16.1	16.6	18.0	18.5	18.8	19.6	17.5	18.2	17.8
South	20.3	19.1	18.4	18.9	19.3	20.3	19.6	19.7	19.4	20.8	20.5	22.4	24.3	23.4	24.2	22.9	24.2	23.8
Midwest	15.1	13.9	13.1	13.3	13.4	14.9	16.8	15.9	16.3	16.6	18.7	19.6	20.5	20.8	19.9	17.0	20.1	18.8
West	21.0	18.1	16.9	16.0	17.1	17.8	17.5	17.5	16.6	16.3	18.6	21.0	22.2	22.5	21.2	19.5	20.8	21.2
Children in married-couple families, total	9.1	8.5	8.0	8.0	8.5	8.6	9.0	8.5	8.2	8.6	9.9	11.1	11.6	11.0	11.2	9.5	10.1	10.6
Ages 0–5	10.2	9.2	8.7	9.2	9.8	9.6	10.1	9.9	9.5	9.6	11.1	13.4	13.4	12.2	12.6	10.3	11.5	11.6
Ages 6–17	8.5	8.2	7.7	7.4	7.9	8.1	8.4	7.7	7.5	8.1	9.3	9.8	10.7	10.4	10.5	9.2	9.4	10.2
White, non-Hispanic	5.4	4.8	4.7	4.7	4.9	4.8	5.2	4.5	4.3	4.8	5.3	6.1	6.4	6.1	6.2	5.0	6.6	6.4
Black, non-Hispanic	12.2	10.5	8.5	9.7	11.1	11.3	12.4	12.4	11.8	11.0	11.0	14.5	16.0	15.6	14.9	16.9	10.3	13.3
Hispanic	23.5	22.1	20.8	19.5	21.3	21.4	20.8	20.1	18.5	19.4	22.2	24.0	25.1	23.3	23.6	20.0	19.6	21.2
Children in female-householder families, no husband present, total	46.6	42.6	40.5	40.0	39.8	42.1	42.4	43.1	42.4	43.0	43.9	45.1	47.1	48.0	47.6	46.1	47.4	46.4
Ages 0–5	55.1	50.6	50.7	49.0	48.8	53.0	52.8	52.9	53.0	54.0	54.0	54.8	58.7	57.7	56.3	55.3	55.3	55.1
Ages 6–17	42.9	39.4	36.3	36.3	36.1	37.6	38.1	38.9	37.7	37.9	39.1	40.5	41.9	43.5	43.7	42.0	43.8	42.4
White, non-Hispanic	34.3	30.7	29.3	30.4	29.7	31.6	33.0	33.8	33.6	32.9	33.1	35.1	36.0	36.5	37.3	34.8	39.6	35.7
Black, non-Hispanic	54.2	51.8	48.9	46.3	47.3	50.0	49.0	50.2	49.9	49.8	51.8	51.1	52.6	54.2	53.9	54.6	49.9	52.9
Hispanic	60.4	52.0	50.5	50.2	48.4	50.6	51.9	51.0	47.5	51.8	52.1	52.9	56.8	52.7	55.4	52.4	53.2	53.3

[a]The source for the traditional income in this column is the portion of the 2014 CPS ASEC sample (about 68,000 households) that received a set of income questions similar to those used in 2013. The 2014 CPS ASEC included redesigned questions for income that were implemented to a subsample of the 98,000 addresses using a probability split panel design.
[b]The source for the redesigned income in this column is the portion of the 2014 CPS ASEC sample (about 30,000 households) that received the redesigned income questions. The 2014 CPS ASEC included redesigned questions for income that were implemented to a subsample of the 98,000 addresses using a probability split panel design. The redesigned income questions were used for the entire 2015 CPS ASEC sample.
[c]From 1980 to 2002, following the 1977 Office of Management and Budget (OMB) standards for collecting and presenting data on race, the Current Population Survey (CPS) asked respondents to choose one race from the following: white, black, American Indian or Alaskan Native, or Asian or Pacific Islander. An "other" category was also offered. Beginning in 2003, the CPS allowed respondents to select one or more race categories. All race groups discussed in this table from 2002 onward refer to people who indicated only one racial identity within the categories presented. For this reason, data from 2002 onward are not directly comparable with data from earlier years. People who reported only one race are referred to as the race-alone population. The use of the race-alone population in this table does not imply that it is the preferred method of presenting or analyzing data. Data on race and Hispanic origin are collected separately. Persons of Hispanic origin may be of any race.
[d]Regions: Northeast includes CT, MA, ME, NH, NJ, NY, PA, RI, and VT. South includes AL, AR, DC, DE, FL, GA, KY, LA, MD, MS, NC, OK, SC, TN, TX, VA, and WV. Midwest includes IA, IL, IN, KS, MI, MN, MO, ND, NE, OH, SD, and WI. West includes AK, AZ, CA, CO, HI, ID, MT, NM, NV, OR, UT, WA, and WY.
Note: Data for 2010 use the Census 2010-based population controls. The 2004 data have been revised to reflect a correction to the weights in the 2005 ASEC. Data for 1999, 2000, and 2001 use Census 2000 population controls. Data for 2000 onward are from the expanded CPS sample. The poverty level is based on money income and does not include noncash benefits, such as food stamps. Poverty thresholds reflect family size and composition and are adjusted each year using the annual average Consumer Price Index level. In 2014, the poverty threshold for a two parent, two child family was $24,008. The levels shown here are derived from the ratio of the family's income to the family's poverty threshold.

SOURCE: Adapted from "Table ECON1.A. Child Poverty: Percentage of Children Ages 0–17 Living below Selected Poverty Levels by Selected Characteristics, 1980–2014," in *America's Children in Brief: Key National Indicators of Well-Being, 2016*, Federal Interagency Forum on Child and Family Statistics, 2016, https://www.childstats.gov/americaschildren/tables.asp (accessed December 27, 2016)

AFCARS reports that more than half (51%) of the children who left foster care in FY 2015 were reunited with their parents. (See Table 1.8.) About 6% of the children were placed in a relative's home, 9% were emancipated, or "aged out" of the system, and 22% of children who left foster care were adopted.

Some observers feel that children in foster care who age out of the system are unprepared and often unable to cope without financial assistance and emotional support. For example, Rita Soronen explains in "We Are Abandoning Children in Foster Care" (CNN.com, April 17, 2014) that programs to assist foster children with transitioning to adulthood and independent living vary from state to state, are often inadequate, and cannot substitute the support of a family. Without support, foster children's futures may be bleak. She notes that one out of five may be

TABLE 1.5

Opposite- and same-sex couples with and without children in the household, 2014

[In percent]

Household characteristics	Married opposite-sex couples Percent	Unmarried opposite-sex couples Percent	Total same-sex couples Percent	Total male-male couples Percent	Total female-female couples Percent
Total households (number)	55,779,842	6,727,206	783,100	377,903	405,197
Age of householder					
15 to 24 years	1.3	12.0	4.1	2.7	5.4
25 to 34 years	13.3	35.3	17.3	15.5	18.9
35 to 44 years	20.0	21.5	19.7	19.6	19.9
45 to 54 years	22.2	15.9	26.6	28.8	24.5
55 to 64 years	21.3	9.5	17.1	18.1	16.2
65 years and over	21.9	5.8	15.2	15.3	15.1
Average age of householder (years)	51.9	39.0	48.4	49.2	47.7
Average age of spouse/partner (years)	51.2	38.1	46.5	46.7	46.4
Race of householder					
White	82.1	76.4	83.6	85.2	82.2
Black or African American	6.9	11.4	7.4	5.8	8.9
American Indian or Alaska Native	0.6	1.1	0.7	0.6	0.9
Asian	5.6	2.4	3.1	3.6	2.7
Native Hawaiian or Pacific Islander	0.1	0.2	0.2	0.2	0.1
Some other race	3.2	5.6	2.5	2.4	2.6
Two or more races	1.5	2.8	2.5	2.4	2.6
Percent of couples interracial	6.8	13.4	14.8	17.3	12.4
Hispanic origin of householder					
Hispanic or Latino origin (of any race)	12.4	18.8	11.7	11.5	11.8
White alone, not Hispanic or Latino	73.4	64.3	75.7	77.1	74.5
Educational attainment					
Householder has at least a bachelor's degree	38.2	24.1	48.6	51.9	45.6
Both partners with at least a bachelor's degree	23.7	12.5	30.7	31.4	30.0
Employment status[a]					
Householder employed	67.1	78.0	74.5	75.5	73.5
Both partners employed	47.8	59.4	59.5	60.5	58.5
Children in the household					
Children in the household[b]	39.6	41.0	17.3	10.4	23.7
Own children in the household	39.5	37.9	16.0	10.0	21.5
Household income					
Less than $35,000	15.1	27.5	14.6	11.0	17.9
$35,000 to $49,999	11.7	15.9	10.4	9.0	11.7
$50,000 to $74,999	19.5	22.3	16.8	15.9	17.7
$75,000 to $99,999	16.1	14.0	15.0	14.7	15.4
$100,000 or more	37.6	20.3	43.2	49.4	37.3
Average household income (dollars)	104,226	71,692	117,768	137,149	99,681
Home tenure					
Own	79.1	41.4	66.9	68.3	65.5
Rent	20.9	58.6	33.1	31.7	34.5

[a]Employed or in the armed forces.
[b]Includes own children and nonrelatives of the householder under 18 years.

SOURCE: Adapted from "Table 1. Household Characteristics of Opposite-Sex and Same-Sex Couple Households: ACS 2014," in *Characteristics of Same-Sex Couple Households: 2014*, U.S. Census Bureau, 2014, https://www.census.gov/hhes/samesex/files/ssex-tables-2014.xlsx (accessed December 27, 2016)

homeless, only half will be employed, and seven out of 10 young women will be pregnant by age 21. Many are at risk for involvement with the criminal justice system. Soronen states that "it is our duty as a nation to end this cycle." Furthermore, she asserts, "We must demand justice and safety at every level for children, not only because it is their basic human right but because those who grow and learn in just environments and with the protection of families ultimately create humane and thriving societies as adults."

According to AFCARS, children who were adopted in FY 2015 were younger on average (6.2 years) than the average age of all children in foster care (7.3 years),

reflecting adoptive parents' preference for younger children. (See Table 1.9.) Of children adopted in FY 2015, more than half (56%) were aged five years and younger. Forty-eight percent of children adopted were white, 22% were Hispanic, and 18% were African American. Although the majority (68%) of children were adopted by married couples, single women adopted 26% of children, single men adopted 3%, and unmarried couples adopted 3%.

Despite financial incentives and subsidies intended to encourage adoption, many children who enter foster care will never have a permanent family, but instead will age out of the system. AFCARS reports there were 111,820 children

TABLE 1.6

Characteristics of opposite-sex unmarried couples with children, 2016

[Numbers in thousands, except for percentages]

			Presence of biological children[a]			
	Total		No biological children		At least one biological child under 18, of either partner	
All opposite sex unmarried couples	Number	%	Number	%	Number	%
Total	8,075	100.0	5,044	100.0	3,031	100.0
Age of male partner						
15–24 years	1,050	13.0	704	13.9	347	11.4
25–29 years	1,702	21.1	1,107	21.9	594	19.6
30–34 years	1,340	16.6	694	13.8	647	21.3
35–39 years	858	10.6	317	6.3	541	17.9
40–44 years	696	8.6	309	6.1	387	12.8
45–49 years	659	8.2	395	7.8	264	8.7
50–54 years	570	7.1	433	8.6	137	4.5
55–64 years	759	9.4	657	13.0	102	3.4
65+ years	440	5.4	429	8.5	11	0.4
Age of female partner						
15–24 years	1,569	19.4	1,023	20.3	546	18.0
25–29 years	1,805	22.4	1,121	22.2	684	22.6
30–34 years	1,222	15.1	583	11.6	639	21.1
35–39 years	781	9.7	278	5.5	503	16.6
40–44 years	695	8.6	312	6.2	383	12.6
45–49 years	564	7.0	392	7.8	172	5.7
50–54 years	481	6.0	404	8.0	77	2.5
55–64 years	594	7.4	569	11.3	25	0.8
65+ years	363	4.5	361	7.2	2	0.1
Age difference						
Male 10+ years older than female	930	11.5	551	10.9	379	12.5
Male 6–9 years older than female	915	11.3	543	10.8	372	12.3
Male 4–5 years older than female	844	10.5	518	10.3	326	10.8
Male 2–3 years older than female	1,366	16.9	821	16.3	546	18.0
Male and female within 1 year	2,460	30.5	1,613	32.0	847	27.9
Female 2–3 years older than male	542	6.7	325	6.4	217	7.2
Female 4–5 years older than male	321	4.0	219	4.4	101	3.3
Female 6–9 years older than male	373	4.6	216	4.3	157	5.2
Female 10+ years older than male	324	4.0	238	4.7	86	2.9
Race of male partner						
White alone—non-Hispanic	5,150	63.8	3,641	72.2	1,509	49.8
Black alone—non-Hispanic	984	12.2	516	10.2	467	15.4
Hispanic[b]	1,523	18.9	649	12.9	875	28.9
All remaining single races and all race combinations, non-Hispanic	417	5.2	238	4.7	180	5.9
Race of female partner						
White alone—non-Hispanic	5,175	64.1	3,624	71.8	1,551	51.2
Black alone—non-Hispanic	822	10.2	410	8.1	412	13.6
Hispanic[b]	1,547	19.2	691	13.7	856	28.3
All remaining single races and all race combinations, non-Hispanic	531	6.6	319	6.3	212	7.0
Race difference[c]						
Both white alone—non-Hispanic	4,520	56.0	3,217	63.8	1,304	43.0
Both black alone—non-Hispanic	704	8.7	339	6.7	366	12.1
Both other alone or any combination—non-Hispanic	213	2.6	110	2.2	103	3.4
Both Hispanic	1,150	14.2	446	8.8	704	23.2
Neither Hispanic	717	8.9	485	9.6	232	7.6
One Hispanic, other non-Hispanic	770	9.5	447	8.9	323	10.7
Race of male partner						
White alone	6,476	80.2	4,187	83.0	2,290	75.5
Black alone	1,059	13.1	559	11.1	500	16.5
Asian alone	201	2.5	128	2.5	73	2.4
All remaining single races and all race combinations	338	4.2	170	3.4	168	5.5
Race of female partner						
White alone	6,495	80.4	4,211	83.5	2,284	75.4
Black alone	918	11.4	458	9.1	461	15.2
Asian alone	280	3.5	174	3.4	106	3.5
All remaining single races and all race combinations	381	4.7	202	4.0	180	5.9

awaiting adoption on September 30, 2015. Almost a quarter (23%) of "waiting children" were African American. More than half (52%) of waiting children were living in foster homes with nonrelatives while waiting to be adopted.

TABLE 1.6

Characteristics of opposite-sex unmarried couples with children, 2016 [CONTINUED]

[Numbers in thousands, except for percentages]

	Total		No biological children		At least one biological child under 18, of either partner	
All opposite sex unmarried couples	**Number**	**%**	**Number**	**%**	**Number**	**%**
Race difference						
Both white alone	6,076	75.3	3,930	77.9	2,146	70.8
Both black alone	807	10.0	389	7.7	418	13.8
Both Asian alone	147	1.8	81	1.6	66	2.2
Both other alone or any comb.	169	2.1	71	1.4	98	3.2
Partners identify as different races	876	10.8	573	11.4	303	10.0
Origin of male partner						
Hispanic	1,523	18.9	649	12.9	875	28.9
Non-Hispanic	6,551	81.1	4,395	87.1	2,156	71.1
Origin of female partner						
Hispanic	1,547	19.2	691	13.7	856	28.3
Non-Hispanic	6,528	80.8	4,353	86.3	2,174	71.7
Origin difference						
Neither Hispanic	6,154	76.2	4,151	82.3	2,004	66.1
Both Hispanic	1,150	14.2	446	8.8	704	23.2
Male Hispanic, female not	373	4.6	203	4.0	171	5.6
Female Hispanic, male not	397	4.9	245	4.8	152	5.0
Labor force status of male partner						
Not in labor force	1,223	15.1	877	17.4	346	11.4
In labor force	6,852	84.9	4,167	82.6	2,685	88.6
Labor force status of female partner						
Not in labor force	2,152	26.7	1,170	23.2	982	32.4
In labor force	5,922	73.3	3,874	76.8	2,048	67.6
Labor force difference						
Both in labor force	5,331	66.0	3,512	69.6	1,819	60.0
Only male in labor force	1,521	18.8	655	13.0	867	28.6
Only female in labor force	591	7.3	362	7.2	230	7.6
Neither in labor force	631	7.8	515	10.2	116	3.8
Employment of male partner						
Not employed	1,665	20.6	1,095	21.7	570	18.8
Employed	6,409	79.4	3,948	78.3	2,461	81.2
Employment of female partner						
Not employed	2,473	30.6	1,363	27.0	1,110	36.6
Employed	5,602	69.4	3,681	73.0	1,921	63.4
Employment difference						
Both in labor force—both employed	4,775	59.1	3,206	63.6	1,569	51.8
Both in labor force—only male employed	221	2.7	142	2.8	79	2.6
Both in labor force—only female employed	267	3.3	132	2.6	135	4.4
Both in labor force—both unemployed	68	0.8	31	0.6	37	1.2
Male in labor force—male employed	1,414	17.5	600	11.9	814	26.9
Male in labor force—male unemployed	108	1.3	55	1.1	53	1.7
Female in labor force—female employed	560	6.9	342	6.8	217	7.2
Female in labor force—female unemployed	32	0.4	19	0.4	13	0.4
Not in labor force—not employed	631	7.8	515	10.2	116	3.8
Male education						
Not high school graduate	1,077	13.3	501	9.9	576	19.0
High school graduate	2,934	36.3	1,606	31.8	1,328	43.8
Some college	2,296	28.4	1,487	29.5	809	26.7
Bachelor's degree or higher	1,767	21.9	1,450	28.7	317	10.5
Female education						
Not high school graduate	873	10.8	369	7.3	504	16.6
High school graduate	2,440	30.2	1,385	27.5	1,056	34.8
Some college	2,688	33.3	1,610	31.9	1,078	35.6
Bachelor's degree or higher	2,073	25.7	1,680	33.3	393	13.0

Living Arrangements of Young Adults

A young person's transition into adult independence does not necessarily occur at age 18. The marriage age has risen since the 1950s, and because obtaining a college education has become the norm, young people have delayed finding employment that allows them to support

TABLE 1.6

Characteristics of opposite-sex unmarried couples with children, 2016 [CONTINUED]

[Numbers in thousands, except for percentages]

All opposite sex unmarried couples	Total		No biological children		At least one biological child under 18, of either partner	
	Number	%	Number	%	Number	%
Education difference						
Neither has bachelor's degree	5,404	66.9	2,964	58.8	2,440	80.5
One has bachelor's degree, other has less	1,501	18.6	1,030	20.4	470	15.5
Both have bachelor's degree or more	1,170	14.5	1,050	20.8	120	4.0
Personal earnings of male partner						
Under $5,000 or loss	213	2.6	120	2.4	93	3.1
Without income	1,221	15.1	838	16.6	383	12.6
$5,000 to $9,999	280	3.5	162	3.2	119	3.9
$10,000 to $14,999	404	5.0	212	4.2	192	6.3
$15,000 to $19,999	496	6.1	273	5.4	223	7.3
$20,000 to $24,999	628	7.8	339	6.7	289	9.5
$25,000 to $29,999	709	8.8	365	7.2	344	11.3
$30,000 to $39,999	1,083	13.4	681	13.5	402	13.3
$40,000 to $49,999	902	11.2	578	11.5	324	10.7
$50,000 to $74,999	1,213	15.0	829	16.4	384	12.7
$75,000 to $99,999	420	5.2	277	5.5	143	4.7
$100,000 and over	505	6.3	370	7.3	135	4.5
Personal earnings of female partner						
Under $5,000 or loss	426	5.3	198	3.9	228	7.5
Without income	1,961	24.3	1,102	21.8	859	28.3
$5,000 to $9,999	422	5.2	240	4.8	182	6.0
$10,000 to $14,999	578	7.2	323	6.4	256	8.4
$15,000 to $19,999	609	7.5	364	7.2	245	8.1
$20,000 to $24,999	596	7.4	331	6.6	264	8.7
$25,000 to $29,999	580	7.2	371	7.4	209	6.9
$30,000 to $39,999	1,011	12.5	710	14.1	301	9.9
$40,000 to $49,999	693	8.6	466	9.2	227	7.5
$50,000 to $74,999	766	9.5	593	11.8	173	5.7
$75,000 to $99,999	218	2.7	173	3.4	44	1.5
$100,000 and over	215	2.7	173	3.4	42	1.4
Personal earnings difference						
Male earns $50,000+ more	913	11.3	565	11.2	348	11.5
Male earns $30,000–$49,999 more	980	12.1	593	11.8	387	12.8
Male earns $10,000–$29,999 more	1,857	23.0	986	19.6	871	28.7
Male earns $5,000–$9,999 more	546	6.8	326	6.5	220	7.3
Male earns within $4,999 of female	1,692	21.0	1,180	23.4	512	16.9
Female earns $5,000–$9,999 more	404	5.0	272	5.4	132	4.4
Female earns $10,000–$29,999 more	983	12.2	605	12.0	378	12.5
Female earns $30,000–$49,999 more	441	5.5	312	6.2	129	4.3
Female earns $50,000+ more	259	3.2	205	4.1	54	1.8

[a]Excludes ever-married children under 18 years.
[b]Hispanics may be of any race.
[c]"White" refers to non-Hispanic white alone, "black" to non-Hispanic black alone, and "other" to non-Hispanic other alone or in combination.

SOURCE: "Table UC3. Opposite Sex Unmarried Couples by Presence of Biological Children under 18, and Age, Earnings, Education, and Race and Hispanic Origin of Both Partners: 2016," in *America's Families and Living Arrangements: 2016: Unmarried couples (UC Table Series)*, U.S. Census Bureau, 2016, https://www.census.gov/hhes/families/data/cps2016UC.html (accessed December 27, 2016)

themselves independently of their parents. A growing number of young adults older than the age of 18 years continue to live in, or return to, their parents' home. Some young people live with their parents until their mid-20s, and others are likely to return to their parents' home at some time after moving out, especially after college or service in the military. Many young adults also share households with other young adults.

Socioeconomic experts attribute this phenomenon to the rising cost of living in the United States. Wages have not increased at the same rate as the cost of living; therefore, the same amount of money buys less than it did in previous years. Furthermore, credit markets tightened during and after the Great Recession, which made it difficult to qualify for a mortgage and may have further delayed young people leaving home. At the same time, there were layoffs and foreclosures; young adults who found themselves jobless or in foreclosure may have returned to their parents' home.

The Census Bureau (2016, https://www.census.gov/hhes/families/files/graphics/AD-1.pdf) observes that the

FIGURE 1.8

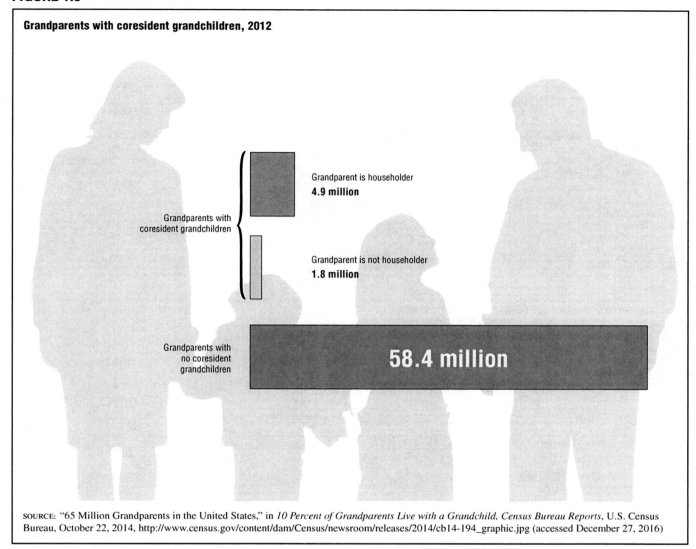

Grandparents with coresident grandchildren, 2012

Grandparents with coresident grandchildren

Grandparent is householder
4.9 million

Grandparent is not householder
1.8 million

Grandparents with no coresident grandchildren

58.4 million

SOURCE: "65 Million Grandparents in the United States," in *10 Percent of Grandparents Live with a Grandchild, Census Bureau Reports*, U.S. Census Bureau, October 22, 2014, http://www.census.gov/content/dam/Census/newsroom/releases/2014/cb14-194_graphic.jpg (accessed December 27, 2016)

percentages of young adults aged 18 to 24 years and those aged 25 to 34 years living with parents increased between 2005 and 2016. For example, Figure 1.9 shows that in 2016 nearly 20% of males aged 25 to 34 years were living with their parents.

Young adults who live by themselves for any length of time are unlikely to return home after experiencing independence. By contrast, those who move in with roommates or who cohabit without marrying are more likely to return to the parental home if the living situation does not work out or the relationship fails. Some young adults struggle on their own, only to return home for respite from financial pressures, because of loneliness, or because they need emotional support or security. Others return home following divorce to get help from their parents with child care.

TABLE 1.7

Children in the foster care system, fiscal years 2011–15

	2011	2012	2013	2014	2015
Number in foster care on September 30 of the fiscal year	397,605	397,301	401,213	414,429	427,910
Number entered foster care during the fiscal year	251,450	251,354	254,712	264,555	269,509
Number exited foster care during the fiscal year	247,543	239,535	238,930	237,554	243,060
Number waiting to be adopted on September 30 of the fiscal year	106,440	101,935	104,387	108,189	111,820
Number waiting to be adopted whose parental rights (for all living parents) were terminated during the fiscal year	61,904	58,187	58,638	61,070	62,378
Number adopted with public child welfare agency involvement during the fiscal year	50,913	52,025	50,820	50,625	53,549

SOURCE: "Adapted from "Numbers at a Glance," in *The AFCARS Report: Preliminary FY 15 Estimates as of June 2016*, no. 23, U.S. Department of Health and Human Services, Administration for Children and Families, Administration on Children, Youth and Families, Children's Bureau, June 2016, https://www.acf.hhs.gov/sites/default/files/cb/afcarsreport23.pdf (accessed December 27, 2016)"

TABLE 1.8

Characteristics of children exiting foster care during fiscal year 2015

Age at exit	Years	
Mean	8.9	
Median	7.9	

Age at exit	Percent	Number
Less than 1 year	5%	10,967
1 year	8%	19,377
2 years	8%	19,593
3 years	7%	16,789
4 years	6%	15,109
5 years	6%	13,796
6 years	6%	13,385
7 years	5%	12,669
8 years	5%	11,594
9 years	4%	10,129
10 years	4%	9,128
11 years	3%	8,137
12 years	3%	7,985
13 years	3%	7,940
14 years	4%	8,911
15 years	4%	10,168
16 years	5%	11,853
17 years	5%	11,698
18 years	7%	18,005
19 years	2%	4,246
20 years	0%	743

Time in care	Months	
Mean	19.0	
Median	13.5	

Time in care	Percent	Number
Less than 1 month	11%	25,640
1–5 months	15%	36,927
6–11 months	20%	47,865
12–17 months	16%	39,727
18–23 months	12%	28,826
24–29 months	8%	19,714
30–35 months	5%	13,172
3–4 years	9%	20,715
5 years or more	4%	10,047

Race/ethnicity	Percent	Number
American Indian/Alaskan Native	2%	5,249
Asian	1%	1,598
Black or African American	23%	54,795
Native Hawaiian/other Pacific Islander	0%	519
Hispanic (of any race)	21%	51,667
White	45%	109,132
Unknown/unable to determine	2%	4,105
Two or more races	6%	15,596

Reasons for discharge	Percent	Number
Reunification with parent(s) or primary caretaker(s)	51%	123,894
Living with other relative(s)	6%	15,621
Adoption	22%	52,931
Emancipation	9%	20,789
Guardianship	9%	22,303
Transfer to another agency	2%	4,363
Runaway	0%	985
Death of child	0%	336

Note: All races exclude children of Hispanic origin. Children of Hispanic ethnicity may be any race.

SOURCE: "Children Exiting Foster Care during FY 2015," in *The AFCARS Report: Preliminary FY 15 Estimates as of June 2016*, no. 23, U.S. Department of Health and Human Services, Administration for Children and Families, Administration on Children, Youth and Families, Children's Bureau, June 2016, https://www.acf.hhs.gov/sites/default/files/cb/afcarsreport23.pdf (accessed December 27, 2016)

TABLE 1.9

Selected characteristics of children adopted in fiscal year 2015

Age at adoption	Years	
Mean	6.2	
Median	5.2	

Age at adoption	Percent	Number
Less than 1 year	2%	1,096
1 year	12%	6,453
2 years	14%	7,624
3 years	11%	5,912
4 years	9%	4,886
5 years	8%	4,249
6 years	7%	3,801
7 years	6%	3,458
8 years	6%	3,004
9 years	5%	2,493
10 years	4%	2,132
11 years	3%	1,809
12 years	3%	1,513
13 years	2%	1,331
14 years	2%	1,160
15 years	2%	919
16 years	2%	872
17 years	1%	666
18 years	0%	136
19 years	0%	17
20 years	0%	10

Time elapsed from termination of parental rights to adoption	Months	
Mean	11.9	
Median	8.7	

Time elapsed from termination of parental rights to adoption	Percent	Number
Less than 1 month	2%	1,207
1–5 months	29%	15,517
6–11 months	35%	18,447
12–17 months	17%	8,876
18–23 months	7%	3,848
24–29 months	4%	1,949
30–35 months	2%	1,014
3–4 years	2%	1,298
5 years or more	1%	580

Race/ethnicity	Percent	Number
American Indian/Alaskan Native	2%	898
Asian	0%	203
Black or African American	18%	9,764
Native Hawaiian/other Pacific Islander	0%	79
Hispanic (of any race)	22%	11,683
White	48%	25,870
Unknown/unable to determine	1%	714
Two or more races	8%	4,316

SOURCE: Adapted from "Children Adopted with Public Agency Involvement in FY 2015," in *The AFCARS Report: Preliminary FY 15 Estimates as of June 2016*, no. 23, U.S. Department of Health and Human Services, Administration for Children and Families, Administration on Children, Youth and Families, Children's Bureau, June 2016, https://www.acf.hhs.gov/sites/default/files/cb/afcarsreport23.pdf (accessed December 27, 2016)

FIGURE 1.9

Young adults living with their parents, 1960–2016

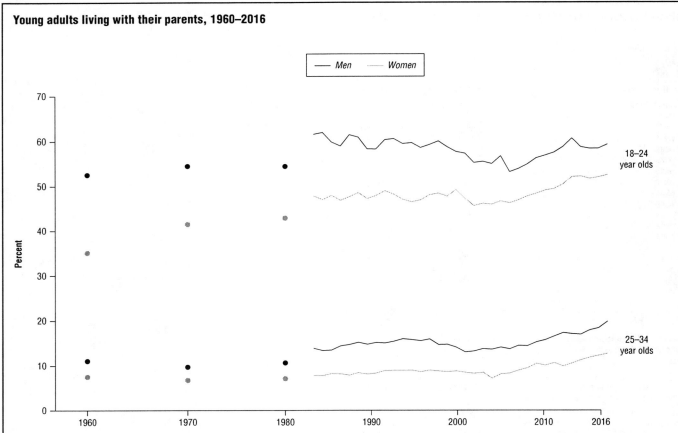

Note: Unmarried college students living in dormitories are counted as living in group quarters in decennial data but as living in their parental home in the Current Population Survey (CPS) data.

SOURCE: "Figure AD-1. Young Adults Living in the Parental Home," in *Families and Living Arrangements—Living Arrangements of Adults*, U.S. Census Bureau, November 16, 2016, https://www.census.gov/hhes/families/files/graphics/AD-1.pdf (accessed December 27, 2016)

CHAPTER 2
CHILDREN, TEENS, AND MONEY

FAMILY INCOME

Almost all children are financially dependent on their parents, and their financial condition directly depends on how much their parents earn. Bernadette D. Proctor, Jessica L. Semega, and Melissa A. Kollar of the U.S. Census Bureau report in *Income and Poverty in the United States: 2015* (September 2016, https://www.census.gov/content/dam/Census/library/publications/2016/demo/p60-256.pdf) that 2014 saw the first increase in real income since before the Great Recession, which spanned from late 2007 to mid-2009. In 2015 median household income (half of all households earned more and half earned less) was 1.6% lower than in 2007 and 2.4% lower than the household income peak in 1999. In 2015 family households (with or without children) had a median income of $72,165, which was slightly higher than the 2014 median of $68,504. (See Table 2.1.)

Median income varied greatly by race and ethnic group. Asian American households had the highest median income, at $77,166, followed by non-Hispanic white households at $62,950. (See Table 2.1.) The median income for Hispanic households was $45,148, and the median income for African American households, at $36,898, was the lowest of any reported racial or ethnic group.

The Cost of Raising a Child

Since the 1960s the Family Economics Research Group of the U.S. Department of Agriculture (USDA) has provided estimates on the cost of rearing a child to adulthood. The estimates are calculated per child in a household with two children and are categorized by the age of the child using different family income levels. Attorneys and judges use these estimates when determining child-support awards in divorce cases as well as in cases involving the wrongful death of a parent. Public officials use the estimates to determine payments for the support of children in foster care and for subsidies to adoptive families. Financial planners and consumer educators use them to help people determine their life insurance needs.

INCOME LEVELS. The estimated annual family expenditures for a child vary widely depending on the income level of the household. The estimated amount a family spends on a child also tends to increase as the child ages. The USDA estimates that in 2013 married-couple households that earned less than $61,530 per year spent amounts ranging from $9,480 for very young children to $10,400 for 15- to 17-year-olds. (See Table 2.2.) Annual spending estimates for middle-income, married-couple families ranged from $12,940 for the youngest children to $14,970 for 15- to 17-year-olds. The estimates for married-couple families with incomes above $106,540 ranged from spending $21,430 annually for the youngest children to $25,700 for the oldest.

The estimated annual expenditures for single-parent families that earned less than $61,530 per year were slightly less than those of two-parent families, most likely because their average incomes were lower ($27,290 for single-parent families and $39,360 for two-parent families). (See Table 2.3 and Table 2.2.) The USDA estimates that in 2013 single parents that earned less than $61,530 spent an annual average of $8,090 to $9,560, depending on the age of the child. Single-parent families that earned $61,530 or more spent an average of $17,550 to $21,550 per child per year.

The USDA estimates that the highest-income households spent more than twice the amount on their children that the lowest-income households did. (See Table 2.2 and Table 2.3.) This difference varied by the type of expense. For example, the estimated annual expense for child care and education for children aged 15 to 17 years in these high-income families ($6,980) was more than seven times that for children the same age in the lowest-income families ($980). There were comparable differences in expenditures

TABLE 2.1

Median income by type of household and race and Hispanic origin of householder, 2014–15

[Income in 2015 dollars. Households and people as of March of the following year.]

Characteristic	2014 Number (thousands)	2014 Median income (dollars) Estimate	2015 Number (thousands)	2015 Median income (dollars) Estimates	Percentage change in real median income (2015 less 2014) Number (thousands)
Households					
All households	124,587	53,718	125,819	56,516	5.2
Type of household					
Family households	81,716	68,504	82,184	72,165	5.3
Married-couple	60,010	81,118	60,251	84,626	4.3
Female householder, no husband present	15,544	36,192	15,622	37,797	4.4
Male householder, no wife present	6,162	53,746	6,310	55,861	3.9
Nonfamily households	42,871	32,084	43,635	33,805	5.4
Female householder	22,728	26,703	23,093	29,022	8.7
Male householder	20,143	39,226	20,542	40,762	3.9
Race[a] and Hispanic origin of householder					
White	98,679	56,932	99,313	60,109	5.6
White, not Hispanic	84,228	60,325	84,445	62,950	4.4
Black	16,437	35,439	16,539	36,898	4.1
Asian	6,040	74,382	6,328	77,166	3.7
Hispanic (any race)	16,239	42,540	16,667	45,148	6.1
Nativity of householder					
Native born	106,191	54,741	107,081	57,173	4.4
Foreign born	18,396	49,649	18,738	52,295	5.3
Naturalized citizen.	9,735	59,329	9,856	61,982	4.5
Not a citizen	8,661	40,842	8,881	45,137	10.5
Region					
Northeast	22,179	59,278	22,347	62,182	4.9
Midwest	27,459	54,330	27,455	57,082	5.1
South	47,040	49,712	47,822	51,174	2.9
West	27,909	57,754	28,195	61,442	6.4
Residence[b]					
Inside metropolitan statistical areas	104,009	55,920	107,615	59,258	N
Inside principal cities	40,578	47,905	42,615	51,378	N
Outside principal cities	63,431	61,671	65,000	64,144	N
Outside metropolitan statistical areas[c]	20,578	45,534	18,204	44,657	N
Earnings of full-time year-round workers					
Men with earnings	62,455	50,441	63,887	51,212	1.5
Women with earnings	46,226	39,667	47,211	40,742	2.7
Female-to-male earnings ratio	X	0.79	X	0.80	1.2

X = Not applicable

N = Not comparable

[a]Federal surveys give respondents the option of reporting more than one race. Therefore, two basic ways of defining a race group are possible. A group such as Asian may be defined as those who reported Asian and no other race (the race-alone or single-race concept) or as those who reported Asian regardless of whether they also reported another race (the race-alone-or-in-combination concept). This table shows data using the first approach (race alone). The use of the single-race population does not imply that it is the preferred method of presenting or analyzing data. The Census Bureau uses a variety of approaches. Information on people who reported more than one race, such as white and American Indian and Alaska Native or Asian and black or African American, is available from Census 2010 through American FactFinder. About 2.9 percent of people reported more than one race in Census 2010. Data for American Indians and Alaska Natives, Native Hawaiians and other Pacific Islanders, and those reporting two or more races are not shown separately.

[b]Once a decade, the Current Population Survey, Annual Social and Economic Supplement (CPS ASEC) transitions to a new sample design and updates all metropolitan statistical area delineations. As a result, the metropolitan/nonmetropolitan estimates for 2014 and 2015 are not comparable. Users may want to use the American Community Survey estimates for metropolitan/nonmetropolitan comparisons.

[c]The "outside metropolitan statistical areas" category includes both micropolitan statistical areas and territory outside of metropolitan and micropolitan statistical areas.

SOURCE: Adapted from Bernadette D. Proctor, Jessica L. Semega, and Melissa A. Kollar, "Table 1. Income and Earnings Summary Measures by Selected Characteristics: 2014 and 2015," in *Income and Poverty in the United States: 2015*, U.S. Census Bureau, September 13, 2016, http://www.census.gov/library/publications/2016/demo/p60-256.html (accessed December 28, 2016)

by income group in single-parent households. Similarly, there were also geographic and regional differences; the cost of housing was significantly lower in rural communities than in urban areas. (See Figure 2.1.)

AGE OF CHILD. The 2013 estimates of family expenditures on a child increased with the child's age, except for housing, child care, and education. (See Table 2.2 and Table 2.3.) The estimates for child care and education were highest for preschoolers (under the age of six years) in most income groups. Many women with children this age are employed and must pay for child care. Once children enter school, child care costs decrease. As school-aged children grow up, the need for after-school

TABLE 2.2

Estimated annual expenditures on a child by husband-wife families, 2013

Age of child	Total expense	Housing	Food	Transportation	Clothing	Health care	Child care and education[a]	Miscellaneous[b]
Before tax income: less than $61,530 (average = $39,360)								
0–2	$9,480	$3,100	$1,210	$1,200	$670	$670	$2,200	$430
3–5	9,520	3,100	1,310	1,250	530	630	2,070	630
6–8	9,130	3,100	1,780	1,380	600	700	920	650
9–11	9,950	3,100	2,050	1,390	610	760	1,400	640
12–14	10,370	3,100	2,220	1,510	720	1,150	950	720
15–17	10,400	3,100	2,210	1,670	760	1,080	980	600
Total	**$176,550**	**$55,800**	**$32,340**	**$25,200**	**$11,670**	**$14,970**	**$25,560**	**$11,010**
Before-tax income: $61,530 to $106,540 (average = $82,790)								
0–2	$12,940	$4,070	$1,450	$1,730	$790	$900	$3,090	$910
3–5	12,970	4,070	1,550	1,780	640	850	2,960	1,120
6–8	12,800	4,070	2,180	1,910	710	990	1,810	1,130
9–11	13,680	4,070	2,490	1,910	740	1,060	2,280	1,130
12–14	14,420	4,070	2,680	2,040	870	1,500	2,060	1,200
15–17	14,970	4,070	2,670	2,200	940	1,410	2,600	1,080
Total	**$245,340**	**$73,260**	**$39,060**	**$34,710**	**$14,070**	**$20,130**	**$44,400**	**$19,710**
Before-tax income: more than $106,540 (average = $186,460)								
0–2	$21,430	$7,370	$1,980	$2,610	$1,100	$1,040	$5,500	$1,830
3–5	21,440	7,370	2,080	2,670	920	990	5,370	2,040
6–8	21,330	7,370	2,740	2,800	1,010	1,140	4,220	2,050
9–11	22,290	7,370	3,100	2,800	1,050	1,220	4,700	2,050
12–14	23,750	7,370	3,320	2,930	1,220	1,710	5,080	2,120
15–17	25,700	7,370	3,310	3,090	1,330	1,620	6,980	2,000
Total	**$407,820**	**$132,660**	**$49,590**	**$50,700**	**$19,890**	**$23,160**	**$95,550**	**$36,270**

[a]Includes only families with child care and education expenses.
[b]Includes personal care items, entertainment, and reading materials.
Notes: Estimates are based on 2005–06 Consumer Expenditure Survey data updated to 2013 dollars by using the Consumer Price Index. For each age category, the expense estimates represent average child-rearing expenditures for each age (e.g., the expense for the 3–5 age category, on average, applies to the 3-year-old, the 4-year-old, or the 5-year-old). The total (0–17) row represents the expenditure sum of all ages (0, 1, 2, 3, …17) in 2013 dollars. The figures represent estimated expenses on the younger child in a two-child family. Estimates are about the same for the older child, so to calculate expenses for two children, figures should be summed for the appropriate age categories. To estimate expenses for an only child, multiply the total expense for the appropriate age category by 1.25. To estimate expenses for each child in a family with three or more children, multiply the total expense for each appropriate age category by 0.78. For expenses on all children in a family, these totals should be summed.

SOURCE: Mark Lino, "Table 1. Estimated Annual Expenditures on a Child by Husband-Wife Families, Overall United States, 2013," in *Expenditures on Children by Families, 2013*, U.S. Department of Agriculture, Center for Nutrition Policy and Promotion, August 2014, https://www.cnpp.usda.gov/sites/default/files/expenditures_on_children_by_families/crc2013.pdf (accessed December 28, 2016)

and summer care also decreases. The estimates do not include expenses related to college attendance, which typically do not occur until the child is at least 18 years old. However, higher income groups tended to spend more on education for 15- to 17-year-olds, suggesting that some disposable income in these groups is spent on providing additional educational opportunities for their children.

FUTURE COSTS. By incorporating an average annual inflation rate of 2.4% (the average annual inflation rate over the previous 20 years), the USDA also estimates the total cost of raising a child born in 2013 who will reach the age of 17 years in 2030. Total family expenses for raising a child born in 2013 are estimated to be $218,680 for the lowest-income group, $304,480 for the middle-income group, and $506,610 for the highest-income group. (See Table 2.4.)

CHILDREN IN POVERTY

Children are the largest group of poor people in the United States. In 1973 they replaced older adults as the poorest age group. (See Figure 2.2.) Proctor, Semega, and Kollar state that in 2015 the poverty rate for all children younger than 18 years of age was 19.7% (14.5 million children). Children under the age of 18 years made up 23.1% of the total U.S. population, but they made up 33.6% of the people living below the poverty line. Children under age six are particularly vulnerable to poverty, and about half (49.5%) of children younger than age six who lived with a single mother were in poverty. This was nearly five times the rate of poverty for children under six years old who lived in married-couple families (10.1%).

The child poverty rate declined between 1995 and 2000, but the rate of children living in poverty (below 100% of the poverty line) and in low-income families (100% to 200% of the poverty line) began to rise again in 2000. By 2015 children represented 19.7% of people in families with an income greater than 200% of the poverty threshold, 28.1% of those in families with an income between 100% and 199% of the poverty threshold, and 33.6% of people in families with an income below 50% of the poverty threshold. (See Figure 2.3.)

TABLE 2.3

Estimated annual expenditures on a child by single-parent families, 2013

Age of child	Total expense	Housing	Food	Transportation	Clothing	Health care	Child care and education[a]	Miscellaneous[b]
Before-tax income: less than $61,530 (average = $27,290)								
0–2	$8,090	$2,940	$1,450	$700	$420	$550	$1,510	$520
3–5	9,010	2,940	1,430	940	340	640	2,090	630
6–8	8,800	2,940	1,910	1,050	360	710	1,030	800
9–11	9,420	2,940	2,090	1,090	420	650	1,470	760
12–14	9,840	2,940	2,240	1,160	440	990	1,210	860
15–17	9,560	2,940	2,360	1,160	480	990	950	680
Total	$164,160	$52,920	$34,440	$18,300	$7,380	$13,590	$24,780	$12,750
Before-tax income: $61,530 or more (average = $111,660)								
0–2	$17,550	$6,100	$2,160	$1,960	$620	$1,040	$3,970	$1,700
3–5	18,490	6,100	2,160	2,210	520	1,150	4,550	1,800
6–8	18,610	6,100	2,780	2,320	550	1,260	3,620	1,980
9–11	19,520	6,100	3,120	2,350	640	1,180	4,200	1,930
12–14	20,570	6,100	3,200	2,430	680	1,650	4,480	2,030
15–17	21,550	6,100	3,350	2,420	760	1,640	5,420	1,860
Total	$348,870	$109,800	$50,310	$41,070	$11,310	$23,760	$78,720	$33,900

[a]Includes only families with child care and education expenses.
[b]Includes personal care items, entertainment, and reading materials.
Notes: Estimates are based on 2005–06 Consumer Expenditure Survey data updated to 2013 dollars by using the consumer price index. For each age category, the expense estimates represent average child-rearing expenditures for each age (e.g., the expense for the 3–5 age category, on average, applies to the 3-year-old, the 4-year-old, or the 5-year-old). The total (0–17) row represents the expenditure sum of all ages (0, 1, 2, 3, ...17) in 2013 dollars. The figures represent estimated expenses on the younger child in a single-parent, two-child family. For estimated expenses on the older child, multiply the total expense for the appropriate age category by 0.97. To estimate expenses for two children, the expenses on the younger child and older child after adjusting the expense on the older child downward should be summed for the appropriate age categories. To estimate expenses for an only child, multiply the total expense for the appropriate age category by 1.29. To estimate expenses for each child in a family with three or more children, multiply the total expense for each appropriate age category by 0.77 after adjusting the expenses on the older children downward. For expenses on all children in a family, these totals should be summed.

SOURCE: Mark Lino, "Table 7. Estimated Annual Expenditures on a Child by Single-Parent Families, Overall United States, 2013," in *Expenditures on Children by Families, 2013*, U.S. Department of Agriculture, Center for Nutrition Policy and Promotion, August 2014, https://www.cnpp.usda.gov/sites/default/files/expenditures_on_children_by_families/crc2013.pdf (accessed December 28, 2016)

Hispanic children and non-Hispanic African American children were especially likely to be poor in 2014. That year 12.3% of non-Hispanic white children, 31.9% of Hispanic children, and 37.3% of non-Hispanic African American children were poor. (See Table 1.4 in Chapter 1.)

Extreme poverty is defined as an income of less than half the poverty level. According to the Children's Defense Fund, in the press release "National Child Poverty Rate Drops; Still Higher Than 2007: Small Relief for Black Children" (September 13, 2016, http://www.childrensdefense.org/news room/cdf-in-the-news/press-releases/2016/NationalChild PovertyRateDropsStillHigherThan2007.html), 6.5 million children were living in extreme poverty in 2015. For a family of four this means living on $33 per day or less than $12,129 annually

Government Aid to Children

Many programs exist in the United States to assist families and children living with economic hardship. Some programs are federally administered, and others operate at the state level. Many programs are mandated at the federal level and administered by the states, which can make tracking them complicated.

TEMPORARY ASSISTANCE FOR NEEDY FAMILIES. Under the Temporary Assistance for Needy Families (TANF) program, states receive a fixed amount from the federal government to "help needy families achieve self-sufficiency." The TANF block grant was created by a welfare reform law, the Personal Responsibility and Work Opportunity Reconciliation Act of 1996.

In *The Temporary Assistance for Needy Families (TANF) Block Grant: Responses to Frequently Asked Questions* (March 18, 2016, https://fas.org/sgp/crs/misc/RL32760.pdf), Gene Falk of the Congressional Research Service explains, "TANF provides fixed funding to states, the bulk of which is provided in a $16.5 billion-per-year basic federal block grant. States are also required in total to contribute, from their own funds, at least $10.4 billion." In March 2015 TANF served 1.6 million families—a total of 4.1 million recipients, of which about 3 million were children. (See Table 2.5.)

States have considerable leeway in how they use TANF funds, and TANF benefits are established by the states. For example, Falk notes that in July 2013 the maximum monthly benefit for a family of three ranged from $923 in Alaska to $170 in Mississippi. In all states TANF benefits are just a fraction of poverty-level income. Each state also decides which families and children receive aid. TANF requires that an adult recipient work in exchange for time-limited assistance. At least 50% of all families and 90% of two-parent families must

FIGURE 2.1

Cost of raising a child from birth to age 18 years, 2013

SOURCE: "The Cost of Raising a Child," in *Expenditures on Children by Families, 2013*, U.S. Department of Agriculture, Center for Nutrition Policy and Promotion, August 2014, https://www.cnpp.usda.gov/sites/default/files/expenditures_on_children_by_families/CRC2013InfoGraphic.pdf (accessed December 28, 2016)

TABLE 2.4

Estimated annual expenditures on children born in 2013, by income group

Year	Age	Lowest	Middle	Highest
			income group	
2013	<1	$9,480	$12,940	$21,430
2014	1	9,710	13,250	21,940
2015	2	9,940	13,570	22,470
2016	3	10,220	13,930	23,020
2017	4	10,470	14,260	23,570
2018	5	10,720	14,600	24,140
2019	6	10,530	14,760	24,590
2020	7	10,780	15,110	25,180
2021	8	11,040	15,470	25,790
2022	9	12,320	16,940	27,590
2023	10	12,610	17,340	28,260
2024	11	12,920	17,760	28,930
2025	12	13,780	19,170	31,570
2026	13	14,110	19,630	32,330
2027	14	14,450	20,100	33,100
2028	15	14,840	21,370	36,680
2029	16	15,200	21,880	37,560
2030	17	15,560	22,400	38,460
Total		**$218,680**	**$304,480**	**$506,610**

Note: Estimates are for the younger child in husband-wife families with two children and assume an average annual inflation rate of 2.4 percent.

SOURCE: Mark Lino, "Table 10. Estimated Annual Expenditures on a Child Born in 2013 by Income Group, Overall United States," in *Expenditures on Children by Families, 2013*, U.S. Department of Agriculture, Center for Nutrition Policy and Promotion, August 2014, https://www.cnpp.usda.gov/sites/default/files/expenditures_on_children_by_families/crc2013.pdf (accessed December 28, 2016)

work. States that fail to meet these work standards risk a reduction in their block grant funding.

TANF is a major funding source for child care. According to Falk, in fiscal year (FY) 2014, 16% of all TANF funds used were either expended on child care or transferred to the child care block grant (the Child Care and Development Fund). TANF also contributes to the child welfare system, which provides foster care, adoption assistance, and services to families with children who either have experienced or are at risk for abuse or neglect.

Historically, the typical family receiving TANF cash assistance was a single mother (who had been unemployed) and her one or two children. Because family structures have changed, TANF assistance may now be given to other families such as those composed of a child and relative caregiver, families with an employed adult, or children with parents who are ineligible for assistance because of their immigration status.

Ife Floyd, LaDonna Pavetti, and Liz Schott of the Center on Budget and Policy Priorities assert in *TANF Continues to Weaken as a Safety Net* (October 27, 2015, http://www.cbpp.org/sites/default/files/atoms/files/6-16-15 tanf.pdf) that although TANF provides a temporary safety net for a few families, it reaches fewer families in need and has placed poor families, and children in

FIGURE 2.2

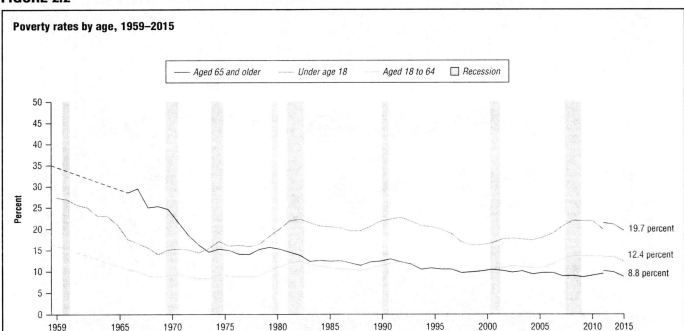

Poverty rates by age, 1959–2015

Note: The data for 2013 and beyond reflect the implementation of the redesigned income questions. The data points are placed at the midpoints of the respective years. Data for people aged 18 to 64 and aged 65 and older are not available from 1960 to 1965.

SOURCE: Bernadette D. Proctor, Jessica L. Semega, and Melissa A. Kollar, "Figure 5. Poverty Rates by Age: 1959 to 2015," in *Income and Poverty in the United States: 2015*, U.S. Census Bureau, September 13, 2016, http://www.census.gov/library/publications/2016/demo/p60-256.html (accessed December 28, 2016)

FIGURE 2.3

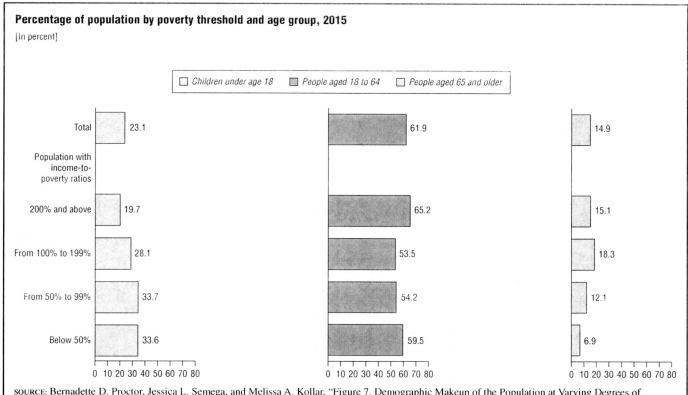

Percentage of population by poverty threshold and age group, 2015

[in percent]

☐ Children under age 18   ▨ People aged 18 to 64   ☐ People aged 65 and older

	Children under age 18	People aged 18 to 64	People aged 65 and older
Total	23.1	61.9	14.9
Population with income-to-poverty ratios			
200% and above	19.7	65.2	15.1
From 100% to 199%	28.1	53.5	18.3
From 50% to 99%	33.7	54.2	12.1
Below 50%	33.6	59.5	6.9

SOURCE: Bernadette D. Proctor, Jessica L. Semega, and Melissa A. Kollar, "Figure 7. Demographic Makeup of the Population at Varying Degrees of Poverty: 2015," in *Income and Poverty in the United States: 2015*, U.S. Census Bureau, September 13, 2016, http://www.census.gov/library/publications/2016/demo/p60-256.html (accessed December 28, 2016).

TABLE 2.5

Temporary Assistance for Needy Families caseload, 2015

Total families	1,618,151
Total recipients	4,067,509
Total adults	1,120,809
Total children	2,946,700

Notes: TANF cash assistance caseload includes families receiving assistance in statue-funded programs counted toward the TANF maintenance of effort (MOE) requirement.

SOURCE: Gene Falk, "Table 3. TANF Cash Assistance Caseload: March 2015," in *The Temporary Assistance for Needy Families (TANF) Block Grant: Responses to Frequently Asked Questions*, Congressional Research Service, March 18, 2016, https://fas.org/sgp/crs/misc/RL32760.pdf (accessed December 28, 2016)

particular, at risk for increased hardship. The researchers aver, "TANF does less to lift families out of deep poverty than its predecessor Aid to Families with Dependent Children (AFDC), and it has contributed to a rise in families living in extreme poverty." They cite the fact that in 2014 just 23 out of 100 families in poverty received cash benefits from TANF, down from 68 out of 100 in 1996.

TANF caseloads varied widely during the Great Recession, growing substantially in some states but not in others. According to Floyd, Pavetti, and Schott, variations in unemployment do not completely explain the variation in state caseloads. For example, the states with the largest caseload increases (Oregon, Colorado, and Illinois) were not states with the highest rates of unemployment; in terms of increased unemployment, they ranked 28th, 14th, and 30th, respectively. Floyd, Pavetti, and Schott note that TANF did not perform well as a safety net during and after the recession, and observe that "TANF benefits are not sufficient to lift families out of poverty in any state, and TANF does far less than AFDC did to lift families out of deep poverty."

Although TANF may not be ideal, strong evidence indicates that the program benefits recipients, especially children. In the presentation "TANF Coverage and Children's Wellbeing" (January 18, 2014, https://sswr.confex.com/sswr/2014/webprogram/Paper20348.html) at the Society for Social Work and Research 2014 Annual Conference in San Antonio, Texas, Julia Shu-Huah Wang of the Columbia University School of Social Work presented the results of a study that considered how relieving parents' financial stress affects children's well-being. Wang finds that TANF coverage may significantly increase the number of times parents or guardians share breakfast with children each week, the likelihood that the family has rules about watching television, and the educational expectations of parents or guardians for their children. TANF coverage was also associated with decreased likelihood of children repeating grades. Wang concludes that TANF may have a positive impact on family life and expectations about educational attainment. She proposes, "To augment current TANF policies, programs and policies supporting low-income families should consider improving familial investment in time and resources for children and enhancing services that will help reduce parental stress."

THE SUPPLEMENTAL NUTRITION ASSISTANCE PROGRAM. The Supplemental Nutrition Assistance Program (SNAP; formerly known as the food stamp program) is administered by the USDA. SNAP provides low-income households with electronic benefit cards that can be used at most grocery stores, much like debit cards, in place of cash. This assistance is intended to ensure that recipients have access to a nutritious diet. It is available to households with a gross monthly income of no more than 130% of the poverty line and a net monthly income (income minus certain legally permitted deductions) at or below the poverty line. Kelsey Farson Gray and Shivani Kochhar of Mathematica Policy Research indicate in *Characteristics of Supplemental Nutrition Assistance Program Households: Fiscal Year 2014* (December 2015, https://www.fns.usda.gov/sites/default/files/ops/Characteristics2014.pdf) that 84% households that received SNAP benefits in FY 2014 lived in poverty and 22% of SNAP households had zero gross income.

The amount of money a family receives on its benefit card is based on the USDA's estimate of how much it costs to provide households with nutritious, low-cost meals, called the Thrifty Food Plan. This estimate changes yearly to reflect inflation. The American Recovery and Reinvestment Act of 2009 increased SNAP maximum allotments 13.6% starting on April 1, 2009. The Food and Nutrition Service (FNS) explains in "Supplemental Nutrition Assistance Program (SNAP): Eligibility" (October 20, 2016, http://www.fns.usda.gov/snap/applicant_recipients/eligibility.htm) that in FY 2016 the maximum monthly benefit for a family of four was $649. (See Table 2.6.)

Gray and Kochhar report that in FY 2014 the majority (57%) of SNAP households contained children and single adults and that nearly half (44%) of all SNAP participants were children.

THE SPECIAL SUPPLEMENTAL NUTRITION PROGRAM FOR WOMEN, INFANTS, AND CHILDREN. The Special Supplemental Nutrition Program for Women, Infants, and Children (WIC) provides food assistance and nutritional screening for low-income pregnant and postpartum women, infants, and children under the age of five years. This program can help women and young children with household incomes that are too high to receive SNAP benefits. Recipients receive food items or vouchers for purchases of certain items in retail stores.

TABLE 2.6

Maximum monthly Supplemental Nutrition Assistance Program allotment by number of people in household, fiscal year 2016

People in household	Maximum monthly allotment
1	$194
2	$357
3	$511
4	$649
5	$771
6	$925
7	$1,022
8	$1,169
Each additional person	$146

Benefit computation	Example
Multiply net income by 30%... (round up)	$1,132 net monthly income × 0.3 = 339.60 (round up to $340)
Subtract 30% of net income from the maximum allotment for the household size...	$649 maximum allotment for 4 − $340 (30% of net income) = $309, **SNAP Allotment** for a full month

SNAP = Supplemental Nutrition Assistance Program

SOURCE: "How Much Could I Receive? Allotments for Households in the 48 Contiguous States and the District of Columbia," in *Supplemental Nutrition Assistance Program (SNAP) Eligibility*, U.S. Department of Agriculture, Food and Nutrition Service, October 20, 2016, https://www.fns.usda.gov/snap/eligibility (accessed December 28, 2016)

In "Women, Infants and Children (WIC): Frequently Asked Questions about WIC" (May 2, 2016, https://www.fns.usda.gov/wic/frequently-asked-questions-about-wic), the FNS explains that eligibility guidelines for the period July 1, 2013, to June 30, 2014, required applicants to have an income at or below 185% of the poverty level. Applicants must also be certified as being "at nutritional risk" by a medical professional, meaning that to be eligible an individual must be at risk for health problems related to inadequate nutrition. Examples of factors that may indicate risk include abnormal weight gain during pregnancy, a history of high-risk pregnancies, being underweight or overweight, anemia, and a history of inadequate nutrition.

Income eligibility guidelines state that a family of one (in other words, a single, pregnant woman) could earn up to $1,832 per month and still qualify for WIC. A family of four could earn $3,747 per month and participate in WIC. Betsy Thorn et al. note in *WIC Participant and Program Characteristics 2014 Final Report* (November 2015, https://www.fns.usda.gov/sites/default/files/ops/WICPC2014.pdf) that nearly three-quarters (74.2%) of WIC participants in 2014 had household incomes at or below the federal poverty level. (See Figure 2.4.)

According to Thorn et al., 9.3 million women and children participated in WIC in 2014. Just over half (53.3%) of WIC participants were children, 23% were infants, and 23.6% were pregnant, postpartum, or breastfeeding women. The WIC program is federally funded but administered by state and local health agencies.

FIGURE 2.4

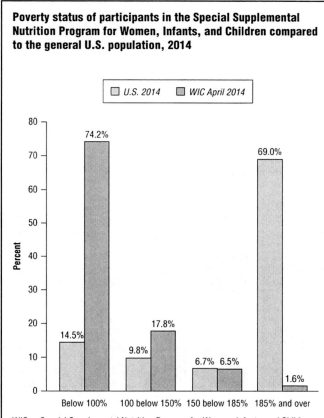

FIGURE 2.4

Poverty status of participants in the Special Supplemental Nutrition Program for Women, Infants, and Children compared to the general U.S. population, 2014

WIC = Special Supplemental Nutrition Program for Women, Infants, and Children.
Note: Percents may not add to 100 percent due to rounding.

SOURCE: Betsy Thorn et al., "Figure ES.3. Poverty Status of WIC Participants Reporting Income Versus General U.S. Population," in *WIC Participant and Program Characteristics 2014 Final Report*, Prepared by Insight Policy Research for the U.S. Department of Agriculture, Food and Nutrition Service, November 2015, https://www .fns.usda.gov/sites/default/files/ops/WICPC2014.pdf (accessed December 28, 2016)

In "WIC Program Participation and Costs" (March 10, 2017, https://www.fns.usda.gov/pd/wic-program), the FNS reports that in FY 2016 the WIC program's expenditures were nearly $6 billion.

SCHOOL NUTRITION PROGRAMS. School nutrition programs offer food assistance to school-aged children. Until the USDA updated its standards for federally subsidized school lunch programs in late 2012, less than 2% of middle or high school meals met nutritional standards aimed at limiting fat, sodium, sugar, and calories. The revised USDA standards stipulate that as of the 2014–15 school year all grains offered in school programs must be whole-grain rich. Both a fruit and a vegetable must be offered daily, and a variety of vegetables must be served each week. Milk is limited to nonfat or low-fat (1%), and sweetened flavored milk may be served only if it is nonfat.

In the press release "Latest Research Shows School Meals Improve Food Security, Dietary Intake, and Weight Outcomes, Says Food Research & Action Center" (August 23, 2016, http://www.frac.org/news/latest-research-shows-school-meals-improve-food-security-dietary-intake-and-weight-outcomes-says-food-research-action-center), the Food Research and Action Center reports that the new nutrition standards have already served to "improve nutrition-related outcomes among students, including improvements in fruit and vegetable selection and consumption." The center also notes that free or reduced-price school lunches and breakfast programs have been shown to reduce food insecurity and that low-income students who eat breakfast and lunch at school have a more healthful diet than their peers who do not eat school meals.

Children living in families that earn no more than 185% of the poverty level are eligible for reduced-price school meals; children living in families that earn no more than 130% of the poverty level are eligible for free school meals. The FNS reports in "Federal Cost of Programs" (March 10, 2017, https://www.fns.usda.gov/sites/default/files/pd/cncost.pdf) that in FY 2016 the U.S. government spent $17.8 billion on school nutrition programs, including the National School Lunch Program, the School Breakfast Program, and the Special Milk Program. In 2016, 30.4 million children took part in the National School Lunch Program.

CHILD SUPPORT

Children living in single-parent families are far more likely to be poor than children living in two-parent households, and the number of children living with only one parent (usually the mother) is increasing. According to Timothy S. Grall of the Census Bureau, in *Custodial Mothers and Fathers and Their Child Support: 2013* (January 2016, https://www.census.gov/content/dam/Census/library/publications/2016/demo/P60-255.pdf), in 2014, 13.4 million parents had custody of 22.1 million children under the age of 21 years whose other parent lived elsewhere. Mothers accounted for 82.5% of these custodial parents, whereas fathers made up only 17.5%. These proportions have not changed significantly since 1994.

Grall indicates that about half (48.7%) of the 13.4 million custodial parents in 2014 had a child support agreement with the other parent. Most agreements required child support payments from the noncustodial parent. In 2013 about two-thirds (68.5%) of all custodial parents due support received at least some payments. Nearly half (45.6%) of custodial parents received all the payments they were due. (See Figure 2.5.) Custodial parents living below the poverty level did not fare as well; just 34.8% received full payment. (See Table 2.7.) Grall notes that in 2013 noncustodial parents who had joint physical or legal custody agreements were more likely to receive the full amount of child support

FIGURE 2.5

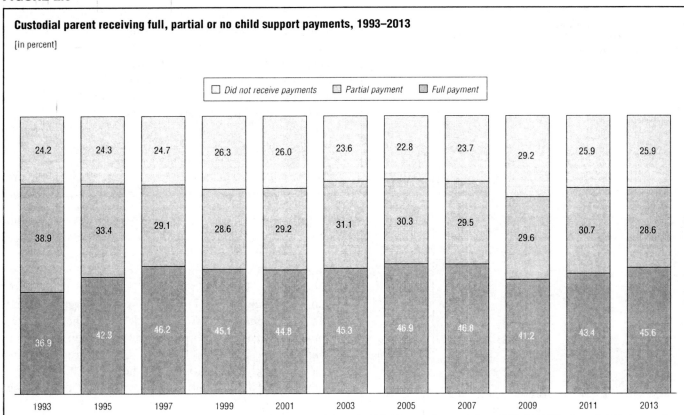

Custodial parent receiving full, partial or no child support payments, 1993–2013

[in percent]

SOURCE: Timothy Grall, "Figure 4. Custodial Parents Receiving Full, Partial, or No Child Support Payments Due: 1993–2013," in *Custodial Mothers and Fathers and Their Child Support: 2013*, U. S. Census Bureau, October 2016, https://www.census.gov/content/dam/Census/library/publications/2016/demo/p60-255.pdf (accessed December 28, 2016)

(58.6%) than parents who had no contact with the non-custodial parent (32%).

Differences existed in the child support arrangements for custodial mothers and custodial fathers. In 2013 custodial mothers were much more likely than custodial fathers to be awarded child support (52.3% and 31.4%, respectively). (See Table 2.7.) On average, custodial mothers with support agreements were due $5,760 in child support in 2013, and received $3,936. Custodial fathers with agreements were due $6,435 on average, and received $4,821. As noted earlier, fewer than half of all custodial parents actually received the full child support due them; only 46.2% of custodial mothers and 40.7% of custodial fathers due support received the total amount due.

Grall explains that receipt of child support payments made a significant difference in the household incomes of single-parent and low-income families. In 2013 the average family income of custodial parents who received at least some of the child support due them was $37,370, and the child support represented 14.3% of the total household income. Child support represented 17.7% of the total household income for those parents who received all the child support due them. Child support

was a larger proportion of income for some low-income parents. Among custodial parents below the poverty level who received the full support owed to them, child support on average accounted for 70.3% of their annual income.

Government Assistance in Obtaining Child Support

Inadequate financial support from noncustodial parents contributes to the high incidence of poverty among children living in single-parent families. When custodial parents are not paid the child support due them, their families suffer financially and often must turn to public welfare. Therefore, government agencies have an interest in recovering child support from delinquent parents.

In 1975 Congress established the Child Support Enforcement (CSE) program, a collaborative effort among local, state, and federal agencies, to ensure that children receive financial support from both parents. Under the Child Support Recovery Act of 1992, non-custodial parents who are delinquent on child support due in another state can be prosecuted. CSE services are automatically provided to families receiving assistance under TANF; any support collected usually reimburses the state and federal governments for TANF payments made to the family. Child support services are

TABLE 2.7

Characteristics of custodial parents by award status and payments received, 2013

[Numbers in thousands, as of spring 2014. Parents living with own children under 21 years of age whose other parent is living in the home.]

		With child support agreements or awards									
				Due child support payments in 2013							
								Received all payments		Did not receive payments	
Characteristics	Total	Total	Percent	Total	Average due	Average received	Percent received	Total	Percent	Total	Percent
All custodial parents											
Total	13,418	6,528	48.7	5,697	$5,774	$3,953	68.5	2,595	45.6	1,475	25.9
Sex											
Male	2,350	739	31.4	648	$6,435	$4,821	74.9	264	40.7	169	26.1
Female	11,069	5,789	52.3	5,049	$5,760	$3,936	68.3	2,331	46.2	1,305	25.8
Age											
Under 30 years	2,971	1,251	42.1	1,072	$4,185	$1,925	46.0	325	30.3	320	29.9
30 to 39 years	4,807	2,579	53.7	2,319	$5,192	$3,437	66.2	922	39.8	648	27.9
40 years and over	5,640	2,698	47.8	2,305	$7,100	$5,414	76.3	1,349	58.5	507	22.0
Race and ethnicity[a]											
White alone	9,173	4,852	52.9	4,202	$6,000	$4,341	72.4	2,050	48.8	963	22.9
White alone, not Hispanic	6,454	3,637	56.4	3,167	$6,166	$4,668	75.7	1,624	51.3	654	20.7
Black alone	3,393	1,268	37.4	1,138	$4,567	$2,320	50.8	383	33.7	405	35.6
Hispanic (any race)	3,103	1,364	44.0	1,164	$5,411	$3,341	61.7	484	41.6	326	28.0
Current marital status[b]											
Married	2,131	1,094	51.3	971	$5,416	$3,896	71.9	457	47.1	241	24.8
Divorced	4,469	2,577	57.7	2,281	$6,772	$5,209	76.9	1,289	56.5	458	20.1
Separated	1,552	634	40.9	530	$6,517	$3,584	55.0	192	36.2	158	29.8
Never married	5,117	2,157	42.2	1,863	$4,486	$2,538	56.6	635	34.1	603	32.4
Educational attainment											
Less than high school diploma	1,799	686	38.1	568	$4,970	$2,373	47.7	172	30.3	218	38.4
High school graduate	4,274	1,965	46.0	1,690	$5,374	$3,232	60.1	588	34.8	501	29.6
Less than 4 years of college	4,706	2,444	51.9	2,132	$5,554	$3,912	70.4	1,021	47.9	509	23.9
Bachelors degree or more	2,640	1,434	54.3	1,306	$7,002	$5,638	80.5	815	62.4	246	18.8
Selected characteristics											
Family income below 2013 poverty level	3,859	1,737	45.0	1,474	$5,021	$2,918	58.1	513	34.8	495	33.6
Worked full-time, year-round	6,660	3,293	49.4	2,922	$5,764	$4,021	69.8	1,414	48.4	680	23.3
Public assistance program participation[c]	5,715	2,687	47.0	2,327	$5,071	$2,858	56.4	801	34.4	777	33.4
With 1 child	7,333	3,062	41.8	2,593	$5,741	$4,050	70.5	1,221	47.1	688	26.5
With 2 or more children	6,086	3,466	57.0	3,104	$5,802	$3,871	66.7	1,374	44.3	786	25.3
Child had contact with other parent in 2013	9,316	4,796	51.5	4,168	$5,937	$4,363	73.5	2,106	50.5	917	22.0
Child had no contact with other parent in 2013	4,102	1,732	42.2	1,529	$5,333	$2,833	53.1	489	32.0	558	36.5
Court ordered physical or legal joint custody	3,503	1,989	56.8	1,771	$6,013	$4,839	80.5	1,037	58.6	312	17.6

[a]Includes those reporting one race alone and not in combination with any other race.
[b]Excludes 150,000 with marital status of widowed.
[c]Received any of the following: Medicaid, food stamps, public housing or rent subsidy, Temporary Assistance for Needy Families (TANF), or general assistance.

SOURCE: Timothy Grall, "Table 2. Demographic Characteristics of Custodial Parents by Award Status and Payments Received: 2013," in *Custodial Mothers and Fathers and Their Child Support: 2013*, U.S. Census Bureau, October 2016, https://www.census.gov/content/dam/Census/library/publications/2016/demo/P60-255.pdf (accessed December 28, 2016)

also available for a small application fee to families not receiving TANF.

Provisions in the Personal Responsibility and Work Opportunity Reconciliation Act of 1996 strengthened and improved child support collection activities. The law established a National Directory of New Hires to track parents across state lines, made the process for establishing paternity faster and easier, and enacted tough new penalties for delinquent parents, including expanded wage garnishment and suspension or revocation of driver's licenses. The law also required single-mother TANF applicants to disclose the paternity of their children and

to assign any child support payments to the state. According to the Administration for Children and Families, in "FY 2015 Preliminary Report" (April 18, 2016, https://www.acf.hhs.gov/css/resource/fy-2015-preliminary-data-report), these efforts have paid off; in FY 2015 CSE handled 14.7 million cases (involving 15.9 million children) and collected $28.6 billion.

TEEN EMPLOYMENT

The U.S. Bureau of Labor Statistics (BLS) reports in the press release "The Employment Situation: November 2016" (March 10, 2017, https://www.bls.gov/news.release/

pdf/empsit.pdf) that in February 2017 among teens aged 16 to 19 years the unemployment rate was 15%. This was much higher than the overall unemployment rate that month of 4.7%.

Employment rates among young people are highest during the summer months, when many full-time students are out of school, and businesses are hiring seasonal workers. For example, the BLS states in the press release "Employment and Unemployment among Youth—Summer 2016" (August 17, 2016, https://www.bls.gov/news.release/pdf/youth.pdf) that the employment of youth between the ages of 16 and 24 years increased by 1.9 million to 20.5 million from April to July 2016. Nevertheless, the BLS reports that in July 2016 unemployed youth numbered 2.6 million. African American youth were more likely to be unemployed (20.6%) than Hispanics (11.3%), Asian Americans (10%), or whites (9.9%). Among youth employed in July 2016, 25% (5.2 million out of 20.5 million total workers aged 16 to 24 years) of them held jobs in the leisure and hospitality industry, which includes food services. (See Table 2.8.) An additional 18% (3.8 million) of youth were in the retail trade

industry and 13% (2.6 million) were in education and health services.

Teens often do not earn as much as older workers. For instance, in "Characteristics of Minimum Wage Workers: 2015" (April 2016, https://www.bls.gov/opub/reports/minimum-wage/2015/home.htm), the BLS reports that in 2015 workers under the age of 25 years were only about one-fifth of all hourly paid workers, but they were about half of those paid the federal minimum wage or less. Of employed teenagers (aged 16 to 19 years) paid by the hour, 11.2% earned the minimum wage or less, compared with 2.2% of workers aged 25 years and older. (See Table 2.9.)

In *After Years of Labor Market Pain, 2015 Finally Gave Millennial Workers Reasons for Optimism* (January 2016, http://genprogress.org/wp-content/uploads/2016/01/14120002/EOY-Jobs-Report.pdf), a report released by Generation Progress, the youth outreach arm of the Center for American Progress, a nonprofit think-tank, Sunny Frothingham and Rachel West analyze BLS data and find the unemployment rate for youth aged 16 to 24 years was more than twice the national unemployment rate. The researchers

TABLE 2.8

Employed teens and young adults aged 16–24 by industry, race and Hispanic ethnicity, July 2015–16

[Numbers in thousands. Data are not seasonally adjusted.]

Industry and class of worker	Total July 2015	Total July 2016	White July 2015	White July 2016	Black or African American July 2015	Black or African American July 2016	Asian July 2015	Asian July 2016	Hispanic or Latino ethnicity July 2015	Hispanic or Latino ethnicity July 2016
Total employed	**20,333**	**20,456**	**15,903**	**15,981**	**2,645**	**2,499**	**855**	**859**	**4,127**	**4,235**
Agriculture and related industries	309	320	294	302	7	5	1	4	47	74
Nonagricultural industries	20,024	20,136	15,609	15,678	2,638	2,493	853	855	4,079	4,162
Private wage and salary workers*	18,223	18,359	14,169	14,314	2,418	2,245	791	774	3,790	3,893
Mining, quarrying, and oil and gas extraction	75	39	68	25	0	13	3	0	9	15
Construction	883	991	799	934	36	24	1	8	267	304
Manufacturing	1,385	1,408	1,133	1,092	162	172	46	71	322	261
Durable goods	882	792	726	653	104	75	33	41	173	136
Nondurable goods	504	616	406	439	58	97	14	30	149	124
Wholesale trade	277	252	228	209	24	20	12	4	94	58
Retail trade	4,005	3,756	2,902	2,871	680	500	206	173	785	781
Transportation and utilities	447	434	337	278	73	100	13	30	133	81
Information	288	278	221	237	30	20	30	20	52	59
Financial activities	725	762	571	581	93	78	39	57	180	145
Professional and business services	1,547	1,690	1,228	1,324	158	189	75	99	332	399
Education and health services	2,236	2,607	1,664	1,951	331	391	137	133	368	497
Leisure and hospitality	5,437	5,213	4,234	4,072	762	638	196	138	1,098	1,104
Other services	918	929	784	741	68	98	33	40	150	190
Government wage and salary workers	1,403	1,395	1,091	1,042	195	221	47	68	189	177
Federal	114	158	82	112	14	23	9	14	3	8
State	541	510	414	366	77	82	19	36	80	58
Local	748	728	595	563	103	116	18	18	106	111
Self-employed, unincorporated, and unpaid family workers	398	382	349	322	26	28	16	14	100	91

*Includes self-employed workers whose businesses are incorporated.

Note: Estimates for the above race groups (white, black or African American, and Asian) do not sum to totals because data are not presented for all races. Persons whose ethnicity is identified as Hispanic or Latino may be of any race. Updated population controls are introduced annually with the release of January data.

SOURCE: "Table 3. Employed Persons 16 to 24 Years of Age by Industry, Class of Worker, Race, and Hispanic or Latino Ethnicity, July 2015–2016," in *Employment and Unemployment among Youth—Summer 2016*, U.S. Department of Labor, Bureau of Labor Statistics, August 17, 2016, https://www.bls.gov/news.release/pdf/youth.pdf (accessed December 28, 2016)

TABLE 2.9

Workers paid hourly rates at or below the federal minimum wage, by selected characteristics, 2015

	Number of workers (in thousands)				Percent distribution				Percent of workers paid hourly rates		
		At or below the minimum wage				At or below the minimum wage				At or below the minimum wage	
Characteristic	Total paid hourly rates	Total	At minimum wage	Below minimum wage	Total paid hourly rates	Total	At minimum wage	Below minimum wage	Total	At minimum wage	Below minimum wage
Age and gender											
Total, 16 years and older	78,232	2,561	870	1,691	100	100	100	100	3.3	1.1	2.2
16 to 24 years	15,562	1,153	475	678	19.9	45	54.6	40.1	7.4	3.1	4.4
16 to 19 years	4,355	487	258	229	5.6	19	29.6	13.6	11.2	5.9	5.3
25 years and older	62,670	1,408	395	1,013	80.1	55	45.4	59.9	2.2	0.6	1.6
Men, 16 years and older	38,732	959	330	629	49.5	37.4	37.9	37.2	2.5	0.9	1.6
16 to 24 years	7,778	417	193	224	9.9	16.3	22.1	13.3	5.4	2.5	2.9
16 to 19 years	2,124	194	107	87	2.7	7.6	12.3	5.1	9.1	5.1	4.1
25 years and older	30,954	542	137	404	39.6	21.2	15.8	23.9	1.8	0.4	1.3
Women, 16 years and older	39,500	1,602	540	1,062	50.5	62.6	62.1	62.8	4.1	1.4	2.7
16 to 24 years	7,784	736	282	454	10	28.7	32.5	26.8	9.5	3.6	5.8
16 to 19 years	2,231	293	150	143	2.9	11.4	17.3	8.4	13.1	6.7	6.4
25 years and older	31,716	866	258	608	40.5	33.8	29.6	36	2.7	0.8	1.9
Race and Hispanic or Latino ethnicity											
White[a]	60,306	1,872	561	1,311	77.1	73.1	64.4	77.5	3.1	0.9	2.2
Men	30,448	667	218	450	38.9	26.1	25	26.6	2.2	0.7	1.5
Women	29,858	1,205	343	862	38.2	47	39.4	51	4	1.1	2.9
Black or African American[a]	11,178	481	247	234	14.3	18.8	28.4	13.9	4.3	2.2	2.1
Men	5,015	212	85	127	6.4	8.3	9.8	7.5	4.2	1.7	2.5
Women	6,163	270	162	108	7.9	10.5	18.6	6.4	4.4	2.6	1.7
Asian[a]	3,690	109	32	78	4.7	4.3	3.6	4.6	3	0.9	2.1
Men	1,715	35	12	23	2.2	1.4	1.4	1.4	2	0.7	1.3
Women	1,975	74	20	55	2.5	2.9	2.3	3.2	3.8	1	2.8
Hispanic or Latino[a]	15,809	459	159	300	20.2	17.9	18.3	17.7	2.9	1	1.9
Men	8,825	188	67	121	11.3	7.3	7.7	7.1	2.1	0.8	1.4
Women	6,984	272	92	179	8.9	10.6	10.6	10.6	3.9	1.3	2.6
Full- and part-time status											
Full-time workers[b]	57,809	1,075	288	787	73.9	42	33.1	46.6	1.9	0.5	1.4
Men	31,662	469	118	351	40.5	18.3	13.6	20.8	1.5	0.4	1.1
Women	26,146	606	170	436	33.4	23.7	19.6	25.8	2.3	0.7	1.7
Part-time workers[b]	20,285	1,477	579	898	25.9	57.7	66.6	53.1	7.3	2.9	4.4
Men	6,989	486	212	274	8.9	19	24.4	16.2	7	3	3.9
Women	13,296	991	367	624	17	38.7	42.2	36.9	7.5	2.8	4.7

[a]Estimates for the above race groups—white, black, or African American, and Asian—do not sum to totals because data are not presented for all races. Persons whose ethnicity is identified as Hispanic or Latino may be of any race.
[b]The distinction between full- and part-time workers is based on hours usually worked. These data will not sum to totals because full- or part-time status on the principal job is not identifiable for a small number of multiple jobholders. Full time is 35 hours or more per week; part time is less than 35 hours.
Note: Data exclude all self-employed workers, whether or not their businesses are incorporated.

SOURCE: "Table 1. Wage and Salary Workers Paid Hourly Rates with Earnings at or below the Prevailing Federal Minimum Wage, by Selected Characteristics, 2015 Annual Averages," in *Characteristics of Minimum Wage Workers, 2015*, U.S. Department of Labor, Bureau of Labor Statistics, April 2016, https://www.bls.gov/opub/reports/minimum-wage/2015/home.htm (accessed December 28, 2016)

observe that more Millennials (people born between 1982 and 2004) live in poverty than members of previous generations did at the same age. Frothingham and West conclude, "The unemployment rates for youth and Millennials of color show that many young people lack opportunities to successfully participate in the current labor market... These challenges and disparities should be a call to action for policy makers to better respond to the needs of Millennial workers."

CHAPTER 3
CARING FOR CHILDREN

SOCIETAL CHANGES AND WORKING MOTHERS

During the first decades of the 21st century, women with young children were much more likely to work outside the home than they had been three decades previously. Jane Lawler Dye of the U.S. Census Bureau reports in *Fertility of American Women: June 2004* (December 2005, https://www.census.gov/prod/2005pubs/p20-555.pdf) that in 1976, 31% of women aged 15 to 44 years with a child under the age of one year old worked. In the press release "Employment Characteristics of Families—2015" (April 22, 2016, https://www.bls.gov/news.release/pdf/famee.pdf), the U.S. Bureau of Labor Statistics (BLS) reports that in 2015 the labor force participation rate (the percentage of the population working or looking for work) for mothers with children under the age of one year was 58.1%. As shown in Table 3.1, the labor force participation rate in 2015 for mothers with children under age six was 64.2%, and for mothers with children between the ages of six and 17 it was 74.4%. The labor force participation rate for all mothers with children under the age of 18 years was 69.9%.

Many factors contributed to the increased proportion of mothers in the workforce. Legislation passed during the late 1970s made it more practical for women to return to work after the birth of a child. In 1976 tax code changes enabled families to take a tax credit for child care costs, making it more financially feasible for women to return to work. In 1978 the Pregnancy Discrimination Act was passed, making it illegal for employers to discriminate in hiring, firing, promoting, or determining pay levels based on pregnancy or childbirth. In 1993 the Family and Medical Leave Act (FMLA) was passed, requiring employers to give eligible employees up to 12 weeks of unpaid leave for childbearing or family care each year. The Affordable Care Act of 2010 (ACA) provides for nursing breaks and requires employers to provide a private, sanitary place for mothers covered by the Fair Labor Standards Act (which includes many hourly workers) to express breast milk until their children's first birthday. The repeal of the ACA promised by President Donald Trump (1946–) may jeopardize the accommodations afforded to working mothers under the legislation.

Societal changes also contributed to the greater number of women with young children in the labor force. Judith Dey of the BLS compares in *How Has Labor Force Participation among Young Moms and Dads Changed? A Comparison of Two Cohorts* (September 2014, https://www.bls.gov/opub/btn/volume-3/pdf/how-has-labor-force-participation-among-young-moms-and-dads-changed.pdf) the work lives of young adults born between 1980 and 1984 (the 1997 cohort) and those born between 1957 and 1964 (the 1979 cohort) after their first children were born. Dey finds that although the differences have narrowed, women continue to take more time off after the birth of a child than do men, largely because of increased labor force participation of mothers in the year after giving birth, not because of decreased labor force participation of new fathers. (See Figure 3.1 and Figure 3.2.)

Dey observes that parents with greater educational attainment spent less time out of the labor force after the birth of their first child. Across education levels, fathers in the 1997 cohort spent more weeks out of the labor force than did fathers in the 1979 cohort. (See Table 3.2.) The reverse was true for new mothers. Mothers in each educational attainment category in the 1997 cohort spent less time out of the labor force compared with the 1979 cohort. In the 1979 cohort mothers with some college or higher spent 41.7% of the weeks during the first year after the birth of their child out of the labor force, but this fell to 37.5% in the 1997 cohort. New mothers with less than a high school diploma in the 1979 cohort spent 72.8% of the weeks during the year out of the labor force, while those in the 1997 cohort spent just 55% of the weeks during the year out of the labor force.

TABLE 3.1

Employment status of the population, by sex, marital status, and presence and age of own children under age 18, 2015

[Numbers in thousands]

Characteristic	2015 Total	Men	Women
With own children under 18 years			
Civilian noninstitutional population	65,564	29,095	36,469
Civilian labor force	52,476	26,978	25,498
Participation rate	80.0	92.7	69.9
Employed	50,238	26,079	24,159
Full-time workers[a]	43,250	24,880	18,370
Part-time workers[b]	6,989	1,199	5,790
Employment-population ratio	76.6	89.6	66.2
Unemployed	2,238	899	1,339
Unemployment rate	4.3	3.3	5.3
Married, spouse present			
Civilian noninstitutional population	49,822	25,122	24,700
Civilian labor force	40,226	23,532	16,694
Participation rate	80.7	93.7	67.6
Employed	39,026	22,889	16,137
Full-time workers[a]	34,148	21,958	12,190
Part-time workers[b]	4,877	931	3,947
Employment-population ratio	78.3	91.1	65.3
Unemployed	1,200	643	557
Unemployment rate	3.0	2.7	3.3
Other marital status[c]			
Civilian noninstitutional population	15,742	3,973	11,769
Civilian labor force	12,250	3,446	8,804
Participation rate	77.8	86.7	74.8
Employed	11,213	3,190	8,022
Full-time workers[a]	9,101	2,922	6,179
Part-time workers[b]	2,111	268	1,843
Employment-population ratio	71.2	80.3	68.2
Unemployed	1,038	256	782
Unemployment rate	8.5	7.4	8.9
With own children 6 to 17 years, none younger			
Civilian noninstitutional population	36,616	16,171	20,445
Civilian labor force	30,057	14,840	15,218
Participation rate	82.1	91.8	74.4
Employed	28,923	14,392	14,531
Full-time workers[a]	25,073	13,785	11,288
Part-time workers[b]	3,850	607	3,243
Employment-population ratio	79.0	89.0	71.1
Unemployed	1,134	448	687
Unemployment rate	3.8	3.0	4.5
With own children under 6 years			
Civilian noninstitutional population	28,948	12,924	16,024
Civilian labor force	22,419	12,138	10,281
Participation rate	77.4	93.9	64.2
Employed	21,315	11,687	9,628
Full-time workers[a]	18,177	11,095	7,082
Part-time workers[b]	3,139	592	2,547
Employment-population ratio	73.6	90.4	60.1
Unemployed	1,104	451	652
Unemployment rate	4.9	3.7	6.3
With no own children under 18 years			
Civilian noninstitutional population	185,237	92,006	93,231
Civilian labor force	104,654	56,643	48,011
Participation rate	56.5	61.6	51.5
Employed	98,595	53,052	45,544
Full-time workers[a]	78,243	44,471	33,772
Part-time workers[b]	20,353	8,581	11,772
Employment-population ratio	53.2	57.7	48.9
Unemployed	6,058	3,591	2,468
Unemployment rate	5.8	6.3	5.1

The presence of fathers in the household influenced maternal labor force status differently in the 1979 and 1997 cohorts. In the 1979 cohort the father's presence was associated with mothers spending fewer weeks out of

TABLE 3.1

Employment status of the population, by sex, marital status, and presence and age of own children under age 18, 2015 [CONTINUED]

[Numbers in thousands]

[a]Usually work 35 hours or more per week at all jobs.
[b]Usually work less than 35 hours per week at all jobs.
[c]Includes never married; married, spouse absent; divorced; separated; and widowed persons.
Notes: Own children include sons, daughters, step-children, and adopted children. Not included are nieces, nephews, grandchildren, and other related and unrelated children. Detail may not sum to totals due to rounding. Updated population controls are introduced annually with the release of January data.

SOURCE: Adapted from "Table 5. Employment Status of the Population by Sex, Marital Status, and Presence and Age of Own Children under 18, 2014–15 Annual Averages," in *Employment Characteristics of Families—2015*, U.S. Department of Labor, Bureau of Labor Statistics, April 22, 2016, https://www.bls.gov/news.release/pdf/famee.pdf (accessed December 29, 2016)

FIGURE 3.1

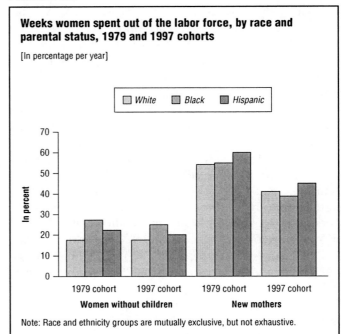

Weeks women spent out of the labor force, by race and parental status, 1979 and 1997 cohorts

[In percentage per year]

Note: Race and ethnicity groups are mutually exclusive, but not exhaustive.

SOURCE: Judith Dey, "Chart 4. Percentage of Weeks per Year Women Spent out of the Labor Force, by Race and Parental Status, 1979 and 1997 Cohorts," in "How Has Labor Force Participation among Young Moms and Dads Changed? A Comparison of Two Cohorts," *Beyond the Numbers*, vol. 3, no. 19, U.S. Department of Labor, Bureau of Labor Statistics, September 2014, https://www.bls.gov/opub/btn/volume-3/pdf/how-has-labor-force-participation-among-young-moms-and-dads-changed.pdf (accessed December 29, 2016)

the labor force, while in the 1997 cohort it was associated with a few more weeks in the labor force. (See Table 3.3.) In both cohorts white mothers were more likely to take more time off from the labor force when the father of the child lived in the household. African American and Hispanic mothers with the father of their child in the household spent less time out of the labor force than did mothers who lived in a household where the father was not present.

Dey concludes that young mothers in the 1997 cohort "worked a greater portion of the year after the birth of their child, creating a markedly different labor market experience from young mothers in the previous cohort. Young fathers' work patterns have also changed, but far less dramatically. They still work slightly more than young men who have not become fathers, but the differences between fathers and men without children are smaller in the more recent generation of young men."

Mothers Work to Support Their Families

The growing number of single mothers means that more women have to work to support their family. In 1970 about 3 million women maintained single-parent households; by 2015 this number had increased to 8.5 million. Changes in government programs that aided poor families also resulted in increasing numbers of single mothers entering the workforce. In 1996 the federal government placed a two-year limit on receiving public assistance benefits while not working, requiring poor parents to work even if they had to place young children in day care. In 2015, 70.8% of single mothers were working. (See Table 3.4.) Nearly two-thirds (65.4%) of single mothers with children under three years old were in the labor force that year, with a 12% unemployment rate. (See Table 3.5.)

FIGURE 3.2

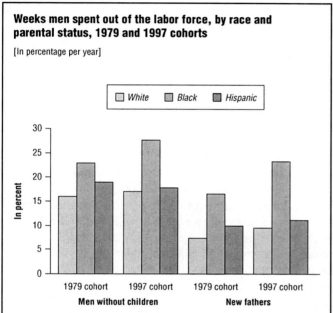

Weeks men spent out of the labor force, by race and parental status, 1979 and 1997 cohorts

[In percentage per year]

Note: Race and ethnicity groups are mutually exclusive, but not exhaustive.

SOURCE: Judith Dey, "Chart 5. Percentage of Weeks per Year Men Spent out of the Labor Force, by Race and Parental Status, 1979 and 1997 Cohorts," in "How Has Labor Force Participation among Young Moms and Dads Changed? A Comparison of Two Cohorts," *Beyond the Numbers*, vol. 3, no. 19, U.S. Department of Labor, Bureau of Labor Statistics, September 2014, https://www.bls.gov/opub/btn/volume-3/pdf/how-has-labor-force-participation-among-young-moms-and-dads-changed.pdf (accessed December 29, 2016)

TABLE 3.3

Percentage of weeks new mothers spent out of the labor force in year following birth of first child, by presence of the father in household and race, 1979 and 1997 cohorts

Characteristic	1979 cohort	1997 cohort
All mothers		
Father not present	56.5	40
Father present	53.6	42.4
White		
Father not present	52.5	37
Father present	53.9	43.7
Black		
Father not present	57.8	42.6
Father present	47.6	30.9
Hispanic		
Father not present	66.8	45
Father present	56.5	44.3

SOURCE: Judith Dey, "Table 6. Percentage of Weeks New Mothers Spent out of the Labor Force in the Year Following Birth of First Child, by Presence of the Father in the Household and Race, 1979 and 1997 Cohorts," in "How Has Labor Force Participation among Young Moms and Dads Changed? A Comparison of Two Cohorts," *Beyond the Numbers*, vol. 3, no. 19, U.S. Department of Labor, Bureau of Labor Statistics, September 2014, https://www.bls.gov/opub/btn/volume-3/pdf/how-has-labor-force-participation-among-young-moms-and-dads-changed.pdf (accessed December 29, 2016)

TABLE 3.2

Percentage of weeks out of the labor force in the year after the birth of the first child, by educational attainment and sex, 1979 and 1997 cohorts

Education	Mothers		Fathers	
	1979 cohort	1997 cohort	1979 cohort	1997 cohort
Less than high school diploma	72.8	55	14.6	20.1
High school diploma	50.6	40.1	6.4	10
Some college or higher	41.7	37.5	3.4	7

Note: Table excludes those enrolled in school anytime in the year after the birth of the first child.

SOURCE: Judith Dey, "Table 4. Percentage of Weeks out of the Labor Force in the Year after the Birth of the First Child, by Educational Status at Time of Birth and Gender, 1979 and 1997 Cohorts," in "How Has Labor Force Participation among Young Moms and Dads Changed? A Comparison of Two Cohorts," *Beyond the Numbers*, vol. 3, no. 19, U.S. Department of Labor, Bureau of Labor Statistics, September 2014, https://www.bls.gov/opub/btn/volume-3/pdf/how-has-labor-force-participation-among-young-moms-and-dads-changed.pdf (accessed December 29, 2016)

TABLE 3.4

Employment status of parents, by age of youngest child and family type, 2015

[Numbers in thousands]

Characteristic	Number 2015	Percent distribution 2015
With own children under 18 years		
Total families	34,363	100.0
Parent(s) employed	30,672	89.3
No parent employed	3,692	10.7
Married-couple families		
Total	23,401	100.0
Parent(s) employed	22,631	96.7
Mother employed	15,420	65.9
Both parents employed	14,174	60.6
Mother employed, not father	1,246	5.3
Father employed, not mother	7,211	30.8
Neither parent employed	771	3.3
Families maintained by mother*		
Total	8,505	100.0
Mother employed	6,024	70.8
Mother not employed	2,481	29.2
Families maintained by father*		
Total	2,457	100.0
Father employed	2,017	82.1
Father not employed	440	17.9
With own children, 6 to 17 years, none younger		
Total families	19,774	100.0
Parent(s) employed	17,762	89.8
No parent employed	2,012	10.2
Married-couple families		
Total	13,306	100.0
Parent(s) employed	12,842	96.5
Mother employed	9,363	70.4
Both parents employed	8,565	64.4
Mother employed, not father	798	6.0
Father employed, not mother	3,479	26.1
Neither parent employed	464	3.5
Families maintained by mother*		
Total	5,080	100.0
Mother employed	3,790	74.6
Mother not employed	1,290	25.4
Families maintained by father*		
Total	1,388	100.0
Father employed	1,130	81.4
Father not employed	258	18.6
With own children under 6 years		
Total families	14,589	100.0
Parent(s) employed	12,910	88.5
No parent employed	1,680	11.5
Married-couple families		
Total	10,096	100.0
Parent(s) employed	9,789	97.0
Mother employed	6,057	60.0
Both parents employed	5,609	55.6
Mother employed, not father	448	4.4
Father employed, not mother	3,732	37.0
Neither parent employed	307	3.0
Families maintained by mother*		
Total	3,425	100.0
Mother employed	2,234	65.2
Mother not employed	1,191	34.8

TABLE 3.4

Employment status of parents, by age of youngest child and family type, 2015 [CONTINUED]

[Numbers in thousands]

Characteristic	Number 2015	Percent distribution 2015
Families maintained by father*		
Total	1,069	100.0
Father employed	887	83.0
Father not employed	182	17.0

*No spouse present.

Note: Own children include sons, daughters, step-children, and adopted children. Not included are nieces, nephews, grandchildren, and other related and unrelated children. Detail may not sum to totals due to rounding. Updated population controls are introduced annually with the release of January data.

SOURCE: Adapted from "Table 4. Families with Own Children: Employment Status of Parents by Age of Youngest Child and Family Type, 2014–2015 Annual Averages," in *Economic News Release*, U.S. Department of Labor, Bureau of Labor Statistics, April 22, 2016, https://www.bls.gov/news.release/famee.t04.htm (accessed December 29, 2016)

Married women have also entered the workforce in larger numbers. A decline in real wages plus a rising cost of living has prompted many two-parent families to maintain two incomes to meet financial obligations and pay for their children's future college expenses. Table 3.1 shows that 67.6% of married women with children under the age of 18 years were in the labor force in 2015 and that 64.2% of married women with children under age six were in the labor force that year. In 60.6% of married-couple families with children under 18 years old, both parents were employed. (See Table 3.4.) The dual-income family (with both parents working and contributing to the financial success of the household) has become commonplace as families have become increasingly dependent on women's economic contributions to the household.

WHO CARES FOR CHILDREN IN THE UNITED STATES?
School-Aged Children

Married parents who both work and single parents who work need reliable child care. The Federal Interagency Forum on Child and Family Statistics (known as the Forum) reports in *America's Children in Brief: Key National Indicators of Well-Being, 2016* (2016, https://www.childstats.gov/americaschildren/tables.asp) that in 2011 most grade school–aged children with employed mothers received child care from someone other than their parents while their mother worked. The percentage of these children who did receive care from their parents was highest for the youngest group (those aged five to eight years) and declined for older children. (See Figure 3.3.) The child care arrangements for children receiving nonparental care also varied by age group in 2011. Children aged five to 11 years were more likely

TABLE 3.5

Employment status of mothers, by age of youngest child and family type, 2015

[Numbers in thousands]

Characteristic	Total	With own children under 3 years old		
		2 years	1 year	Under 1 year
Total mothers				
Civilian noninstitutional population	9,308	2,920	3,254	3,134
Civilian labor force	5,714	1,869	2,024	1,821
Participation rate	61.4	64.0	62.2	58.1
Employed	5,336	1,741	1,897	1,698
Full-time workers[a]	3,882	1,280	1,370	1,232
Part-time workers[b]	1,455	462	526	466
Employment-population ratio	57.3	59.6	58.3	54.2
Unemployed	377	127	128	123
Unemployment rate	6.6	6.8	6.3	6.7
Married, spouse present				
Civilian noninstitutional population	6,341	1,974	2,252	2,114
Civilian labor force	3,772	1,198	1,356	1,218
Participation rate	59.5	60.7	60.2	57.6
Employed	3,628	1,149	1,300	1,179
Full-time workers[a]	2,698	864	961	873
Part-time workers[b]	931	285	339	306
Employment-population ratio	57.2	58.2	57.7	55.8
Unemployed	144	49	55	39
Unemployment rate	3.8	4.1	4.1	3.2
Other marital status[c]				
Civilian noninstitutional population	2,967	946	1,001	1,020
Civilian labor force	1,942	670	669	603
Participation rate	65.4	70.9	66.8	59.1
Employed	1,708	592	596	519
Full-time workers[a]	1,184	415	409	359
Part-time workers[b]	524	177	187	160
Employment-population ratio	57.6	62.6	59.5	50.9
Unemployed	234	78	72	84
Unemployment rate	12.0	11.6	10.8	13.9

[a]Usually work 35 hours or more per week at all jobs.
[b]Usually work less than 35 hours per week at all jobs.
[c]Includes never married; married, spouse absent; divorced; separated; and widowed persons.
Note: Own children include sons, daughters, step-children, and adopted children. Not included are nieces, nephews, grandchildren, and other related and unrelated children. Detail may not sum to totals due to rounding. Updated population controls are introduced annually with the release of January data.

SOURCE: Adapted from "Table 6. Employment Status of Mothers with Own Children under 3 Years Old by Single Year of Age of Youngest Child and Marital Status, 2014—2015 Annual Averages," in *Economic News Release*, U.S. Department of Labor, Bureau of Labor Statistics, April 22, 2016, https://www.bls.gov/news.release/famee.t06.htm (accessed December 29, 2016)

than children aged 12 to 14 years to be cared for by their grandparents. Children aged nine to 11 years were more likely than other age groups to receive care through enrichment activities: 21.1% of nine- to 11-year-olds received care this way, compared with 17.9% of five- to eight-year-olds and 17.8% of 12- to 14-year-olds. Children aged 12 years and older were significantly more likely than younger children to care for themselves: 2.4% of five- to eight-year-olds cared for themselves, compared with 10.2% of nine- to 11-year-olds, and 32.5% of 12- to 14-year-olds.

SELF-CARE—LATCHKEY KIDS. The term *latchkey kids* is used to describe children who are left alone or unsupervised either during the day or before or after school. In the factsheet "Afterschool Essentials: Research and Polling" (2014, http://www.afterschoolalliance.org/documents/Essentials_and_Polling_2014_010714.pdf), the Afterschool Alliance, an advocacy group that aims to ensure that all youth have access to affordable, quality after-school programs, indicates that 11.3 million school-aged children were "on their own" after school in 2014; 800,000 of these latchkey kids were in grades kindergarten to five. The Afterschool Alliance reports that 10.2 million children in kindergarten through 12th grade were in after-school programs in 2014, and that an additional 19.4 million children would participate in after-school programs were they available.

21ST CENTURY COMMUNITY LEARNING CENTERS. Many families rely on after-school care to provide a safe and nurturing place for their children while they are working. In response to concerns about the availability of quality after-school programs, the U.S. Department of Education initiated 21st Century Community Learning Centers (21st CCLC), authorized under Title X, Part I, of the Elementary and Secondary Education Act and reauthorized under Title IV, Part B, of the No Child Left

FIGURE 3.3

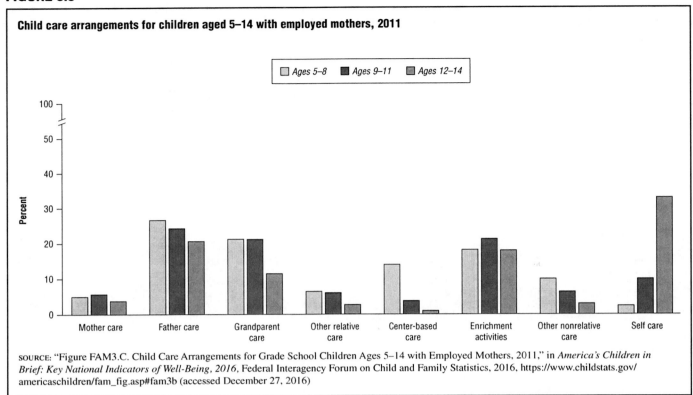

Child care arrangements for children aged 5–14 with employed mothers, 2011

SOURCE: "Figure FAM3.C. Child Care Arrangements for Grade School Children Ages 5–14 with Employed Mothers, 2011," in *America's Children in Brief: Key National Indicators of Well-Being, 2016*, Federal Interagency Forum on Child and Family Statistics, 2016, https://www.childstats.gov/americaschildren/fam_fig.asp#fam3b (accessed December 27, 2016)

Behind Act. This initiative gives grants to low-performance elementary and middle schools in rural and urban areas to provide after-school opportunities for their students, both educational and recreational. In 1997 the 21st CCLC had a budget of only $1 million; however, by fiscal year (FY) 2014 the program's budget had increased to nearly $1.2 billion. In *21st Century Community Learning Centers (21st CCLC) Analytic Support for Evaluation and Program Monitoring: An Overview of the 21st CCLC Performance Data: 2013–14* (2015, https://www2.ed.gov/programs/21stcclc/performance.html), Sylvia Lyles reports that in 2014 the 21st CCLC after-school programs served more than 2.2 million children throughout the country. More than one-third (35.5%) of regular attendees were Hispanic, 29.6% were white, and 22.4% were African American.

Participation improves academic performance. According to Lyles, more than one-third of students reported improvement in mathematics (36.5%) and English (36.8%) grades. Nearly half (49.4%) of teachers reported improvement in homework completion and 36.5% reported improvement in student behavior.

Children Younger Than Five (Preschoolers)

Amy Rathbun and Anlan Zhang report in *Primary Early Care and Education Arrangements and Achievement at Kindergarten Entry* (June 2016, https://nces.ed.gov/pubs2016/2016070.pdf) the percentages of children aged four to five years who received different types

of early childhood and education (ECE) care before entering kindergarten between 1995 and 2012. A higher percentage of young children were in center-based care in 2012 than in 1995, while the percentage cared for by nonrelatives in home-based settings was lower in 2012 than in 1995. The percentages of young children who received care from relatives in home settings and those who had no regular ECE care and were largely cared for by their parents the year before kindergarten in 2012 were comparable to the percentages in 1995.

As their children grow from infancy to school age, working mothers often change child care arrangements to meet the needs of their children, their families, and their employers. Making child care arrangements for infants and toddlers is often more difficult than for older children because fewer organized child care facilities admit infants and very young children, primarily due to the cost of hiring enough workers and adapting facilities to provide adequate care for babies. In addition, many parents prefer, if possible, to keep their infants in a home environment for as long as possible. Also, many mothers view center-based programs, which often have an educational focus, as most appropriate for older preschoolers.

FACTORS THAT AFFECT CHILD CARE
Preschool Child Care

RACIAL AND ETHNIC DIFFERENCES. In 2012 non-Hispanic African American (68%) and Asian or Pacific

TABLE 3.6

Percentage of children aged 3–6 in center-based care, by child and family characteristics and region, selected years 1995–2012

Characteristic	1995	2001	2005	2007	2012
Total	**55.0**	**56.3**	**57.1**	**55.3**	**60.6**
Race and Hispanic origin[a]					
White, non-Hispanic	56.9	58.9	59.0	58.4	63.0
Black, non-Hispanic	59.5	63.0	66.5	65.2	68.0
Asian or Pacific Islander, non-Hispanic	59.4	63.4	72.5	65.1	67.8
Hispanic	37.2	39.8	43.5	38.9	51.5
Poverty status					
Below 100% poverty	45.6	46.6	47.2	40.6	45.2
100–199% poverty	43.2	48.7	46.5	45.1	51.0
200% poverty and above	65.8	64.0	66.2	65.3	71.9
Family type					
Two parents[b]	54.8	56.5	56.9	55.4	61.4
Two parents, married	—	57.3	58.3	56.8	63.6
Two parents, unmarried	—	46.4	42.8	39.8	47.3
One parent	56.0	55.8	57.7	54.3	57.4
No parents	50.5	55.9	59.6	57.2	64.6
Mother's highest level of education[c]					
Less than high school	34.8	38.0	34.9	28.7	42.0
High school diploma or equivalent	47.6	47.3	48.6	43.1	49.1
Some college, including vocational/technical/associate's degree	56.8	61.4	56.2	54.4	57.9
Bachelor's degree or higher	74.5	70.0	72.9	71.3	79.2
Mother's employment status[c]					
35 hours or more per week	60.2	62.9	63.7	65.4	67.1
Less than 35 hours per week	62.1	61.4	60.8	61.7	66.3
Looking for work	51.8	46.2	42.0	37.8	57.9
Not in the labor force	46.5	46.9	50.2	43.9	51.0
Region[d]					
Northeast	56.3	63.8	67.0	66.3	69.4
South	58.4	59.1	56.4	55.0	63.4
Midwest	53.8	55.5	54.4	55.8	58.1
West	49.9	47.4	54.2	47.6	53.0

—Not available.

[a]In 1995 and 2001, the 1977 Office of Management and Budget (OMB) Standards for Data on Race and Ethnicity were used to classify persons into one of the following four racial groups: white, black, American Indian or Alaskan Native, or Asian or Pacific Islander. In 2005 and later years, the revised 1997 OMB standards were used. Under these standards, persons could select one or more of five racial groups: white, black, or African American, American Indian or Alaska Native, Asian, or Native Hawaiian or other Pacific Islander. For 2005 and later years, when separate reporting was possible, respondents who reported the child being Asian or Native Hawaiian or other Pacific Islander were combined for continuity purposes. Included in the total but not shown separately are American Indian or Alaska Native respondents and respondents of two or more races. Data on race and Hispanic origin are collected separately. Persons of Hispanic origin may be of any race.
[b]Refers to adults' relationship to child and does not indicate marital status. Data for 2007 and 2012 include same-sex parents.
[c]Children without mothers or female guardians in the home are not included in estimates.
[d]Regions: Northeast includes CT, MA, ME, NH, NJ, NY, PA, RI, and VT. South includes AL, AR, DC, DE, FL, GA, KY, LA, MD, MS, NC, OK, SC, TN, TX, VA, and WV. Midwest includes IA, IL, IN, KS, MI, MN, MO, ND, NE, OH, SD, and WI. West includes AK, AZ, CA, CO, HI, ID, MT, NM, NV, OR, UT, WA, and WY.
Note: Center-based programs include day care centers, prekindergartens, nursery schools, Head Start programs, and other early childhood education programs. The 2012 National Household Education Survey (NHES:2012) was a self-administered paper-and-pencil questionnaire that was mailed to respondents, while NHES administrations prior to 2012 were administered via telephone with an interviewer. Measurable differences in estimates between 2012 and prior years could reflect actual changes in the population, or the changes could be due to the mode change from telephone to mail. Some data have been revised from previously published figures.

SOURCE: "Table FAM3.B. Child Care: Percentage of Children Ages 3–6, Not Yet in Kindergarten, in Center-Based Care Arrangements by Child and Family Characteristics and Region, Selected Years 1995–2012," in *America's Children in Brief: Key National Indicators of Well-Being, 2016*, Federal Interagency Forum on Child and Family Statistics, 2016, https://www.childstats.gov/americaschildren/fam_fig.asp#fam3b (accessed December 27, 2016)

Islander (67.8%) mothers with preschool-aged children relied more on center-based child care than did non-Hispanic white (63%) and Hispanic (51.5%) mothers. (See Table 3.6.)

INCOME AND POVERTY MAKE A DIFFERENCE. The type of child care arrangements made vary by poverty status. (See Table 3.6.) For example, families at or above the poverty level in 2012 were the most likely to have children in center-based care, presumably because they were better able to pay for this care. Among families with preschoolers, 67.1% of mothers who were employed 35

hours or more per week and 66.3% of mothers who worked less than 35 hours per week used center-based care.

Although estimates vary, more than 40% of children under the age of five years are in home-based care, and a substantial number of children from low-income families are cared for in home-based settings that are often unregulated. (In every state, family members who provide care only to children who are related to them are legally exempt from regulation.) The main types of home-based care are care provided by a relative in the child's home or the caregiver's home; care provided by a nonrelative in the caregiver's home; and care provided in the child's home by babysitters, neighbors, friends, and other nonrelatives. Many parents use a combination of home- and center-based child care. According to Rachel A. Gordon et al., in "Beyond an 'Either-Or' Approach to Home- and Center-Based Child Care: Comparing Children and Families Who Combine Care Types with Those Who Use Just One" (*Early Childhood Research Quarterly*, vol. 28, no. 4, October 1, 2013), about 20% of four-year-olds attended both home- and center-based care. The researchers find that mothers for whom school readiness was a priority were more likely to combine home-based care with a center than use home care only, and children who attended centers, exclusively or along with home care, had higher average reading and math scores than those who had home care only.

Rebekah Levine Coley et al. analyzed data on 4,250 low-income children to compare how children fared in public and private early education and care (EEC) arrangements and published their results in "Comparing Public, Private, and Informal Preschool Programs in a National Sample of Low-Income Children" (*Early Childhood Research Quarterly*, vol. 36, Third Quarter 2016). The researchers observe that EEC programs improve school readiness skills for children. Their analysis reveals that low-income children who attended private EEC centers showed the highest math, reading, and language skills at age five. Children attending public EEC centers also had higher math and reading skills when compared with children who were only cared for by parents.

FORMAL CHILD CARE FACILITIES

Although no comprehensive data exist on the types or quality of formal or informal child care arrangements in the United States, Child Care Aware of America (CCAA) estimates in *Parents and the High Cost of Child Care: 2016* (2016, http://usa.childcareaware.org/wp-content/uploads/2016/12/CCA_High_Cost_Report.pdf) that in 2015 nearly 11 million children under the age of five years were in some type of child care arrangement. More than one-third (35%) were in center-based care, 32% were cared for by a grandparent, 10% received care from another relative, 8% were in family child care homes, 5% received care in their own home, and 5% were cared for in the home of a neighbor or friend. The CCAA estimates that 26% of children receive care in more than one setting each week.

In *Child Care in America: 2016 State Fact Sheets* (http://usa.childcareaware.org/wp-content/uploads/2016/07/2016-Fact-Sheets-Full-Report-02-27-17.pdf), the CCAA notes that child care funding is insufficient to meet the need. Fewer than 18% of eligible children receive the child care assistance funds for which they qualify.

The care providers of children in formal care settings are major influences in their lives. The CCAA notes that "despite tremendous responsibilities, the average income for a full-time child care professional in 2015 was only $10.72 an hour, putting the wages of child care workers below those of 97% of all occupations in the American economy." Many parents discover that quality and affordable care is difficult to find. In some communities child care is hard to find at any cost. Shortages of child care for infants, sick children, and children with special needs and for schoolchildren before and after school pose problems for many parents.

Licensing Requirements

CCAA explains that federal law requires the states to protect the health and safety of children in terms of preventing and controlling infectious diseases, ensuring building and physical safety, and providing health and safety training to child care workers. Because these federal requirements are broad, the standards that states set for licensing child care centers and child care homes vary. For example, requirements for obtaining a license, necessary training, and the number of children the facility can care for are different from state to state.

The National Resource Center for Health and Safety in Child Care and Early Education lists in *Caring for Our Children: National Health and Safety Performance Standards; Guidelines for Early Care and Education Programs* (August 2011, http://cfoc.nrckids.org/WebFiles/CFOC3_updated_final.pdf) 686 national standards and guidelines that "represent the best evidence, expertise, and experience in the country on quality health and safety practices and policies that should be followed in today's early care and education settings."

These standards and guidelines are intended to ensure safety, promote accountability, and encourage quality child care. Examples of staffing guidelines include requiring background screening before employing any staff member and mandating that all center teachers have current certification in first aid and cardiopulmonary resuscitation and that lead teachers have a Child Development Associate credential, college courses in early childhood education, or an associate's degree in early childhood education or a related field. Staff with food handling responsibilities should be trained in food service and safety. Examples of facility guidelines include ensuring adequate clearance space for swings and other play equipment, installing shock-absorbing surfaces to prevent head-impact injuries, and using U.S. Consumer Product Safety Commission–approved helmets when children ride toys with wheels such as tricycles and skateboards.

Regulations and Quality of Care

Federal assistance to low-income families to pay for child care eroded during the late 20th century at the same time that the government imposed requirements that more low-income parents work. The 1996 welfare reform law, the Personal Responsibility and Work Opportunity Reconciliation Act, eliminated the guarantee that families on welfare would receive subsidized child care, and although the legislation gave states wide discretion in the use of federal funds, it also imposed penalties if states failed to meet criteria for getting low-income parents into the workforce.

This legislation pushed the issue of regulation of child care facilities to the forefront. In 1989 the National Institute of Child Health and Human Development (NICHD) initiated the Study of Early Child Care and Youth Development. This ongoing study aimed to answer many questions about the relationship between child care experiences and children's developmental outcomes. The 1999 phase of the study examined whether the amount of time children spent in child care affected their interactions with their mothers. The results showed that the number of hours infants and toddlers spent in child care was modestly linked to the sensitivity of the mother to her child, as well as to the engagement of the child with the mother in play activities. Children in consistent quality day care showed fewer problem behaviors, whereas those who switched day care arrangements showed more problem behaviors. Children in quality care centers had higher cognitive and language development than those in lower-quality centers.

The second phase of the study, which was described in *The NICHD Study of Early Child Care and Youth Development: Findings for Children up to Age 4½ Years* (January 2012, https://www.nichd.nih.gov/publications/pubs/documents/seccyd_06.pdf), found that the quality of child care had an impact on children's social and intellectual development. The study defined quality care as care that met ideal adult-to-child ratios, maintained ideal group sizes, and had well-trained child care providers. It focused on the quality of children's actual day-to-day experiences in child care by observing children's social interactions and their activities.

The study found that children in higher-quality child care had better cognitive function and language development during the first three years of life, as well as greater school readiness by age four and a half. Children in higher-quality care were more sensitive to other children, more cooperative, and less aggressive and disobedient than were children in lower-quality care. Lastly, the study found that children who were cared for in child care centers rather than in home-based care had better cognitive and language development but also showed an increased number of behavior problems both in the child care setting and once they began kindergarten.

In "Early Child Care and Adolescent Functioning at the End of High School: Results from the NICHD Study of Early Child Care and Youth Development" (*Developmental*

Psychology, vol. 52, no. 10, October 2016), Deborah Lowe Vandell, Margaret Burchinal, and Kim M. Pierce examine the relationship between early child care and how adolescents function at the end of high school. The researchers find that more experience in center-based care was linked to higher class rank and that higher-quality child care was associated with higher grades. They also note a link between admission to more selective colleges and students who received center-based and higher-quality child care and who spent fewer hours in child care. Vandell, Burchinal, and Pierce assert that their findings "suggest long-term benefits of higher quality child care, center-type care, and lower child-care hours for measures of academic standing at the end of high school."

THE COST OF CHILD CARE

The CCAA documents in *Parents and the High Cost of Child Care: 2016* the increasing cost of child care and observes that it is "out of reach for many families and comprises a significant portion of family income." Although the U.S. Department of Health and Human Services established up to 7% of family income as the standard of affordability, the CCAA's nationwide survey found that the average cost of full-time center-based care for an infant ranges from just about 7% to roughly 16% of the state median income for a couple. In every state, the average cost of center-based infant care is more than 24% of the median income for single parents.

The CCAA's survey found that in 2015 the average yearly cost to have a four-year-old cared for in a child care center varied by state, from $3,997 in Mississippi to $12,781 in Massachusetts. For an infant, annual costs ranged from $4,882 in Mississippi to $17,062 in Massachusetts. Throughout the United States, average child care costs for an infant in a child care center were higher than the average amount that families spent on food.

Government Assistance with Child Care

BLOCK GRANTS. The federal government makes grants to states through the Child Care and Development Block Grant (CCDBG) to help low-income and poor parents pay for child care. Recognizing that child care assistance helps contribute to a productive workforce, every state has a child care assistance program that subsidizes some child care expenses using this federal block grant money and state funds. The states distribute these funds in the form of monthly subsidies or vouchers to low-income families to help them pay for child care.

In November 2014 the CCDBG was reauthorized for the first time in nearly two decades. New provisions of the law aim to improve the quality of child care, increase the number of low-income children accessing quality child care, and help ensure that low-income families have stable, reliable sources of child care.

In some states parents receive a voucher that they can use to pay for a portion of child care costs; in other states payments are made directly to the child care provider of the parents' choice. However, according to Hannah Matthews and Christina Walker of the Center for Law and Social Policy, an advocacy organization for low-income people, in *Child Care Assistance Spending and Participation in 2014* (March 2016, http://www.clasp.org/resources -and-publications/publication-1/CC-Spending-and-Partici pation-2014-1.pdf), in 2014 child care assistance spending and participation in CCDBG-funded child care were at all-time lows; spending was $11.3 billion, the lowest level since 2002. The monthly average of 1.4 million children receiving CCDBG-funded child care was the smallest number of children served since 1998. Twenty-four states served fewer children in 2014 than in 2013, and in nine states (Alabama, Hawaii, Kansas, Kentucky, Louisiana, Michigan, Nevada, West Virginia, and Wyoming) child care spending decreased for three consecutive years between 2011 and 2014.

Matthews and Walker observe that the states are contending with increased costs associated with the CCDBG Act of 2014. In FY 2016 Congress increased funding for the CCDBG by $326 million, which will help the states implement the new law. However, the researchers assert that an estimated $503 million in additional funding is needed to reverse the continuing decrease in CCDBG participation in 2017. Matthews and Walker aver, "Even further investments will be needed over time to implement additional provisions of the reauthorization and expand assistance for more eligible families."

HEAD START. Perhaps the best-known and most successful government-funded child care program is Head Start, a federal program begun in 1965 under the Administration for Children and Families (ACF), a part of the Department of Health and Human Services. The free program provides early education, health care, social services, and free meals to preschool children in families whose incomes are below the poverty line or who receive public assistance. In *Head Start Program Facts Fiscal Year 2015* (May 2016, https://eclkc.ohs.acf.hhs.gov/hslc/ data/factsheets/docs/head-start-fact-sheet-fy-2015.pdf), the ACF indicates that Head Start operates in every state and that in 2015 it served nearly 945,000 people, most of them children aged birth to five years but also a small number of pregnant women.

In 2015 Head Start issued *Head Start Early Learning Outcomes Framework: Ages Birth to Five* (https://eclkc .ohs.acf.hhs.gov/hslc/hs/sr/approach/pdf/ohs-framework .pdf), which is a revised guidance about what young children should learn, know, and be able to do to be successful in school. The framework is based on research that has improved educators' and caregivers' understanding of early development and school readiness. The guiding principles of the framework are:

- Children are individuals and are influenced by their environments, temperaments, and life experiences; with appropriate support they can be successful learners.

- Learning occurs in the context of caring relationships with families, teachers, and other adults in young children's lives.

- Families must be respected as children's primary influence because their knowledge, skills, and culture contribute to children's school readiness.

- Children learn best in nurturing, supportive environments where they feel safe and valued.

- Children learn new skills simultaneously. For example, as they gain verbal skills, they are better able to express their emotions and form friendships.

- Teaching must be appropriate to children's stage of development and should provide opportunities for children to explore and play.

- Learning environments must welcome, respect, and respond to children's cultural backgrounds and beliefs. Optimal learning occurs when it builds on each child's experiences.

TAX CREDITS. The federal Child and Dependent Care Credit helps families by allowing them to claim an income tax credit for part of their child care expenses for children under the age of 13 years. According to the Internal Revenue Service, in "Topic 602—Child and Dependent Care Credit" (February 17, 2017, https://www .irs.gov/taxtopics/tc602.html), in 2016 parents could claim up to $3,000 in qualified expenses for one child or $6,000 for two or more children.

FAMILY LEAVE. In 1993 Congress enacted the FMLA, requiring employers with 50 or more employees to give unpaid time off (12 weeks in any 12-month period) to employees to care for newborn or newly adopted children, sick family members, or for personal illness. The employee must be allowed to return to the same position (or one equivalent in pay, benefits, and other terms of employment) and must receive uninterrupted health benefits. The U.S. Department of Labor reports that before this legislation, fewer than a quarter of all workers received family leave benefits and that most of those who did worked in establishments with more than 100 employees.

In October 2009 President Barack Obama (1961–) signed legislation to expand the FMLA so that workers with a family member who is in the armed forces or a reserve component of the armed forces are now entitled to leave "because of any qualifying exigency arising out of the fact that the spouse, or a son, daughter, or parent, of the employee is on covered active duty (or has been notified of an impending call or order to covered active duty)" in a foreign country. Workers can take up to 26 weeks of unpaid, job-protected leave to care for a veteran during the five years after he or she leaves military service if the veteran suffered, became ill, or was injured while on active duty or had an injury or illness aggravated while on active duty.

In February 2015 the Department of Labor's Wage and Hour Division revised the definition of *spouse* under the FMLA so that eligible workers in legal same-sex marriages are able to take FMLA leave to care for their spouse or family members.

In *Paid Family and Medical Leave in New Hampshire: Who Has It? Who Takes It?* (Summer 2016, http://scholars.unh.edu/cgi/viewcontent.cgi?article=1282&context=carsey), Kristin Smith and Nicholas Adams of the University of New Hampshire analyze use of the FMLA in New Hampshire and find that access to paid leave is uneven. Thirty-seven percent of workers do not have extended paid leave for their own illnesses, 48% do not have parental leave, and 63% do not have paid leave to care for a sick family member. Only 37% of workers in New Hampshire have access to all three types of unpaid leave. Women are less likely to have paid leave but are more likely to take leave. Sixty percent of working women have taken paid or unpaid leave, compared with 40% of men. Smith and Adams conclude, "A statewide paid family and medical leave insurance program could increase access to such leave, reduce inequality among workers, improve economic security among families, reduce women's caregiving burden, strengthen men's caregiving options, and help level the playing field for couples, workers, and businesses alike."

CHAPTER 4

HEALTH AND SAFETY

FACTORS AFFECTING CHILDREN'S HEALTH

A variety of factors affect children's health. These range from prenatal influences; access to and quality of health care; poverty, homelessness, and hunger; childhood diseases; and diet and exercise. This chapter discusses these factors and looks at the leading causes of death among infants, children, and adolescents.

Birth Defects

The Centers for Disease Control and Prevention (CDC) reports in "Facts about Birth Defects" (October 11, 2016, https://www.cdc.gov/ncbddd/birthdefects/facts.html) that birth defects affect about one out of every 33 babies born. Birth defects are the leading cause of infant deaths and increase the risk for illness and disability. Although many birth defects cannot be prevented, some such as neural tube defects (serious problems with development of the brain and spine) and fetal alcohol syndrome are in large part preventable. Many neural tube defects can be prevented by the adequate intake of folic acid (400 micrograms per day of this B vitamin) before and during early pregnancy, and fetal alcohol syndrome can be prevented by expectant mothers limiting their alcohol consumption.

Specific birth defects include:

- Anencephaly—a type of neural tube defect in which a baby is born without parts of the brain and skull

- Anophthalmia/microphthalmia—birth defects of a baby's eyes; anophthalmia is when a baby is born without one or both eyes and microphthalmia is when one or both eyes do not fully develop

- Anotia/microtia—birth defects involving the ears

- Cleft lip/cleft palate—birth defects that occur when a baby's lip or mouth do not form properly

- Congenital heart defects—birth defects that affect the structure of a baby's heart

- Craniosynostosis—a birth defect in which the bones in a baby's skull join too early, before the brain is fully formed

- Down syndrome—babies are born with an extra chromosome, causing physical and mental health challenges

- Encephalocele—a neural tube defect that affects the brain, causing physical and mental problems such as loss of strength in the limbs, delayed growth, and intellectual disability

- Gastroschisis—a baby's intestines protrude through an opening near the navel; surgery is needed to repair the defect

- Hypospadias—in baby boys the opening of the urethra, which carries urine from the bladder, is not at the tip of the penis; most cases require surgery to correct the defect

- Microcephaly—a baby's head and brain are smaller than usual, causing a range of problems, such as developmental delays, intellectual disability, and hearing and vision problems

- Omphalocele—a baby's intestines, liver, or other organs protrude from the body through the navel; surgery is performed to correct the defect

- Spina bifida—a type of neural tube defect that can cause mild to severe physical and intellectual disabilities; surgery is often performed to correct the defect

- Upper and lower limb reduction defects—parts of limbs or entire limbs do not develop properly

Expectant mothers infected with the Zika virus, which is transmitted primarily by mosquitoes but may also be spread through sexual intercourse, may pass the infection onto their unborn children. Infection during pregnancy can cause microcephaly and other birth defects, such as damage to the brain and the back of the eye and joints with limited range of motion. In "Zika

Virus and Birth Defects—Reviewing the Evidence for Causality" (*New England Journal of Medicine*, vol. 374, no. 20, May 19, 2016), Sonja A. Rasmussen et al. of the CDC explain that the Zika virus has spread rapidly since its identification in Brazil in early 2015. The researchers assert that because infection causes birth defects, intensified efforts are needed to prevent the infection of expectant mothers.

Health Care

IMMUNIZATIONS. The CDC's National Immunization Survey tracks immunization coverage among preschool children aged 19 months to 35 months. Holly A. Hill et al. of the CDC report in "Vaccination Coverage among Children Aged 19–35 Months—United States, 2015" (*Morbidity and Mortality Weekly Report*, vol. 65, no. 39, October 7, 2016) that in 2015 the overall vaccination coverage of young children was high: greater than 90% for vaccines against measles, mumps, and rubella (MMR); hepatitis B; polio; and varicella (chicken pox). For the recommended doses of hepatitis A vaccine (HepA) and rotavirus vaccines, the percentages of children immunized were 59.6% and 73.2%, respectively, considerably below the 90% target established in Healthy People 2020, the 10-year U.S. government objectives for improving Americans' health. Less than 1% of children received no vaccinations. In general, children living below the poverty level had lower coverage for many vaccines than children living at or above the poverty level. (See Table 4.1.)

The Federal Interagency Forum on Child and Family Statistics (known simply as the Forum) explains in *America's Children in Brief: Key National Indicators of Well-Being, 2016* (2016, https://www.childstats.gov/america schildren/tables.asp) that in 2014, 87.6% of adolescents aged 13 to 17 years had received the recommended dose of Tdap vaccine to protect against diphtheria, tetanus, and pertussis (whooping cough). (See Table 4.2.) This was a marked increase from 2006, when only 10.8% had received the vaccine. The MenACWY vaccine prevents bacterial meningitis (inflammation of the membranes covering the brain and spinal cord caused by bacterial infection as opposed to viral or fungal infection). In 2006 only 11.7% of 13- to 17-year-olds had received one or more doses of the MenACWY vaccine (two doses are recommended—one at age 11 or 12 and a second at age 16); by 2014 this had risen to 79.3%. Table 4.2 also shows that the percentage of adolescent females who received at least one of the three recommended doses of the human papillomavirus (HPV) vaccine, which protects against the human papillomavirus, increased from 25.1% in 2007 to 60% in 2014. (HPV is the most common sexually transmitted virus and can cause cervical, vaginal, and vulvar cancers in females and penile cancer in males; it can also cause anal cancer, throat cancer, and genital warts in males and females.)

Although adolescent males are also advised to receive the HPV vaccine, in 2014 just 41.7% had had at least one of the three recommended doses.

Like any medication, vaccinations are not without risks, such as rare but serious allergic reactions. In 1988 the National Vaccine Injury Compensation Program (VICP) was established to provide compensation to individuals who are injured by certain vaccines. The Health Resources and Services Administration lists the VICP-covered injuries in *What You Need to Know about the National Vaccine Injury Compensation Program* (September 2016, https://www.hrsa.gov/vaccinecompensation/resources/84521booklet.pdf). Covered injuries include anaphylactic shock (a severe, rapid, and sometimes fatal hypersensitivity reaction), which is associated with the diphtheria, tetanus, pertussis, polio, hepatitis B, and MMR vaccines; encephalopathy (a disease or disorder of the brain), which is associated with the pertussis and MMR vaccines; and infection, which is associated with the MMR and polio vaccines.

In 1998 Andrew Wakefield et al. ignited a controversy over vaccine safety when they published the study "Ileal-Lymphoid-Nodular Hyperplasia, Non-specific Colitis, and Pervasive Developmental Disorder in Children" (*Lancet*, vol. 351, no. 9103), linking the MMR vaccine to autism. Other scientists failed to replicate Wakefield et al.'s findings. Gardiner Harris reports in "Journal Retracts 1998 Paper Linking Autism to Vaccines" (NYTimes.com, February 2, 2010) that the *Lancet* retracted the paper in February 2010 after ethical conflicts in Wakefield et al.'s study had been uncovered. In January 2011 the article "Journal: Study Linking Vaccine to Autism Was Fraud" (Associated Press, January 5, 2011) indicated that a new comparison of the study's reported diagnoses to hospital records showed that Wakefield et al. had altered facts about some of the children in their study. Wakefield et al. had reported that the 12 children studied showed no signs of autism until receiving the MMR vaccine, whereas five of the children had previously documented developmental problems. Furthermore, all the children's cases had been misrepresented in some way.

Harris reports that prior to the *Lancet*'s retraction of Wakefield et al.'s paper, parent groups in the United States had mobilized to oppose certain vaccinations based on various theories about how vaccinations could trigger autism. Although large population studies have found no link between vaccines and autism, the damage has been done. Many parents are choosing not to vaccinate their children. As a result, there have been serious outbreaks of pertussis, measles, and other preventable infectious diseases.

For example, in "Measles Cases and Outbreaks" (March 6, 2017, https://www.cdc.gov/measles/cases-out breaks.html), the CDC reports that in 2015, 188 cases

TABLE 4.1

Vaccination coverage among children aged 19–35 months by race and ethnicity and poverty level, 2015

Vaccine/Dose	White, non-Hispanic (Referent) %	Black, non-Hispanic %	Hispanic %	American Indian/ Alaska Native %	Asian %	Native Hawaiian or other Pacific Islander %	Multiracial %	At or above poverty (Referent) %	Below poverty %	MSA, central city (Referent) %	MSA, non-central city %	Non-MSA %
	Race/ethnicity							Poverty level		MSA status		
DTaP[a]												
≥3 doses	94.8	94.3	95.5	92.3	97.3	92.2	93.6	96.0	93.1	95.3	95.0	93.5
≥4 doses	85.2	82.0	84.5	79.6	90.0		82.5	87.1	80.2	85.4	84.3	82.7
Poliovirus (≥3 doses)	93.1	93.3	94.5	91.8	96.9	92.8	92.4	94.6	91.8	93.9	94.0	91.7
MMR (≥1 dose)	91.8	90.7	92.3	88.5	92.5	92.0	93.0	92.9	90.3	92.4	91.7	90.7
Hib[b]												
≥3 doses	93.3	92.1	94.0	88.2	93.7	91.8	92.0	94.7	90.5	93.6	93.3	91.8
Primary series	94.4	93.3	95.1	89.8	94.8	92.8	93.1	95.6	91.9	94.6	94.3	93.2
Full series	83.0	78.9	83.0	81.4	87.0		82.4	85.5	78.1	82.3	83.6	80.9
HepB												
≥3 doses	92.0	93.3	93.2	92.4	95.5	94.1	91.4	92.7	92.5	92.9	92.5	92.1
Birth dose[c]	68.2	74.2	77.8	80.7	76.7		72.8	70.2	76.3	72.1	71.7	75.6
Varicella (≥1 dose)	91.2	91.8	92.7	87.8	93.4	91.8	92.1	92.5	90.6	92.5	91.5	89.9
PCV												
≥3 doses	93.2	92.5	94.4	89.7	92.4	90.6	92.5	94.6	91.2	93.1	93.9	91.8
≥4 doses	85.0	81.4	84.0	77.1	85.0		83.7	87.2	78.9	83.9	85.5	80.4
HepA (≥2 doses)	58.7	59.3	60.9	61.3	67.8		54.1	61.7	56.0	60.5	59.6	55.7
Rotavirus[d]	74.6	69.7	72.9		75.6		70.6	76.8	66.8	72.7	75.1	68.6
Combined series[e]	72.7	69.1	71.7	68.2	77.9		73.7	74.7	68.7	72.5	72.5	70.2

DTaP = diphtheria, tetanus toxoids, and acellular pertussis vaccine
HepA = hepatitis A vaccine
HepB = hepatitis B vaccine
Hib = *Haemophilus influenzae* type b vaccine
MMR = measles, mumps, and rubella vaccine
PCV = pneumococcal conjugate vaccine

Notes: Children's race/ethnicity was reported by parent or guardian. Children identified in this report as white, black, Asian, American Indian/Alaska Native, Native Hawaiian or other Pacific Islander, or multiracial were reported by the parent or guardian as non-Hispanic. Children identified as multiracial had more than one race category selected. Children identified as Hispanic might be of any race.
Children were classified as below poverty if their total family income was less than the poverty threshold specified for the applicable family size and number of children aged <18 years. Children with total family income at or above the poverty threshold specified for the applicable family size and number of children aged <18 years were classified as at or above poverty. A total of 492 children with adequate provider data and missing data on income were excluded from the analysis. Poverty thresholds reflect yearly changes in the Consumer Price Index.
Metropolitan Statistical Area as defined by the US Office of Management and Budget.
Children in the 2015 National Immunization Survey were born January 2012–May 2014.
[a]Includes children who might have been vaccinated with diphtheria and tetanus toxoids vaccine, or diphtheria, tetanus toxoids, and pertussis vaccine.
[b]Hib primary series: receipt of ≥2 or ≥3 doses, depending on product type received; full series: primary series and booster dose includes receipt of ≥3 or ≥4 doses, depending on product type received.
[c]One dose HepB administered from birth through age 3 days.
[d]Includes ≥2 or ≥3 doses, depending on product type received (≥2 doses for Rotarix [RV1], or ≥3 doses for RotaTeq [RV5]).
[e]The combined seven-vaccine series (4:3:1:3*:3:1:4) includes ≥4 doses of DTaP, ≥3 doses of poliovirus vaccine, ≥1 dose of measles-containing vaccine, full series of Hib (≥3 or ≥4 doses, depending on type), ≥3 doses of HepB, ≥1 dose of varicella vaccine, and ≥4 doses of PCV.

SOURCE: Adapted from Holly A. Hill et al., "Table 2. Estimated Vaccination Coverage among Children Aged 19–35 Months, by Selected Vaccines and Dosages, Race/Ethnicity and Poverty Level, and Metropolitan Statistical Area (MSA) Status—National Immunization Survey, United States, 2015," in "Vaccination Coverage among Children Aged 19–35 Months—United States, 2015," *Morbidity and Mortality Weekly Report*, vol. 65, no. 39, October 7, 2016, https://www.cdc.gov/mmwr/volumes/65/wr/pdfs/mm6539a4.pdf (accessed January 2, 2017)

of measles were reported. The 2015 cases were linked to an amusement park in California. The CDC speculates that an infected traveler caused this outbreak, which was the same virus type that caused a large outbreak in the Philippines the preceding year. In 2016, 70 cases of measles were reported.

PHYSICIAN VISITS. Children's health depends on access to and use of medical care. The National Center for Health Statistics (NCHS) finds that in 2015, 86.6% of children under the age of four years visited the doctor during the six months prior to the survey, as did 74.4% of children aged five to 11 years and 72.2% of youth aged 12 to 17 years. (See Table 4.3.)

HEALTH INSURANCE. According to Jessica C. Barnett and Marina S. Vornovitsky of the U.S. Census Bureau, in *Health Insurance Coverage in the United States: 2015*

TABLE 4.2

Percentage of adolescents aged 13–17 vaccinated for selected diseases by poverty status[a], race and Hispanic origin[b], 2006–14

Characteristic	Total 2006[c]	2007[c]	2008	2009	2010	2011	2012	2013	2014	Below 100% poverty 2006[c]	2007[c]	2008	2009	2010	2011	2012	2013	2014	100% poverty and above 2006[c]	2007[c]	2008	2009	2010	2011	2012	2013	2014
Total																											
MMR (2 doses or more)[d]	86.9	88.9	89.3	89.1	90.5	91.4	91.8	91.8	90.7	—	—	87.1	87.8	87.8	90.3	89.7	91.7	90.5	—	—	89.6	89.3	91.1	91.4	92.0	91.8	90.8
HepB (3 doses or more)[e]	81.3	87.6	87.9	89.9	91.6	92.3	92.8	93.2	91.4	—	—	86.7	88.3	89.0	91.4	91.3	93.2	91.4	—	—	88.0	90.3	92.4	92.6	93.3	93.1	91.9
Var (1 dose or more)[f]	65.5	75.7	81.9	87.0	90.5	92.3	94.7	94.9	95.2	—	—	77.0	82.9	86.7	91.1	92.5	94.7	95.0	—	—	82.9	87.6	91.2	92.6	95.3	95.2	95.2
Var (2 doses or more)[g]	—	—	34.1	48.6	58.1	68.3	74.9	78.5	81.0	—	—	35.8	46.2	53.8	67.2	72.0	77.3	82.7	—	—	33.9	48.7	58.9	68.4	75.8	79.0	80.8
Td or Tdap (1 dose or more)[h]	60.1	72.3	72.2	76.2	81.2	85.3	88.5	89.1	89.8	—	—	70.9	71.8	76.8	81.5	88.1	88.6	88.7	—	—	72.7	77.0	82.2	86.5	88.6	89.2	90.4
Tdap (1 dose or more)[i]	10.8	30.4	40.8	53.6	68.7	78.2	84.6	86.0	87.6	—	—	38.6	52.8	64.7	74.0	83.6	85.2	85.8	—	—	41.2	56.1	69.5	79.5	85.1	86.4	88.4
MenACWY (1 dose or more)[j]	11.7	32.4	41.8	53.6	62.7	70.5	74.0	77.8	79.3	—	—	40.8	52.5	62.0	69.0	73.2	78.4	79.0	—	—	42.0	53.8	62.9	70.7	74.1	77.5	79.5
HPV (1 dose or more)—females only[k]	—	25.1	37.2	44.3	48.7	53.0	53.8	57.3	60.0	—	—	46.4	51.9	51.8	62.1	64.9	66.8	67.2	—	—	35.8	42.5	47.7	50.1	50.4	54.6	57.7
HPV (3 doses or more)—females only[l]	—	—	17.9	26.7	32.0	34.8	33.4	37.6	39.7	—	—	14.9	25.5	28.2	39.0	36.2	41.5	44.7	—	—	18.6	26.8	32.9	33.4	32.5	36.4	37.9
HPV (1 dose or more)—males only[m]	—	—	—	—	1.4	8.3	20.8	34.6	41.7	—	—	—	—	—	14.1	29.9	46.7	51.6	—	—	—	—	—	6.7	17.3	30.8	39.5
HPV (3 doses or more)—males only[n]	—	—	—	—	—	1.3	6.8	13.9	21.6	—	—	—	—	—	2.5	10.7	16.7	27.2	—	—	—	—	—	1.1	5.5	13.0	20.2
White, non-hispanic																											
MMR (2 doses or more)[d]	—	—	89.9	90.2	91.6	91.4	92.4	92.8	91.0	—	—	89.2	86.7	90.4	88.5	89.9	93.3	87.7	—	—	89.7	90.4	91.7	91.9	92.8	92.7	91.4
HepB (3 doses or more)[e]	—	—	88.1	89.9	92.7	92.8	93.7	93.8	92.2	—	—	88.4	87.4	90.8	90.7	91.7	94.6	89.7	—	—	87.9	90.5	92.8	93.1	94.0	93.7	92.5
Var (1 dose or more)[f]	—	—	82.8	88.5	91.2	92.9	95.3	95.3	95.1	—	—	74.4	79.3	85.6	91.2	91.9	95.6	93.2	—	—	82.9	88.9	91.7	93.2	95.7	95.5	95.4
Var (2 doses or more)[g]	—	—	31.6	48.8	59.2	67.3	74.0	77.7	80.0	—	—	—	34.2	42.9	60.8	61.8	73.1	75.1	—	—	—	49.1	60.4	68.1	75.6	78.5	80.5
Td or Tdap (1 dose or more)[h]	—	—	71.6	76.5	80.9	85.1	87.9	88.8	90.3	—	—	64.5	68.6	70.2	77.5	84.9	88.7	85.6	—	—	72.3	77.1	82.1	86.2	88.3	89.0	91.0
Tdap (1 dose or more)[i]	—	—	41.7	55.8	68.6	78.6	84.4	85.9	88.6	—	—	32.8	49.5	57.5	70.7	80.7	84.9	83.9	—	—	42.5	56.1	69.9	79.6	85.0	86.3	89.3
MenACWY (1 dose or more)[j]	—	—	39.7	53.1	61.2	68.4	71.3	75.6	78.2	—	—	32.8	47.1	50.3	58.5	63.2	72.3	72.9	—	—	40.3	53.3	62.5	69.7	72.5	76.2	79.1
HPV (1 dose or more)—females only[k]	—	—	35.0	43.9	45.8	47.5	51.1	53.1	56.1	—	—	33.6	52.5	39.4	53.6	52.9	53.9	56.7	—	—	35.7	43.0	46.6	46.7	50.6	53.4	56.6
HPV (3 doses or more)—females only[l]	—	—	19.5	29.1	32.4	33.0	33.7	34.9	37.5	—	—	—	25.7	25.7	32.5	30.8	34.1	37.0	—	—	—	—	32.8	33.0	34.3	35.0	38.1
HPV (1 dose or more)—males only[m]	—	—	—	—	—	5.6	15.2	26.7	36.4	—	—	—	—	—	8.9	18.1	30.9	39.4	—	—	—	—	—	5.3	14.5	26.1	36.5
HPV (3 doses or more)—males only[n]	—	—	—	—	—	0.8	4.6	11.1	18.8	—	—	—	—	—	—	5.2	11.4	20.5	—	—	—	—	—	0.7	4.4	11.2	18.8
Black, non-hispanic																											
MMR (2 doses or more)[d]	—	—	89.1	86.3	90.8	90.6	91.1	91.1	91.1	—	—	89.1	84.4	92.1	90.7	91.0	90.6	89.8	—	—	88.6	86.9	90.2	90.8	91.5	91.5	91.7
HepB (3 doses or more)[e]	—	—	86.0	88.9	90.9	91.7	92.5	93.2	91.4	—	—	86.6	86.6	90.0	91.3	91.6	92.5	89.2	—	—	85.8	89.8	91.3	92.3	93.1	94.0	92.8
Var (1 dose or more)[f]	—	—	74.0	82.4	89.2	91.3	93.3	94.3	95.3	—	—	72.7	79.8	87.0	91.1	93.1	92.8	96.4	—	—	74.8	82.8	89.5	89.6	93.3	95.4	95.2
Var (2 doses or more)[g]	—	—	35.0	43.9	55.3	65.3	75.2	77.9	84.6	—	—	—	44.4	60.3	64.7	71.7	77.6	87.7	—	—	—	44.2	51.8	65.3	76.5	77.8	83.3
Td or Tdap (1 dose or more)[h]	—	—	71.4	72.5	80.5	83.1	87.7	87.4	89.6	—	—	68.9	69.5	80.1	79.1	87.5	84.8	88.8	—	—	71.9	74.8	80.1	85.4	87.6	88.9	89.9
Tdap (1 dose or more)[i]	—	—	36.0	52.7	66.9	75.7	83.7	84.1	87.6	—	—	39.0	47.7	68.1	72.1	84.1	82.5	86.7	—	—	33.4	55.6	66.0	77.7	84.0	84.7	88.0
MenACWY (1 dose or more)[j]	—	—	43.1	53.0	63.4	72.1	75.8	77.0	80.3	—	—	38.8	52.0	66.5	72.0	75.3	72.4	79.5	—	—	44.4	53.8	61.4	71.5	76.6	79.6	80.4
HPV (1 dose or more)—females only[k]	—	—	35.7	44.6	48.9	56.0	50.1	55.8	66.4	—	—	45.9	51.6	55.7	60.2	59.9	64.0	70.6	—	—	31.2	40.7	44.5	52.5	46.2	50.8	62.3
HPV (3 doses or more)—females only[l]	—	—	14.9	23.1	30.2	31.7	29.0	34.2	39.0	—	—	—	—	31.6	36.6	33.8	39.0	41.1	—	—	—	—	28.6	28.0	26.4	31.6	36.0
HPV (1 dose or more)—males only[m]	—	—	—	—	—	10.6	25.9	42.2	42.1	—	—	—	—	—	10.2	29.9	44.3	46.9	—	—	—	—	—	10.4	22.9	41.3	40.7
HPV (3 doses or more)—males only[n]	—	—	—	—	—	5.4	15.7	20.4	20.4	—	—	—	—	—	—	—	15.1	18.6	—	—	—	—	—	—	6.2	16.0	22.4
Hispanic																											
MMR (2 doses or more)[d]	—	—	87.5	87.6	86.2	90.6	89.1	90.2	90.5	—	—	83.9	90.6	83.5	91.7	87.7	91.2	92.1	—	—	90.4	85.4	88.1	89.4	90.2	89.5	89.9
HepB (3 doses or more)[e]	—	—	89.8	90.0	88.9	91.7	91.1	92.8	90.5	—	—	86.2	90.3	87.8	93.0	91.1	93.0	90.9	—	—	92.1	89.8	91.0	90.7	91.0	92.2	90.9
Var (1 dose or more)[f]	—	—	84.5	85.5	90.6	91.0	94.1	94.5	95.5	—	—	80.0	84.6	88.1	92.5	92.1	95.3	95.2	—	—	88.9	85.6	92.1	89.6	95.7	94.0	95.4
Var (2 doses or more)[g]	—	—	38.5	49.7	56.2	71.4	76.3	80.3	82.5	—	—	—	49.7	55.8	73.8	76.8	80.2	85.9	—	—	—	49.4	56.7	69.4	76.2	80.7	80.0
Td or Tdap (1 dose or more)[h]	—	—	74.1	76.7	82.4	86.7	89.6	90.5	90.4	—	—	74.8	74.2	78.9	85.0	89.3	90.1	91.1	—	—	75.7	77.4	85.0	80.6	90.0	90.3	90.5
Tdap (1 dose or more)[i]	—	—	41.9	55.6	69.6	78.4	85.4	87.1	86.7	—	—	40.4	55.8	67.4	76.1	84.1	86.6	86.4	—	—	44.0	54.8	70.6	80.6	86.8	87.2	87.2
MenACWY (1 dose or more)[j]	—	—	46.8	55.9	66.1	75.3	77.6	83.4	82.1	—	—	45.0	56.2	67.4	77.2	78.3	86.5	83.2	—	—	48.9	55.9	64.4	73.6	76.4	80.0	81.3
HPV (1 dose or more)—females only[k]	—	—	44.4	45.5	56.2	65.0	62.9	67.5	66.3	—	—	53.0	52.2	57.9	69.2	73.9	76.1	72.4	—	—	39.3	42.0	53.5	61.9	52.2	60.4	59.8
HPV (3 doses or more)—females only[l]	—	—	14.7	23.4	29.5	41.6	35.5	44.8	46.9	—	—	—	—	27.1	44.9	40.9	47.2	51.2	—	—	—	—	32.9	39.5	30.3	42.2	41.2
HPV (1 dose or more)—males only[m]	—	—	—	—	—	14.9	31.7	49.6	54.2	—	—	—	—	—	20.4	39.8	59.1	61.1	—	—	—	—	—	11.2	23.5	42.7	50.6
HPV (3 doses or more)—males only[n]	—	—	—	—	—	2.7	12.9	20.3	27.8	—	—	—	—	—	3.2	19.1	22.3	33.7	—	—	—	—	—	7.6	18.6	18.6	24.1

TABLE 4.2

Percentage of adolescents aged 13–17 vaccinated for selected diseases by poverty status[a], race and Hispanic origin[b], 2006–14 [CONTINUED]

—Not available.

[a]Based on family income and household size using Census Bureau poverty thresholds for the year of data collection.

[b]The revised 1997 Office of Management and Budget (OMB) Standards for Data on Race and Ethnicity were used. Persons could select one or more from the following racial groups: white, black or African American, American Indian or Alaska Native, Asian, or Native Hawaiian or other Pacific Islander. Persons of Hispanic origin may be of any race. Included in the total but not shown separately are American Indian or Alaska Native, Asian, Native Hawaiian or other Pacific Islander and "Two or more races" due to the small sample size. Data on race and Hispanic origin are collected separately but combined for reporting.

[c]Data collection for 2006 and 2007 was only performed during the fourth quarter of each year.

[d]Includes 2 doses (or more) of measles-mumps-rubella vaccine received at any age.

[e]Includes 3 doses (or more) of hepatitis B vaccine received at any age.

[f]Includes 1 dose (or more) of varicella vaccine received at any age and without a history of varicella disease.

[g]Includes 2 doses (or more) of varicella vaccine received at any age and without a history of varicella disease.

[h]Includes 1 dose (or more) of tetanus toxoid-diphtheria vaccine (Td) or tetanus toxoid, reduced diphtheria toxoid, and acellular pertussis (Tdap) since age 10.

[i]Includes 1 dose (or more) of tetanus toxoid, reduced diphtheria toxoid, and acellular pertussis (Tdap) since age 10.

[j]Includes 1 dose (or more) of meningococcal conjugate vaccine (MenACWY) and meningococcal-unknown type vaccine.

[k]Includes 1 dose (or more) quadrivalent or bivalent human papillomavirus vaccine (HPV). Percentages reported among females only.

[l]Includes 3 doses (or more) quadrivalent or bivalent human papillomavirus vaccine (HPV). Percentages reported among females only.

[m]Includes 1 dose (or more) quadrivalent or bivalent human papillomavirus vaccine (HPV). Percentages reported among males only.

[n]Includes 3 doses (or more) quadrivalent or bivalent human papillomavirus vaccine (HPV). Percentages reported among males only.

Note: Data include routinely recommended vaccines (Tdap, MenACWY, HPV) and early childhood vaccines (MMR, HepB, Var) for catch-up coverage estimates. A revised adequate provider data definition was implemented in 2014 NIS-Teen. Estimates prior to 2014 are not directly comparable to those from 2014 and beyond.

SOURCE: "Table HC3.B. Immunization: Percentage of Adolescents Ages 13–17 Years Vaccinated for Selected Diseases by Poverty Status and Race and Hispanic Origin, 2006–2014," in *America's Children in Brief: Key National Indicators of Well-Being, 2016*, Federal Interagency Forum on Child and Family Statistics, 2016, https://www.childstats.gov/americaschildren/tables.asp (accessed January 2, 2017)

TABLE 4.3

Time since last contact with a doctor or other health care professional for children under age 18, 2015

Selected Characteristic	All children under age 18 years	6 months or less[a]	More than 6 months but not more than 1 year[a]	More than 1 year but not more than 2 years[a]	More than 2 years but not more than 5 years[a]	More than 5 years or never[a]
Total	100.0	77.0	16.0	4.3	0.9	1.8
Sex						
Male	100.0	77.5	15.8	4.0	1.0	1.7
Female	100.0	76.4	16.1	4.7	0.9	1.9
Age						
0–4 years	100.0	86.6	9.9	1.5	0.3*	1.7
5–11 years	100.0	74.4	18.3	4.8	0.8	1.6
12–17 years	100.0	72.2	18.1	6.0	1.6	2.0

*Estimates are considered unreliable.

[a]Based on the question, "About how long has it been since anyone in the family last saw or talked to a doctor or other health care professional about [child's name]'s health? Include doctors seen while [he\she] was a patient in a hospital."

Notes: Based on household interviews of a sample of the civilian noninstitutionalized population. This table is based on responses about the sample child, not all children in the family. Data came from the Sample Child File and were weighted using the Sample Child weight. Estimates are age adjusted using the projected 2000 U.S. population as the standard population and using age groups 0–4 years, 5–11 years, and 12–17 years. Estimates for age groups are not age-adjusted. Unknowns for the columns were not included in the denominators when calculating percentages. Percentages may not add to totals due to rounding. "Total" includes children of other races not shown separately and children with unknown family structure, parent's education, family income, poverty status, health insurance, or current health status.

SOURCE: "Table C-8a. Age-Adjusted Percent Distribution (with Standard Errors) of Length of Time since Last Contact with a Doctor or Other Health Care Professional for Children under Age 18 Years, by Selected Characteristics: United States, 2015," in *Summary Health Statistics: National Health Interview Survey, 2015*, National Center for Health Statistics, November 9, 2016, https://ftp.cdc.gov/pub/Health_Statistics/NCHS/NHIS/SHS/2015_SHS_Table_C-8.pdf (accessed January 2, 2017)

(September 2016, https://www.census.gov/content/dam/Census/library/publications/2016/demo/p60-257.pdf), 5.3% of American children under the age of 19 years had no health insurance coverage in 2015. (See Figure 4.1.) Factors affecting children's access to coverage included their age, race, and ethnicity and their family's socioeconomic status. Children in poverty were more likely to be uninsured (7.5%) than children not in poverty (4.8%). In 2015 more Hispanic children were uninsured (7.3%) than African American children (5.2%), non-Hispanic white children (4.3%), or Asian American children (4.2%).

During the first decade of the 21st century the percentage of children who were covered by health insurance increased to the highest rate in 25 years, rising to 91.8% in 2014. (See Table 4.4.) The percentage of children who were covered by private health insurance declined from 67% in 2000 to 53.7% in 2014. In contrast, public health insurance coverage increased from 18.4% in 2000 to 38.1% in 2014. Public health insurance for children was primarily provided by Medicaid, but some children were covered by Medicare, State Children's Health Insurance Programs (CHIP), and the armed forces' Tricare program.

To remain in the Medicaid program, families must have their eligibility reassessed at least every six months. If family income increases above a certain level or other circumstances change even slightly, the family can lose its eligibility for the Medicaid program, disrupting health care coverage.

From the late 1980s through the mid-1990s the numbers of uninsured American children rose as coverage rates for employer-sponsored health insurance declined, even though the proportion of children covered by Medicaid also rose. In 1997, as part of the Balanced Budget Act, Congress created CHIP to expand health insurance to children whose families earned too much money to be eligible for Medicaid but not enough money to pay for private insurance. CHIP provides funding to states to insure children. States may use CHIP funds to establish separate coverage programs, to expand their Medicaid coverage, or to use a combination of both approaches. By September 1999 all 50 states had CHIP plans in place, and over the next decade the program gradually expanded.

The Children's Health Insurance Program Reauthorization Act was signed into law by President Barack Obama (1961–) in 2009. The Centers for Medicare and Medicaid Services notes in "Children's Health Insurance Program" (2017, https://www.medicaid.gov/chip/chip-program-information.html) that 8.9 million children were enrolled in CHIP in fiscal year 2016.

AFFORDABLE CARE ACT BENEFITS FOR CHILDREN. The Affordable Care Act (ACA) of 2010 made major changes to health care in the United States. Many of these changes benefited children, and some improved children's access to health care. One example is that the ACA specified that the CHIP eligibility standards then in place would be extended through 2019. The law also extended CHIP funding until October 1, 2015, after which date the CHIP federal matching rate is gradually increased by up to 23 percentage points. The ACA also provided an additional $40 million in federal funding to prevent eligibility rollbacks or major premium increases

FIGURE 4.1

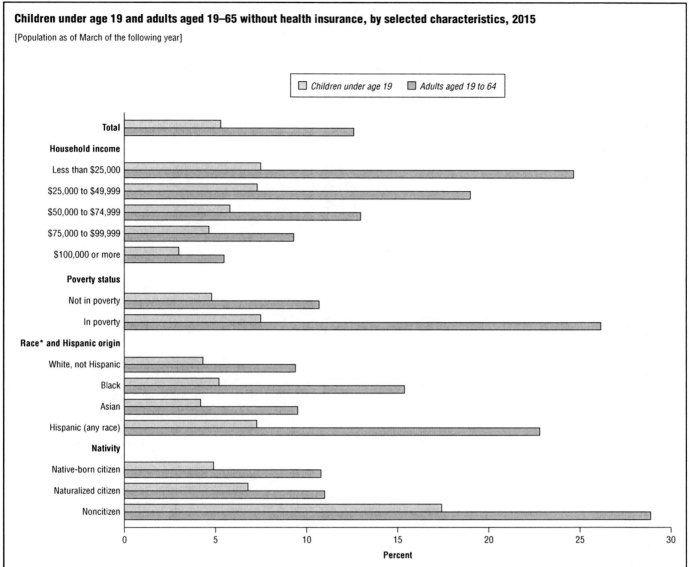

Children under age 19 and adults aged 19–65 without health insurance, by selected characteristics, 2015

[Population as of March of the following year]

*Federal surveys give respondents the option of reporting more than one race. This figure shows data using the race-alone concept. For example, Asian refers to people who reported Asian and no other race.

SOURCE: Jessica C. Barnett and Marina S. Vornovitsky, "Figure 6. Children under Age 19 and Adults Aged 19 to 64 without Health Insurance Coverage by Selected Characteristics: 2015," in *Health Insurance Coverage in the United States: 2015*, U.S. Census Bureau, September 2016, https://www.census.gov/content/dam/Census/library/publications/2016/demo/p60-257.pdf (accessed January 2, 2017).

and to continue efforts to promote enrollment in Medicaid and CHIP.

The ACA also made significant changes in how the private health care industry treats children. It ended health insurance discrimination against children with preexisting conditions. This means that insurance companies cannot deny coverage to children up to age 19 with conditions such as asthma, diabetes, or a disability. The ACA enabled young adults to remain on their parents' health insurance plans until they are 26 years old, and in 2014 Medicaid coverage for former foster children was extended until age 26. The ACA also required that all new health plans cover dental and vision care for children.

The November 2016 election of Donald Trump (1946–) and the Republican Party's promise to repeal or at least substantially revise the ACA may impact health insurance coverage for millions of children.

Homelessness

The U.S. Conference of Mayors discusses the problem of homelessness in *Hunger and Homelessness Survey: A Status Report on Hunger and Homelessness in America's Cities* (December 2016, https://endhomelessness.atavist.com/mayorsreport2016). The report indicates that between 2015 and 2016 there was a 5.6% decrease in homeless families nationally. However, some cities such

TABLE 4.4

Percentage of children under age 18 covered by health insurance at some time during the year by type of insurance and selected characteristics, 1993–2014

Characteristic	1993	1994	1995	1996	1997	1998	1999	2000	2001	2002	2003	2004	2005	2006	2007	2008	2009	2010	2011	2012	2013	2014
Any health insurance																						
Total	13.6	14.6	13.0	12.7	14.0	12.7	11.9	12.4	11.0	10.7	9.8	9.2	9.3	9.5	9.0	9.0	8.2	7.8	7.0	6.6	6.6	5.4
Gender																						
Male	13.8	14.5	12.8	12.8	13.8	12.7	11.9	12.3	11.0	11.0	9.5	9.2	9.1	9.7	9.0	9.0	8.2	8.0	7.0	6.4	6.7	5.6
Female	13.4	14.7	13.3	12.7	14.1	12.7	11.8	12.5	11.0	10.5	10.1	9.2	9.4	9.2	9.1	9.1	8.2	7.6	6.9	6.7	6.5	5.3
Age																						
Ages 0–5	12.4	13.2	11.5	11.5	12.5	11.5	11.0	11.7	9.7	9.1	8.2	8.2	7.7	7.5	7.3	7.6	6.6	6.3	5.0	4.6	5.0	4.1
Ages 6–11	13.8	14.8	12.8	12.9	14.2	12.8	12.1	12.3	11.3	11.0	9.7	9.3	9.2	9.8	8.8	9.0	7.9	7.4	7.0	6.4	6.0	5.2
Ages 12–17	14.8	16.0	14.9	13.9	15.2	13.9	12.5	13.3	12.0	12.0	11.4	10.0	10.8	11.1	10.9	10.6	10.1	9.8	9.0	8.7	8.9	6.9
Race and Hispanic origin[b]																						
White, non-Hispanic	11.0	12.0	10.4	10.0	10.7	8.9	8.1	8.7	7.2	7.5	6.4	6.4	6.5	6.2	7.1	6.7	6.0	5.8	4.8	5.2	4.7	4.1
Black non-Hispanic	14.7	13.5	12.6	13.0	13.8	14.0	11.9	12.2	10.6	10.0	8.9	6.9	8.9	7.8	6.2	7.5	6.6	6.4	5.5	4.4	5.1	3.5
Hispanic	25.3	25.3	24.2	23.4	26.7	26.2	26.7	25.8	24.6	21.9	20.2	19.5	17.5	19.4	15.3	16.8	14.7	13.0	12.3	10.9	11.8	9.7
Region[c]																						
Northeast	9.9	10.6	10.2	10.2	8.9	7.3	7.2	7.0	5.8	7.4	5.1	5.4	5.5	4.3	5.2	6.0	4.4	4.4	3.0	3.5	3.7	3.6
South	18.7	18.9	17.1	16.4	18.0	16.3	15.8	16.1	14.1	13.1	12.1	11.5	12.5	12.7	11.4	10.7	10.7	9.7	8.1	8.0	8.0	7.1
Midwest	8.4	9.0	9.1	8.8	10.0	8.4	7.9	8.1	7.2	7.1	6.5	6.8	6.6	6.3	6.5	8.2	6.7	4.9	5.2	5.5	5.1	3.4
West	14.8	17.6	13.7	13.8	16.4	16.6	14.0	15.9	14.4	13.6	13.1	10.9	10.0	11.6	10.4	9.5	8.6	9.9	9.7	7.5	7.9	5.8
Private health insurance[c]																						
Total	66.3	63.5	65.5	66.5	66.1	68.4	68.8	67.0	66.7	63.9	63.0	63.2	62.1	59.4	59.8	58.4	55.8	54.1	53.7	53.4	53.2	53.7
Gender																						
Male	66.3	63.7	66.2	66.7	66.3	68.2	69.0	67.7	67.0	63.6	63.4	63.7	62.3	59.3	59.8	58.1	56.2	54.0	53.6	54.1	53.3	53.8
Female	66.3	63.3	64.8	66.4	65.9	68.5	68.7	66.2	66.4	64.1	62.5	62.7	61.9	59.4	59.8	58.8	55.4	54.2	53.8	52.7	53.0	53.6
Age																						
Ages 0–5	60.3	57.8	59.7	61.0	61.3	64.7	64.7	63.1	63.4	60.7	58.2	58.1	56.6	54.7	54.1	53.2	50.1	48.3	47.8	48.4	47.3	50.2
Ages 6–11	68.0	64.9	66.8	67.7	66.2	68.8	69.0	67.5	66.8	64.1	63.2	63.4	62.1	59.5	61.0	58.7	57.0	54.7	54.2	53.6	53.6	53.1
Ages 12–17	71.2	68.4	70.6	71.1	71.0	71.7	72.8	70.3	69.7	66.8	67.4	67.7	67.2	63.8	64.2	63.5	60.7	59.7	59.4	58.0	58.3	57.6
Race and Hispanic origin[b]																						
White, non-Hispanic	76.9	74.5	76.5	77.4	76.9	79.1	79.7	77.7	78.2	75.6	75.7	76.3	75.0	72.4	73.8	72.8	70.5	69.1	68.6	68.5	68.8	68.2
Black non-Hispanic	42.2	39.9	43.3	46.0	46.1	47.1	49.1	47.6	48.3	45.0	46.2	45.5	42.3	41.4	41.3	38.4	36.3	34.5	35.1	33.3	33.6	34.3
Hispanic	43.3	41.7	40.1	40.9	42.0	45.3	44.7	44.6	41.1	38.9	36.3	36.1	36.8	34.2	35.3	33.4	30.5	29.2	29.1	29.5	28.2	31.4
Region[c]																						
Northeast	72.2	69.9	70.3	70.8	71.0	74.2	74.3	72.3	73.2	69.4	70.5	70.2	69.6	64.3	67.1	65.8	64.7	61.4	59.3	60.6	58.7	57.8
South	60.5	57.0	59.9	60.0	61.2	63.1	62.7	60.9	60.5	57.4	56.4	57.1	54.5	53.3	54.3	53.2	50.0	48.8	49.4	47.3	47.2	47.9
Midwest	72.9	72.4	72.5	75.5	73.9	76.5	77.7	75.8	74.1	72.8	71.2	71.8	69.2	66.4	65.5	63.4	60.7	60.4	60.9	61.7	62.2	60.1
West	62.9	58.1	62.4	62.7	60.6	62.3	64.2	62.3	63.5	60.0	59.5	58.5	60.6	58.2	57.6	56.2	53.6	51.4	49.5	50.0	50.5	54.5
Public health insurance[d]																						
Total	18.2	19.8	19.6	19.0	17.4	16.3	17.1	18.4	20.4	23.5	25.1	25.4	26.3	28.8	28.6	30.1	33.1	35.2	37.0	37.6	37.7	38.1
Gender																						
Male	18.1	19.7	19.3	18.7	17.4	16.4	17.0	17.7	20.1	23.6	25.0	25.1	26.3	28.7	28.6	30.6	32.7	35.2	37.2	36.9	37.4	37.9
Female	18.3	20.0	19.9	19.2	17.5	16.3	17.3	19.1	20.6	23.3	25.2	25.7	26.4	29.0	28.6	29.6	33.5	35.2	36.9	38.3	38.0	38.3

TABLE 4.4

Percentage of children under age 18 covered by health insurance at some time during the year by type of insurance and selected characteristics, 1993–2014 [CONTINUED]

Characteristic	1993	1994	1995	1996	1997	1998	1999	2000	2001	2002	2003	2004	2005	2006	2007	2008	2009	2010	2011	2012	2013	2014
Age																						
Ages 0–5	25.1	26.7	26.7	25.7	23.4	21.4	22.2	23.1	24.6	28.2	31.3	31.3	33.0	35.3	35.4	36.6	40.2	42.3	45.1	44.4	44.5	42.6
Ages 6–11	16.7	18.6	18.6	17.7	17.2	15.9	16.6	18.1	20.2	23.0	24.9	25.1	26.3	28.6	27.5	30.0	32.5	35.3	36.5	37.7	38.1	39.0
Ages 12–17	12.1	13.5	13.0	13.2	11.6	11.7	12.6	14.2	16.3	19.3	19.3	20.2	19.9	22.9	23.0	23.7	26.3	27.6	29.2	30.7	30.6	33.0
Race and Hispanic origin[b]																						
White, non-Hispanic	10.1	11.3	11.4	11.0	10.1	9.6	10.3	11.5	12.7	15.0	15.8	15.4	16.4	19.4	16.4	18.1	20.6	22.2	24.5	24.0	23.7	24.8
Black, non-Hispanic	41.5	44.6	42.0	38.4	37.1	35.0	35.4	37.3	38.8	42.3	42.7	44.5	45.3	47.0	49.3	50.9	53.9	56.0	56.5	59.4	58.8	59.2
Hispanic	30.0	31.6	34.0	34.2	29.2	26.6	27.0	28.0	32.9	38.2	41.7	42.8	43.8	44.4	47.9	47.7	52.6	55.5	56.6	57.5	58.2	56.5
Region[c]																						
Northeast	17.4	18.9	19.1	18.7	19.0	16.7	17.7	19.9	20.4	22.4	23.5	23.2	23.4	30.2	26.6	27.6	29.8	33.5	36.1	34.3	36.7	37.3
South	18.1	20.5	19.9	20.5	16.9	16.7	18.0	19.5	22.7	26.2	28.5	28.3	29.3	30.1	30.0	32.1	34.7	37.3	39.6	41.4	41.3	41.4
Midwest	18.3	18.0	17.8	15.2	14.7	14.0	13.5	14.9	17.1	19.4	21.3	20.4	23.2	26.6	26.9	27.1	31.3	33.0	32.6	31.4	31.4	34.4
West	19.0	21.5	21.5	20.9	20.2	18.3	19.3	19.3	20.0	24.3	24.8	27.7	27.1	26.9	29.5	32.0	34.7	35.4	38.1	39.7	38.3	36.9

[a] A child was considered to be uninsured if he or she did not have any private health insurance, Medicare, Medicaid, Children's Health Insurance Program (CHIP), state-sponsored or other government-sponsored health plan, or military plan. A child was also defined as uninsured if he or she had only Indian Health Service coverage or had only a private plan that paid for one type of service such as accidents or dental care.

[b] Respondents are asked whether they are of Hispanic origin and about their race separately. Information from these two sources is used to create a four-category race/ethnicity indicator, which distinguishes between "white, non-Hispanic," "black, non-Hispanic," "Other, non-Hispanic," and "Hispanic" children. For this report, estimates for children who are "other, non-Hispanic" are not shown separately but are included in the total. For years 1993–1996, race is based on the main race of the child following the 1977 Office of Management and Budget (OMB) standards for collecting and presenting data on race. From 1997 onward, estimates are presented for children for whom a single race was indicated; following the 1997 OMB standards for collecting and presenting data on race, the National Health Interview Survey asked respondents to choose one or more races from the following: White, Black or African American, Asian, American Indian or Alaska Native, and Native Hawaiian or other Pacific Islander. The use of the race-alone population in this table does not imply that it is the preferred method of presenting or analyzing data. Data from 1997 onward are not directly comparable with data from earlier years. Persons of Hispanic origin may be of any race.

[c] Regions: Northeast includes CT, MA, ME, NH, NJ, NY, PA, RI, and VT. South includes AL, AR, DC, DE, FL, GA, KY, LA, MD, MS, NC, OK, SC, TN, TX, VA, and WV. Midwest includes IA, IL, IN, KS, MI, MN, MO, ND, NE, OH, SD, and WI. West includes AK, AZ, CA, CO, HI, ID, MT, NM, NV, OR, UT, WA, and WY.

[d] Private health insurance includes children covered by any comprehensive private insurance plan (including health maintenance organizations and preferred provider organizations). These plans include those obtained through an employer, purchased directly or obtained through local or community programs. Excludes plans that only paid for one type of service such as accidents or dental care.

[e] Public health insurance includes children who do not have private coverage, but who have Medicaid or other state-sponsored health plans, including CHIP.

Note: A small percentage of children have coverage other than private or public health insurance. They are not shown separately in the report, but they are included in the total.

SOURCE: "Table HC1. Health Insurance Coverage: Percentage of Children Ages 0–17 Covered by Health Insurance Coverage Status at Time of the Year and Selected Characteristics, 1993–2014," in *America's Children in Brief: Key National Indicators of Well-Being, 2016*, Federal Interagency Forum on Child and Family Statistics, 2016. https://www.childstats.gov/americaschildren/tables.asp (accessed January 2, 2017)

as New York City and Wichita, Kansas, reported increases in homeless families between 2009 and 2016. City officials cited lack of affordable housing as the leading cause of homelessness among families with children, followed by poverty, unemployment, and low-paying jobs.

Children are negatively affected by homelessness in a variety of ways. In "Promoting Resilience for Children Who Experience Family Homelessness: Opportunities to Encourage Developmental Competence" (*Cityscape: A Journal of Policy Development and Research*, vol. 16, no. 1, 2014), J. J. Cutuli and Janette E. Herbers explain that homeless children are at increased risk for lower levels of academic achievement, emotional and behavioral problems, and problems in language development and cognitive functioning, as well as illness and chronic disease. This increased risk persists even when accounting for differences in other factors such as poverty.

Homeless adolescents are more likely than their housed peers to suffer from mental health problems; use illegal drugs, alcohol, and cigarettes; and engage in sexual behaviors that increase their risk of pregnancy and of sexually transmitted infections (STIs). In "Mental Health and Health Risk Behaviours of Homeless Adolescents and Youth: A Mixed Methods Study" (*Child and Youth Care Forum*, vol. 45, no. 3, June 2016), Kwaku Oppong Asante, Anna Meyer-Weitz, and Inge Petersen of the University of KwaZulu-Natal collected data from 227 homeless youth to find out why youth engage in behavior that places their health at risk and to determine the relationship between substance use and high-risk sexual behavior. They also look at the factors related to the psychological functioning of homeless youth. The researchers find that most (87.6%) study subjects had moderate to severe psychological problems and that those engaging in violent behavior or thinking about suicide were the most likely to suffer from severe psychological problems. Oppong Asante, Meyer-Weitz, and Petersen conclude that "engagements in risky behaviours were primarily focused on survival strategies, and the emotional impact of homelessness was evidenced in their feelings of exclusion due to social stigma and feelings of despondency and depression."

Hunger

Food insecurity is defined as the lack of access to enough food to meet basic needs. Alisha Coleman-Jensen et al. of the U.S. Department of Agriculture report in *Household Food Security in the United States in 2015* (September 2016, https://www.ers.usda.gov/webdocs/pub lications/err215/err-215.pdf) that in 2015, 87.3% of U.S. households were food secure, which remained essentially unchanged from the year before. However, the remaining 12.7% (15.8 million) of U.S. households experienced food insecurity at some point during the year. Most of these households used a variety of coping strategies to obtain adequate food, such as eating less varied diets, participating in food assistance programs, or getting food from community food pantries or soup kitchens. Both food insecurity and very low food security among children decreased from 2014. Children and adults were food insecure in 7.8% (3 million) of households with children in 2015, down from 9.4% in 2014. Very low food security among children was 0.7% (274,000) of households in 2015, down from 1.1% in 2014.

Coleman-Jensen et al. note that in households with incomes near or below the poverty line, households with children headed by a single mother or father, and African American and Hispanic households were the most likely to experience food insecurity in 2015. Food insecurity varied by state; between 2013 and 2015 it ranged from a low of 8.5% in North Dakota to a high of 20.8% in Mississippi.

It is important to note that homeless people were not included in this study. If they had been included, then it would most likely have increased the percentage of individuals and families counted as food insecure.

EMERGENCY FOOD ASSISTANCE. Feeding America, the nation's largest charitable hunger-relief organization, reports in "Child Hunger Facts" (2017, http://www.feed ingamerica.org/hunger-in-america/impact-of-hunger/child -hunger/child-hunger-fact-sheet.html) that 13.1 million children lived in food insecure households in 2015. Twelve million children, more than 3.5 million of whom were under five years of age, received emergency food assistance from Feeding America.

Exposure to Toxins

Another threat to children's health is exposure to environmental toxins. Two toxins that children are most frequently exposed to are lead and secondhand smoke.

LEAD POISONING. Because they have smaller bodies and are growing, children suffer the effects of lead exposure more acutely than adults do. Lead poisoning causes nervous system disorders, reduction in intelligence, fatigue, inhibited infant growth, and hearing loss. Toxic levels of lead in a parent can also affect unborn children.

In "Toys" (October 15, 2013, http://www.cdc.gov/nceh/ lead/tips/toys.htm), the CDC indicates that children are primarily exposed to lead in paint and plastics. Although leaded paint was banned in the United States in 1978, children may still be exposed to leaded paint in older homes. Leaded paint is not used on toys manufactured in the United States, but it is still widely used on toys that are manufactured in other countries. Therefore, children may be exposed to lead when playing with imported toys. In addition, the use of lead in plastics, which makes them more flexible and able to return to their original shape, has not been banned. The CDC explains that "when the plastic is exposed to substances such as sunlight, air, and detergents, the chemical bond between the lead and plastics breaks down and forms a dust."

In 2008 the Consumer Product Safety Improvement Act (CPSIA) became law. It established new, stricter rules for children's products and included imported toys. The U.S. Consumer Product Safety Commission (CPSC) describes in "The Consumer Product Safety Improvement Act" (December 6, 2013, https://www.cpsc.gov/regulations-laws--standards/statutes/the-consumer-product-safety-improvement-act/) the effects of the CPSIA. Beginning in 2012 all children's products had to be certified by CPSC-approved laboratories as containing no more than 100 parts per million of lead in accessible parts. Nevertheless, in "Recent Recalls" (2017, https://www.cpsc.gov/Recalls), the CPSC indicates that in 2016 it recalled children's M&M's-branded jewelry, Things Remembered children's jewelry, water bottles, children's chairs, swings, and musical instruments because of excessive lead content.

In "CDC's National Surveillance Data (1997–2015)" (October 28, 2016, http://www.cdc.gov/nceh/lead/data/national.htm), the CDC states that in 2015, 11,681 children in the United States aged five years and younger had confirmed blood lead levels greater than the CDC's recommended level of 10 micrograms per deciliter of blood. This was less than 1% of all children tested. Although children from all social and socioeconomic levels can be affected by lead poisoning, children in families with low incomes who live in older, deteriorated housing are at higher risk. Paint produced before 1978 frequently contained lead, so federal legislation requires owners to disclose any information they may have about lead-based paint before renting or selling a home built earlier than 1978.

SECONDHAND SMOKE. Environmental tobacco smoke is a major hazard for children, whose respiratory, immune, and other systems are not as well developed as those of adults. Secondhand smoke (smoke produced by other people's cigarettes) increases the number of attacks and severity of symptoms in children with asthma and can even cause asthma in preschool-aged children. It also causes lower respiratory tract infections, middle-ear infections, and a reduction in lung function in children and increases the risk of sudden infant death syndrome.

The results of research conducted by Jocelyn M. Biagini Myers et al. and reported in "Asking the Right Questions to Ascertain Early Childhood Secondhand Smoke Exposures" (*Journal of Pediatrics*, vol. 160, no. 6, June 2012) reveal that children in families with lower socioeconomic status have much higher levels of secondhand smoke exposures than do children of families with higher socioeconomic status. Table 4.5 shows that between 1988–94 and 2011–12 the percentage of children

exposed to secondhand smoke decreased dramatically. However, in 2011–12, 60.6% of non-Hispanic African American children were still being exposed to this health hazard.

In "Thirdhand Tobacco Smoke: Emerging Evidence and Arguments for a Multidisciplinary Research Agenda" (*Environmental Health Perspectives*, vol. 119, no. 9, September 2011), George E. Matt et al. define thirdhand smoke as "residual tobacco smoke pollutants that remain on surfaces and in dust after tobacco has been smoked, are re-emitted into the gas phase, or react with oxidants and other compounds in the environment to yield secondary pollutants." The researchers explain that infants and young children are 100 times more sensitive than adults to pollutants in house dust and may be at greater risk of thirdhand smoke exposure than adolescents and adults because they spend more time indoors and in areas, such as on carpet, where dust collects and may be resuspended. Infants and toddlers are also more likely to put nonfood items in their mouth.

DISEASES OF CHILDHOOD

Infants, toddlers, children, and teens suffer from many of the same diseases and conditions as adults do—colds, flu, conjunctivitis (pink eye), strep infections, foodborne diseases, vision impairment, and cancer.

The following sections describe common diseases and conditions that afflict toddlers, children, and teens and focus on two increasingly common conditions affecting them: obesity and asthma. These two conditions are often related because overweight and obesity increase the risk of developing asthma.

Infants and Toddlers

Besides birth defects and developmental delays and disabilities, infants and toddlers may suffer from infectious diseases such as hand, foot, and mouth disease (HFMD), a viral illness that causes fever, mouth sores, a rash, and jaundice (a condition in which bilirubin builds up in a baby's blood, causing the skin and eyes to look yellow). There is no treatment for HFMD. Jaundice is treated by placing the baby under special lights.

Children

Although most children are immunized against infectious diseases such as measles, mumps, and rubella (German measles), children commonly suffer from sore throats, ear and sinus infections, colds and flu, and asthma. They may also be diagnosed with depression, learning disorders, or attention-deficit/hyperactivity disorder (ADHD; a condition that makes it hard for children to pay attention, listen, remember instructions, and control their impulses).

TABLE 4.5

Percentage of children aged 4–17 with nicotine in their blood as a result of exposure to secondhand smoke, selected years 1988–2012

Characteristic	1988–1994	1999–2000	2001–2002	2003–2004	2005–2006	2007–2008	2009–2010	2011–2012
Ages 4–17—Any detectable cotinine at or above 0.05 ng/mL								
Total[‡]	84.4	64.2	52.6	61.1	48.9	50.0	39.6	37.3
White, non-Hispanic	83.7	62.7	48.8	63.3	48.9	53.8	39.1	36.9
Black, non-Hispanic	94.7	83.6	80.6	78.2	69.6	62.0	63.7	60.6
Mexican American	76.5	48.2	44.4	38.0	33.2	28.0	25.6	25.3
Ages 4–17—Blood cotinine above 1.0 ng/mL								
Total[‡]	22.5	16.9	16.1	17.1	11.6	15.3	9.0	8.1
White, non-Hispanic	23.1	20.0	18.0	19.5	11.5	19.3	8.9	8.7
Black, non-Hispanic	33.7	22.3	22.6	21.5	21.2	15.4	20.7	16.5
Mexican American	8.3	4.9	5.4*	4.3	4.1	5.1*	3.5	[†]
Ages 4–11—Any detectable cotinine at or above 0.05 ng/mL								
Total[‡]	84.5	64.4	55.1	63.7	51.4	52.6	41.7	40.5
White, non-Hispanic	83.3	62.8	53.7	67.7	52.3	57.4	42.0	37.4
Black, non-Hispanic	94.7	86.2	81.3	81.5	69.7	65.1	67.6	68.7
Mexican American	76.7	48.6	45.3	37.6	32.0	29.1	27.6	29.6
Ages 4–11—Blood cotinine above 1.0 ng/mL								
Total[‡]	24.3	17.7	18.1	18.7	12.3	16.7	9.4	9.7
White, non-Hispanic	25.6	21.0	20.8	22.3	11.8	21.7	9.1	10.1
Black, non-Hispanic	34.2	23.5	24.1	22.7	25.0	18.9	25.8	20.6
Mexican American	8.9	4.7	[†]	3.6	[†]	[†]	2.6*	[†]
Ages 12–17—Any detectable cotinine at or above 0.05 ng/mL								
Total[‡]	84.3	63.9	49.6	57.9	46.0	47.0	37.2	33.8
White, non-Hispanic	84.3	62.5	43.1	58.2	45.1	49.6	36.1	36.4
Black, non-Hispanic	94.8	79.9	79.5	73.9	69.5	58.7	59.2	50.9
Mexican American	76.3	47.5	43.2	38.6	34.7	26.6	23.0	20.0
Ages 12–17—Blood cotinine above 1.0 ng/mL								
Total[‡]	20.1	16.0	13.6	15.0	10.8	13.7	8.4	6.3
White, non-Hispanic	19.7	18.6	14.8	16.3	11.2	16.4	8.7*	7.2
Black, non-Hispanic	33.1	20.7	20.7	20.0	17.1	11.6	14.8*	11.7
Mexican American	7.4	5.1	6.8*	[†]	5.2	7.2	4.7*	[†]

*Estimate is considered unstable.
[†]Reporting standards not met; the estimate is considered unreliable.
[‡]Totals include data for racial/ethnic groups not shown separately.

Notes: Cotinine levels are reported for nonsmoking children only (non-smoker defined as those with cotinine less than or equal to 10 ng/mL). "Any detectable cotinine" indicates blood cotinine levels at or above 0.05 nanograms per milliliter (ng/mL), the detectable level of cotinine in the blood in 1988–1994. The average (geometric mean) blood cotinine level in children living in homes where someone smoked was 1.0 ng/mL in 1988–1994 and in 2003–2006. For 1988–1994, the 1977 Office of Management and Budget (OMB) Standards for Data on Race and Ethnicity were used to classify persons into one of the following four racial groups: White, Black, American Indian or Alaskan Native, or Asian or Pacific Islander. For 1999–2012, the revised 1997 OMB Standards were used. Persons could select one or more of five racial groups: white, black or African American, American Indian or Alaska Native, Asian, and Native Hawaiian or other Pacific Islander. Included in the total but not shown separately are American Indian or Alaska Native, Asian, Native Hawaiian or other Pacific Islander, and "Two or more races." Data on race and Hispanic origin are collected separately but combined for reporting. Beginning in 2007, the National Health and Nutrition Examination Survey allows for reporting of both total Hispanics and Mexican Americans; however, estimates reported here are for Mexian Americans to be consistent with earlier years. Persons of Mexican origin may be of any race.

SOURCE: "Table PHY2.A. Secondhand Smoke: Percentage of Children Ages 4–17 with Specified Blood Cotinine Levels by Age and Race and Hispanic Origin, Selected Years 1988–2012," in *America's Children in Brief: Key National Indicators of Well-Being, 2016*, Federal Interagency Forum on Child and Family Statistics, 2016, https://www.childstats.gov/americaschildren/tables.asp (accessed January 2, 2017)

Teens

Teens contract the same conditions as children do, and if they are sexually active, they are susceptible to STIs such as HPV and the human immunodeficiency virus (HIV; the virus that if left untreated causes the acquired immunodeficiency syndrome [AIDS]). Youth who inject drugs may contract hepatitis, an inflammation of the liver. Hepatitis may also be transmitted via sexual contact.

HOW MANY CHILDREN AND TEENS HAVE AIDS? According to the CDC, in *HIV Surveillance Report, 2014* (November 2014, https://www.cdc.gov/hiv/pdf/library/reports/surveillance/cdc-hiv-surveillance-report-us.pdf), at year-end 2014 an estimated cumulative total of 10,014 children under the age of 13 years had been diagnosed with stage 3 HIV infection (AIDS) since the beginning of the epidemic in 1981. (See Table 4.6.) African American children made up the overwhelming majority of these cases (5,703 cases), followed by Hispanic children (2,406 cases), white children (1,556 cases), Asian American children (47 cases), Native American or Alaskan Native children (27 cases), and Native Hawaiian or Other Pacific Islander children (six cases).

Figure 4.2 shows the numbers of AIDS diagnoses among teens aged 13 to 19 years between 1985 and

TABLE 4.6

Diagnoses of AIDS in children younger than 13 years of age, by year of diagnosis, race, and Hispanic origin, 2010–14 and cumulative

Race/ethnicity	2010		2011		2012		2013		2014		Cumulative[a]	
	No.	Est. no.[b]	No.	Est. no.[b]	No.	Est. no.[b]	No.	Est. no.[b]	No.	Est. no.[b]	No.	Est. no.[b]
American Indian/Alaska Native	0	0	0	0	0	0	0	0	1	1	27	27
Asian[c]	1	1	0	0	0	0	0	0	1	1	47	47
Black/African American	13	13	11	11	9	9	4	4	56	62	5,686	5,703
Hispanic/Latino[d]	4	4	2	2	0	0	2	2	11	12	2,400	2,406
Native Hawaiian/other Pacific Islander	0	0	0	0	0	0	0	0	0	0	6	6
White	3	3	2	2	1	1	0	0	6	6	1,554	1,556
Multiple races	0	0	0	0	0	0	2	2	19	21	266	269
Total[e]	21	21	15	15	10	10	8	8	94	104	9,986	10,014

[a]From the beginning of the epidemic through 2014.
[b]Estimated numbers resulted from statistical adjustment that accounted for reporting delays, but not for incomplete reporting.
[c]Includes Asian/Pacific Islander legacy cases.
[d]Hispanics/Latinos can be of any race.
[e]Because column totals for estimated numbers were calculated independently of the values for the subpopulations, the values in each column may not sum to the column total.
Note: Reported numbers less than 12, as well as estimated numbers (and accompanying trends) based on these numbers, should be interpreted with caution because the numbers have underlying relative standard errors greater than 30% and are considered unreliable.
The criteria for stage 3 (AIDS) classification among pediatric cases were expanded in 2014.

SOURCE: "Table 8b. Stage 3 (AIDS) among Children Aged <13 Years, by Race/Ethnicity, 2010–2014 and Cumulative—United States and 6 Dependent Areas," in *HIV Surveillance Report, 2014*, vol. 26, Centers for Disease Control and Prevention, November 2014, https://www.cdc.gov/hiv/pdf/library/reports/surveillance/cdc-hiv-surveillance-report-us.pdf (accessed January 2, 2017)

2013. Because of the long incubation period between the time of infection and the onset of symptoms, it is highly probable that many people who develop AIDS during their early 20s became infected with HIV during their adolescence.

Overweight and Obese Children

The number of overweight and obese Americans has reached epidemic proportions. The percentage of obese children and adolescents has grown significantly since the 1970s. In 1976–80, 6.5% of children aged six to 11 years were obese, which is defined as having a body mass index (BMI) at or above the 95th percentile of the sex-specific BMI growth charts. (See Table 4.7.) In 2011–14, 17.5% of children were obese.

An upward trend was also seen in the rates of obese adolescents; 4.5% of boys and 5.4% of girls aged 12 to 17 years were obese in 1976–80, compared with 20.1% of adolescent boys and 22.5% of adolescent girls in 2011–14. (See Table 4.7.) The proportion of all children between the ages of six and 17 years who were obese more than tripled, from 5.7% in 1976–80 to 19.5% in 2011–14.

The percentages of overweight high school students (in the 85th percentile or above for BMI) and obese high school students (in the 95th percentile or above for BMI) vary by race and ethnicity. For example, in 2015 non-Hispanic African American (16.8%) and Hispanic (16.4%) adolescents were more likely to be obese than non-Hispanic white (12.4%) adolescents. (See Table 4.8.) In general, younger students were more likely than older students to be either overweight or obese.

Overweight and obese children and adolescents have an increased risk for premature death in adulthood as well as for many chronic diseases, including coronary heart disease, hypertension, diabetes mellitus (type 2), gallbladder disease, respiratory disease, some cancers, and arthritis. Type 2 diabetes, once considered an adult disease, has increased dramatically in children and adolescents. Being overweight or obese may also lead to poor self-esteem and depression in children and teens.

Weight problems in children are caused by a combination of lack of physical activity, unhealthy eating habits, and genetics. Watching television and playing computer and video games contribute to the inactive lifestyles of some children. Laura Kann et al. indicate in "Youth Risk Behavior Surveillance—United States, 2015" (*Morbidity and Mortality Weekly Report*, vol. 65, no. 6, June 10, 2016) that in 2015, 41.7% of high school students spent three or more hours per school day on the computer or playing video games, and 24.7% spent three or more hours per school day watching television, often not getting a sufficient amount of physical exercise as a consequence.

Physical activity patterns established during youth may extend into adulthood and may decrease the risk of illnesses such as coronary heart disease, diabetes, and cancer. Regular physical activity is also associated with improved mental health and life satisfaction. More than 11% of high school boys and 17.5% of high school girls had not been physically active for a total of 60 minutes or more on one of the seven days preceding the 2015 survey. (See Table 4.9.) Non-Hispanic white students were somewhat less likely to have been physically inactive

FIGURE 4.2

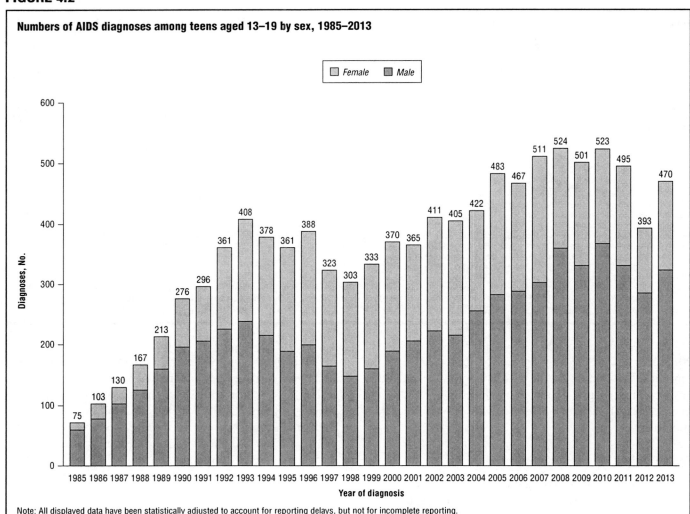

Numbers of AIDS diagnoses among teens aged 13–19 by sex, 1985–2013

Note: All displayed data have been statistically adjusted to account for reporting delays, but not for incomplete reporting.

SOURCE: "Stage 3 (AIDS) Classifications among Adolescents Aged 13–19 Years, by Sex, 1985–2013—United States and 6 Dependent Areas," in *HIV Surveillance—Adolescents and Young Adults*, National Center for HIV/AIDS, Viral Hepatitis, STD & TB Prevention, Division of HIV/AIDS Prevention, 2015, https://www.cdc.gov/hiv/pdf/statistics_surveillance_Adolescents.pdf (accessed January 2, 2017)

(11.6%) than were Hispanic (15.6%) or non-Hispanic African American (20.4%) students. Attending physical education (PE) classes declined with each year of high school; in ninth grade 71.4% of students attended at least one PE class per week, but by 12th grade the percentage fell to 36.1%. (See Table 4.10.)

Asthma

Another serious disease affecting children is asthma (a chronic respiratory disease that causes attacks of difficulty breathing). According to the CDC, in "Most Recent Asthma Data" (February 27, 2017, https://www.cdc.gov/asthma/most_recent_data.htm), 8.4% of children and teens aged one to 18 years were suffering from asthma in 2015. The Forum reports in *America's Children in Brief* that 13.5% of children had ever been diagnosed with asthma in 2014, and 4.3% suffered an asthma attack that year. The prevalence of asthma was higher among

children in families with incomes below 100% of the poverty level (10.5%) than among children in families with incomes at 200% of poverty or above (8.1%) and higher among non-Hispanic African American children (13.4%) than among Hispanic children (8.5%), non-Hispanic white children (7.6%), or non-Hispanic Asian American children (5.6%).

MENTAL HEALTH ISSUES IN YOUNG PEOPLE
Marital Conflict and Divorce

Divorce can cause stressful situations for children in several ways. Experiencing the breakup of their parents' marriage is likely to be stressful for children. One or both parents may have to move to a new home, removing the children from family and friends who could have given them support. Divorce and custody issues can generate hostility between parents, burdening children with additional stress.

TABLE 4.7

Percentage of children aged 6–17 who were obese, by sex, age, race and Hispanic origin, selected years 1976–2014

Characteristic	1976–1980	1988–1994	1999–2002	2003–2006	2007–2010	2011–2014
Ages 6–17						
Total	5.7	11.2	16.0	17.3	18.6	19.5
Race and Hispanic origin*						
White, non-Hispanic	4.9	10.5	13.2	15.5	16.0	17.1
Black, non-Hispanic	8.2	14.0	20.7	21.5	24.0	22.5
Asian, non-Hispanic	—	—	—	—	—	9.8
All Hispanics	—	—	—	—	23.7	24.3
Mexican American	—	15.4	23.0	22.7	23.8	25.2
Gender						
Male	5.5	11.8	17.2	18.1	20.4	18.9
Female	5.8	10.6	14.7	16.3	16.7	20.0
Ages 6–11						
Total	6.5	11.3	15.8	17.0	18.8	17.5
Gender						
Male	6.7	11.6	16.9	18.0	20.7	17.6
Female	6.4	11.0	14.7	15.8	16.9	17.5
Ages 12–17						
Total	4.9	11.1	16.1	17.5	18.4	21.3
Gender						
Male	4.5	12.0	17.5	18.2	20.1	20.1
Female	5.4	10.2	14.7	16.8	16.6	22.5

—Not available.

*From 1976 to 1994, the 1977 Office of Management and Budget (OMB) Standards for Data on Race and Ethnicity were used to classify persons into one of the following four racial groups: White, Black, American Indian or Alaskan Native, or Asian or Pacific Islander. For 1999–2014, the revised 1997 OMB Standards were used. Persons could select one or more of five racial groups: white, black or African American, American Indian or Alaska Native, Asian, and Native Hawaiian or other Pacific Islander. Included in the total but not shown separately are American Indian or Alaska Native, Asian, Native Hawaiian or other Pacific Islander, and "Two or more races." Beginning in 1999, those in each racial category represent those reporting only one race. Data from 1999 onward are not directly comparable with data from earlier years. Data on race and Hispanic origin are collected separately but are combined for reporting. Persons of Mexican origin may be of any race. From 1976 to 2006, the National Health and Nutrition Examination Survey (NHANES) sample was designed to provide estimates specifically for persons of Mexican origin. Beginning in 2007, NHANES allows for reporting of both total Hispanics and Mexican Americans. Beginning 2011–2012, the NHANES sample was designed to provide estimates for Asian Americans.

Note: All estimates have a relative standard error of less than 30 percent and meet agency standards for publication. Previously a body mass index (BMI) at or above the 95th percentile of the sex-specific BMI growth charts was termed overweight. Beginning with America's Children, 2010, a BMI at or above the 95th percentile is termed obese to be consistent with other National Center for Health Statistics publications. Estimates of obesity are comparable to estimates of overweight in past reports.

SOURCE: "Table HEALTH7. Obesity: Percentage of Children Ages 6–17 Who Had Obesity by Age, Race and Hispanic Origin, and Gender, Selected Years 1976–2014," in *America's Children in Brief: Key National Indicators of Well-Being, 2016*, Federal Interagency Forum on Child and Family Statistics, 2016, https://www.childstats.gov/americaschildren/tables.asp (accessed January 2, 2017)

TABLE 4.8

High school students who were overweight or obese, by sex, race/ethnicity, and grade, 2015

	Obesity			Overweight		
	Female	Male	Total	Female	Male	Total
Category	%	%	%	%	%	%
Race/ethnicity						
White*	9.1	15.6	12.4	14.6	15.9	15.2
Black*	15.2	18.2	16.8	21.2	13.6	17.2
Hispanic	13.3	19.4	16.4	20.0	17.0	18.4
Grade						
9	10.3	15.4	13.0	17.6	16.0	16.8
10	12.1	18.2	15.2	16.3	14.8	15.5
11	10.2	18.4	14.5	15.3	16.4	15.9
12	10.5	15.0	12.7	17.0	15.0	16.0
Total	**10.8**	**16.8**	**13.9**	**16.6**	**15.5**	**16.0**

*Non-Hispanic.

Notes: Overweight refers to students who were ≥85th percentile but ≤95th percentile for body mass index, based on sex- and age-specific reference data from the 2000 Centers for Disease Control growth charts. Obese refers to students who were ≥95th percentile for body mass index, based on sex- and age-specific reference data from the 2000 Centers for Disease Control growth charts.

SOURCE: Adapted from Laura Kann et al., "Table 115. Percentage of High School Students Who Had Obesity and Who Were Overweight, by Sex, Race/Ethnicity, and Grade—United States, Youth Risk Behavior Survey, 2015," in "Youth Risk Behavior Surveillance—United States, 2015," *Morbidity and Mortality Weekly Report*, vol. 65, no. 6, June 10, 2016, https://www.cdc.gov/healthyyouth/data/yrbs/pdf/2015/ss6506_updated.pdf (accessed January 3, 2017)

TABLE 4.9

High school students who did not participate in at least 60 minutes of physical activity on at least 1 day and students who were physically active at least 60 minutes/day on 5 or more days, by sex, race/ethnicity, and grade, 2015

| | Did not participate in at least 60 minutes of physical activity on at least 1 day | | | Physically active at least 60 minutes/day on 5 or more days | | |
| | Female | Male | Total | Female | Male | Total |
Category	%	%	%	%	%	%
Race/ethnicity						
White*	14.3	8.8	11.6	43.5	62.0	52.7
Black*	25.2	16.2	20.4	33.4	52.2	43.5
Hispanic	19.2	11.9	15.6	33.1	53.5	43.4
Grade						
9	14.7	9.5	12.0	43.9	62.3	53.7
10	15.8	10.4	13.1	41.9	58.7	50.2
11	18.2	12.4	15.5	36.6	56.3	46.5
12	21.4	12.4	16.9	33.4	53.3	43.5
Total	**17.5**	**11.1**	**14.3**	**39.1**	**57.8**	**48.6**

*Non-Hispanic.

Notes: Sixty minutes of physical activity is doing any kind of physical activity that increased their heart rate and made them breathe some of the time during the 7 days before the survey. Because of changes in question context starting in 2011, national Youth Risk Behavior Survey (YRBS) prevalence estimates derived from the 60 minutes of physical activity question in 2011, 2013, and 2015 are not comparable to those reported in 2009 or earlier. On the 2005–2009 national YRBS questionnaire, physical activity was assessed with three questions (in the following order) that asked the number of days students participated in 1) at least 20 minutes of vigorous physical activity; 2) at least 30 minutes of moderate physical activity; and 3) at least 60 minutes of aerobic (moderate and vigorous) physical activity. On the 2011, 2013, and 2015 national YRBS questionnaires, only the 60 minutes of aerobic physical activity question was included.

SOURCE: Adapted from Laura Kann et al., "Table 105. Percentage of High School Students Who Did Not Participate in at Least 60 Minutes of Physical Activity on at Least 1 Day and Who Were Physically Active at Least 60 Minutes/Day on 5 or More Days, by Sex, Race/Ethnicity, and Grade—United States, Youth Risk Behavior Survey, 2015," in "Youth Risk Behavior Surveillance—United States, 2015," *Morbidity and Mortality Weekly Report*, vol. 65, no. 6, June 10, 2016, https://www.cdc.gov/healthyyouth/data/yrbs/pdf/2015/ss6506_updated.pdf (accessed January 3, 2017)

TABLE 4.10

Percentage of high school students who attended physical education classes on one or more days per week, by sex, grade, and race and ethnicity, 2015

| | Attended PE classes | | | Attended PE classes daily | | |
| | Female | Male | Total | Female | Male | Total |
Category	%	%	%	%	%	%
Race/ethnicity						
White*	45.9	51.0	48.4	21.1	29.6	25.4
Black*	52.2	65.4	59.2	32.2	38.9	35.8
Hispanic	50.1	60.5	55.4	33.0	42.4	37.7
Grade						
9	70.4	72.2	71.4	39.5	44.6	42.2
10	53.9	61.3	57.5	27.0	36.1	31.5
11	34.6	42.2	38.5	18.1	25.2	21.8
12	29.1	42.9	36.1	16.0	27.9	21.9
Total	**47.8**	**55.3**	**51.6**	**25.5**	**33.8**	**29.8**

PE = physical education
*Non-Hispanic.
Note: Percentage refers to attendance in an average week when students were in school.

SOURCE: Adapted from Laura Kann et al., "Table 111. Percentage of High School Students Who Attended Physical Education (PE) classes on ≥1 days and Who Attended PE classes on All 5 Days, by Sex, Race/Ethnicity, and Grade—United States, Youth Risk Behavior Survey, 2015," in "Youth Risk Behavior Surveillance—United States, 2015," *Morbidity and Mortality Weekly Report*, vol. 65, no. 6, June 10, 2016, https://www.cdc.gov/healthyyouth/data/yrbs/pdf/2015/ss6506_updated.pdf (accessed January 3, 2017)

When one or both parents remarry, children are faced with more adjustments to their living arrangements.

Marital conflict hurts children independent of whether it results in the breakup of marriages. Nearly all studies on children of divorce have focused on the period after the parents separated. Recent studies, however, suggest that the negative effects children experience may not come so much from the divorce itself as from the marital discord between parents before the divorce. In fact, some research suggests that many problems reported with troubled teens not only began during the marriage but also may have contributed to the breakup of the marriage. Some children and teens experience longer-term negative outcomes, including physical and emotional health problems, poor educational achievement, and socioeconomic disadvantage.

In "Parental Divorce and Adult Longevity" (*International Journal of Public Health*, vol. 58, no. 1, February 2013), Kandyce Larson and Neal Halfon confirm that divorce affects not only overall well-being in later life but also educational attainment, social network ties, and health behaviors. The researchers conclude that parental divorce in childhood is associated with worse health in adulthood, which in turn affects long-term survival.

Linda J. Luecken et al. hypothesize in "A Longitudinal Study of the Effects of Child-Reported Maternal Warmth on Cortisol Stress Response 15 Years after Parental Divorce" (*Psychosomatic Medicine*, vol. 78, no. 2, February–March 2016) that the quality of mother-child relationships influence children's biological stress response systems—specifically, the regulation of cortisol, a hormone made in the adrenal gland, which governs many of the changes that occur in the body in response to stress. The researchers followed 240 youth from recently divorced families and asked the children to rate the warmth of their relationship with their mother at six time points during childhood, adolescence, and young adulthood. They also measured cortisol in young adulthood before and after a stressful situation. The researchers find that higher ratings of maternal warmth in adolescence predicted lower cortisol responses to stressful tasks in young adulthood. Luecken et al. conclude that these findings "suggest that for children from divorced families, a warm mother-child relationship post-divorce and across development, as perceived by the child, may promote efficient biological regulation later in life."

Eating Disorders

Overweight and obesity are among the most stigmatizing and least socially acceptable conditions in childhood and adolescence. Society, culture, and the media reinforce messages about ideal body shape and size and encourage dieting and exercise to achieve these ideals.

Although multiple factors including genetics have been implicated in the development of eating disorders, an overemphasis on thinness during childhood and adolescence may contribute to eating disorders such as anorexia nervosa (a disorder characterized by voluntary starvation) and bulimia nervosa (a disorder in which a person eats large amounts of food then forces vomiting or uses laxatives to prevent weight gain). Girls are both more likely to have a distorted view of their weight and more likely to have eating disorders than boys.

High school students as a whole have a fairly accurate view of their weight. In 2015, 16% of students were overweight (having a BMI between the 85th and 95th percentile for their age and sex) and 13.9% were obese (having a BMI equal to or greater than the 95th percentile for their age and sex). (See Table 4.8.) By contrast, 31.5% of high school students said they were slightly or very overweight. (See Table 4.11.) Girls, however, were much more likely than boys to have a skewed perception of their body size. Although 15.5% of male students were overweight and 16.8% were obese, only 25.3% perceived themselves as being overweight and 31.4% were trying to lose weight. Among female students, 16.6% were over-

TABLE 4.11

Percentage of high school students who thought they had a problem with weight and were trying to lose weight, by sex, race/ethnicity, and grade, 2015

	Described themselves as overweight			Were trying to lose weight		
	Female	Male	Total	Female	Male	Total
Category	%	%	%	%	%	%
Race/ethnicity						
White*	35.7	24.9	30.3	59.5	28.8	44.1
Black*	34.9	20.0	27.0	54.2	26.2	39.4
Hispanic	45.3	28.0	36.4	66.4	40.0	53.1
Grade						
9	35.8	25.5	30.3	59.4	31.1	44.3
10	38.9	25.2	32.0	59.3	32.0	45.7
11	38.5	25.2	31.6	61.7	31.0	45.7
12	39.6	25.0	32.3	62.6	31.9	47.3
Total	**38.2**	**25.3**	**31.5**	**60.6**	**31.4**	**45.6**

*Non-Hispanic.

SOURCE: Adapted from Laura Kann et al., "Table 117. Percentage of High School Students Who Described Themselves As Slightly or Very Overweight and Who Were Trying to Lose Weight, by Sex, Race/Ethnicity, and Grade—United States, Youth Risk Behavior Survey, 2015," in "Youth Risk Behavior Surveillance—United States, 2015," *Morbidity and Mortality Weekly Report*, vol. 65, no. 6, June 10, 2016, https://www.cdc.gov/healthyyouth/data/yrbs/pdf/2015/ss6506_updated.pdf (accessed January 3, 2017)

weight and 10.8% were obese, but 38.2% described themselves as being overweight and fully 60.6% were trying to lose weight.

Hyperactivity

ADHD is one of the most common neurobehavioral or psychiatric disorders to appear in childhood. No one knows precisely what causes ADHD, although research has focused on biological causes and the role of genetics. Symptoms include restlessness, inability to concentrate, aggressiveness, and impulsivity. Lack of treatment can lead to problems in school, at work, and in making friends. In "ADHD throughout the Years" (February 7, 2017, http://www.cdc.gov/ncbddd/adhd/timeline.html), the CDC explains that the percentage of children diagnosed with ADHD has changed over time in response to changing criteria used to diagnose the disorder, whether health professionals or parents determine the diagnosis, and the development of drug treatment. Figure 4.3 shows key dates in the history of ADHD, including changing diagnostic codes, the dates various drug treatments were approved, and estimates of the percentage of children affected.

Drug and Alcohol Use

Few factors negatively influence the health and well-being of young people more than the use of drugs, alcohol, and tobacco. Monitoring the Future, a long-term study on the use of drugs, alcohol, and tobacco conducted by the University of Michigan's Institute for Social Research, annually surveys eighth, 10th, and 12th graders on their use of these substances. According to Lloyd D. Johnston et al. of the Institute for Social Research, in *Monitoring the Future National Survey Results on Drug Use, 1975–2015: Overview, Key Findings on Adolescent Drug Use* (February 2016, http://www.monitoringthefuture.org/pubs/monographs/mtf-overview2015.pdf), the percentage of high school students who had used an illicit drug during that past year declined between 1997 and 2015, after sharp increases during the early 1990s. Johnston et al. find that in 2015, 38.6% of 12th graders (who were more likely than eighth [14.8%] or 10th [27.9%] graders to have used an illicit drug) had used an illicit drug during the previous 12 months.

Alcohol, which Monitoring the Future does not classify as an illicit drug, had been used by 26% of students by the eighth grade, and 64% had consumed alcohol by the end of high school. Alcohol use in general, binge drinking, and heavy drinking (defined as five or more drinks in a row at least once in the two-week period preceding the survey) fell to their lowest levels in the history of the study.

Kann et al. also examined drug use among high school students. They report that in 2015, 63.2% of all high school students had tried alcohol, and 17.2% had tried it for the first time before the age of 13. (See Table 4.12.) The researchers also note that 38.6% of high school students reported they had tried marijuana and that 7.5% had tried it for the first time before the age of 13.

TOBACCO. Most states prohibit the sale of cigarettes to anyone under the age of 18 years, but the laws are often ignored and may carry no penalties for youths who buy cigarettes or smoke in public. In fact, 12.6% of high school students under the age of 18 years who smoke reported in 2015 that they had bought cigarettes in a store or gas station and 1% purchased them on the Internet. (See Table 4.13.) The American Lung Association reports in "Tobacco Use among Children and Teens" (2017, http://www.lung.org/stop-smoking/smoking-facts/tobacco-use-among-children.html) that each day 2,900 children smoke their first cigarette and that more than 700 of them will become regular smokers. According to Kann et al., 32.3% of all high school students in 2015 said they had tried cigarettes at some point during their lifetime, and 6.6% said they had smoked a whole cigarette before they were 13 years old. (See Table 4.14.) Kann et al. report that 31.4% of students said they were current tobacco users and 12% said they currently smoked cigars or cigarettes. A greater percentage of non-Hispanic white students (32.9%) were tobacco users, compared with Hispanic students (31.8%) or non-Hispanic African American students (26.3%). (See Table 4.15.)

It is important to intervene to keep children from smoking. The American Lung Association reports that 87% of smokers started smoking regularly when they were 18 years old or younger and that 95% began when they were 21 years old or younger. Teens say they smoke for a variety of reasons (they find it relaxing and want to belong), and many young women who are worried about their weight say they smoke because it decreases their appetite. Many young people have seen their parents and grandparents smoke. Children in smoking households are at risk not only from secondhand smoke but also from this greater likelihood to take up smoking themselves.

The CDC is alarmed by a recent trend: young people's growing use of electronic cigarettes (e-cigarettes; battery-powered electronic nicotine delivery systems that use vapor to simulate tobacco smoking), vape pipes, vaping pens, and hookah pens. In "E-cigarette Ads and Youth" (January 5, 2016, https://www.cdc.gov/vitalsigns/ecigarette-ads/), the CDC reports that about 2.4 million middle and high school students were current e-cigarette users in 2015. In 2014, seven out of 10 middle and high school students were exposed to advertising for e-cigarettes from a variety of sources, including retail stores, the Internet, television/movies, and magazines/newspapers. (See Figure 4.4.) The advertising is effective: Figure 4.5 shows how escalating advertising spending has resulted in increasing e-cigarette use among youth.

FIGURE 4.3

Timeline of attention-deficit/hyperactivity disorder diagnostic criteria, prevalence, and treatment, 1902–2013

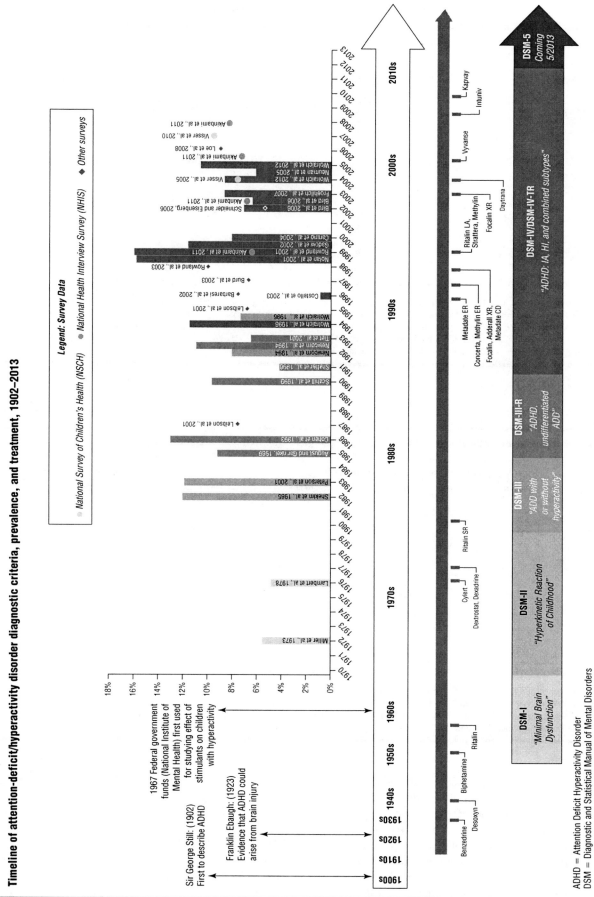

ADHD = Attention Deficit Hyperactivity Disorder
DSM = Diagnostic and Statistical Manual of Mental Disorders

SOURCE: "Timeline of ADHD Diagnostic Criteria, Prevalence, and Treatment," in *ADHD throughout the Years*, Centers for Disease Control and Prevention, National Center on Birth Defects and Developmental Disabilities, Division of Human Development, October 5, 2016, http://www.cdc.gov/ncbddd/adhd/documents/timeline.pdf (accessed January 3, 2017)

TABLE 4.12

Percentage of high school students who ever used alcohol and marijuana and tried either before age 13, by sex, race/ethnicity, and grade, 2015

	Alcohol						Marijuana					
	Ever drank alcohol			Drank alcohol before age 13 years			Ever used marijuana			Tried marijuana before age 13 years		
	Female	Male	Total	Female	Male	Total	Female	Male	Total	Female	Male	Total
Category	%	%	%	%	%	%	%	%	%	%	%	%
Race/ethnicity												
White*	66.7	64.0	65.3	11.7	17.3	14.5	34.3	36.2	35.2	4.2	6.7	5.4
Black*	57.9	51.0	54.4	16.9	18.7	18.0	40.5	49.7	45.5	7.4	13.0	10.6
Hispanic	68.6	63.4	65.9	19.0	23.6	21.3	45.3	46.0	45.6	8.2	13.6	10.9
Grade												
9	53.0	48.9	50.8	18.8	21.5	20.3	25.3	26.5	25.9	6.8	9.9	8.5
10	62.7	58.8	60.8	15.8	21.3	18.6	33.8	37.1	35.5	7.2	9.4	8.3
11	72.1	68.7	70.3	12.9	17.5	15.2	43.6	46.9	45.2	4.5	8.9	6.7
12	75.2	71.5	73.3	9.9	17.0	13.5	48.8	50.9	49.8	3.7	8.5	6.1
Total	**65.3**	**61.4**	**63.2**	**14.6**	**19.7**	**17.2**	**37.5**	**39.8**	**38.6**	**5.6**	**9.2**	**7.5**

*Non-Hispanic.
Note: Students who had at least one drink of alcohol on at least one day during their life, other than a few sips. Students who used marijuana once or more times during their life.

SOURCE: Adapted from Laura Kann et al., "Table 47. Percentage of High School Students Who Ever Drank Alcohol and Who Drank Alcohol for the First Time before Age 13 Years, by Sex, Race/Ethnicity, and Grade—United States, Youth Risk Behavior Survey, 2015," and "Table 53. Percentage of High School Students Who Ever Used Marijuana and Who Tried Marijuana for the First Time before Age 13 Years, by Sex, Race/Ethnicity, and Grade—United States, Youth Risk Behavior Survey, 2015" in "Youth Risk Behavior Surveillance—United States, 2015," *MMWR*, vol. 65, no. 6, June 10, 2016, https://www.cdc.gov/healthyyouth/data/yrbs/pdf/2015/ss6506_updated.pdf (accessed January 3, 2017)

TABLE 4.13

Percentage of high school students who bought cigarettes in a store or gas station, by sex, race/ethnicity, and grade, 2015

	Bought cigarettes in a store or gas station			Bought cigarettes on the Internet		
	Female	Male	Total	Female	Male	Total
Category	%	%	%	%	%	%
Race/ethnicity						
White*	6.6	12.8	9.7	0.1	0.2	0.1
Black*	—N/A	—	—	—	—	—
Hispanic	9.8	21.9	17.5	0.6	0.9	0.8
Grade						
9	6.4	6.2	6.3	0.0	0.3	0.2
10	5.6	6.7	6.1	0.4	2.5	1.3
11	8.8	27.1	20.2	0.0	0.5	0.5
12	10.7	22.8	16.5	0.9	3.8	2.3
Total	**7.7**	**16.5**	**12.6**	**0.3**	**1.4**	**1.0**

N/A = not available
*Non-Hispanic.
Notes: Percentage refers to a period during the 30 days before the survey, amonth the 8.5% of students nationwide who currently smoked cigarettes and who were aged <18 years.

SOURCE: Adapted from Laura Kann et al., "Table 35. Percentage of High School Students Who Usually Obtained Their Own Cigarettes by Buying Them in a Store or Gas Station, and Who Usually Obtained Their Own Cigarettes by Buying Them on the Internet, by Sex, Race/Ethnicity, and Grade—United States, Youth Risk Behavior Survey, 2015," in "Youth Risk Behavior Surveillance—United States, 2015," *Morbidity and Mortality Weekly Report*, vol. 65, no. 6, June 10, 2016, https://www.cdc.gov/healthyyouth/data/yrbs/pdf/2015/ss6506_updated.pdf (accessed January 3, 2017)

Kann et al. report that in 2015 nearly half (44.9%) of students had ever used electronic vapor products (including e-cigarettes, e-cigars, e-pipes, vape pipes, vaping pens, e-hookahs, and hookah pens). (See Table 4.16.) More upper-grade students had used electronic vapor products—43.3% of 10th graders, 49.5% of 11th graders, and 50.9% of 12th graders, compared with 37.2% of ninth graders. More Hispanic (51.9%) students than non-Hispanic white (43.2%) and non-Hispanic African American (42.4%) students reported ever having used electronic vapor products.

CHILDHOOD DEATHS

Infant Mortality

The NCHS defines the infant mortality rate as the number of deaths of babies younger than one year old per

TABLE 4.14

Percentage of high school students who ever smoked cigarettes, and students who smoked a cigarette before age 13, by sex, race/ethnicity, and grade, 2015

Category	Ever tried cigarette smoking			Smoked a whole cigarette before age 13 years		
	Female	Male	Total	Female	Male	Total
	%	%	%	%	%	%
Race/ethnicity						
White*	30.4	33.2	31.8	5.3	6.6	6.0
Black*	29.5	30.6	30.1	3.8	10.1	7.0
Hispanic	32.7	37.8	35.2	4.9	9.2	7.1
Grade						
9	24.5	25.8	25.1	6.1	8.2	7.2
10	28.2	30.0	29.1	6.0	9.1	7.6
11	34.4	40.5	37.5	4.5	6.8	5.6
12	36.3	40.4	38.3	3.0	7.3	5.2
Total	**30.7**	**33.8**	**32.3**	**5.0**	**8.0**	**6.6**

*Non-Hispanic.
Note: Ever tried cigarette smoking includes even one or two puffs.

SOURCE: Adapted from Laura Kann et al., "Table 29. Percentage of High School Students Who Ever Tried Cigarette Smoking and Who Smoked a Whole Cigarette for the First Time before Age 13 Years, by Sex, Race/Ethnicity, and Grade—United States, Youth Risk Behavior Survey, 2015," in "Youth Risk Behavior Surveillance—United States, 2015," *Morbidity and Mortality Weekly Report*, vol. 65, no. 6, June 10, 2016, https://www.cdc.gov/healthyyouth/data/yrbs/pdf/2015/ss6506_updated.pdf (accessed January 3, 2017)

TABLE 4.15

Percentage of high school students who currently used tobacco, by sex, race/ethnicity, and grade, 2015

Category	Female	Male	Total
	%	%	%
Race/ethnicity			
White*	29.4	36.6	32.9
Black*	21.2	30.6	26.3
Hispanic	29.4	34.2	31.8
Grade			
9	23.0	26.9	25.1
10	26.3	31.7	28.9
11	30.0	39.4	34.9
12	32.2	43.0	37.5
Total	**27.7**	**34.9**	**31.4**

*Non-Hispanic.
Note: Tobacco use refers to cigarette, smokeless tobacco, cigar, or electronic vapor products use on at least 1 day during the 30 days before the survey.

SOURCE: Adapted from Laura Kann et al., "Table 45. Percentage of High School Students Who Currently Used Tobacco, by Sex, Race/Ethnicity, and Grade—United States, Youth Risk Behavior Survey, 2015," in "Youth Risk Behavior Surveillance—United States, 2015," *Morbidity and Mortality Weekly Report*, vol. 65, no. 6, June 10, 2016, https://www.cdc.gov/healthyyouth/data/yrbs/pdf/2015/ss6506_updated.pdf (accessed January 3, 2017)

1,000 live births. Neonatal deaths occur within 27 days after birth and postneonatal deaths occur 28 to 365 days after birth. According to the NCHS, in *Health, United States, 2015: With Special Feature on Racial and Ethnic Health Disparities* (May 2016, https://www.cdc.gov/nchs/data/hus/hus15.pdf), between 2004 and 2014 the infant mortality rate decreased 14%, from 6.8 to 5.8 deaths per 1,000 live births, and the neonatal mortality rate fell 13%, from 4.5 to 3.9. Improved access to health care, advances in neonatal medicine, better public health practices, and improved health of pregnant mothers all contributed to the overall decline in infant mortality during the 20th and early 21st centuries. Nevertheless, not all racial and ethnic groups have reached that record-low infant mortality rate. In 2013 the infant mortality rate for non-Hispanic white infants was 5.1 deaths per 1,000 live births, less than half the rate of 11.1 deaths per 1,000 live births for non-Hispanic African American infants. (See Table 4.17.)

SUDDEN INFANT DEATH SYNDROME. In "About SUID and SIDS" (February 1, 2017, https://www.cdc.gov/sids/aboutsuidandsids.htm), the CDC defines sudden infant death syndrome (SIDS) as the sudden death of an infant that cannot be explained even after a thorough medical examination. SIDS is sometimes known as crib death. SIDS

FIGURE 4.4

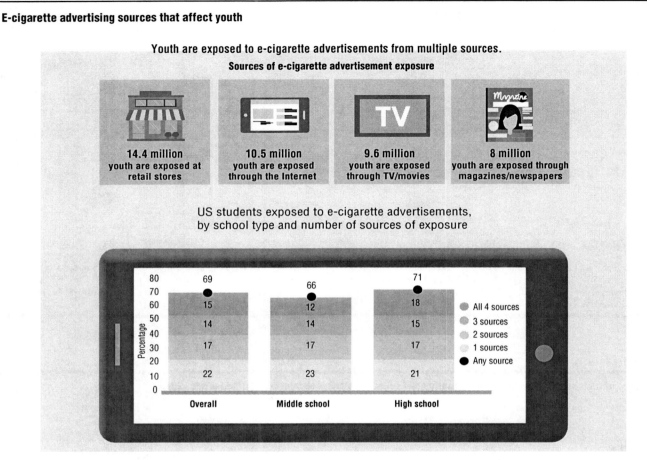

E-cigarette advertising sources that affect youth

Youth are exposed to e-cigarette advertisements from multiple sources.

Sources of e-cigarette advertisement exposure

| 14.4 million youth are exposed at retail stores | 10.5 million youth are exposed through the Internet | 9.6 million youth are exposed through TV/movies | 8 million youth are exposed through magazines/newspapers |

US students exposed to e-cigarette advertisements, by school type and number of sources of exposure

All 4 sources
3 sources
2 sources
1 sources
Any source

Note: Percentages may not add up exactly to any source due to rounding.

SOURCE: "Youth Are Exposed to E-Cigarette Advertisements from Multiple Sources," in "E-cigarette Ads and Youth," *Vital Signs*, Centers for Disease Control and Prevention, National Centers for Chronic Disease Prevention and Health Promotion, January 5, 2016, https://www.cdc.gov/vitalsigns/ecigarette-ads/ (accessed January 3, 2017)

is the leading cause of death among infants aged one month to 12 months and is the third-leading cause of infant mortality in the United States. In 2015 there were 1,600 SIDS deaths, and along with other types of sudden unexpected infant deaths (e.g., those from unknown causes and those due to accidental suffocation or strangulation in bed), sudden unexpected infant deaths claimed 3,700 infants.

In 1992 the American Academy of Pediatrics (AAP) recommended that to reduce the danger of SIDS, infants should not sleep prone (lying face down). In 2005 the AAP refined its recommendation to state that infants should sleep supine (lying face upward). This helps ensure that nothing obstructs the infants' breathing. In October 2011 the AAP's Task Force on Sudden Infant Death Syndrome published the policy statement "SIDS and Other Sleep-Related Infant Deaths: Expansion of Recommendations for a Safe Infant Sleeping Environment" (*Pediatrics*, vol. 128, no. 5) to address additional possible causes of sleep-related infant death. The task force advises "use of a firm sleep surface, breastfeeding,

room-sharing without bed-sharing, routine immunization, consideration of a pacifier, and avoidance of soft bedding, overheating, and exposure to tobacco smoke, alcohol, and illicit drugs."

In November 2016 the Task Force on Sudden Infant Death Syndrome updated its recommendations in "SIDS and Other Sleep-Related Infant Deaths: Updated 2016 Recommendations for a Safe Infant Sleeping Environment" (*Pediatrics*, vol. 138, no. 5). The new recommendations advise that infants sleep in the parents' room "close to the parents' bed, but on a separate surface designed for infants, ideally for the first year of life, but at least for the first 6 months." The recommendations also caution against infants sleeping on couches and armchairs to prevent suffocation through entrapment and advise returning infants to their crib or bassinet after feeding. Bed-sharing with infants younger than four months is not advised and twins and other multiples should have separate sleep surfaces. The task force is skeptical about devices, such as cardiorespiratory mon-

FIGURE 4.5

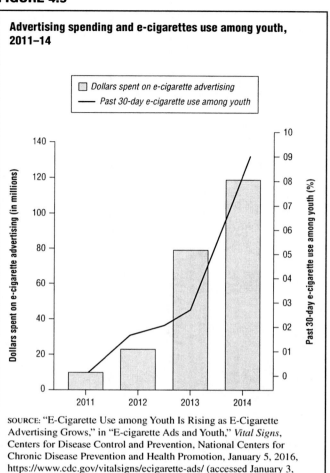

Advertising spending and e-cigarettes use among youth, 2011–14

☐ Dollars spent on e-cigarette advertising
— Past 30-day e-cigarette use among youth

SOURCE: "E-Cigarette Use among Youth Is Rising as E-Cigarette Advertising Grows," in "E-cigarette Ads and Youth," *Vital Signs*, Centers for Disease Control and Prevention, National Centers for Chronic Disease Prevention and Health Promotion, January 5, 2016, https://www.cdc.gov/vitalsigns/ecigarette-ads/ (accessed January 3, 2017)

itors to detect heart or breathing problems, that claim to reduce the risk of SIDS because their efficacy has not been proven. Similarly, there is no evidence that swaddling (wrapping the infant in a light blanket) reduces SIDS. In fact, the risk of death increases if a swaddled infant is placed or rolls to a prone position.

In "Hypoxia at the Heart of Sudden Infant Death Syndrome?" (*Pediatric Research*, vol. 74, no. 4, October 2013), Marianne T. Neary and Ross A. Breckenridge posit that a lack of adequate oxygen causing an abnormal heart rhythm may be responsible for SIDS. Lack of adequate oxygen may delay development of the heart, making it more likely to suffer from electrical conduction problems and abnormal rhythms. If this hypothesis is correct, then simple measures such as using a fan to promote air circulation and the use of oxygen tents for infants at high altitudes where oxygen is scarce might help prevent some cases of SIDS.

Mortality among Older Children

During the second half of the 20th century childhood death rates declined dramatically. Most childhood deaths are from injuries and violence. Although death rates for all ages decreased, the largest declines were among children.

In 2013 the three leading causes of death among one- to nine-year-olds were unintentional injuries, cancer, and congenital anomalies (birth defects). (See Figure 4.6.) Among those aged 10 to 24 years the three leading causes of death were unintentional injuries, suicide, and homicide. The remaining deaths were spread across a variety

TABLE 4.16

Percentage of high school students who ever used electronic vapor products and current users by sex, race/ethnicity, and grade, 2015

Category	Ever used electronic vapor products			Current electronic vapor products use		
	Female	Male	Total	Female	Male	Total
	%	%	%	%	%	%
Race/ethnicity						
White*	42.3	44.0	43.2	24.2	26.3	25.2
Black*	37.7	46.5	42.4	14.5	21.2	18.0
Hispanic	51.2	52.6	51.9	25.0	27.4	26.3
Grade						
9	37.4	37.0	37.2	19.8	19.6	19.7
10	41.2	45.3	43.3	22.3	24.2	23.2
11	47.8	51.1	49.5	24.1	27.4	25.9
12	49.0	52.6	50.9	24.6	31.9	28.2
Total	**43.6**	**46.1**	**44.9**	**22.6**	**25.6**	**24.1**

*Non-Hispanic.
Note: Electronic vapor products include e-cigarettes, e-cigars, e-pipes, vape pipes, vaping pens, e-hookahs, and hookah pens. Use occurred on at least 1 day during the 30 days before the survey.

SOURCE: Adapted from Laura Kann et al., "Table 41. Percentage of High School Students Who Ever Used Electronic Vapor Products and Who Currently Used Electronic Vapor Products, by Sex, Race/Ethnicity, and Grade—United States, Youth Risk Behavior Survey, 2015," in "Youth Risk Behavior Surveillance—United States, 2015," *Morbidity and Mortality Weekly Report*, vol. 65, no. 6, June 10, 2016, https://www.cdc.gov/healthyyouth/data/yrbs/pdf/2015/ss6506_updated.pdf (accessed January 3, 2017)

TABLE 4.17

Death rates among infants by race and Hispanic origin of mother, 1983–1991 and 1995–2013

[Infant deaths per 1,000 live births]

Characteristic	1983[a]	1984[a]	1985[a]	1986[a]	1987[a]	1988[a]	1989[a]	1990[a]	1991[a]	1995	1996	1997	1998	1999	2000	2001	2002	2003[b]	2004[b]	2005[b]	2006[b]	2007[b]	2008[b]	2009[b]	2010[b]	2011[b]	2012[b]	2013[b]
Total	10.9	10.4	10.4	10.1	9.8	9.6	9.5	8.9	8.6	7.6	7.3	7.2	7.2	7.0	6.9	6.8	7.0	6.8	6.8	6.9	6.7	6.8	6.6	6.4	6.1	6.1	6.0	6.0
Race and Hispanic origin[c]																												
White, non-Hispanic	9.2	8.6	8.6	8.3	8.1	7.8	7.8	7.2	7.0	6.3	6.0	6.0	6.0	5.8	5.7	5.7	5.8	5.7	5.7	5.8	5.6	5.6	5.5	5.3	5.2	5.1	5.0	5.1
Black, non-Hispanic	19.1	18.1	18.3	18.0	17.5	18.0	18.0	16.9	16.6	14.7	14.2	13.7	13.9	14.1	13.6	13.5	13.9	13.6	13.6	13.6	13.4	13.3	12.7	12.4	11.5	11.5	11.2	11.1
American Indian or Alaska Native	15.2	13.4	13.1	13.9	13.0	12.7	13.4	13.1	11.3	9.0	10.0	8.7	9.3	9.3	8.3	9.7	8.6	8.7	8.6	8.1	8.3	9.2	8.4	8.5	8.3	8.2	8.4	7.6
American Indian or Alaska Native, non-Hispanic	—	—	—	—	—	—	—	—	—	—	—	—	—	9.4	8.2	9.7	8.7	8.7	8.6	8.3	8.6	9.4	8.7	9.2	8.6	8.5	8.7	7.7
Asian or Pacific Islander	8.3	8.9	7.8	7.8	7.3	6.8	7.4	6.6	5.8	5.3	5.2	5.0	5.5	4.8	4.9	4.7	4.8	4.8	4.7	4.9	4.6	4.8	4.5	4.4	4.3	4.4	4.1	4.1
Asian or Pacific Islander, non-Hispanic	—	—	—	—	—	—	—	—	—	—	—	—	—	4.7	4.8	4.6	4.7	4.7	4.6	4.8	4.4	4.6	4.4	4.3	4.2	4.2	4.0	3.9
Hispanic[d]	9.5	9.3	8.8	8.4	8.2	8.3	8.1	7.5	7.1	6.3	6.1	6.0	5.8	5.7	5.6	5.4	5.6	5.6	5.5	5.6	5.4	5.5	5.6	5.3	5.3	5.2	5.1	5.0
Mexican American	9.1	8.9	8.5	7.9	8.0	7.7	7.2	7.2	6.9	6.0	5.8	5.8	5.6	5.5	5.4	5.2	5.4	5.5	5.5	5.5	5.3	5.4	5.6	5.1	5.1	5.0	5.0	4.9
Puerto Rican	12.9	12.9	11.2	11.8	9.9	11.6	11.7	9.9	9.7	8.9	8.6	7.9	7.8	8.3	8.2	8.5	8.2	8.2	7.8	8.3	8.0	7.7	7.3	7.2	7.1	7.8	6.9	5.9
Cuban	7.5	8.1	8.5	7.6	7.1	7.3	6.2	7.2	5.2	5.3	5.1	5.5	3.6	4.7	4.5	4.2	3.7	4.6	4.6	4.4	5.1	5.2	4.9	5.8	3.8	4.3	5.0	3.0
Central and South American	8.5	8.3	8.0	7.7	7.6	7.2	7.4	6.8	5.9	5.5	5.0	5.5	5.3	4.7	4.6	5.0	5.1	5.0	4.6	4.7	4.5	4.6	4.8	4.5	4.4	4.4	4.1	4.3
Other and unknown Hispanic	10.6	9.5	9.2	8.7	9.1	7.2	8.4	8.0	8.2	7.4	7.7	6.2	6.5	7.2	6.9	6.0	7.1	6.7	6.7	6.4	5.8	6.4	5.9	6.1	6.1	5.4	5.6	—

— Not available.

[a] Prior to 1995, rates are on a cohort basis. Beginning in 1995, rates are on a period basis. Data for 1995 onward are weighted to account for unmatched records.

[b] Beginning in 2003, infant mortality rates are reported to two decimal places in National Center for Health Statistics reports, so the rates reported here will vary from those in other reports. This difference in reporting could affect significance testing.

[c] The 1977 Office of Management and Budget (OMB) Standards for Data on Race and Ethnicity were used to classify persons into one of the following four racial groups: white, black, American Indian or Alaskan Native, or Asian or Pacific Islander. CA, HI, OH (for December only), PA, UT, and WA reported multiple-race data in 2003, following the revised 1997 OMB Standards. In 2004, the following states began to report multiple-race data: FL, ID, KY, MI, MN, NH, NY State (excluding New York City), SC, and TN. The multiple-race data for these states were bridged to the single-race categories of the 1977 OMB Standards for comparability with other states. In addition, note that data on race and Hispanic origin are collected and reported separately. Persons of Hispanic origin may be of any race.

[d] Trends for the Hispanic population are affected by an expansion in the number of registration areas that included an item on Hispanic origin on the birth certificate. The number of states in the reporting area increased from 22 states in 1980 to 23 states and the District of Columbia (DC) in 1983–1987, 30 states and DC in 1988, 47 states and DC in 1989, 48 states and DC in 1990, 49 states and DC in 1991, and all 50 states and DC from 1993 onward.

Note: Infant deaths are deaths before an infant's first birthday. Rates for race groups from the National Linked Files of Live Births and Infant Deaths vary slightly from those obtained via unlinked infant death records using the National Vital Statistics System because the race reported on the death certificate sometimes does not match the race on the infant's birth certificate. Rates obtained from linked data (where race is obtained from the birth, rather than the death, certificate) are considered more reliable, but linked data are not available before 1983 and are also not available for 1992–1994.

SOURCE: "Table HEALTH2. Infant mortality: Death Rates among Infants by Detailed Race and Hispanic Origin of Mother, 1983–1991 and 1995–2013," in *America's Children in Brief: Key National Indicators of Well-Being, 2016,* Federal Interagency Forum on Child and Family Statistics, 2016, https://www.childstats.gov/americaschildren/tables.asp (accessed January 2, 2017)

FIGURE 4.6

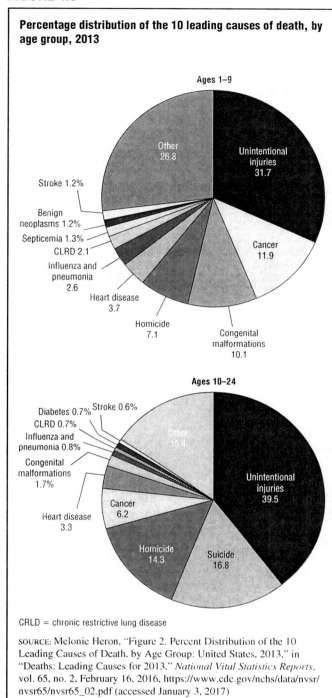

Percentage distribution of the 10 leading causes of death, by age group, 2013

Ages 1–9

Other 26.8
Stroke 1.2%
Benign neoplasms 1.2%
Septicemia 1.3%
CLRD 2.1
Influenza and pneumonia 2.6
Heart disease 3.7
Homicide 7.1
Congenital malformations 10.1
Cancer 11.9
Unintentional injuries 31.7

Ages 10–24

Diabetes 0.7%
Stroke 0.6%
CLRD 0.7%
Influenza and pneumonia 0.8%
Congenital malformations 1.7%
Heart disease 3.3
Cancer 6.2
Other 15.4
Homicide 14.3
Suicide 16.8
Unintentional injuries 39.5

CRLD = chronic restrictive lung disease

SOURCE: Melonie Heron, "Figure 2. Percent Distribution of the 10 Leading Causes of Death, by Age Group: United States, 2013," in "Deaths: Leading Causes for 2013," *National Vital Statistics Reports*, vol. 65, no. 2, February 16, 2016, https://www.cdc.gov/nchs/data/nvsr/nvsr65/nvsr65_02.pdf (accessed January 3, 2017)

of diseases, including heart disease, chronic lower respiratory disease, influenza and pneumonia, septicemia (blood poisoning), and other types of noncancerous growths (benign neoplasms and neoplasms of uncertain or unknown behavior).

MOTOR VEHICLE INJURIES. The CDC reports that motor vehicle crashes were the leading cause of death among 16- to 19-year-olds in 2014. In "Teen Drivers: Get the Facts" (October 13, 2016, https://www.cdc.gov/ motorvehiclesafety/teen_drivers/teendrivers_factsheet.html), the CDC estimates that 2,270 teens aged 16 to 19 years were killed in traffic accidents in 2014, and that 221,313 were treated in hospital emergency departments for injuries sustained in motor-vehicle crashes. In 2014 male teens were more than twice as likely as female teens to die in a motor-vehicle crash. Teens in their first months of licensed driving, as well as teens driving with other teen passengers, were at increased risk of being in a motor-vehicle crash. Teens aged 16 to 19 years were three times as likely as older drivers to be in a crash.

The CDC identifies the following risk factors for teen drivers:

- Underestimating or failing to recognize dangerous situations

- Speeding and driving too close to the vehicle in front of them

- Failing to wear seat belts—in 2015 just 61% of high school students said they always wore a seat belt when riding as a passenger in a vehicle

- Drinking and driving—Figure 4.7 outlines the effects of alcohol on driving

Kann et al. state that in 2015, during the month before the survey, 32.8% of teen drivers had drunk alcohol and 21.7% had used marijuana. Distracted driving was also a problem, as 41.5% of high school students who drove reported having texted or e-mailed while driving.

SUICIDE. According to Sally C. Curtin et al. of the CDC, in "*QuickStats*: Death Rates for Motor Vehicle Traffic Injury, Suicide, and Homicide among Children and Adolescents Aged 10–14 Years—United States, 1999–2014" (*Morbidity and Mortality Weekly Report*, vol. 65, no. 43, November 4, 2016), in 2014 the deaths from suicide (425) were comparable to the deaths (384) from motor-vehicle traffic injuries among children aged 10 to 14 years. (See Figure 4.8.) Nevertheless, suicide was the leading cause of death among children in this age group. The CDC reports in "Suicide Prevention: Youth Suicide" (March 10, 2015, https://www.cdc.gov/Violence Prevention/suicide/youth_suicide.html) that young people are most likely to commit suicide using firearms (45%), suffocation (40%), and poisoning (8%). Many young people survive suicide attempts; each year about 157,000 youths aged 10 to 24 years are treated for self-inflicted injuries in emergency departments.

Females are more likely to attempt suicide than males, but males are more likely than females to die as a result of suicide. Among young people aged 10 to 24 years, the CDC notes that about 81% of suicide deaths are males and 19% are females. Kann et al. questioned high school students regarding their thoughts about suicide. In 2015, 17.7% of high school students surveyed

FIGURE 4.7

Likely effects of alcohol on driving

About 4 beers = 0.08% blood alcohol level*

Typical effects

- Muscle coordination becomes poor (e.g., balance, speech, vision, reaction time, and hearing)
- Harder to detect danger
- Judgment, self-control, reasoning, and memory are impaired

Predictable effects on driving

- Concentration
- Short-term memory loss
- Speed control
- Reduced information processing capability (e.g., signal detection, visual search)
- Impaired perception

*The number of beers listed represents the approximate amount of alcohol that a 160-pound man would need to drink in one hour to reach the BAC.

SOURCE: "Likely Effects of Alcohol on Driving," in "What factors put teen drivers at risk?" *Teen Drivers: Get the Facts*, Centers for Disease Control and Prevention, National Center for Injury Prevention and Control, Division of Unintentional Injury Prevention, October 13, 2016, https://www.cdc.gov/motorvehiclesafety/teen_drivers/teendrivers_factsheet.html (accessed January 3, 2017)

claimed that they had seriously thought about attempting suicide during the previous 12 months. (See Table 4.18.) Females (23.4%) were more likely to have considered suicide than males (12.2%). Of all students, 14.6% (19.4% of females and 9.8% of males) had made a specific plan to attempt suicide. Approximately 8.6% of students (11.6% of females and 5.5% of males) said they had attempted suicide during the previous year, and 2.8% of high school students (3.7% of females and 1.9% of males) said they had suffered injuries from the attempt that required medical attention. (See Table 4.19.) These numbers reflect the fact that females of all ages tend to choose less fatal methods when attempting suicide, such as overdosing and cutting veins, than do males, who tend to choose more deadly methods, such as shooting or hanging. Students whose suicide attempts resulted in their death were not counted in Kann et al.'s analysis of survey data.

Youth suicide rates reflect the fact that a large proportion of students, particularly female students, feel sad or hopeless. In 2015, 39.8% of female students and 20.3% of male students reported these feelings. (See Table 4.20.) The likelihood that a child or adolescent will commit suicide increases with the presence of certain risk factors. According to the CDC, these risk factors include a history of previous suicide attempts; a family history of suicide, depression, or mental health problems; alcohol or drug abuse; stressful life events or loss; easy access to lethal methods, such as firearms; exposure to suicidal behavior in other people; and incarceration. Although depression alone does not predict suicide attempts, it is important to note that the percentage of youth aged 12 to 17 years who reported having at least one major depressive episode during the past year has steadily increased from 9% in 2004 to 11.4% in 2014. (See Table 4.21.)

In addition, sexual minority status (having a sexual orientation or engaging in sexual activities that are not part of the mainstream) is considered to be a risk factor for suicide among youths. In "Non-suicidal Self-Injury and Suicidal Thoughts and Behaviors in Heterosexual and Sexual Minority Young Adults" (*Comprehensive Psychiatry*, vol. 65, February 2016), Aliona Tsypes et al. explain that factors associated with increased risk for depression and suicidal thoughts and behaviors among sexual minority youth include stigmatization and less social support, as well as "interpersonal stress in the form of discrimination and rejection from sexual majority peers [and] ostracism by groups that rigidly define sexual orientation identities."

Bullying, continuous taunts, and victimization may drive many sexual minority teens to consider suicide and some to act on it. Increasingly, bullying occurs electronically via e-mail, texting, and social media, and it can be crueler and even more damaging than physical bullying. It is also harder to combat because cyberbullies can remain anonymous while harassing and abusing their victims. Social media can also fan the flames of depression and suicidal thinking. Websites, blogs, and online communities that glorify depression, self-injury, and even suicide can encourage troubled or isolated young people to engage in substance abuse, unsafe sex, or other self-destructive behaviors.

Kann et al. report in "Sexual Identity, Sex of Sexual Contacts, and Health-Related Behaviors among Students in Grades 9–12—United States and Selected Sites, 2015" (*Morbidity and Mortality Weekly Report*, vol. 65, no. 9, August 12, 2016) that twice as many gay, lesbian, and bisexual high school students (28%) reported being bullied via e-mail, chat rooms, instant messaging, websites, or texting during the past year as did heterosexual students (14.2%). Similarly, just 4.6% of heterosexual students said they had not gone to school on at least one day during the 30 days before the survey because of safety concerns, compared with 12.5% of gay, lesbian, and bisexual students.

Sadly, but not surprisingly, Kann et al. indicate that the rate of serious consideration of suicide among gay, lesbian, and bisexual students (42.8%) and among students not sure about their sexual identity (31.9%) was markedly higher than among heterosexual students (14.8%). In 2015, 32.8% of gay, lesbian, and bisexual students and 13.7% of students not sure about their sexual identity had attempted suicide one or more times during

FIGURE 4.8

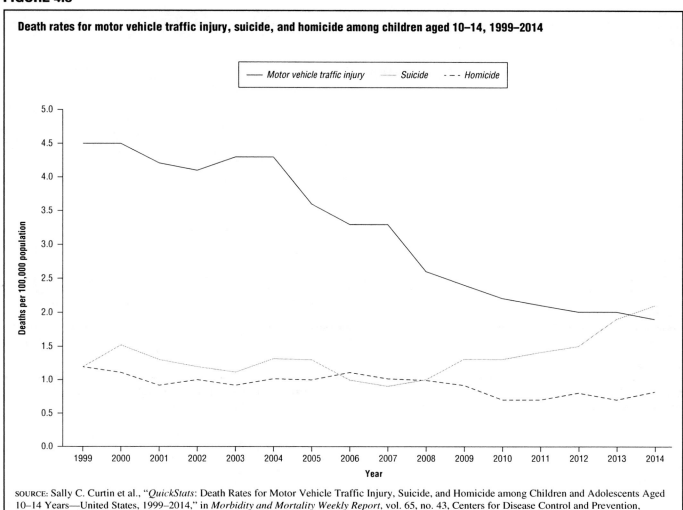

Death rates for motor vehicle traffic injury, suicide, and homicide among children aged 10–14, 1999–2014

SOURCE: Sally C. Curtin et al., "*QuickStats*: Death Rates for Motor Vehicle Traffic Injury, Suicide, and Homicide among Children and Adolescents Aged 10–14 Years—United States, 1999–2014," in *Morbidity and Mortality Weekly Report*, vol. 65, no. 43, Centers for Disease Control and Prevention, November 4, 2016, https://www.cdc.gov/mmwr/volumes/65/wr/mm6543a8.htm (accessed January 3, 2017)

the 12 months before the survey, compared with 6.4% of heterosexual students. (See Table 4.22.)

Research supports the observation that social media can help friendships, but there is also evidence of a connection between depression and excessive texting, viewing video clips, video gaming, chatting, e-mailing, and other media use. Researchers have even coined the term *Facebook depression* to describe depression that is associated with the use of this social networking site. Some research finds that the more people use the Internet, and Facebook in particular, the lonelier and more depressed they feel. There is also a theory of "emotional contagion," whereby depression appears to be transmissible via online interactions with negative content and depressed peers.

Although for many teens participation in social networks may increase social connectedness and social engagement, for some it may worsen feelings of depression, isolation, and alienation. In "Association between Social Media Use and Depression among U.S. Young Adults" (*Depression and Anxiety*, vol. 33, no. 4, April 2016), Liu yi Lin et al. report the results of a survey of young adults aged 19 to 32 years to determine the relationship between social media use and mental health. The researchers find that social media use "was significantly associated with increased depression" and that the more time young adults spent using social media, the more likely they were to be depressed. Mark L. Hatzenbuehler, Katie A. McLaughlin, and Ziming Xuan find in "Social Networks and Risk for Depressive Symptoms in a National Sample of Sexual Minority Youth" (*Social Science & Medicine*, vol. 75, no. 7, October 1, 2013) an association between social networks and symptoms of depression among sexual minority adolescents. They report, "Sexual minority youths' social networks were more isolated, less connected, and of lower status than majority youths' networks," especially for males. Hatzenbuehler, McLaughlin, and Xuan observe that peer social networks can increase stigma and discrimination, placing sexual minority youth at increased risk for mental health problems.

TABLE 4.18

Percentage of high school students who seriously considered attempting suicide, and made a suicide plan, by sex, race and ethnicity, and grade, 2015

	Seriously considered attempting suicide			Made a suicide plan		
	Female	Male	Total	Female	Male	Total
Category	%	%	%	%	%	%
Race/ethnicity						
White*	22.8	11.5	17.2	18.4	9.3	13.9
Black*	18.7	11.0	14.5	17.3	10.6	13.7
Hispanic	25.6	12.4	18.8	20.7	10.9	15.7
Grade						
9	26.5	10.7	18.2	22.5	8.1	15.0
10	25.7	10.8	18.3	21.6	9.2	15.4
11	22.1	13.3	17.7	17.2	10.4	13.9
12	18.6	14.0	16.3	15.7	12.0	13.8
Total	**23.4**	**12.2**	**17.7**	**19.4**	**9.8**	**14.6**

*Non-Hispanic.
Note: Timeframe is during the 12 months before the survey.

SOURCE: Adapted from Laura Kann et al., "Table 25. Percentage of High School Students Who Seriously Considered Attempting Suicide and Who Made a Plan about How They Would Attempt Suicide, by Sex, Race/Ethnicity, and Grade—United States, Youth Risk Behavior Survey, 2015," in "Youth Risk Behavior Surveillance—United States, 2015," *Morbidity and Mortality Weekly Report*, vol. 65, no. 6, June 10, 2016, https://www.cdc.gov/healthyyouth/data/yrbs/pdf/2015/ss6506_updated.pdf (accessed January 3, 2017)

TABLE 4.19

Percentage of high school students who attempted suicide and whose suicide attempt resulted in an injury that required medical treatment, by sex, race and ethnicity, and grade, 2015

	Attempted suicide			Suicide attempt treated by a doctor or nurse		
	Female	Male	Total	Female	Male	Total
Category	%	%	%	%	%	%
Race/ethnicity						
White*	9.8	3.7	6.8	3.4	0.9	2.1
Black*	10.2	7.2	8.9	3.6	4.0	3.8
Hispanic	15.1	7.6	11.3	4.5	2.9	3.7
Grade						
9	15.1	5.1	9.9	4.7	1.9	3.2
10	13.0	5.7	9.4	3.9	2.2	3.1
11	10.2	5.8	8.0	3.4	2.0	2.6
12	7.2	5.2	6.2	2.3	1.4	1.9
Total	**11.6**	**5.5**	**8.6**	**3.7**	**1.9**	**2.8**

*Non-Hispanic.
Note: Attempted suicide refers to attempting one or more times during the 12 months before the survey.

SOURCE: Adapted from Laura Kann et al., "Table 27. Percentage of High School Students Who Attempted Suicide and Whose Suicide Attempt Resulted in an Injury, Poisoning, or Overdose That Had to Be Treated by a Doctor or Nurse, by Sex, Race/Ethnicity, and Grade—United States, Youth Risk Behavior Survey, 2015," in "Youth Risk Behavior Surveillance—United States, 2015," *Morbidity and Mortality Weekly Report*, vol. 65, no. 6, June 10, 2016, http://www.cdc.gov/healthyyouth/data/yrbs/pdf/2015/ss6506_updated.pdf (accessed January 3, 2017)

TABLE 4.20

Percentage of high school students who felt sad or hopeless, by sex, race and ethnicity, and grade, 2015

Category	Female %	Male %	Total %
Race/ethnicity			
White*	37.9	19.2	28.6
Black*	33.9	17.6	25.2
Hispanic	46.7	24.3	35.3
Grade			
9	41.5	16.7	28.4
10	40.1	19.2	29.8
11	40.9	22.1	31.4
12	36.3	23.9	30.0
Total	**39.8**	**20.3**	**29.9**

*Non-Hispanic.
Note: The time that a high school student felt sad or hopeless is almost every day for >2 weeks in a row so that they stopped doing some usual activities during the 12 months before the survey.

SOURCE: Adapted from Laura Kann et al., "Table 23. Percentage of High School Students Who Felt Sad or Hopeless, by Sex, Race/Ethnicity, and Grade—United States, Youth Risk Behavior Survey 2015," in "Youth Risk Behavior Surveillance—United States, 2015," *Morbidity and Mortality Weekly Report*, vol. 65, no. 6, June 10, 2016, https://www.cdc.gov/healthyyouth/data/yrbs/pdf/2015/ss6506_updated.pdf (accessed January 3, 2017)

TABLE 4.21

Percentage of youth aged 12–17 who had at least one major depressive episode in the past year by age, sex, race, Hispanic origin, and poverty status, 2004–14

Characteristic	2004	2005	2006	2007	2008	2009	2010	2011	2012	2013	2014
Total	**9.0**	**8.8**	**7.9**	**8.2**	**8.3**	**8.1**	**8.0**	**8.2**	**9.1**	**10.7**	**11.4**
Age											
Ages 12–13	5.4	5.2	4.9	4.3	4.9	4.6	4.3	4.1	5.4	6.1	7.2
Ages 14–15	9.2	9.5	7.9	8.4	8.5	8.8	9.0	8.6	10.2	12.4	11.9
Ages 16–17	12.3	11.5	10.7	11.5	11.2	10.4	10.6	11.7	11.4	13.2	14.6
Gender											
Male	5.0	4.5	4.2	4.6	4.3	4.7	4.4	4.5	4.7	5.3	5.7
Female	13.1	13.3	11.8	11.9	12.5	11.7	11.9	12.1	13.7	16.2	17.3
Race and Hispanic origin[a]											
White, non-Hispanic	9.2	9.1	8.2	8.7	8.8	8.4	8.6	8.6	9.1	10.9	12.0
Black, non-Hispanic	7.7	7.6	6.4	7.8	7.1	7.9	6.8	7.0	7.9	8.6	9.1
American Indian or Alaska Native	7.8	6.1	9.3	4.6	10.1	7.5	7.4	11.4	5.2	4.5	6.9
Asian	8.3	6.0	7.7	6.6	7.7	7.6	5.5	7.6	4.2	10.2	10.4
Two or more races	11.7	10.5	13.0	9.9	12.0	8.0	9.4	10.6	11.3	13.0	12.5
Hispanic	9.1	9.1	8.0	7.1	7.5	7.7	7.8	8.1	10.5	11.4	11.5
Poverty status[b]											
Below 100% poverty	8.7	8.1	7.6	7.6	7.7	7.4	7.2	8.1	10.2	10.2	10.9
100–199% poverty	8.7	9.6	9.0	8.9	9.1	8.6	9.0	8.9	9.0	11.3	12.3
200% poverty and above	9.1	8.7	7.6	8.0	8.2	8.2	7.9	8.1	8.7	10.6	11.2

[a]1997 Office of Management and Budget (OMB) standards were used to collect race and ethnicity data. Persons could select one or more of five racial groups: white, black or African American, American Indian or Alaska Native, Native Hawaiian or other Pacific Islander, or Asian. Respondents could choose more than one race. Those reporting more than one race were classified as "Two or more races." Data on Hispanic origin are collected separately. Persons of Hispanic origin may be of any race. Included in the total but not shown separately are persons of Native Hawaiian or other Pacific Islander origin.
[b]Estimates are based on a definition of poverty level that incorporates information on family income, size, and composition and is calculated as a percentage of the U.S. Census Bureau's poverty thresholds.
Note: A major depressive episode (MDE) is defined as in the 4th edition of the *Diagnostic and Statistical Manual of Mental Disorders (DSM-IV)*, which specifies a period of at least 2 weeks when a person experienced a depressed mood or loss of interest or pleasure in daily activities and had a majority of specified depression symptoms. Respondents with unknown past-year MDE were excluded.

SOURCE: "Table HEALTH4.A. Adolescent Depression: Percentage of Youth Ages 12–17 Who Had at Least One Major Depressive Episode (MDE) in the Past Year by Age, Gender, Race and Hispanic Origin, and Poverty Status, 2004–2014," in *America's Children in Brief: Key National Indicators of Well-Being, 2016*, Federal Interagency Forum on Child and Family Statistics, 2016, https://www.childstats.gov/americaschildren/tables.asp (accessed January 2, 2017)

TABLE 4.22

Percentage of high school students who attempted suicide, by sexual identity and sex of sexual contacts, 2015

National survey (all students)	%
	8.6

	Sexual identity			Sex of sexual contacts		
	Heterosexual (straight)	Gay, lesbian, or bisexual	Not sure	Opposite sex only	Same sex only or both sexes	No Sexual contact
Size	%	%	%	%	%	%
National survey						
Total	**6.4**	**29.4**	**13.7**	**9.7**	**27.6**	**4.2**
Male	4.5	19.4	16.0	6.9	17.0	2.3
Female	8.4	32.8	11.7	13.1	31.0	6.1

NA = not available
Note: Occurrence of one or more times during the 12 months before the survey.

SOURCE: Adapted from Laura Kann et al., "Table 27. Percentage of High School Students Who Attempted Suicide, by Sexual Identity and Sex of Sexual Contacts—United States and Selected U.S. Sites, Youth Risk Behavior Survey, 2015," in "Sexual Identity, Sex of Sexual Contacts, and Health-Related Behaviors among Students in Grades 9–12—United States and Selected Sites, 2015," *Morbidity and Mortality Weekly Report*, vol. 65, no. 9, August 12, 2016, https://www.cdc.gov/mmwr/volumes/65/ss/pdfs/ss6509.pdf (accessed January 4, 2016)

CHAPTER 5

TEEN SEXUALITY AND PREGNANCY

EARLY SEXUAL ACTIVITY

Many teenagers are sexually active. Laura Kann et al. report in "Youth Risk Behavior Surveillance—United States, 2015" (*Morbidity and Mortality Weekly Report*, vol. 65, no. 6, June 10, 2016) that 41.2% of high school students surveyed in grades nine through 12 had ever had sexual intercourse. (See Table 5.1.) Boys (43.2%) were slightly more likely than girls (39.2%) to have had intercourse. Non-Hispanic African American students (48.5%) were more likely than Hispanic (42.5%) or non-Hispanic white students (39.9%) to have ever had intercourse.

The proportion of students who had ever had intercourse rose with age; 24.1% of ninth graders, 35.7% of 10th graders, 49.6% of 11th graders, and 58.1% of 12th graders had ever had intercourse at the time of the survey in 2015. (See Table 5.1.) Kann et al. report that 3.9% of students had intercourse for the first time before age 13. This early sexual activity is of concern, especially for girls. In "The Double Standard at Sexual Debut: Gender, Sexual Behavior and Adolescent Peer Acceptance" (*Sex Roles*, vol. 75, no. 7, October 2016), Derek A. Kreager et al. observe that there continues to be a sexual double standard: female teens who have sexual intercourse suffer decreases in peer acceptance, whereas male teens reporting the same behavior gain peer acceptance.

Theo G. M. Sandfort et al. find in "Long-Term Health Correlates of Timing of Sexual Debut: Results from a National U.S. Study" (*American Journal of Public Health*, vol. 98, no. 1, January 2008) that early sexual initiation has long-term negative sexual health outcomes for both boys and girls, including a higher likelihood of engaging in sexually risky behaviors and problems in sexual functioning, and Sonia Jovic et al. observe in "Associations between Life Contexts and Early Sexual Initiation among Young Women in France" (*Perspectives on Sexual and Reproductive Health*, vol. 46, no. 1,

March 2014) that sexual activity before age 16 has been linked to increased risk of teen pregnancy and sexually transmitted diseases.

Risk Factors for Early Sexual Activity

The quality of parent-child relationships is a significant factor in the age of sexual initiation. In "Family Cohesion and Romantic and Sexual Initiation: A Three Wave Longitudinal Study" (*Journal of Youth and Adolescence*, vol. 41, no. 5, May 2012), Hanneke de Graaf et al. find that young girls aged 12 to 14 years who have negative relationships with their parents turn to romantic relationships for intimacy and emotional support, which creates the opportunity for early sexual relationships. Interestingly, among boys and older adolescent girls, de Graaf et al. find no connection between family relationships and early sexual behavior. Deborah J. Jones et al. indicate in "Linking Childhood Sexual Abuse and Early Adolescent Risk Behavior: The Intervening Role of Internalizing and Externalizing Problems" (*Journal of Abnormal Child Psychology*, vol. 41, no. 11, January 2013) that childhood sexual abuse and neglect are also linked to early sexual activity.

Kelly L. Donahue et al. report the results of a twin study focusing on risk factors for early sexual intercourse in "Testing Putative Causal Associations of Risk Factors for Early Intercourse in the Study of Twin Adults: Genes and Environment" (*Archives of Sexual Behavior*, vol. 42, no. 1, January 2013). The researchers indicate that history of exposure to early physical and sexual trauma, cigarette smoking, and marijuana use were correlated with early sexual activity.

In "Early Adolescent African American Girls' Perceptions of Virginity and Romantic Relationships" (*Nursing*, vol. 2, October 2012), Gwendolyn D. Childs et al. of the University of Alabama, Birmingham, School of Nursing observe that the 2011 National Youth Risk

TABLE 5.1

Percentage of high school students who ever had sexual intercourse and who had sexual intercourse for the first time before age 13, by sex, race and ethnicity, and grade, 2015

Category	Ever had sexual intercourse			Had first sexual intercourse before age 13 years		
	Female	Male	Total	Female	Male	Total
	%	%	%	%	%	%
Race/ethnicity						
White*	40.3	39.5	39.9	1.6	3.5	2.5
Black*	37.4	58.8	48.5	4.3	12.1	8.3
Hispanic	39.8	45.1	42.5	3.1	6.8	5.0
Grade						
9	20.7	27.3	24.1	2.5	4.6	3.6
10	33.5	37.9	35.7	2.7	6.8	4.7
11	48.2	51.2	49.6	1.6	4.8	3.2
12	57.2	59.0	58.1	1.7	5.5	3.6
Total	**39.2**	**43.2**	**41.2**	**2.2**	**5.6**	**3.9**

*Non-Hispanic.

SOURCE: Adapted from Laura Kann et al., "Table 69. Percentage of High School Students Who Ever Had Sexual Intercourse and Who Had Sexual Intercourse for the First Time before Age 13 Years, by Sex, Race/Ethnicity, and Grade—United States, Youth Risk Behavior Survey, 2015," in "Youth Risk Behavior Surveillance—United States, 2015," *Morbidity and Mortality Weekly Report*, vol. 65, no. 6, June 10, 2016, https://www.cdc.gov/healthyyouth/data/yrbs/pdf/2015/ss6506_updated.pdf (accessed January 3, 2017)

Behavior Survey reports that about 7% of African American females engaged in sexual activity before the age of 13. The researchers also cite data from the National Longitudinal Study of Adolescent Health showing that African American adolescents are less likely than white adolescents to be involved in romantic relationships. Childs et al. posit that when African American adolescents are involved in romantic relationships, they are more likely to be involved in long-term relationships rather than in multiple short-term relationships. Because the probability of sexual activity increases with the duration of a relationship, early sexual behavior among African American adolescents may in part be associated with their involvement in long-term relationships.

Regret

Many studies report that both sexes consider social pressure a major factor in engaging in early sexual activity. Peer pressure and a belief that "everyone is doing it" have often been cited as explanations. In "Awkward or Amazing: Gender and Age Trends in First Intercourse Experiences" (*Psychology of Women Quarterly*, vol. 35, no. 1, March 2011), Jennifer L. Walsh et al. indicate that most females' descriptions of their first sexual experiences were generally less positive than those of males, and their reasons were more likely to emphasize relationships and emotions. Those who had their first sexual experiences in early adolescence were more likely to describe it as awkward, and less likely to describe it as positive than those who had their first experiences later in adolescence.

Marie-Aude Boislard, Daphne van de Bongardt, and Martin Blais observe in "Sexuality (and Lack Thereof) in Adolescence and Early Adulthood: A Review of the Literature" (*Behavioral Science*, vol. 6, no. 1, March 2016) that thinking about adolescents' first sexual experiences has changed over time, and rather than focusing exclusively on the risks associated with early sexual activity, acknowledges that sexual initiation during adolescence and young adulthood are not necessarily risky. The researchers observe that "the field of youth sexual development has recently shifted toward an increased recognition of sexual intimacy with one's partner as a developmental task in adolescence and emerging adulthood." Boislard, van de Bongardt, and Blais cite studies that find female sexual self-esteem and other positive measures of self-worth increase with sexual experience to support the notion of sexual initiation as a positive, healthy developmental milestone. They note that other research finds "a more positive body image among male college students after their first experience of intercourse, and lower psychological distress among both male and female college students." The researchers do, however, concede that youth who initiate sexual activity early are more vulnerable and may not be ready for safe and consensual sexual relationships.

Boislard, van de Bongardt, and Blais identify seven common themes present in a review of 268 studies of youth sexual behavior that spanned multiple countries and cultures, specifically:

1. young people assess potential sexual partners as "clean" or "unclean";

2. sexual partners influence behavior in general;

3. condoms are associated with lack of trust;

4. gender stereotypes are important determinants of social expectations and behavior;

5. society both condemns and rewards sexual behavior;

6. sexual activity or inactivity influences social standing and reputations; and

7. social expectations get in the way of useful communication about sex.

The Media and Teen Concepts of Sexuality

Children and teens are bombarded with a multitude of images, information, and messages about sex and sexuality in the media. Along with posters, billboards, print advertising, magazines, and books, electronic media including television, CDs, DVDs, movies, video games, smartphones, computers, notebooks, readers, and any device that can access the Internet convey sexual content to young people. Media messages can and do powerfully shape the attitudes, beliefs, and behaviors of children and adolescents.

In "Are Sexual Media Exposure, Parental Restrictions on Media Use and Co-viewing TV and DVDs with Parents and Friends Associated with Teenagers' Early Sexual Behaviour?" (*Journal of Adolescence*, vol. 36, no. 6, December 2013), Alison Parkes et al. observe that research demonstrates that media exposure to sexual content (in films, on television, online, and in video games) predicts earlier sexual activity. Parkes et al. find that teens who watched TV/DVDs with friends more often than with parents were more likely to report sexual intercourse. Viewing sexual media content with same-sex friends was associated with lower risk for sexual intercourse but frequent viewing with mixed-sex peers was a strong risk factor. Teens who said their parents restricted their access to sexual content were less likely to report intercourse than their peers with unrestricted access. The frequency of parents viewing sexual media content with their teens was not associated with risk for sexual intercourse.

In September 2010 the American Academy of Pediatrics (AAP) released the policy statement "Sexuality, Contraception, and the Media" (*Pediatrics*, vol. 126, no. 3). The AAP stresses that adolescent exposure to the portrayal of "casual sex and sexuality with no consequences" on television; in music, movies, and magazines; and on the Internet are "important factors in the initiation of sexual intercourse." The AAP urges pediatricians to give adolescents straightforward information about human sexuality and contraception rather than promoting abstinence-only, which the AAP argues is ineffective in the face of overwhelming media messages about nonabstinence.

Some studies, such as Victor C. Strasburger, Amy B. Jordan, and Ed Donnerstein's "Health Effects of Media on Children and Adolescents" (*Pediatrics*, vol. 125, no. 1, April 1, 2010), find a correlation between media exposure to sexual themes and pornography and early sexual activity. These studies assert that media play a key role in delivering sexual information to adolescents, shaping their beliefs about how males and females interact in romantic relationships, and often conveying the message that sex is risk free. However, a meta-analysis (a review of multiple studies considering all of their data) performed by Christopher J. Ferguson, Rune K. L. Nielsen, and Patrick M. Markey presented in "Does Sexy Media Promote Teen Sex? A Meta-analytic and Methodological Review" (*Psychiatric Quarterly*, June 29, 2016) finds little relationship between media exposure—even sexy media (defined as "media depicting or discussing sexual encounters")—and the sexual behavior of adolescents and young adults.

Sexual Activity and Substance Use

Research suggests a link between substance use and sexual activity among adolescents. Researchers find that both sexual activity and a history of multiple partners correlate with some use of drugs, alcohol, and cigarettes. However, Kann et al. indicate in "Youth Risk Behavior Surveillance" that among sexually active students, only 20.6% reported in 2015 that they had used alcohol or drugs at the time of their last sexual intercourse. (See Table 5.2.) Males (24.6%) were more likely than females (16.4%) to report this behavior. Hispanics (22.8%) and non-Hispanic African Americans (21.8%) were more likely than non-Hispanic whites (19.3%) to report using alcohol or drugs before their last sexual intercourse.

Arielle R. Deutsch et al. examined whether earlier onset of drinking and smoking predicted early sexual intercourse and reported their findings in "Substance Use and Sexual Intercourse Onsets in Adolescence: A Genetically Informative Discordant Twin Design" (*Journal of Child and Adolescent Substance Abuse*, vol. 54, no. 1, January 2014). Deutsch et al. interviewed more than 3,400 same-sex twins to determine whether the timing of smoking, drinking, drunkenness, and conduct disorder symptoms was related to the onset of sexual activity. The researchers find that although smoking and drinking did not predict sexual intercourse, drunkenness was associated with sexual intercourse. Twins who experienced their first alcohol intoxication at younger ages than their co-twins were more likely to have sex earlier than their co-twins. Deutsch et al. conclude, "Early smoking and drinking onset do not predict earlier intercourse onset. Relationships between early substance use and sexual intercourse onsets may have been previously overstated."

Voluntary and Nonvoluntary Experiences

The Centers for Disease Control and Prevention (CDC) conduct the National Survey of Family Growth (NSFG), and the 1995 and 2002 NSFG both asked young women whether their first sexual experience was voluntary. In "A Demographic Portrait of Statutory Rape" (2005, https://www.researchgate.net/profile/Kristin_Moore/publication/268042180_A_Demographic_Portrait_of_Statutory_Rape/links/54d8c3710cf24647581b89fe.pdf), Kristin Moore

TABLE 5.2

Percentage of high school students who did not use any method to prevent pregnancy during last sexual intercourse and who drank alcohol or used drugs before last sexual intercourse, by sex, race and ethnicity, and grade, 2015

| | Did not use any method to prevent pregnancy | | | Drank alcohol or used drugs before last sexual intercourse | | |
| | Female | Male | Total | Female | Male | Total |
Category	%	%	%	%	%	%
Race/ethnicity						
White*	10.2	10.3	10.4	14.7	24.4	19.3
Black*	25.6	9.9	15.9	19.0	23.1	21.8
Hispanic	22.7	17.2	20.0	17.7	27.7	22.8
Grade						
9	22.0	12.1	16.5	16.8	27.2	22.7
10	12.9	11.7	12.3	15.6	23.3	19.7
11	12.3	9.9	11.1	16.7	23.0	19.8
12	16.2	14.2	15.5	16.1	25.6	20.8
Total	**15.2**	**12.2**	**13.8**	**16.4**	**24.6**	**20.6**

*Non-Hispanic.

Note: Percentage is among the 30.1% of students nationwide who were currently sexually active.

SOURCE: Adapted from Laura Kann et al., "Table 79. Percentage of High School Students Who Did Not Use Any Method to Prevent Pregnancy during Last Sexual Intercourse and Who Drank Alcohol or Used Drugs before Last Sexual Intercourse by Sex, Race/Ethnicity, and Grade—United States, Youth Risk Behavior Survey, 2015," in "Youth Risk Behavior Surveillance—United States, 2015," *Morbidity and Mortality Weekly Report*, vol. 65, no. 6, June 10, 2016, https://www.cdc.gov/healthyyouth/data/yrbs/pdf/2015/ss6506_updated.pdf (accessed January 3, 2017)

and Jennifer Manlove find that 18% of girls whose first sexual experience occurred at the age of 13 years or younger said it was nonvoluntary, compared with 10% of those whose first sexual experience was at age 15 or 16 years and 5% of those whose first experience was between the ages of 17 and 19 years.

The next NSFG, conducted from 2006 to 2010, asked the same question about first sexual experience. The results are described by Gladys Martinez, Casey E. Copen, and Joyce C. Abma in *Teenagers in the United States: Sexual Activity, Contraceptive Use, and Childbearing, 2006–2010 National Survey of Family Growth* (October 2011, https://www.cdc.gov/nchs/data/series/sr_23/sr23_031.pdf). Among female survey respondents aged 18 to 24 years, nearly half (48%) had mixed feelings about their first sexual intercourse, 41.2% reported that they really wanted it to happen at the time, and 10.8% did not want it to happen at the time. In contrast, 62.5% of males really wanted their first sexual intercourse to happen at the time, 32.5% reported mixed feelings, and 5% said they did not want it to happen at the time. The younger the age at which first sexual intercourse occurred, the more likely respondents were to state they did not want it to happen or had mixed feelings about it at the time it happened.

In the 2011–13 NSFG, 6.2% of female respondents aged 18 to 24 years who had sex before age 20 said their first intercourse was not voluntary. Kann et al. find that 6.7% of high school students (10.3% of females and 3.1% of males) had been forced to have sex when they did not want it.

Childhood and adolescent sexual abuse has been shown to lead to increased likelihood of high-risk sexual

behaviors, sexually transmitted infections (STIs), and early pregnancy. For example, Yuko Homma et al. find in "The Relationship between Sexual Abuse and Risky Sexual Behavior among Adolescent Boys: A Meta-analysis" (*Journal of Adolescent Health*, vol. 51, no. 1, July 2012) that sexually abused boys were significantly more likely than nonabused boys to report risky behaviors such as unprotected sexual intercourse, multiple partners, and unplanned pregnancy. The researchers conclude that because childhood and adolescent sexual abuse of males can exert a strong influence on future sexual behavior, "we should strengthen sexual abuse prevention initiatives, raise awareness about male sexual abuse survivors' existence and sexual health issues, improve sexual health promotion for abused young men, and screen all people, regardless of gender, for a history of sexual abuse."

Early sexual initiation for teenage girls has also been linked to adverse outcomes. In "Early Onset of Sexual Intercourse Is an Indicator for Hazardous Lifestyle and Problematic Life Situation" (*Scandinavian Journal of Caring Sciences*, vol. 27, no. 1, March 2013), Marlene Makenzius and Margareta Larsson observe that girls who have sexual intercourse may be at greater risk for depression, which in turn might lead to risky sexual behavior and drug or alcohol consumption when they have sex. Sexual abuse, smoking, and use of illicit drugs are reported more frequently among teens with early sexual intercourse.

In "Internalizing and Externalizing Behaviors as Predictors of Sexual Onset in Early Adolescence" (*Journal of Early Adolescence*, vol. 33, no. 7, 2013), Marie-Aude P. Boislard et al. observe that younger teens engaging in

TABLE 5.3

Percentage of high school students who experienced physical dating violence and sexual dating violence by sex, race and ethnicity, and grade, 2015

	Physical dating violence				Sexual dating violence		
	Female	Male	Total		Female	Male	Total
Category	%	%	%		%	%	%
Race/ethnicity							
White*	11.9	5.9	9.0		16.6	3.5	10.1
Black*	12.2	9.0	10.5		11.7	8.0	10.0
Hispanic	11.4	8.0	9.7		14.2	7.0	10.6
Grade							
9	11.1	5.3	8.1		17.6	4.5	10.8
10	10.9	8.2	9.6		15.8	7.4	11.8
11	11.6	7.9	10.1		14.9	5.1	10.3
12	12.9	8.2	10.5		13.9	4.6	9.2
Total	**11.7**	**7.4**	**9.6**		**15.6**	**5.4**	**10.6**

*Non-Hispanic.
Notes: Experience of physical dating violence occurred one or more times during the 12 months before the survey. Percentage of students is among the 68.6% of students nationwide who dated or went out with someone during the 12 months before the survey, being physically hurt on purpose (counting being hit, slammed into something, or injured with an object or weapon) by someone they were dating or going out with. Experience of sexual dating violence among the 69% of students nationwide who dated or went out with someone during the 12 months before the survey, being forced to do sexual things (counting kissing, touching, or being physically forced to have sexual intercourse) they did not want to do by someone they were dating or going out with. The prevalence of dating or going out with someone during the 12 months before the survey varies slightly for physical dating violence and sexual dating violence because of differences in the number of usable responses to each question.

SOURCE: Adapted from Laura Kann et al., "Table 21. Percentage of High School Students Who Experienced Physical Dating Violence and Sexual Dating Violence by Sex, Race/Ethnicity, and Grade—United States, Youth Risk Behavior Survey, 2015," in "Youth Risk Behavior Surveillance—United States, 2015," *Morbidity and Mortality Weekly Report*, vol. 65, no. 6, June 10, 2016, https://www.cdc.gov/healthyyouth/data/yrbs/pdf/2015/ss6506_updated.pdf (accessed January 3, 2017)

sexual activity are less likely to have accurate knowledge and confidence to use contraceptives effectively and may have difficulty obtaining contraceptives. They also have more sexual partners, more STIs, and more unintended pregnancies than older teens.

In "Youth Risk Behavior Surveillance," Kann et al. report that in 2015 nearly one out of 10 (9.6%) high school students said they had been physically hurt on purpose by a boyfriend or girlfriend (hit, slammed into something, or injured with an object or weapon) one or more times during the previous 12 months. Non-Hispanic African American female students (12.2%) were the most likely to have been hurt by a dating partner, followed by white female (11.9%) and Hispanic female students (11.4%). The survey also asked students if they had ever experienced sexual dating violence—being forced to do sexual things such as kissing, touching, or being physically forced to have sexual intercourse they did not want to do by someone they were dating. Nearly 16% of female and more than 5% of male students said they had experienced sexual dating violence. (See Table 5.3.)

CONTRACEPTIVE USE
Too Few Use Contraceptives

In "Youth Risk Behavior Surveillance" Kann et al. find that 56.9% of sexually active high school students reported in 2015 that they or their partners had used condoms during their last sexual intercourse. (See Table 5.4.) Non-Hispanic African American students reported the highest rate of condom use (63.4%) among sexually active youth. Non-Hispanic white students reported a rate of 56.8%, and Hispanic students reported a rate of 55.6%. Males (61.5%) were significantly more likely than females (52%) to report condom use. However, the use of condoms decreased from the ninth grade (60.5%) to the 12th grade (52.9%), a period during which the frequency of sexual intercourse increased, probably because older adolescents turned to alternative methods of birth control, such as oral contraception.

Among sexually active students nationwide in 2015, 18.2% reported that they or their partners used oral contraceptives, or "the pill." (See Table 5.4.) Although this form of contraception protects against pregnancy, it does not protect against STIs. More than twice as many non-Hispanic white students (23.5%) reported using birth control pills than did Hispanic (11.8%) or non-Hispanic African American (9%) students. This disparity may be due to the need for a prescription for birth control pills; non-Hispanic white students tend to have greater access to medical care than minority students do. Among students who were sexually active in 2015, the use of oral contraceptives increased between ninth grade (10.9%) and 12th grade (20.1%).

REASONS FOR USE OR NONUSE OF CONDOMS. Research indicates that adolescents' attitudes and beliefs about their relationships with their partners influence whether they will use condoms. Drawing on a national survey of male adolescents in "Condom Use: Indicators

TABLE 5.4

Percentage of high school students who used a condom during last sexual intercourse and who used birth control pills before last sexual intercourse, by sex, race and ethnicity, and grade, 2015

	Condo use			Birth control pill use		
	Female	Male	Total	Female	Male	Total
Category	%	%	%	%	%	%
Race/ethnicity						
White*	55.9	58.1	56.8	25.4	21.4	23.5
Black*	46.7	73.6	63.4	9.0	9.0	9.0
Hispanic	48.3	62.5	55.6	15.4	8.1	11.8
Grade						
9	56.7	63.3	60.5	11.2	10.8	10.9
10	54.0	65.6	59.9	20.2	11.6	15.9
11	52.9	62.5	57.7	23.9	19.1	21.5
12	48.8	57.4	52.9	23.2	16.9	20.1
Total	**52.0**	**61.5**	**56.9**	**21.3**	**15.2**	**18.2**

*Non-Hispanic.
Note: Percentage of students among the 30.1% of students nationwide who were currently sexually active. Condom use and birth control pills were used to prevent pregnancy.

SOURCE: Adapted from Laura Kann et al., "Table 73. Percentage of High School Students Who Used a Condom during Last Sexual Intercourse and Who Used Birth Control Pills before Last Sexual Intercourse, by Sex, Race/Ethnicity, and Grade—United States, Youth Risk Behavior Survey, 2015," in "Youth Risk Behavior Surveillance—United States, 2015," *Morbidity and Mortality Weekly Report*, vol. 65, no. 6, June 10, 2016, https://www.cdc.gov/healthyyouth/data/yrbs/pdf/2015/ss6506_updated.pdf (accessed January 3, 2017)

in Children and Youth" (October 2016, https://www.childtrends.org/wp-content/uploads/2016/10/28_Condom_Use.pdf), Child Trends Data Bank reports that condom use among high school students rose from 46% in 1991 to 63% in 2003 and then fell to 57% in 2015. Factors associated with lower likelihood of condom use include a large age difference between partners, a history of sexual abuse, and substance abuse. Factors linked to higher rates of condom use are higher educational attainment of parents, increased communication with parents about contraception, attending a sex education course that covered contraception, and believing that condoms effectively prevent pregnancy and STIs.

The 2011–13 NSFG (April 20, 2015, https://www.cdc.gov/nchs/nsfg/key_statistics/a.htm#condom) questioned males aged 15 to 24 years about their attitudes toward condom use. More than one-quarter of the survey respondents said there was a "pretty good chance" or "almost certain chance" they would feel less physical pleasure if they used a condom during sex, which might deter them from using condoms. In contrast, the majority of survey respondents said there was "no chance" (58.7%) that discussing condom use with a new partner would be embarrassing, and another 20.1% said there was "little chance" of embarrassment. Roughly 80% reported there was a good or a certain chance that a new partner "would appreciate" the use of a condom.

SEXUALLY TRANSMITTED INFECTIONS

Adolescents and young adults have a higher risk of acquiring STIs than older adults. Female adolescents may have an increased susceptibility to chlamydia, a bacterial infection that can cause pelvic inflammatory disease and is a contributing factor in the transmission of HIV. In *Sexual Risk Behavior: HIV, STD, & Teen Pregnancy Prevention* (July 18, 2016, https://www.cdc.gov/healthyyouth/sexualbehaviors/), the CDC reports that half of the nearly 20 million new STIs reported each year and 22% of all new HIV diagnoses are among young people aged 15 to 24 years.

Rates of many STIs among youth increased in 2015. For example, rates of chlamydia infection among females aged 15 to 19 years decreased steadily between 2011 and 2014, but increased 1.5% in 2015. (See Table 5.5.) Among 20- to 24-year-old females, the rate increased 2.7% in 2015. Males aged 15 to 19 years also saw decreasing rates between 2011 and 2014 but increased 6.3% in 2015. Among young men aged 20 to 24 years, the rate increased 7.8% in 2015.

In *Sexually Transmitted Disease Surveillance 2015* (October 2016, https://www.cdc.gov/std/stats15/std-surveillance-2015-print.pdf), the CDC reports that in 2015, people aged 15 to 44 years accounted for 92.7% of reported gonorrhea cases in which age was known. Although rates among 15- to 19-year-olds decreased between 2011 and 2014, in 2015 the rate increased 5.2% among these teens and 7.2% among young adults aged 20 to 24 years.

The CDC further reports in *Sexually Transmitted Disease Surveillance 2015* that rates of syphilis among teens aged 15 to 19 years increased 10.2% during in 2015, and rose 14.9% among young adults aged 20 to 24 years. Rates among young men aged 20 to 24 years have risen each year since 2002, from 5.2 cases per 100,000 males to 35.7 cases in 2015.

TABLE 5.5

Reported cases and rates of chlamydia by age group and sex, 2011–15

Year	Age group	Cases				Rates*		
		Total	Male	Female	Unknown sex	Total	Male	Female
2011	0–4	747	284	458	5	3.7	2.8	4.6
	5–9	143	24	118	1	0.7	0.2	1.2
	10–14	15,405	1,743	13,588	74	74.4	16.5	134.3
	15–19	459,029	90,764	366,818	1,447	2,120.8	816.3	3,485.2
	20–24	542,947	147,948	393,534	1,465	2,450.8	1,307.8	3,630.0
2012	0–4	774	272	495	7	3.9	2.7	5.1
	5–9	151	17	134	0	0.7	0.2	1.3
	10–14	14,355	1,655	12,673	27	69.5	15.7	125.5
	15–19	433,239	86,150	346,430	659	2,028.2	785.8	3,331.7
	20–24	554,173	152,772	400,629	772	2,453.9	1,322.8	3,630.9
2013	0–4	681	266	402	13	3.4	2.6	4.1
	5–9	145	20	123	2	0.7	0.2	1.2
	10–14	12,585	1,554	11,001	30	60.9	14.7	108.9
	15–19	395,612	78,404	316,438	770	1,869.7	722.9	3,068.4
	20–24	553,658	153,102	399,545	1,011	2,428.8	1,310.9	3,594.2
2014	0–4	603	200	388	15	3.0	2.0	4.0
	5–9	181	26	152	3	0.9	0.2	1.5
	10–14	11,406	1,342	10,041	23	55.2	12.7	99.2
	15–19	381,717	77,908	303,294	515	1,811.9	722.4	2,949.3
	20–24	566,385	159,804	405,876	705	2,472.0	1,361.3	3,632.7
2015	0–4	518	196	322	0	2.6	1.9	3.3
	5–9	148	18	130	0	0.7	0.2	1.3
	10–14	10,642	1,216	9,394	32	51.5	11.5	92.8
	15–19	391,396	82,775	307,937	684	1,857.8	767.6	2,994.4
	20–24	589,963	172,313	416,772	878	2,574.9	1,467.8	3,730.3

*No population data are available for unknown sex and age; therefore, rates are not calculated.
Note: This table should be used only for age comparisons. Cases in the 0–4 age group may include cases due to perinatal transmission.

SOURCE: Adapted from "Table 10. Chlamydia—Reported Cases and Rates of Reported Cases by Age Group and Sex, United States, 2011–2015," in *Sexually Transmitted Diseases Surveillance 2015*, Centers for Disease Control and Prevention, National Center for HIV/AIDS, Viral Hepatitis, STD, and TB Prevention, Division of STD Prevention, October 2016, https://www.cdc.gov/std/stats15/std-surveillance-2015-print.pdf (accessed January 4, 2017)

Human Papillomavirus Vaccine

The human papillomavirus (HPV) is an STI that can cause genital warts and cervical cancer in women. The CDC does not require that cases of HPV be reported, but HPV is the most common STI in the United States. HPV has been linked to development of several types of cancer, including cervical, vulvar, vaginal, penile, anal, and oropharyngeal (back of the throat, including the base of the tongue and tonsils). The CDC reports (October 5, 2016, https://www.cdc.gov/cancer/hpv/) that each year, more than 30,000 HPV-associated cancers are diagnosed; cervical cancer is the most common HPV-associated cancer in women.

A vaccine against the strains of HPV that cause genital warts in males and females and cervical cancer in females was approved in 2006. It may be administered to males and females aged nine to 26 years and is nearly 100% effective. (See Chapter 4 for the percentage of adolescents who received the recommended doses of the vaccine from 2008 to 2014.)

TEEN CHILDBEARING TRENDS

Brady E. Hamilton, Lauren M. Rossen, and Amy M. Branum of the CDC report in "Teen Birth Rates for Urban and Rural Areas in the United States, 2007–2015" (November 2016, https://www.cdc.gov/nchs/data/databriefs/db264.pdf) that birth rates for teens have declined since 2007, with the largest decreases in large urban areas and the smallest decreases in rural counties. From 2007 through 2015, teen birth rates plummeted 50% in large urban counties, from 38.1 births to 18.9 births per 1,000 females aged 15 to 19 years. Teen birth rates were lowest in large urban counties and highest in rural counties. (See Figure 5.1.)

Consequences for Teen Mothers and Their Children

Teenage mothers and their babies face more health risks than older women and their babies. Teenagers who become pregnant are more likely than older women to suffer from pregnancy-induced hypertension and eclampsia (a life-threatening condition that sometimes results in convulsions and/or coma). Teenagers are more likely to have their labor induced, and an immature pelvis can cause prolonged or difficult labor, possibly resulting in bladder or bowel damage to the mother, infant brain damage, or even death of the mother and/or the child.

Although many health risks are similar for children regardless of the mother's age, children born to teen mothers are more likely to have a low birth weight and to die as infants, compared with children born to older mothers. In "About Teen Pregnancy" (April 5, 2016, https://www.cdc.gov/teenpregnancy/about/index.htm),

FIGURE 5.1

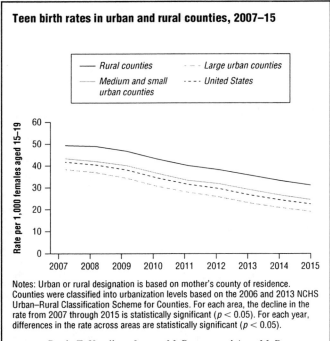

Teen birth rates in urban and rural counties, 2007–15

Notes: Urban or rural designation is based on mother's county of residence. Counties were classified into urbanization levels based on the 2006 and 2013 NCHS Urban–Rural Classification Scheme for Counties. For each area, the decline in the rate from 2007 through 2015 is statistically significant ($p < 0.05$). For each year, differences in the rate across areas are statistically significant ($p < 0.05$).

SOURCE: Brady E. Hamilton, Lauren M. Rossen, and Amy M. Branum, "Figure 1. Teen Birth Rates, by Urbanization Level of County: United States, 2007–2015," in "Teen Birth Rates for Urban and Rural Areas in the United States, 2007–2015," *NCHS Data Brief*, no. 264, Centers for Disease Control and Prevention, National Center for Health Statistic, November 2016, https://www.cdc.gov/nchs/data/databriefs/db264.pdf (accessed January 4, 2017)

the CDC also observes that children of teenage mothers are more likely to drop out of high school, be incarcerated at some time during adolescence, give birth as a teenager, and face unemployment as a young adult than are children of older mothers.

Few teenage mothers are ready for the emotional, financial, and psychological responsibilities and challenges of parenthood. Teen parents are typically more disadvantaged before and after becoming parents, which may account for many of the negative outcomes associated with teen births. Becoming a parent at a young age usually cuts short a teenage mother's education, limiting her ability to support herself and her child. The CDC reports in "About Teen Pregnancy" that just half of teen mothers receive a high school diploma by age 22, compared with 90% of young women who had not become teen mothers. As a result of lower educational attainment, teen mothers are more likely than older mothers to depend on public assistance after giving birth and to experience family and economic instability.

In "The Intergenerational Effects of Abuse and Neglect: Maltreatment Risk among Young Children of Adolescent Mothers" (Society for Social Work and Research 2014 Annual Conference, January 15–19, 2014, https://sswr .confex.com/sswr/2014/webprogram/Paper22361.html),

Emily Putnam-Hornstein et al. report that infants of teen mothers also are at increased risk of abuse and neglect, with as many as 25% reported to child protective services for maltreatment before age five.

In "A Content Analysis of Teen Parenthood in 'Teen Mom' Reality Programming" (*Health Communication*, vol. 31, no. 12, 2016), Nicole Martins et al. analyze the content of MTV shows *16 and Pregnant*, *Teen Mom*, and *Teen Mom 2* to see if these shows offer an accurate image of teen pregnancy. The researchers find that the teen mothers on television were younger, more often white, and had healthier babies compared with national averages. In addition, the babies' fathers on television were more involved in daily infant care than is typical in real life. The teen mothers on these shows were more likely to obtain high school diplomas and had more active social lives than national averages. Martins et al. also note that the shows never discuss financial or health care concerns and speculate that the teen mothers on reality television shows have higher earnings than most teen mothers because of their appearance on the shows and income from speaking engagements, endorsements, and appearances on other MTV shows. This explains how they can afford child care, live on their own as opposed to living with relatives, and pay college tuition. The researchers conclude, "these shows do not provide young people with an accurate portrayal of the trials and tribulations of teen parenthood, but rather offer a somewhat sanitized version of it, softening some of the hardships experienced by real teen parents and their children."

Teen Fathers

Jennifer Manlove et al. report an analysis of data that included information about male teens who fathered children in "Male Involvement in Family Planning: The Estimated Influence of Improvements in Condom Use and Efficacy on Nonmarital Births among Teens and Young Adults" (September 17, 2014, https://www.child trends.org/wp-content/uploads/2014/09/2014-36MaleInvolve mentFamilyPlanning.pdf). The researchers find that young unmarried fathers are less likely than older and married fathers to live with their children. Fewer than half of teen fathers live with their first child at the time of the child's birth, and among those fathers, only about a quarter will be living with their children when the father reaches his early 20s.

Unmarried men and men who have children when they are still adolescents are more likely to go on to have additional children with new partners than are men who are older or are married when their first child is born. As is the case with teen mothers, much research also indicates that first and additional births in adolescence and young adulthood have the potential to further compromise young fathers' opportunities for educational attainment and economic stability, both of which are very closely linked to their children's future health, well-being, and opportunities for success.

In "Differential Social Evaluation of Pregnant Teens, Teen Mothers and Teen Fathers by University Students" (*Adolescence and Youth*, October 2014), Keri Weed and Jody S. Nicholson assert that stigmatization of teen parents is common, and young fathers may be assessed more negatively than teen mothers and with different stereotypes. Weed and Nicholson observe, "While teen mothers are depicted as being 'poor, lone, vulnerable and morally suspect,' teen fathers have been portrayed as 'being absent, criminal, violent and socially excluded.'" The concern that young fathers will be unable to financially support their children may contribute to the negative stereotypes.

TEEN ABORTION

The CDC reports that 664,435 abortions were performed in 2013. The rate of abortions per 1,000 live births decreased from a high of 359 in 1980 to 200 in 2013. The highest abortion rates were among women aged 20 to 29 years. Girls under the age of 15 years accounted for the smallest percentage of abortions (0.3%) and had the lowest abortion rates (0.6 per 1,000). Adolescents aged 15 to 19 years accounted for 11.4% and had an abortion rate of 8.2 per 1,000.

In "Abortion Surveillance—United States, 2013" (November 25, 2016, https://www.cdc.gov/mmwr/volumes/65/ss/ss6512a1.htm), Tara C. Jatlaoui et al. report, "From 2004 to 2013, the percentage of abortions accounted for by adolescents aged 15–19 years decreased 31% and their abortion rate decreased 46%. These decreases were greater than the decreases for women in any older age group." (See Table 5.6.)

States have varying laws on parental involvement in minors' abortion decisions. In "An Overview of Abortion Laws" (2017, https://www.guttmacher.org/state-policy/explore/overview-abortion-laws), the Guttmacher Institute reports that as of January 2017, 37 states required some form of parental involvement in a minor's decision to have an abortion: 26 states required that one or both parents must give consent, and 11 states required that one or both parents be notified.

HOMOSEXUALITY

In *Just the Facts about Sexual Orientation and Youth: A Primer for Principals, Educators, and School Personnel* (2008, http://www.apa.org/pi/lgbt/resources/just-the-facts.pdf), the American Psychological Association (APA) stresses that sexual orientation is one aspect of the identity of adolescents, not a mental disorder. According to the APA, sexual orientation is developed across a lifetime and along a continuum; in other words,

TABLE 5.6

Abortions, by age group and year, 2004–13

Age group (yrs)	2004	2005	2006	2007	2008	2009	2010	2011	2012	2013	2004 to 2008	2009 to 2013	2012 to 2013	2004 to 2013
					Year						% change			
% of abortions														
<15	0.6	0.6	0.5	0.5	0.5	0.5	0.5	0.4	0.4	0.3	−16.7	−40.0	−25.0	−50.0
15–19	16.6	16.5	16.5	16.5	16.1	15.5	14.6	13.4	12.2	11.4	−3.0	−26.5	−6.6	−31.3
20–24	33.2	32.8	32.7	32.6	32.7	32.6	32.8	32.9	32.8	32.7	−1.5	0.3	−0.3	−1.5
25–29	23.1	23.5	24.1	24.2	24.4	24.4	24.5	24.9	25.3	25.9	5.6	6.1	2.4	12.1
30–34	14.8	14.6	14.2	14.1	14.4	14.8	15.3	15.8	16.4	16.8	−2.7	13.5	2.4	13.5
35–39	8.5	8.8	8.9	8.9	8.8	8.9	8.9	8.9	9.1	9.2	3.5	3.4	1.1	8.2
≥40	3.2	3.2	3.2	3.2	3.1	3.3	3.4	3.6	3.7	3.6	−3.1	9.1	−2.7	12.5
Abortion rate[a]														
<15	1.3	1.2	1.2	1.2	1.2	1.1	1.0	0.9	0.8	0.6	−7.7	−45.5	−25.0	−53.8
15–19	15.1	14.5	14.7	14.4	14.0	12.9	11.8	10.6	9.3	8.2	−7.3	−36.4	−11.8	−45.7
20–24	30.3	29.4	30.2	29.6	29.7	28.0	27.1	25.2	23.6	22.0	−2.0	−21.4	−6.8	−27.4
25–29	22.8	22.3	22.9	22.2	22.1	21.0	20.4	19.6	19.0	18.3	−3.1	−12.9	−3.7	−19.7
30–34	13.9	13.7	14.0	13.8	14.0	13.5	13.4	12.8	12.5	11.9	0.7	−11.9	−4.8	−14.4
35–39	7.6	7.8	8.0	7.9	8.0	7.7	7.7	7.5	7.4	7.0	5.3	−9.1	−5.4	−7.9
≥40	2.6	2.6	2.7	2.7	2.7	2.8	2.8	2.9	2.8	2.6	3.8	−7.1	−7.1	0.0
Total (no.)	714,398	701,984	724,407	714,139	718,037	686,006	664,857	632,824	603,745	570,399	—	—	—	—

*Number of abortions obtained by women in a given age group per 1,000 women in that same age group. Women aged 13–14 years were used as the denominator for the group of women aged <15 years, and women aged 40–44 years were used as the denominator for the group of women aged ≥40 years. Women aged 15–44 years were used as the denominator for the overall rate. For each reporting area, abortions for women of unknown age were distributed according to the distribution of abortions among women of known age for that area.

Note: Data from 42 reporting areas; by year, these reporting areas represent 96%–98% of all abortions reported to Center for Disease Control (CDC) by age during 2004–2013. Excludes 10 reporting areas (California, District of Columbia, Florida, Louisiana, Maine, Maryland, New Hampshire, Vermont, West Virginia, and Wyoming) that did not report, did not report by age, or did not meet reporting standards for ≥1 year.

SOURCE: Adapted from Tara C. Jatlaoui et al., "Table 4. Reported Abortions, by Known Age Group and Year—Selected Reporting Areas, United States, 2004–2013," in "Abortion Surveillance—United States, 2013," *Morbidity and Mortality Weekly Report*, vol. 65, no.12, November 25, 2016, https://www.cdc.gov/mmwr/volumes/65/ss/pdfs/ss6512.pdf (accessed January 4, 2017)

teens are not necessarily simply homosexual or heterosexual, but may feel varying degrees of attraction to people of both genders. The APA explains that lesbian, gay, bisexual, and transgender (LGBT) adolescents face prejudice and discrimination that negatively affect their educational experiences and emotional and physical health. Their legitimate fear of being hurt as a result of disclosing their sexuality often leads to feelings of isolation. All these factors account for higher rates of emotional distress, suicide attempts, risky sexual behavior, and substance use among LGBT adolescents. The APA underscores the need for school personnel to be as open and accepting as possible to support these adolescents.

Programs to Support LGBT Teens

Because adolescence can be an especially difficult time for LGBT youth, several initiatives and programs have been developed to support them through the challenges of the teen years. For example, the It Gets Better Project was created after the columnist Dan Savage (1964–) and his partner Terry Miller created a YouTube video to offer hope to gay teens confronting harassment in 2010. The video inspired a global support program, with more than 50,000 user-created videos, a book, and the website ItGetsBetter.org, to communicate with LGBT youth and offer them inspiring visions of happy, productive, and fulfilling adult lives.

The Trevor Project (http://www.thetrevorproject.org) was launched in 1998 by James Lecesne, Peggy Rajski, and Randy Stone, the creators of the Academy Award–winning short film *TREVOR*, the story of a 13-year-old boy who attempts suicide after being bullied and harassed about his feelings for another boy. The project began as a telephone lifeline and grew to become a national leader in providing crisis intervention and suicide prevention services to LGBT youth. It has been honored by the White House as a "Champion of Change."

The Point Foundation (https://pointfoundation.org) offers scholarships to promising LGBTQ (the Q is for "queer" or "questioning") students to help them realize their academic and leadership potential. Along with financial support, the foundation matches students with mentors (successful professionals who can help guide them in their chosen fields). It also offers community education programs that are aimed at increasing awareness and understanding and "that affect social change by challenging attitudes that contribute to social stigma and its resulting prejudice, which is often experienced by those in the LGBTQ community."

The CDC website LGBT Youth Resources (October 28, 2015, https://www.cdc.gov/lgbthealth/youth-resources .htm) offers a list of resources for LGBT children, teens, and their families. These include:

- Gay-Straight Alliance (GSA Network, 2017, https:// gsanetwork.org/) is a grassroots, youth-led organization that advocates for racial and gender justice

- GLSEN (Gay, Lesbian & Straight Education Network, 2017, https://www.glsen.org/) conducts research, develops resources for educators, and partners with national education organizations to improve school climate and champion LGBT issues in K–12 education

- National Alliance to End Homelessness (2017, http:// www.endhomelessness.org/) is a nonprofit, nonpartisan organization dedicated to preventing and ending homelessness

- SIECUS (Sexuality Information and Education Council of the United States, 2017, http://www.siecus.org/) educates and informs schools, communities, and policy makers about sexuality and sexual and reproductive health

STI AND PREGNANCY PREVENTION PROGRAMS FOR TEENS

Abstinence

In response to the growing concern about nonmarital births and the threat of AIDS, several national youth organizations and religious groups began campaigns during the 1990s to encourage teens to sign an abstinence pledge (a promise to abstain from sexual activity until marriage). Debra Hauser of Advocates for Youth indicates in *Five Years of Abstinence-Only-until-Marriage Education: Assessing the Impact* (2004, http://www.advocates foryouth.org/component/content/article/623-five-years-of-abstinence-only-until-marriage-education-assessing-the-impact) that in 1996 the federal government committed $250 million over five years to fund state initiatives to promote abstinence as Title V of the Social Security Act. Only 11 states made the results of their evaluations of the effectiveness of these programs public. Hauser indicates that Advocates for Youth examined these evaluations and found that the programs "showed few short-term benefits and no lasting, positive impact.... No program was able to demonstrate a positive impact on sexual behavior over time."

In fact, some studies of abstinence-only education programs find that they have a negative impact on teens' sexual health. In "A Farewell to Abstinence and Fidelity?" (*Lancet Global Health*, vol. 4, no. 9, September 2016), Kent Buse, Mikaela Hildebrand, and Sarah Hawkes report that the *Lancet*'s Commission on Adolescent Health and Wellbeing concluded that there is "'high-quality evidence that abstinence-only education is ineffective in preventing HIV, incidence of sexually transmitted infections, and adolescent pregnancy' and that there is 'high-quality evidence of some benefit' of comprehensive school-based sex education when combined with contraception provision."

Many question if abstinence-only education is the best approach to prevent teen pregnancy or the spread of STIs. For example, Jillian B. Carr and Analisa Packham report in "The Effects of State-Mandated Abstinence-Based Sex Education on Teen Health Outcomes" (*Health Economics*, vol. 166, no. 2, February 2016) that their analysis of the relationship between state-level policies and teen health outcomes finds that "state-level abstinence education mandates have no effect on teen birth rates or abortion rates."

Researchers at the University of North Georgia (UNG) compared the effects of abstinence only and comprehensive sex education on rates of STIs and presented the results at the UNG 18th Annual Research Conference held in April 2013. In "No Sex, Please: Comprehensive vs. Abstinence-Only Sex Education" (http://digitalcommons .northgeorgia.edu/ngresearchconf/2013/trialtrack/51), Stacy C. Smith, Sarah Vogt, and Velma Faircloth find "no difference in effectiveness between abstinence-only education and those students receiving no sex education." The researchers assert that comprehensive sex education is much more effective than abstinence only and exhort nurses to advocate for it.

FUNDING ABSTINENCE-ONLY EDUCATION. In a February 9, 2016, media release, "President's Budget Supports Adolescent Sexual Health Promotion Programs and Calls for End to 'Abstinence Education,'" SIECUS commends the fiscal year (FY) 2017 federal budget because it underscores the efforts of President Barack Obama (1961–) "to rid our nation of abstinence-only-until-marriage (AOUM) funding once and for all by not only eliminating the competitive AOUM program, but also including a legislative proposal to eliminate the Title V AOUM state grant program currently authorized at $75 million for FY 2017."

The FY 2017 budget emphasizes investment in programs that inform and educate youth about how to lead sexually healthy lives. It increases funding for the Office of Adolescent Health's Teen Pregnancy Prevention Program and maintains current funding for the CDC Division of Adolescent and School Health.

Sex and STI/HIV Education in Schools

The Guttmacher Institute reports in "Sex and HIV Education" (https://www.guttmacher.org/state-policy/explore/ sex-and-hiv-education) that as of March 1, 2017, 22 states and the District of Columbia required schools to provide both sex education and HIV education, two states required sex education only, and 12 states mandated HIV education only. Twenty-seven states required that any sex education and HIV education that was provided meet specific requirements; 13 states required instruction that is medically accurate; 26 states and the District of Columbia required that instruction be age-appropriate; eight states required culturally sensitive instruction that is not biased against any race, sex, or ethnicity; and two states prohibited the promotion of religion. Parental involvement in whatever sex or HIV education was provided was a requirement in 38 states and the District of Columbia. In most states this meant parental notification and the ability for parents to remove their children from instruction.

When sex education is taught, 18 states and the District of Columbia required that education about contraception be included. There were 37 states that required abstinence be included in sex education. Of these, 25 states required that it be stressed and 11 that it be covered in the program. Information about skills for healthy sexuality, such as how to avoid coerced sex and how to make healthy decisions, were a required part of sex education in 28 states. In 19 states it was required that sex education include instruction on the importance of restricting sexual activity to marriage. Sexual orientation was a required part of sex education instruction in 13 states. Among these, four states required only negative information about sexual orientation (e.g., the Alabama code states that education should emphasize "in a factual manner and from a public health perspective, that homosexuality is not a lifestyle acceptable to the general public and that homosexual conduct is a criminal offense under the laws of the state"). Some states also had content requirements in place for HIV education. In 20 states, when HIV education was taught, information on contraception was required. It was required that abstinence be stressed in HIV education in 27 states, and 12 states simply required that it be covered as part of HIV instruction.

According to the Guttmacher Institute, in the fact sheet "American Teens' Sources of Sexual Health Education" (April 2016, https://www.guttmacher.org/fact-sheet/facts-american-teens-sources-information-about-sex), almost all U.S. teenagers received some formal sex education. However, nearly half (43%) of teenage boys and more than half (57%) of teenage girls reported receiving no information on methods of birth control before they first had sex.

CHAPTER 6
GETTING AN EDUCATION

Despite the controversies surrounding the quality and direction of American education, the United States remains one of the most highly educated nations in the world. According to Grace Kena et al., in *The Condition of Education 2016* (May 2016, https://nces.ed.gov/pubs2016/2016144.pdf), between 1995 and 2015 the percentage of people aged 25 to 29 years who had received a high school diploma rose from 87% to 91%. The percentage in that age group that had earned a bachelor's degree or higher increased from 25% to 36%. Among people in the 25-to-29 age group, females (39%) were more likely than males (32%) to have completed a bachelor's or higher degree in 2015. (See Figure 6.1.)

THE NO CHILD LEFT BEHIND ACT

During the 1980s there was growing concern that Americans were falling behind other developed countries in educational achievement. In response, the National Education Goals Panel was created in 1989 to advance several national objectives, including increasing the high school graduation rate and competency in English, mathematics, science, history, and geography. Although a task force recommended the panel's reauthorization in 1999, the passage of the No Child Left Behind (NCLB) Act closed the panel in 2002.

The NCLB changed the laws defining and regulating the federal government's role in kindergarten through 12th-grade education. The law is based on four basic education reform principles. According to the U.S. Department of Education, in "Four Pillars of NCLB" (July 1, 2004, https://www2.ed.gov/nclb/overview/intro/4pillars.html), these principles are:

- Stronger accountability for results

- Increased flexibility and local control

- Expanded options for parents

- An emphasis on teaching methods that have been proven to work

Accountability

Under the NCLB, schools are required to demonstrate "adequate yearly progress" toward statewide proficiency goals, including closing the achievement gap between advantaged and disadvantaged students. Schools that do not demonstrate progress face corrective action and restructuring measures. Progress reports are public, so parents can remain informed about their school and school district. Schools that make or exceed yearly targets are eligible for awards.

The accountability outlined under the NCLB is measured through standards testing, and federal financing of schools depends on the results of these mandated tests. The testing provisions of the NCLB are the subject of debate. Advocates view testing as a means to ensure that all children are held to the same high standards. They argue that many young people have passed through school without acquiring basic reading and math skills and are ill equipped to function in an information-oriented economy. By contrast, Jennifer L. Jennings and Douglas Lee Lauen note in "Accountability, Inequality, and Achievement: The Effects of the No Child Left Behind Act on Multiple Measures of Student Learning" (*RSF: The Russell Sage Foundation Journal of the Social Sciences*, vol. 2, no. 5, September 2016) that several studies have found that accountability systems improve students' scores on state and national tests, and others have found small but positive effects of No Child Left Behind on measures of student achievement other than state test scores. Jennings and Lauen analyzed test scores of sixth- through eighth-grade students in the Houston Independent School District between 2003 and 2007 and find higher scores on math state tests, but lower math and reading scores on audit tests that are not tied to the accountability system. The researchers explain that although they

FIGURE 6.1

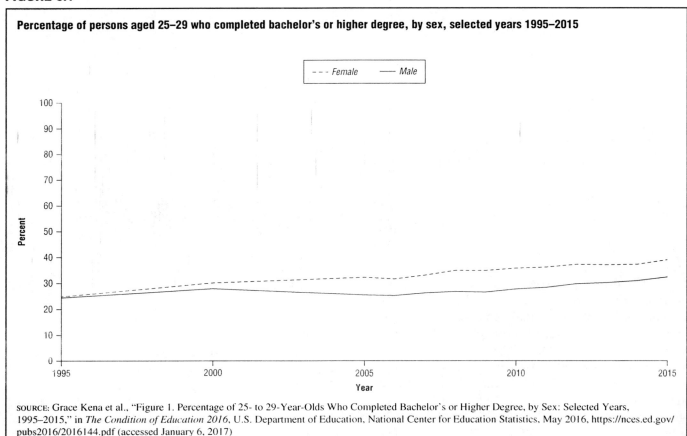

Percentage of persons aged 25–29 who completed bachelor's or higher degree, by sex, selected years 1995–2015

SOURCE: Grace Kena et al., "Figure 1. Percentage of 25- to 29-Year-Olds Who Completed Bachelor's or Higher Degree, by Sex: Selected Years, 1995–2015," in *The Condition of Education 2016*, U.S. Department of Education, National Center for Education Statistics, May 2016, https://nces.ed.gov/pubs2016/2016144.pdf (accessed January 6, 2017)

cannot determine why gains in state test scores are not reflected in audit test scores, this finding should prompt further investigation about "how instruction changes when schools face accountability pressure, why gains vary across different measures of achievement, and why gains vary across different subgroups of students."

In "What Parents Still Do Not Know about No Child Left Behind and Why It Matters" (*Journal of Education Policy*, vol. 31, no. 3, 2016), Lesley E. Lavery reports that 10 years after NCLB was instituted, more than half of the nation's 100,000 public schools failed to make sufficient progress toward state standards and one-third of schools have repeatedly failed to meet NCLB targets. Lavery notes that nearly half of Americans do not support NCLB and cites the fact that "few families have taken advantage of the policy's purported opportunities through formally designated channels such as school choice and tutoring services" as further evidence of flagging enthusiasm for the policy.

The Common Core State Standards

Until the second decade of the 21st century, states established their own academic standards, and their standards varied widely. The Common Core standards aim to ensure that all students in public schools are similarly educated when they graduate from high school. Common Core writing assignments emphasize evidence-based arguments rather than personal narratives like "how I spent my summer vacation." Math standards are intended to help students understand mathematical principles rather than simply memorizing ways to solve problems.

Released in 2010, the Common Core state standards (CCSS) detail what students in kindergarten through 12th grade should know in language arts and mathematics at the end of each grade. The Bill & Melinda Gates Foundation contributed about $200 million to fund the development, evaluation, implementation, and promotion of the CCSS. More than 40 states adopted the CCSS, a consistent set of K–12 standards, created by the states, that outline what students should know at each grade level in math and English.

Stephen Sawchuk observes in "What to Make of the Debate over Common Core" (Smithsonian.com, September 4, 2013) that Common Core standards require students to think critically about what they are learning and to analyze and apply it rather than simply committing material to memory. Sawchuk explains that the standards aim to equip students completing high school to "succeed in college or entry-level jobs without remediation."

STANDARDS HAVE SUPPORTERS AND OPPONENTS. CCSS advocates believe common standards and consistent benchmarks will ensure equitable education and that "raising the bar" will improve students' academic performance. In "An Examination of the Debate Surrounding Core Curriculum State Standards in American Education" (*Paideia*, vol. 3, no. 20, Spring 2016), Kristen Henry explains that supporters maintain that CCSS effectively address curriculum variation, promote educational equity by ensuring that all students benefit from a uniform curriculum, and enable accurate comparisons between state school systems. Proponents also believe that CCSS will reduce the percentage of postsecondary students requiring remedial coursework in college and prepare them to compete in the global economy.

Critics of CCSS think their adoption is an example of federal government overreach that takes control away from the states, local communities, and families. (It is important to remember that the federal government did not develop the CCSS but does support them.) Detractors also cite the high costs of the program and observe that even though states' participation in CCSS is voluntary, the financial incentives to participate are so great that states with inadequate education budgets cannot afford to pass up the opportunity. Critics also think that funding for CCSS should be more equitably distributed to address other issues that influence academic performance such as poverty, food insecurity, health care, and access to books.

Interestingly, the CCSS has supporters and detractors on both sides of the aisle. President Donald Trump (1946–) and the U.S. senators Ted Cruz (1970–; R-TX), Rand Paul (1963–; R-KY), and Marco Rubio (1971–; R-FL) oppose CCSS, along with Republican governors Scott Walker of Wisconsin (1967–) and Bobby Jindal of Louisiana (1971–). Conservative groups such as the Republican National Committee, the Cato Institute, and the Heritage Foundation also oppose the CCSS. Other Republicans, however, including the former Florida governor Jeb Bush (1953–) and Ohio governor John Kasich (1952–), support CCSS. Many Democrats, including former president Barack Obama (1961–) and former U.S. secretary of state Hillary Clinton (1947–), support CCSS, as does the Democratic-affiliated Center for American Progress.

Liberal detractors view CCSS as a rigid, one-size-fits-all approach to education that does not reflect how teachers teach in the classroom and how students learn. For example, Diane Ravitch, a senior fellow at the Brookings Institution and research professor of education at New York University, is skeptical about the standards. In "Everything You Need to Know about Common Core—Ravitch" (WashingtonPost.com, January 18, 2014), Ravitch observes that it will be at least a decade before the results of the adoption of these standards can

be analyzed, but she is not optimistic that the outcomes will be universally favorable. She concludes, "I believe in standards, but they must not be rigid, inflexible, and prescriptive. Teachers must have the flexibility to tailor standards to meet the students in their classrooms, the students who can't read English, the students who are two grade levels behind, the students who are homeless, the students who just don't get it and just don't care, the students who frequently miss class. Standards alone cannot produce a miraculous transformation."

Testing Assesses Student Performance

National Assessment of Educational Progress (NAEP) levels define what students should know and do at different grade levels, and looking at changes in test scores over time is one way to gauge the performance of the education system. In *The Condition of Education 2016*, Kena et al. describe how the NAEP assesses student performance in reading at grades 4, 8, and 12 in public and private schools and compares test results over time. NAEP reading scores range from 0 to 500.

Among fourth-grade students, the average reading scores for white (232), African American (206), Hispanic (208), and Asian/Pacific Islander students (239) and the percent of students performing at the "proficient" level were higher in 2015 (36%) than in 1992 (29%). Among eighth-grade students in 2015, average reading scores for white (274), African American (248), and Hispanic (253) students were lower than the scores in 2013 (276, 250, and 256, respectively), but still higher than they were in 1992. Similarly, the percentage of eighth graders considered proficient increased from 29% in 1992 to 34% in 2015.

Another way to evaluate the U.S. educational system is to compare how its students perform to the performance of students in other countries. The Program for International Student Assessment (PISA) measures the performance of 15-year-olds in reading, mathematics, and science literacy. Kena et al. compare the average results of U.S. teens on the 2012 PISA against the results of teens from other countries in the Organisation for Economic Co-operation and Development (OECD), which have highly developed economies and democratic governments. They report that on the 2012 PISA, U.S. teens achieved an average reading score of 498. This was close to the overall OECD average of 496 and was lower than the average score of 19 educational systems in other OECD countries. The U.S. average score of 481 in mathematics literacy was below the OECD average score of 494 and was lower than the average score in 29 educational systems of the OECD countries. The average score of U.S. teens in science literacy was 497, compared with an average among OECD countries of 501. U.S. teens were outperformed by 22 educational systems in OECD countries in science literacy.

The Voucher Controversy

Many people believe that problems such as large class sizes, inadequate teacher training, and lack of computers and supplies in public schools are unsolvable within the current public school system. One solution touted during the early 1990s was the school voucher system: the government would provide a certain amount of money each year to parents in the form of a voucher to enroll their children at the schools of their choice, either public or private. School vouchers became a highly polarized issue, with strong opinions both for and against the idea.

The National Education Association (NEA), the largest teachers' union in the country, objected to school vouchers, arguing that voucher programs would divert money from the public education system and make existing problems worse. The union declared that giving money to parents who choose to send their child to a religious or parochial school is unconstitutional. Furthermore, the NEA and other voucher opponents claimed there was little evidence to support the idea that voucher programs lead to better educational outcomes. For example, in *Keeping Informed about School Vouchers: A Review of Major Developments and Research* (July 2011, http://files.eric .ed.gov/fulltext/ED522161.pdf), Alexandra Usher and Nancy Kober of the Center on Education Policy conclude that a decade of research reveals "that vouchers have had no clear positive effect on student academic achievement, and mixed outcomes for students overall."

Voucher supporters maintain that parents should be able to choose the best educational environments for their children. They argue that vouchers give everyone, not just the wealthy or middle class, an opportunity for a better education for their children in private schools. They also believe that making the educational system a free-market enterprise, in which parents may choose which school their children will attend, would force the public education system to provide a higher standard of education to compete.

The National Conference of State Legislatures reports in "School Voucher Laws: State-by-State Comparison" (2017, http://www.ncsl.org/research/education/ voucher-law-comparison.aspx) that in addition to the District of Columbia, 13 states operated school voucher programs in 2017: Arkansas, Florida, Georgia, Indiana, Louisiana, Maine, Mississippi, North Carolina, Ohio, Oklahoma, Utah, Vermont, and Wisconsin.

Public School Choice: No Child Left Behind and Charter Schools

In lieu of a voucher program, the NCLB offered a public-school choice program. Parents of students enrolled in "failing" public schools were allowed to move their children to a better-performing public or charter school. Local school districts were required to provide this choice and provide students with transportation to the alternative school.

The NCLB also expanded the creation and use of charter schools. Public charter schools are funded by government money and run by a management group under an agreement, or charter, with the state that exempts it from many state or local regulations that govern most public schools. In return for these exemptions and funding, the school must meet certain standards. The National Alliance for Public Charter Schools estimates in "The Public Charter Schools Dashboard" (2016, http://www.publiccharters .org/dashboard/schools/page/overview/year/2016) that there were 6,440 charter schools, including 642 new schools, operating during the 2013–14 school year.

In "A Meta-analysis of the Literature on the Effect of Charter Schools on Student Achievement" (Society for Research on Educational Effectiveness, Spring 2016 Conference, http://files.eric.ed.gov/fulltext/ED566972.pdf), Julian R. Betts and Y. Emily Tang of the University of California, San Diego, reviewed research to determine whether charter schools produce higher academic achievement than traditional public schools. Betts and Tang find no significant differences for reading achievement but find that charter schools produce higher achievement gains in math compared with public schools. They also note that "A tiny but growing literature on non-achievement outcomes suggests positive influences of charter schools on educational attainment and behavioral outcomes."

RACE TO THE TOP

The American Recovery and Reinvestment Act (ARRA), which was signed into law by President Obama in February 2009, included $4.4 billion for a new program called the Race to the Top Fund. According to the U.S. Department of Education, in "Race to the Top Program: Executive Summary" (November 2009, https:// www2.ed.gov/programs/racetothetop/executive-summary .pdf), the program was "designed to encourage and reward States that are creating the conditions for education innovation and reform." The program awarded grants to states that developed educational reform plans that could accomplish four key objectives:

- Prepare students to succeed in college and the workplace

- Measure student growth and success to help teachers improve instruction

- Recruit and retain the best teachers

- Help the lowest-achieving schools succeed

In "Fundamental Change: Innovation in America's Schools under Race to the Top" (November 2015, https:// www2.ed.gov/programs/racetothetop/rttfinalrptfull.pdf), the U.S. Department of Education, Office of Elementary and Secondary Education analyzes the impact of the program and notes positive trends such as higher graduation rates and higher rates of participation and success in advanced placement (AP) courses. (See Figure 6.2.)

FIGURE 6.2

Participation and success in advanced placement courses, 2011 and 2015

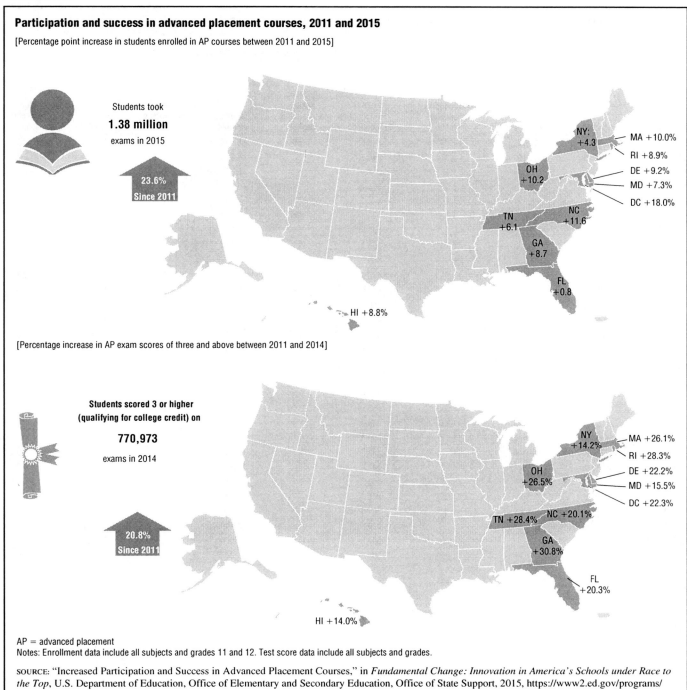

[Percentage point increase in students enrolled in AP courses between 2011 and 2015]

Students took
1.38 million
exams in 2015

23.6%
Since 2011

NY:
+4.3

OH
+10.2

TN
+6.1

NC
+11.6

GA
+8.7

FL
+0.8

HI +8.8%

MA +10.0%
RI +8.9%
DE +9.2%
MD +7.3%
DC +18.0%

[Percentage increase in AP exam scores of three and above between 2011 and 2014]

Students scored 3 or higher
(qualifying for college credit) on

770,973

exams in 2014

20.8%
Since 2011

NY
+14.2%

OH
+26.5%

TN +28.4%

NC +20.1%

GA
+30.8%

FL
+20.3%

HI +14.0%

MA +26.1%
RI +28.3%
DE +22.2%
MD +15.5%
DC +22.3%

AP = advanced placement
Notes: Enrollment data include all subjects and grades 11 and 12. Test score data include all subjects and grades.

SOURCE: "Increased Participation and Success in Advanced Placement Courses," in *Fundamental Change: Innovation in America's Schools under Race to the Top*, U.S. Department of Education, Office of Elementary and Secondary Education, Office of State Support, 2015, https://www2.ed.gov/programs/racetothetop/rttfinalrptfull.pdf (accessed January 7, 2017).

Participating states made progress toward their goals, which included improving relationships between states and districts, improving communication between teachers, parents, administrators, and other stakeholders, and adoption of higher academic standards.

THE COST OF PUBLIC EDUCATION

The average annual expenditure per student in the public-school system in constant 2012–13 dollars rose from $8,459 per pupil in school year (SY) 1989–90 to $11,230 per pupil in SY 2014–15. (See Table 6.1.) Each year, when the federal budget is determined by Congress, the debate over funding for public education is fierce. Public school officials and teachers stress the importance of investing in the public education system, arguing that more money will provide more teachers, educational materials, and (eventually) a better education to students. They point to school buildings in need of repair, and classes that meet in hallways and other cramped areas

TABLE 6.1

Expenditures per pupil in public elementary and secondary schools, 1989–90 through 2023–24

| | Current expenditures in unadjusted dollars[a] | | | Current expenditures in constant 2012–13 dollars[b] | | | | | |
| | | | | Total current expenditures | | Per pupil in fall enrollment | | Per pupil in average daily attendance (ADA) | |
School year	Total, in billions	Per pupil in fall enrollment	Per pupil in average daily attendance (ADA)	In billions	Annual percentage change	Per pupil enrolled	Annual percentage change	Per pupil in ADA	Annual percentage change
1989–90	$188.2	$4,643	$4,980	$343.0	3.8	$8,459	2.9	$9,073	2.3
1990–91	202.0	4,902	5,258	349.0	1.8	8,468	0.1	9,083	0.1
1991–92	211.2	5,023	5,421	353.6	1.3	8,409	−0.7	9,075	−0.1
1992–93	220.9	5,160	5,584	358.7	1.4	8,375	−0.4	9,064	−0.1
1993–94	231.5	5,327	5,767	366.4	2.1	8,429	0.6	9,126	0.7
1994–95	243.9	5,529	5,989	375.1	2.4	8,504	0.9	9,212	0.9
1995–96	255.1	5,689	6,147	382.0	1.8	8,519	0.2	9,205	−0.1
1996–97	270.2	5,923	6,393	393.3	3.0	8,624	1.2	9,307	1.1
1997–98	285.5	6,189	6,676	408.4	3.8	8,853	2.7	9,549	2.6
1998–99	302.9	6,508	7,013	425.9	4.3	9,151	3.4	9,861	3.3
1999–2000	323.9	6,912	7,394	442.6	3.9	9,446	3.2	10,104	2.5
2000–01	348.4	7,380	7,904	460.3	4.0	9,751	3.2	10,443	3.4
2001–02	368.4	7,727	8,259	478.3	3.9	10,033	2.9	10,723	2.7
2002–03	387.6	8,044	8,610	492.4	3.0	10,219	1.9	10,938	2.0
2003–04	403.4	8,310	8,900	501.5	1.8	10,332	1.1	11,064	1.2
2004–05	425.0	8,711	9,316	513.0	2.3	10,513	1.8	11,243	1.6
2005–06	449.1	9,145	9,778	522.2	1.8	10,632	1.1	11,368	1.1
2006–07	476.8	9,679	10,336	540.4	3.5	10,969	3.2	11,714	3.0
2007–08	506.9	10,298	10,982	553.9	2.5	11,254	2.6	12,001	2.5
2008–09	518.9	10,540	11,239	559.3	1.0	11,359	0.9	12,113	0.9
2009–10	524.7	10,636	11,427	560.1	0.1	11,353	−0.1	12,198	0.7
2010–11	527.2	10,658	11,418	551.6	−1.5	11,153	−1.8	11,948	−2.0
2011–12[c]	527.5	10,650	11,400	536.3	−2.8	10,830	−2.9	11,590	−3.0
2012–13[c]	542.2	10,920	11,680	542.2	1.1	10,920	0.8	11,680	0.8
2013–14[c]	556.6	11,190	11,970	548.4	1.1	11,020	0.9	11,790	0.9
2014–15[c]	576.8	11,590	12,400	558.8	1.9	11,230	1.9	12,020	1.9
2015–16[c]	—	—	—	570.0	2.0	11,440	1.8	12,240	1.8
2016–17[c]	—	—	—	582.8	2.2	11,670	2.0	12,480	2.0
2017–18[c]	—	—	—	598.3	2.7	11,900	2.0	12,730	2.0
2018–19[c]	—	—	—	610.7	2.1	12,080	1.5	12,930	1.5
2019–20[c]	—	—	—	622.4	1.9	12,240	1.3	13,100	1.3
2020–21[c]	—	—	—	633.0	1.7	12,370	1.0	13,240	1.0
2021–22[c]	—	—	—	643.2	1.6	12,490	1.0	13,370	1.0
2022–23[c]	—	—	—	654.2	1.7	12,630	1.1	13,510	1.1
2023–24[c]	—	—	—	662.9	1.3	12,720	0.7	13,610	0.7

—Not available.
[a]Unadjusted (or "current") dollars have not been adjusted to compensate for inflation.
[b]Constant dollars based on the consumer price index, prepared by the Bureau of Labor Statistics, U.S. Department of Labor, adjusted to a school-year basis.
[c]Projected.
Note: Current expenditures include instruction, support services, food services, and enterprise operations. Some data have been revised from previously published figures.

SOURCE: "Table 236.15. Current Expenditures and Current Expenditures per Pupil in Public Elementary and Secondary Schools: 1989–90 through 2023–24," in *Digest of Education Statistics, 2013*, U.S. Department of Education, Institute of Education Sciences, National Center for Education Statistics, 2014, https://nces.ed.gov/programs/digest/d13/tables/dt13_236.15.asp (accessed February 6, 2017)

because of space constraints. Opponents of increasing public school funding suggest that more money does not create a better education—better teachers do. To support their argument, they point to the increase in spending per pupil while some measures of academic achievement remain low.

PREPRIMARY SCHOOL
Preprimary Growth

Participating in early childhood programs such as nursery school, Head Start, prekindergarten, and kindergarten helps prepare children for the academic challenges of first grade. In contrast to declining elementary and secondary school enrollment between 1970 and 1980, preprimary enrollment showed substantial growth, as reported by Thomas D. Snyder and Cristobal de Brey of the National Center for Education Statistics (NCES) in *Digest of Education Statistics 2014* (April 2016, https://nces.ed.gov/pubs2016/2016006.pdf), increasing from 4.1 million in 1970 to 4.9 million in 1980. By 2013 enrollment had grown to 7.9 million.

The percentage of all children aged three to five years enrolled in preprimary programs also increased substantially between 1965 and 2010. In 1965, 27.1% of three- to five-year-olds were enrolled in nursery school or kindergarten. Snyder and de Brey report that by 2013, 60.3% of three- to five-year-olds were enrolled in full-day and 39.7% in part-day programs.

Preschool enrollment rates are correlated with parents' educational attainment. In 2014 the enrollment rate of children in preprimary programs whose parents had not earned a high school diploma was 28%. (See Figure 6.3.) The enrollment rate of children whose parents had a high school diploma or equivalent was 32%, for those whose parents had advanced beyond high school to vocational/technical training or some college it

was 35%, for those whose parents had an associate's degree it was 38%, for those whose parents had a bachelor's degree it was 43%, and for those whose parents had any graduate or professional school it was 49%. These percentages likely reflect three things: parents with higher educational levels are more likely to continue working after becoming parents, they are better able to pay for preprimary programs, and they value the educational benefits of preprimary programs for their children.

Head Start

The Head Start program, which was established as part of the Economic Opportunity Act of 1964, is one of the most durable and successful federal programs for low-income and at-risk children. Directed by the Administration for Children and Families, Head Start aims to improve the social competence, learning skills, health, and nutrition of children from low-income households, so they can begin school on a more level footing with children from higher-income households. Regulations require that 90% of children enrolled in Head Start be from low-income households.

The Administration for Children and Families notes in *Office of Head Start—Services Snapshot* (2014, https://eclkc.ohs.acf.hhs.gov/hslc/data/psr/2014/NATIONAL_SNAPSHOT_ALL_PROGRAMS.pdf) that in 2013–14,

FIGURE 6.3

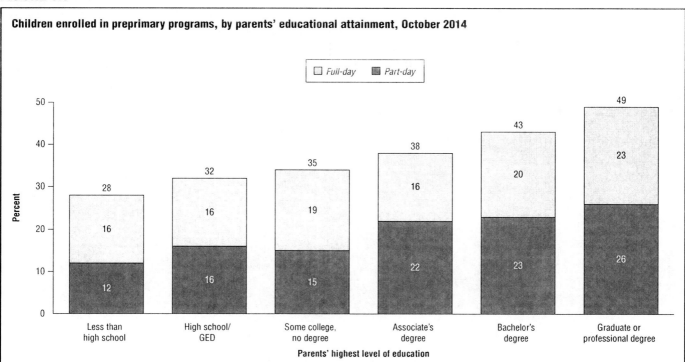

Children enrolled in preprimary programs, by parents' educational attainment, October 2014

Note: Enrollment data include only those children in preschool programs and do not include those enrolled in kindergarten or primary programs. Parents' highest level of education is defined as the highest level of education attained by the most educated parent who lives in the household with the child. Data are based on sample surveys of the civilian noninstitutionalized population. Detail may not sum to totals because of rounding.

SOURCE: Grace Kena et al., "Figure 5. Percentage of 3- to 5-Year Old Children Enrolled in Preschool Programs, by Parents' Highest Level of Education and Attendance Status, October 2014," in *The Condition of Education 2016*, U.S. Department of Education, National Center for Education Statistics, May 2016, https://nces.ed.gov/pubs2016/2016144.pdf (accessed January 7, 2017)

nearly 1 million children were served by Head Start programs. Of the children and families served, 43% were white, 29% were African American, 10% were multiracial, 4% were Native American or Alaskan Native, 2% were Asian American or Pacific Islander, and 13% were of an unspecified or other race. In addition, 38% were of Hispanic ethnicity. A significant portion (12%) of enrolled children had disabilities, including developmental disabilities, health impairments, visual or hearing impairments, emotional disturbances, speech and language impairments, orthopedic handicaps, and learning disabilities.

ELEMENTARY AND SECONDARY SCHOOL
Enrollment

All U.S. states require students to attend school through at least the age of 16 years; therefore, preprimary, elementary, and secondary school enrollments reflect the number of births over a specified period. Because of the baby boom following World War II (1939–1945), school enrollment grew rapidly during the 1950s and 1960s, when those children reached school age. Elementary enrollment reached a then-record high in 1969, as did high school enrollment in 1971.

During the late 1960s the birth rate began to decline, resulting in steadily falling school enrollment. An echo effect occurred during the late 1970s and early 1980s,

when those born during the baby boom began their own families. This echo effect triggered an increase in school enrollment starting in the mid-1980s. In 1985 public elementary and secondary school enrollment increased for the first time since 1971. It continued to increase in the following years. Kena et al. report that total public school enrollment reached 50 million in 2013 and is projected to increase to 51.4 million in 2025–26. (See Figure 6.4.)

Private Schools

Enrollment in public schools far surpasses enrollment in private schools. The NCES indicates in "Private School Enrollment" (May 2016, https://nces.ed.gov/programs/coe/indicator_cgc.asp) that the proportion of students enrolled in private elementary and secondary schools decreased to 10% in 2013–14 from 12% in 1995–96 and is expected to decrease to 9% in 2025–26.

RELIGIOUS SCHOOLS. In "United States Catholic Elementary and Secondary Schools, 2015–2016: The Annual Statistical Report on Schools, Enrollment, and Staffing" (2016, http://www.ncea.org/NCEA/Proclaim/Catholic _School_Data/Catholic_School_Data.aspx), the National Catholic Educational Association reports that in 2015 there were 6,525 Catholic schools in the United States with roughly 2 million students.

Kena et al. report that the numbers of students enrolled in conservative Christian (707,000) and affiliated religious

FIGURE 6.4

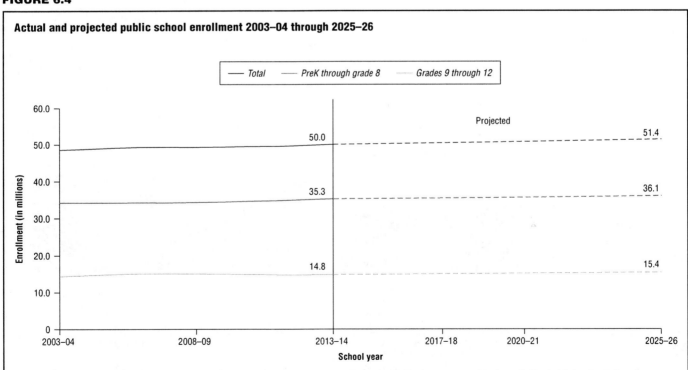

Actual and projected public school enrollment 2003–04 through 2025–26

SOURCE: Grace Kena et al., "Figure 1. Actual and Projected Public School Enrollment in Prekindergarten (PreK) through Grade 12, by Grade Level: Selected School Years 2003–04 through 2025–26," in *The Condition of Education 2016*, U.S. Department of Education, National Center for Education Statistics, May 2016, https://nces.ed.gov/pubs2016/2016144.pdf (accessed January 7, 2017)

(565,000) schools in 2013–14 were lower than in 2003–04, whereas the 758,000 students enrolled in unaffiliated religious schools (schools with a religious orientation that are not classified as Catholic or conservative Christian) represented an increase in enrollment from 2003–04.

Dropping Out

DROPOUT RATES. Status dropouts are people aged 16 to 24 years who have not finished high school and are not enrolled in school. Kena et al. report that status dropout rates decreased from 1990, when 12% of young people were status dropouts, to 2014, when 6.5% were status dropouts. In 2014 the Hispanic status dropout rate, 10.6%, was considerably higher than that of non-Hispanic African Americans (7.4%) or non-Hispanic whites (5.2%). (See Figure 6.5.)

Dropout rates also vary greatly according to family income. In 2014 nearly 12% of people aged 16 to 24 years who were from families that had the lowest quartile incomes (the lowest 25% of incomes) had dropped out of school. (See Figure 6.6.) This was four times the dropout rate (2.8%) of 16- to 24-year-olds whose families had the highest quartile incomes.

RETURNING TO SCHOOL OR GETTING AN ALTERNATIVE DIPLOMA. The decision to drop out of high school does not necessarily mean the end of a young person's education. Many former students return to school to get their diploma or to take the test necessary to obtain an alternative credential or degree, such as a general equivalency diploma (GED). The GED Testing Service reports in *2013 Annual Statistical Report on the GED Test* (2014, http://www.gedtestingservice.com/uploads/files/5b49fc887db0c075da20a68b17d313cd.pdf) that in 2013, 560,000 people passed GED tests. Nearly two-thirds (64%) of test takers cited an educational reason for pursuing the certification; many people who earn a GED continue their education by earning associate's, bachelor's, or advanced degrees.

Special Populations

STUDENTS WITH DISABILITIES. In 1976 Congress passed the Education of the Handicapped Act, which required schools to develop programs for children with

FIGURE 6.5

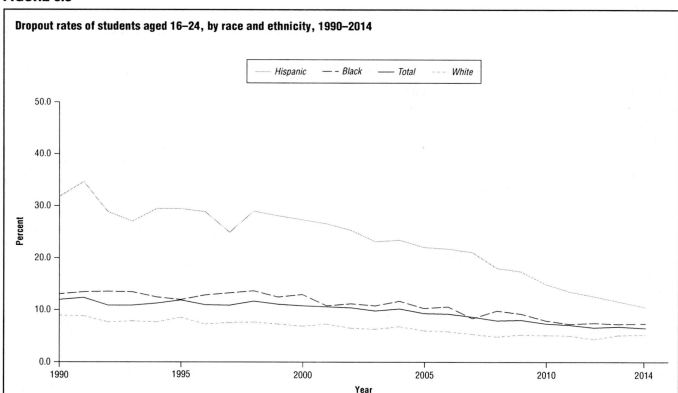

Dropout rates of students aged 16–24, by race and ethnicity, 1990–2014

Note: The "status dropout rate" is the percentage of 16- to 24-year-olds who are not enrolled in school and have not earned a high school credential (either a diploma or an equivalency credential such as a GED certificate). Data are based on sample surveys of the civilian noninstitutionalized population, which excludes persons in prisons, persons in the military, and other persons not living in households. Data for all races include other racial/ethnic categories not separately shown. Race categories exclude persons of Hispanic ethnicity.

SOURCE: Grace Kena et al., "Figure 2. Status Dropout Rates of 16- to 24-Year-Olds, by Race/Ethnicity: 1990 through 2014," in *The Condition of Education 2016*, U.S. Department of Education, National Center for Education Statistics, May 2016, https://nces.ed.gov/pubs2016/2016144.pdf (accessed January 7, 2017)

FIGURE 6.6

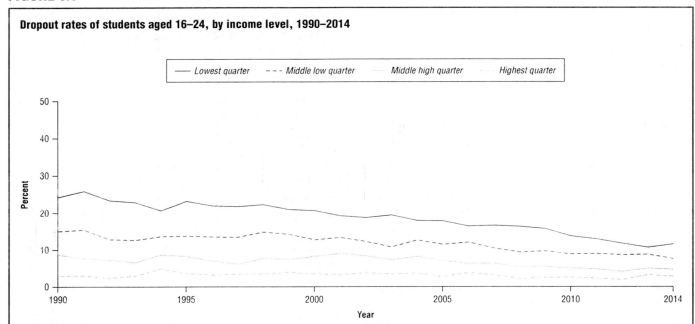

Dropout rates of students aged 16–24, by income level, 1990–2014

— Lowest quarter   - - - Middle low quarter   ⋯ Middle high quarter   ⋯ Highest quarter

Note: The "status dropout rate" is the percentage of 16- to 24-year-olds who are not enrolled in school and have not earned a high school credential (either a diploma or an equivalency credential such as a GED certificate). The "lowest" quarter represents the bottom 25 percent of family incomes. The "middle low" quarter represents families between the 25th percentile and the median (50th percentile). The "middle high" quarter represents families with incomes between the median (50th percentile) and the 75th percentile. The "highest" quarter represents the top 25 percent of all family incomes. Data are based on sample surveys of the civilian noninstitutionalized population, which excludes persons in prisons, persons in the military, and other persons not living in households.

SOURCE: Grace Kena et al., "Figure 3. Status Dropout Rates of 16- to 24-Year-Olds, by Income Level: 1990 through 2014," in *The Condition of Education 2016*, U.S. Department of Education, National Center for Education Statistics, May 2016, https://nces.ed.gov/pubs2016/2016144.pdf (accessed January 7, 2017)

disabilities. Formerly, parents of many students with disabilities had few options other than institutionalization or nursing care. The Education of the Handicapped Act required that children with disabilities be placed in the "least restrictive environment," which led to increased efforts to educate them in regular classrooms (known as mainstreaming). The law defined *handicapped* as children who were intellectually disabled, hard of hearing or deaf, orthopedically impaired, speech- and language-impaired, visually impaired, seriously emotionally disturbed, or otherwise health-impaired. It also included children with specific learning disabilities who require special education and related services.

In 1990 the Individuals with Disabilities Education Act was passed. This reauthorized and expanded the earlier Education of the Handicapped Act. It added autism and traumatic brain injury to the list of disabilities covered by the law, and amendments added in 1992 and 1997 increased coverage for infants and toddlers and for children with attention-deficit disorder and attention-deficit/hyperactivity disorder. The law required public school systems to develop an Individualized Education Program for each child with disabilities, reflecting the needs of individual students. In December 2004 the Individuals with Disabilities Education Improvement Act was signed into law by President George W. Bush (1946–),

which reauthorized the Individuals with Disabilities Education Act and brought it in line with the provisions of the NCLB.

Because of legislation that enforces their rights, more children with disabilities have been served in public schools. Between SY 1990–91 and SY 2004–05 enrollment of students with disabilities grew from 4.7 million (11% of total public school enrollment) to 6.7 million (14% of total public school enrollment). In 2013–14, the number of students served fell to 6.5 million (13% of total public school enrollment). Of students served under the Individuals with Disabilities Education Act, about one-third (35%) had a specific learning disability and one-fifth (21%) had a speech or language impairment. (See Figure 6.7.)

HOMELESS CHILDREN. Homelessness harms children in many ways, including hindering their ability to attend and succeed in school. Homeless children have difficulty with transportation to school, maintaining necessary documents, and attaining privacy needed for homework, sleep, and interaction with parents. Compared with children who are poor but housed, homeless children miss more days of school, more often repeat a grade, and are more often put into special education classes.

The McKinney-Vento Homeless Assistance Act of 1987 required in Title VII, subtitle B, that each state

FIGURE 6.7

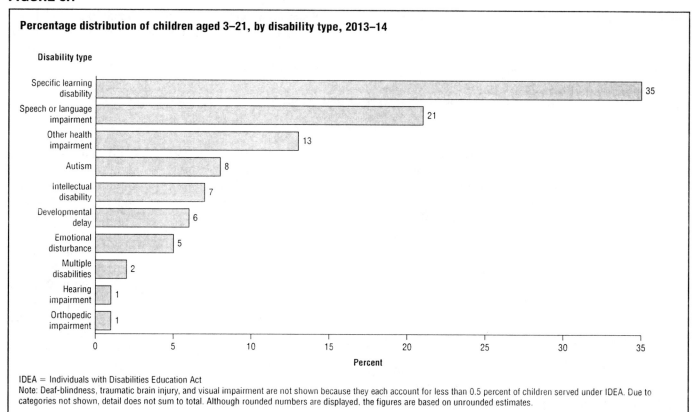

Percentage distribution of children aged 3–21, by disability type, 2013–14

IDEA = Individuals with Disabilities Education Act

Note: Deaf-blindness, traumatic brain injury, and visual impairment are not shown because they each account for less than 0.5 percent of children served under IDEA. Due to categories not shown, detail does not sum to total. Although rounded numbers are displayed, the figures are based on unrounded estimates.

SOURCE: Grace Kena et al., "Figure 1. Percentage Distribution of Children Ages 3–21 Served under the Individuals with Disabilities Education Act (IDEA). Part B, by Disability Type: School Year 2013–14," in *The Condition of Education 2016*, U.S. Department of Education, National Center for Education Statistics, May 2016, https://nces.ed.gov/pubs2016/2016144.pdf (accessed January 7, 2017)

provide "free, appropriate, public education" to homeless youth. The law further required that all states develop a plan to address the denial of access to education experienced by homeless children.

The McKinney-Vento Homeless Education Assistance Improvements Act of 2001 went further to address inequities that affect homeless children in the public-school system. New guidance for states and school systems released by the U.S. Department of Education in April 2003 noted the main differences between the old and new programs:

- Homeless children may no longer be segregated in a separate program on the basis of their homeless status.

- Schools must immediately enroll homeless students even if they are missing some of the documentation normally required.

- Upon parental request, states and school districts must provide transportation for homeless children to the school they attended before they became homeless.

- School districts must designate a local liaison for homeless children and youths.

HOMESCHOOLED CHILDREN. Some parents choose to teach their children at home. Brian D. Ray of the NCES

reports in "Research Facts on Homeschooling" (March 23, 2016, https://www.nheri.org/research/research-facts-on-homeschooling.html) that the most common motivation is to "customize or individualize the curriculum and learning environment for each child." Ray reports that approximately 2.3 million children were homeschooled in 2014–15, up from 2 million in 2010.

States have differing requirements for parents who teach their children at home. According to the Homeschool Legal Defense Association (2017, https://www.hslda.org/laws/default.asp), some states, such as Idaho and New Jersey, give parents the right to educate their children as they see fit, and impose only minor controls or none at all. Other states have stricter regulations. Highly regulated states, such as New York, Pennsylvania, and Vermont, require parents to obtain and use approved curriculum, submit achievement test scores, or meet qualification requirements. Critics of homeschooling argue that parents may not be qualified to be teachers, but proponents believe that parents can gain teaching skills through experience, just as other teachers do.

HIGHER EDUCATION: OFF TO COLLEGE

Formal schooling beyond high school is increasingly viewed as a necessity, not only for young people's development but also for their economic success. Many parents consider supporting their children to attend college to be a financial priority and responsibility.

College Entrance Examinations

Most students who want to enter a college or university in the United States must take either the ACT (formerly American College Testing) or the SAT (once known as the Scholastic Aptitude Test, then the Scholastic Assessment Test, now simply the SAT) as part of their admission requirements. The ACT is a curriculum-based achievement test, measuring proficiency in reading, math, English, and science, whereas the SAT is the primary admissions test to measure a student's mathematical skills, verbal reasoning, and writing ability in a way intended to assess readiness for college. Students who take these tests usually plan to continue their education beyond high school; therefore, these tests do not profile all high school students.

MORE STUDENTS ARE TAKING SAT AND ACT EXAMS, WITH MIXED RESULTS. Performance on the SAT is measured on a scale of 200 to 800 for each of three sections, with the established average score being about 500 for each. According to the College Board, the SAT benchmark score of 1550 signals a 65% chance of achieving a B− average or higher during the first year of college, which research suggests is a strong predictor of college success and earning an undergraduate degree. Fewer than half (43%) of SAT test takers in the high school class of 2014 met the SAT benchmark. The College Board indicates that students who meet the benchmark are more likely than those who do not to enroll in a four-year college, 78% versus 46%, respectively. Similarly, 56% of students who meet the benchmark complete their degree within four years, compared with 27% of those who did not meet the benchmark.

The College Board notes in *Class of 2016 SAT Results* (September 2016, https://reports.collegeboard.org/sat-suite-program-results/class-of-2016-results) that in 2016 nearly 1.7 million students took the SAT. For the class of 2016, the average scores were 494 for reading, 508 for math, and 482 for writing.

According to ACT, Inc., in *The Condition of College and Career Readiness 2016* (August 24, 2016, http://www.act.org/content/act/en/newsroom/act-scores-down-for-2016-us-grad-class-due-to-increased-percentage-of-students-tested.html), nearly 2.1 million students took the ACT in 2016, representing 64% of all high school graduates that year. The ACT's four subject tests are scored on a scale of one to 36, with 36 being the highest possible score. ACT College Readiness Benchmarks are the scores for each test that indicate a student has at least a 50% chance of earning a B grade or higher, or a 75% chance of earning a C grade or higher, in first-year

college courses in the subjects covered by that test. ACT research demonstrates that students meeting three or four ACT College Readiness Benchmarks are very likely to be successful in first-year college courses. In 2016, 38% of the graduates tested met three benchmarks and just 34% did not meet any of the benchmarks, indicating that they may be very challenged in first-year college courses.

DO TEST SCORES ACCURATELY PREDICT ACADEMIC SUCCESS? Although the College Board and ACT, Inc., claim that exam scores correlate with academic success in college, some educators take issue with this assertion. Lyndsey Layton and Emma Brown report in "SAT Reading Scores Hit a Four-Decade Low" (WashingtonPost.com, September 24, 2012) that there are concerns the SAT favors middle-class and wealthier students because average SAT test scores increase with each additional $20,000 in family income. They also observe that the disappointing 2012 test scores raise questions about the success of the decade-long NCLB effort to raise test scores. In "Beyond Correlations: Usefulness of High School GPA and Test Scores in Making College Admissions Decisions" (*Applied Measurement in Education*, vol. 26, no. 2, 2013), Richard Sawyer asserts that high school grade point average (GPA) is better than test scores in terms of predicting first-year college GPA but observes that in some instances such as predicting high levels of academic success, the ACT score may be better. Sawyer concludes that in most instances, using high school grades and ACT together has better predictive value than either alone.

Projected Enrollment

In the NCES publication *Projections of Education Statistics to 2023* (April 2016, https://nces.ed.gov/pubs2015/2015073.pdf), William J. Hussar and Tabitha M. Bailey project enrollment in institutions of higher education to rise through 2023. This is due not only to large numbers of students who are college age but also to the increasing number of people of all ages who seek advanced learning. Enrollment in degree-granting postsecondary institutions is expected to increase 15% from 2012 to 2023.

Community College Enrollment and the Great Recession

During times of economic distress, people often turn to community colleges for job retraining or to learn different skills to pursue new careers. This trend was observed during the Great Recession of 2007–09. In "The Financial Crisis and College Enrollment: How Have Students and Their Families Responded?" (Jeffrey Brown and Caroline Hoxby, eds., *How the Great Recession Affected Higher Education*, 2013), Bridget Terry Long analyzes data from the Integrated Postsecondary

Education Data System, an annual survey of colleges and universities to determine how college attendance was influenced by the recession. Long finds that college attendance increased, especially in states hardest hit by unemployment and declining home values; however, it was part-time enrollment that increased while full-time enrollment actually decreased.

The American Association of Community Colleges reports in "2016 Community College Fact Sheet" (February 2016, http://www.aacc.nche.edu/AboutCC/Documents/AACCFactSheetsR2.pdf) that in 2016, nearly half of all undergraduate students attended community colleges. In 2016 there were 1,108 community colleges. The association estimates that more than 12 million students attended the nation's community colleges during SY 2014–15. On average, students were 28 years of age, and 36% of students were the first generation in their family to attend college. In SY 2011–12, 22% of community college students worked full time, 17% were single parents, and 12% were students with disabilities.

College Costs

In 2016 paying for a college education, even at public four-year institutions, ranked as one of the costliest investments for families in the United States. The NCES indicates in "Fast Facts: Back to School Statistics" (August 2016, https://nces.ed.gov/fastfacts/display.asp?id=372) that in SY 2014–15 the average annual in-state cost at a public four-year institution, including tuition and room and board, was $16,188. For one year at a private, nonprofit four-year institution, the average cost for tuition and room and board was $41,970; at a private for-profit institution it was $23,372. The College Board reports in "Trends in College Prices" (2017, https://trends.collegeboard.org/college-pricing/figures-tables/average-published-undergraduate-charges-sector-2016-17#Key%20Points) that in SY 2016–17 average tuition and fees rose more for out-of-state students than for in-state students; the out-of-state premium increased by 4.3%, from $14,650 to $15,280. Average tuition and fees of $33,480 at private, nonprofit four-year institutions were $8,550 (34%) higher than the average public four-year out-of-state price, and average charges, including tuition, fees, and room and board of $45,370 in the private sector were $10,000 (28%) higher than the same costs at the out-of-state rate at a public four-year institution.

Because it is often difficult for students to accurately predict college costs and future indebtedness as a result of student loans, the U.S. Department of Education created a "College Scorecard" (2015, https://collegescorecard.ed.gov) that enables individuals to learn about a college's "affordability and value," so they can make more informed choices about which college to attend.

FINANCIAL ASSISTANCE FOR STUDENTS. According to the NCES (2016, https://nces.ed.gov/fastfacts/display.asp?id=31), during the 2013–14 academic year, 85% of full-time undergraduates enrolled in postsecondary institutions were receiving some type of financial aid (e.g., grants, loans, or work-study programs) from federal, state, institutional, or other sources to meet their educational expenses. More than half (56%) of full-time undergraduates received some form of federal assistance, and 49% received some type of nonfederal aid. (Some students received aid from both federal and nonfederal sources.) Federal assistance that goes directly to students includes Pell Grants (the annual maximum was increased to $5,815 for the 2016–17 academic year), the Stafford Student Loan Program (ranges from an annual maximum loan of $5,500 per year for dependent freshmen to $12,500 for independent juniors or seniors), and Supplemental Educational Opportunity Grants (which range from $100 to $4,000 per year).

A national study of college students and parents conducted by Ipsos Public Affairs for the financial services company Sallie Mae, *How America Pays for College 2016* (2016, http://news.salliemae.com/files/doc_library/file/HowAmericaPaysforCollege2016FNL.pdf), finds that families with students spent an average of $23,688 on college in 2015–16. The average amount spent for students at four-year private colleges was $41,762; at four-year public colleges, it was $23,290.

Out-of-pocket contributions by families covered 41% of student costs for college in 2015–16; student loans were used to pay 13% of costs, and parent borrowing covered 7% of costs. About 70% of students relied on scholarship and grant funding, with about one-quarter using both. The majority (85%) of families filed a Free Application for Federal Student Aid; half of college students had scholarships, and 47% received grant money.

As reported in *How America Pays for College 2016*, two-thirds of families (67%) considered the price of a college when deciding where students should apply, and 44% waited to receive financial aid awards before choosing which school to attend. Thirty percent of students and 24% of parents said cost was "the primary driver for choosing the school they attend." Many families took one or more steps to save money, such as choosing in-state schools with lower tuition (80%). Other strategies students used to reduce costs included living at home (49%), working (77%), reducing personal spending (62%), and earning their degrees in shorter periods than their programs typically take (27%). Others opted to live closer to home (61%) or at home/with relatives (54%), file for education tax credits (42%), live with a roommate (41%), or accelerate the pace of coursework (28%).

AMERICAN OPPORTUNITY TAX CREDIT. The Obama administration included the American Opportunity Tax

Credit in the ARRA. This credit allowed students or their parents to receive a federal income tax refund of up to $2,500 per year in college costs for the tax years 2009 through 2017. The full amount was available to Americans whose adjusted gross income was $80,000 or less ($160,000 or less for joint filers). The credit is reduced if a taxpayer's modified adjusted gross income exceeds those amounts. Taxpayers whose modified adjusted gross income exceeds $90,000 ($180,000 for joint filers) cannot claim the credit.

EDUCATIONAL ATTAINMENT AND EARNINGS

The educational attainment of the U.S. population has risen steadily since the 1940s. In "Fast Facts: Degrees Conferred by Race and Sex" (2015, https://nces.ed.gov/fastfacts/display.asp?id=72), the NCES states that from 2002 to 2013, educational attainment rates increased at all levels of certification and degrees. The number of certificates conferred grew 49%, from 646,000 in 2002 to 966,000 in 2013; associate's degrees increased 59%, from 634,000 to 1 million, and 36% more bachelor's degrees were granted (1.3 million to 1.8 million). Forty-five percent more master's degrees (519,000 in 2002 to 752,000 in 2013) and 44% more doctorate level degrees (122,000 to 175,000) were awarded.

Education is a good investment because earning levels rise with increased education. In "Work-Life Earnings by Field of Degree and Occupation for People with a Bachelor's Degree: 2011" (October 2012, https://www.census.gov/prod/2012pubs/acsbr11-04.pdf), Tiffany Julian of the U.S. Census Bureau observes that "educational attainment is by far the most important social characteristic for predicting earnings."

Interestingly, Michael T. French et al. find that high school GPA not only predicts educational attainment but also earnings in adulthood. In "What You Do in High School Matters: High School GPA, Educational Attainment, and Labor Market Earnings as a Young Adult" (*Eastern Economic Journal*, May 19, 2014), French et al. find that students with higher high school GPAs consistently earned more than their peers with lower GPAs.

The Census Bureau calculates Synthetic Work-Life Earnings (SWE), which estimate the amount of money a person might expect to make over the course of a 40-year career. SWE estimates do not aim to predict individual earnings and make assumptions that may not be realistic for everyone (e.g., full-time, year-round employment for 40 years). The purpose of SWE estimates is to illustrate potential differences in earnings based on factors such as education and occupation over the course of a person's work life. For example, the difference between earning $60,000 per year and $72,500 per year might not seem particularly large, but over a 40-year work life it is $500,000. Using SWE estimates helps show how relatively small differences in annual income add up over the course of a person's work life.

Julian notes that educational attainment dramatically influences SWE. People who attain no more than an eighth-grade education have SWE of $936,000; for those who graduate from high school it increases to $1.4 million. An associate's degree increases SWE to $1.8 million, and a bachelor's degree brings it to $2.4 million. Individuals with a master's degree have SWE of $2.8 million. Those with doctorate degrees have SWE of $3.5 million. Professional degrees such as law or medical degrees offer the highest SWE, at $4.2 million.

CHAPTER 7
JUVENILE CRIME AND VICTIMIZATION

THE UNIFORM CRIME REPORTS AND THE NATIONAL CRIME VICTIMIZATION SURVEY

Two main government sources collect crime statistics in the United States: the Federal Bureau of Investigation (FBI) and the Bureau of Justice Statistics (BJS). The FBI compiles the annual Uniform Crime Reporting (UCR) Program. The FBI notes in *Crime in the United States, 2015* (September 26, 2016, https://ucr.fbi.gov/crime-in -the-u.s/2015/crime-in-the-u.s.-2015) that the UCR began in 1930 and now collects data from more than 18,000 city, county, and state law enforcement agencies.

The second set of crime statistics is the National Crime Victimization Survey (NCVS), which is prepared by the BJS. Since 1973 the annual survey measures the levels of victimization resulting from criminal activity in the United States. According to the BJS, in "Data Collection: National Crime Victimization Survey" (2015, https:// www.bjs.gov/index.cfm?ty=dcdetail&iid=245), the survey collects data from a nationally representative sample of approximately 90,000 households each year on the "frequency, characteristics and consequences of criminal victimization in the United States."

The NCVS complements the UCR. It measures the levels of criminal victimization of people and households for the crimes of rape, robbery, assault, burglary, motor vehicle theft, and larceny. Murder is not included because the NCVS data are gathered through interviews with victims. Definitions for these crimes are the same as those established by the UCR.

Some observers believe the NCVS is a better indicator of the volume of crime in the United States than the UCR. Nonetheless, like all surveys, it is subject to error. The survey depends on people's memories of incidents that happened up to six months earlier. Many times, a victim is not certain what happened, even moments after the crime occurred. In addition, the NCVS limits the data to victims aged 12 years and older, an admittedly arbitrary age selection.

CRIME TRENDS
Violent and Property Crimes

Jennifer L. Truman and Rachel E. Morgan of the BJS report in *Criminal Victimization, 2015* (October 2016, https://www.bjs.gov/content/pub/pdf/cv15.pdf) that in 2015 U.S. residents experienced 5 million violent victimizations and 14.6 million property crimes (burglary, motor vehicle theft, and theft).

According to Truman and Morgan, in 2015 the rate of violent crime was 20.1 violent incidents per 1,000 people aged 12 years and older, down from 23.2 per 1,000 in 2013. Victimization rates for rape, sexual assault, and robbery were essentially unchanged during this period. The rate of violent crime was much lower in 2015 than it was roughly two decades earlier. The violent crime victimization rate stood at 79.8 in 1993, more than three times the 20.1 rate in 2015. The rate of property crime decreased from 118.1 victimizations per 1,000 households in 2014 to 110.7 per 1,000 households in 2015.

The UCR cataloged 1,197,704 million violent crimes (including murder, nonnegligent manslaughter, rape, robbery, and aggravated assault) in 2015, up 3.9% from the 2014 estimate. According to the UCR, there were an estimated 8 million property crimes (including burglary, larceny-theft, and motor vehicle theft) in 2015, down 2.6% from 2014. This decline continued a long-term trend. The property crime rate decreased 20.2% from 2006 to 2015.

Trends in Juvenile Crime

In *Juvenile Offenders and Victims: 2014 National Report* (December 2014, https://www.ojjdp.gov/ojstatbb/ nr2014/downloads/NR2014.pdf), Melissa Sickmund and Charles Puzzanchera observe that in 2010 U.S. law enforcement agencies arrested 1.6 million youth under the age of 18 years. Still, juvenile arrests in 2010 were at their lowest levels in 30 years and for most offenses, juvenile arrests fell proportionately more than adult arrests between 2001 and 2010.

Sickmund and Puzzanchera report that after 10 years of declines between 1994 and 2004, juvenile arrests for violent offenses increased between 2004 and 2006 but then declined each year through 2010. In 2010 the number of juvenile arrests was 21% fewer than the number of arrests in 2001. Nevertheless, the late 20th-century surge in youth crime and violence caused much concern in society. Various groups, both public and private, undertook the mission of trying to uncover the reasons juvenile crime was on the rise. Lawmakers responded by toughening existing laws and finding ways to try more juveniles as adults, and courts levied stricter sentences. (See Chapter 10.)

JUVENILE OFFENDERS

For some young people, the teenage and young adult years are difficult and challenging times. While their peers are playing sports, going to proms, participating in school activities, heading to college, and making plans for the future, some juveniles and youths are, for a variety of reasons, committing crimes and having brushes with the law. A juvenile delinquent is someone who has committed a crime but is below the age at which an individual carries adult responsibilities and can be sentenced as an adult. When dealing with young offenders, each state has its own definition of the term *juvenile*: most states put the upper age limit at 17 years of age, although some states set it as low as 14 years of age.

When reporting its national crime statistics, the FBI considers those under the age of 18 years to be juveniles. The FBI often divides its juvenile crime statistics into age-based subcategories, such as aged 16 years and older and aged 15 years and younger, to demonstrate how juvenile offenses vary by age. The FBI does the same with youth, who are often defined as those aged 18 to 24 years. Some organizations and studies, however, classify youth age ranges differently, citing youths as those aged 18 to 21 years or aged 18 to 25 years.

The U.S. Department of Justice (DOJ) defines crime as all behaviors and acts for which society provides formally approved punishments. Written law, both federal and state, defines which behaviors are criminal. Some actions, such as murder, robbery, and burglary, have always been considered criminal. Others, such as domestic violence or driving under the influence of drugs or alcohol, were more recently classified as criminal actions. Other changes in society have also influenced crime. For example, the widespread use of computers provides new opportunities for white-collar cybercrime, such as identity theft and the malicious spread of computer viruses and worms.

Crime can range from actions as simple as taking a candy bar from a store without paying for it, to those as severe and violent as murder. Most people have broken some law, wittingly or unwittingly, at some time during their life. Therefore, the true extent of criminality is impossible to measure. Researchers can only analyze crime reported by victims or known to law enforcement authorities.

Risk Factors for Youth Violence and Delinquency

Various government entities, schools, student and parent organizations, and research groups have devoted countless hours to the issue of youth violence. One of their goals is to find ways to recognize the potential for violent behavior in youth before it becomes a serious problem. They work individually and sometimes collectively to outline trends in youth violence and to determine which factors lead to violent behavior.

The Centers for Disease Control and Prevention (CDC) outlines the risk factors that increase the likelihood that a young person will become violent in the fact sheet "Understanding Youth Violence" (2015, https://www.cdc.gov/violenceprevention/pdf/yv-factsheet-a.pdf). These factors include a history of violent victimization or prior violence; drug, alcohol, or tobacco use; association with delinquent peers; a dysfunctional family life; poor grades; and poverty in the family or community. The CDC recommends several approaches to stopping youth violence, including programs to improve family relationships, teaching children nonviolent means for resolving social problems, role modeling through mentoring programs, and changes to physical and social environments to address the social and economic causes of violence.

In "Fact Sheet: Juvenile Delinquency" (September 2008, https://aspe.hhs.gov/pdf-report/what-challenges-are-boys-facing-and-what-opportunities-exist-address-those-challenges-fact-sheet-juvenile-delinquency), the U.S. Department of Health and Human Services outlines individual, familial, and community risk factors for juvenile delinquency among boys. Individual risk factors include early aggressive behavior, concentration problems, drug or alcohol abuse, association with antisocial peers, and too much unstructured leisure time. Familial risk factors include childhood maltreatment, dysfunctional parenting, lack of supervision, and parental criminality. Community risk factors include exposure to community violence and poverty.

Margaret A. Zahn et al. examine the risk factors for girls' delinquency in *Girls Study Group: Understanding and Responding to Girls' Delinquency* (April 2010, https://www.ncjrs.gov/pdffiles1/ojjdp/226358.pdf). The researchers point out that certain types of trauma (particularly sexual abuse) occur more often among delinquent girls. Mental disorders diagnosed among girls that result from trauma, such as depression, anxiety, and post-traumatic stress disorder, have a strong relationship to female delinquency. Other risk factors include physical abuse, early onset of puberty, inconsistent or lax parental supervision, parental criminality, family instability, and poverty.

In "Risk, Promotive, and Protective Factors in Youth Offending: Results from the Cambridge Study in Delinquent Development" (*Journal of Criminal Justice*, no. 45, 2016), David P. Farrington, Maria M. Ttofi, and Alex R. Piquero report the results of a long-term study of males from age eight onward to identify factors that increase risk for delinquency and may predict convictions between ages 10 and 18. The researchers find that high troublesomeness (i.e., getting into trouble more often than average) and having a criminally convicted parent increased risk for delinquency as did high levels of dishonesty and high daring (willingness to take risks).

Homicide

The UCR defines murder and nonnegligent manslaughter as "the willful (nonnegligent) killing of one human being by another." It also stipulates, however, that "deaths caused by negligence, suicide, or accident; justifiable homicides; and attempts to murder or assaults to murder" are not counted in this category of crime. Approximately 15,698 murders and nonnegligent manslaughters occurred in 2015, up 10.8% from 2014 but down 9.3% from 2006.

In 2015, 15,326 people were identified as homicide offenders, including 667 juveniles under age 18. (See Table 7.1.) (Because the identity of all murder offenders is not known, these statistics are lower than they would be if all offenders were identified.) Those under age 18 represented 4.3% of all reported homicide offenders in 2015. (These percentages do not reflect the fact that some murder offenders of unknown age were presumably younger than age 18.) Table 7.1 shows that in 2015, of known offenders, 12 homicides were committed by children aged 12 years and younger, 341 by youth aged 13 to 16 years, and 1,263 by those aged 17 to 19 years.

Among the 667 known homicide offenders under the age of 18 years, 61.8% (412) were African American, 35.4% (236) were white, 15.6% (104) were Hispanic, 2.1% (14) were Alaskan Native, Asian American, native Hawaiian, or other Pacific Islander, and 0.75% (5) were of unknown race.

TABLE 7.1

Murder offenders by age, sex, race, and ethnicity, 2015

Age	Total	Sex			Race				Ethnicity[a]		
		Male	Female	Unknown	White	Black or African American	Other[b]	Unknown	Hispanic or Latino	Not Hispanic or Latino	Unknown
Total	15,326	9,553	1,180	4,593	4,636	5,620	283	4,787	1,312	4,598	4,408
Percent distribution[c]	100.0	62.3	7.7	30.0	30.2	36.7	1.8	31.2	12.7	44.6	42.7
Under 18[d]	667	616	51	0	236	412	14	5	104	269	91
Under 22[d]	2,648	2,403	239	6	916	1,638	69	25	404	1,108	322
18 and over[d]	9,456	8,327	1,109	20	4,324	4,755	268	109	1,183	4,125	1,169
Infant (under 1)	0	0	0	0	0	0	0	0	0	0	0
1 to 4	1	1	0	0	0	1	0	0	0	0	0
5 to 8	2	1	1	0	1	1	0	0	0	0	1
9 to 12	9	8	1	0	4	5	0	0	2	2	2
13 to 16	341	320	21	0	119	210	9	3	54	147	44
17 to 19	1,263	1,143	119	1	442	784	28	9	193	527	156
20 to 24	2,448	2,180	262	6	844	1,513	66	25	330	1,030	273
25 to 29	1,814	1,607	204	3	739	997	52	26	214	756	244
30 to 34	1,251	1,082	165	4	610	584	40	17	175	509	173
35 to 39	840	733	107	0	449	368	17	6	104	382	115
40 to 44	594	506	88	0	350	223	17	4	79	269	69
45 to 49	449	384	63	2	251	175	20	3	47	200	56
50 to 54	453	390	60	3	295	128	16	14	46	225	46
55 to 59	278	248	29	1	174	94	9	1	23	148	30
60 to 64	149	136	13	0	103	41	1	4	5	74	23
65 to 69	88	77	11	0	60	27	0	1	7	44	12
70 to 74	52	42	10	0	37	10	4	1	3	32	7
75 and over	91	85	6	0	82	6	3	0	5	49	9
Unknown	5,203	610	20	4,573	76	453	1	4,673	25	204	3,148

[a]Not all agencies provide ethnicity data; therefore, the race and ethnicity totals will not equal.
[b]Includes American Indian or Alaska Native, Asian, and Native Hawaiian or other Pacific Islander.
[c]Because of rounding, the percentages may not add to 100.0.
[d]Does not include unknown ages.

SOURCE: "Expanded Homicide Data Table 3. Murder Offenders by Age, Sex, Race, and Ethnicity, 2015," in *Crime in the United States, 2015*, U.S. Department of Justice, Federal Bureau of Investigation, 2016, https://ucr.fbi.gov/crime-in-the-u.s/2015/crime-in-the-u.s.-2015/tables/expanded_homicide_data_table_3_murder_offenders_by_age_sex_and_race_2015.xls (accessed January 9, 2017)

Rape and Sex Offenses

The FBI states in *Crime in the United States, 2015* that there were an estimated 90,185 rapes reported in 2015 (a 6.3% increase from the previous year but 4.5% lower than in 2006). Arrests, however, were much below that figure, and not all law enforcement agencies reported data regarding rape arrests. The FBI reports that of the 12,304 suspects arrested for sex offenses (these include but are not limited to rape) in 2015 for whom age data are known (not all law enforcement agencies reported all arrests or all age statistics), 2,072 (16.8%) were aged 16 to 20 years, 1,655 (13.5%) were aged 11 to 15 years, and 53 (0.4%) were aged 10 years or younger. (See Table 7.2.)

Aggravated and Simple Assault

The FBI in its Uniform Crime Reporting Program defines aggravated assault as "an unlawful attack by one person upon another for the purpose of inflicting severe or aggravated bodily injury.... This type of assault is usually accompanied by the use of a weapon or by other means likely to produce death or great bodily harm. Attempted aggravated assault that involves the display of—or threat to use—a gun, knife, or other weapon is included in this crime category because serious personal injury would likely result if the assault were completed." In 2015 an estimated 764,449 aggravated assaults were reported. By contrast, simple assaults are assaults or attempted assaults not involving a weapon and not resulting in serious injury to the victim. These include acts such as assault and battery, resisting or obstructing the police, and hazing. In its UCR arrest reports, the FBI lists a category called "other assaults" (to differentiate between these types of assaults and aggravated assaults). Of the 418,534 suspects arrested for assault that year for whom age information was provided to the UCR, 26,215 (6.3%) were aged 11 to 15 years and 947 (0.2%) were aged 10 years or younger. (See Table 7.2.)

Robbery, Burglary, and Larceny-Theft

Robbery, burglary, and larceny-theft are different crimes under the UCR. Robbery is "the taking or attempting to take anything of value from the care, custody, or control of a person or persons by force or threat of force or violence and/or by putting the victim in fear" and is categorized as a violent crime. Burglary involves "the unlawful entry of a structure to commit a felony or theft" and is classified as a property crime. Larceny-theft, also a property crime, is "the unlawful taking, carrying, leading, or riding away of property from the possession or constructive possession of another" and includes crimes such as shoplifting, pocket picking, purse snatching, thefts from motor vehicles, thefts of motor vehicle parts and accessories, and bicycle thefts. These offenses, taken together, are disproportionately committed by young people.

Based on UCR data, the FBI estimates that 1,683,005 larceny-theft offenses, 69,150 robbery offenses, 37,465 stolen property offenses, and 449,006 burglary/breaking and entering offenses were committed in 2015. In 2015 the FBI reports that of the 354,609 people who were arrested for larceny-theft offenses for whom age information is known more than one-quarter were youth: 23,086 (6.5%) were aged 15 years or younger and 68,877 (19.4%) were aged 16 to 20 years. There were 18,653 arrests for robbery; 1,479 (8%) were of people aged 15 years or younger and 5,494 (29.5%) were aged 16 to 20 years. There were 21,025 arrests made for stolen property; 1,329 (6.3%) were of people aged 15 years or younger and 4,268 (20.3%) were aged 16 to 20 years. More than 30% of arrests for breaking and entering were of youth. There were 47,260 arrests for burglary/breaking and entering; 150 (0.3%) were children aged 10 years or younger, 4,261 (9.1%) were aged 11 to 15 years, and 10,461 (22.1%) were aged 16 to 20 years. (See Table 7.2.)

Motor vehicle theft (a separate category in the UCR) is also disproportionately perpetrated by young people, usually in urban areas. In 2015 there were 178,116 motor vehicle thefts nationwide, and 16,229 people were arrested in association with these thefts. The FBI notes that, based on data provided to the UCR, of those arrested for motor vehicle theft in 2015, 1,701 (10.5%) were aged 11 to 15 years and 3,696 (22.8%) were aged 16 to 20 years. (See Table 7.2.)

Computer Crime

Illegally accessing a computer, known as hacking, is a crime committed frequently by juveniles. When it involves manipulation or theft of the information in private, corporate, or government databases and networks, it can be quite costly. Some hackers use malware, such as computer viruses, worms, or spyware, to help them compromise targets' computers, servers, and networks, create havoc, or otherwise assist them in illegal activities. Juvenile hackers who break into their peers' e-mail or post on their Facebook accounts without permission may view their actions as pranks when, in fact, they are crimes.

Cases of juvenile hacking have been reported since the 1980s; however, as of 2017, there were no published reports describing the magnitude of the problem. In "Hacking in High School: Cybercrime Perpetration by Juveniles" (*Deviant Behavior*, vol. 35, no. 7, 2014), Catherine D. Marcum et al. explain that because hacker culture is secretive, it is difficult to fully characterize the typical offender. However, the researchers state that adolescent males with a high level of computer skills and low self-control who are impulsive, risk seeking, and shortsighted may be attracted to the thrill of increasingly more challenging hacking. Marcum et al. find that low self-control and deviant peer associations (i.e., friends

TABLE 7.2

Arrestee's age, by offense category, 2015

Arrest offense category	Total arrestees	10 and under	11–15	16–20	21–25	26–30	31–35	36–40	41–45	46–50	51–55	56–60	61–65	66 and over	Unknown age
Total	3,081,609	2,974	122,384	465,840	566,915	487,505	404,230	291,285	230,170	190,970	157,368	90,256	40,677	28,783	2,252
Crimes against persons	441,326	1,006	28,100	54,999	75,191	67,844	58,004	43,319	35,620	29,319	23,377	13,055	5,944	5,045	503
Assault offenses	418,534	947	26,215	51,045	71,259	64,827	55,301	41,284	34,064	28,075	22,410	12,461	5,607	4,551	488
Homicide offenses	2,733	0	43	578	678	422	341	191	143	114	100	47	36	39	1
Human trafficking offenses	8	0	0	2	2	0	1	0	2	0	1	0	0	0	0
Kidnapping/abduction	6,132	1	83	731	1,277	1,136	972	714	449	326	219	128	49	44	3
Sex offenses	12,304	53	1,655	2,072	1,614	1,297	1,274	1,033	883	764	618	401	244	388	8
Sex offenses, nonforcible	1,615	5	104	571	361	162	115	97	79	40	29	18	8	23	3
Crimes against property	569,563	1,065	39,624	111,873	100,122	87,681	71,041	48,090	36,803	29,526	22,555	11,949	5,152	3,522	560
Arson	2,145	61	487	356	236	213	200	151	103	114	104	67	28	25	0
Bribery	177	0	3	22	28	33	26	22	18	7	13	3	1	1	0
Burglary/breaking & entering	47,260	150	4,261	10,461	8,374	7,322	5,824	3,730	2,642	2,090	1,442	619	213	111	21
Counterfeiting/forgery	14,461	0	52	1,672	2,830	2,797	2,436	1,589	1,171	855	600	283	84	61	31
Destruction/damage/vandalism	55,732	355	7,164	11,693	10,235	7,681	5,954	3,921	2,860	2,363	1,749	950	439	334	34
Embezzlement	6,177	0	9	1,312	1,435	992	716	540	397	319	246	123	58	26	4
Extortion/blackmail	232	1	16	41	31	35	32	27	19	10	14	3	1	2	0
Fraud offenses	32,863	6	520	3,981	6,260	6,211	5,119	3,534	2,591	1,947	1,407	747	306	208	26
Larceny/theft offenses	354,609	466	22,620	68,877	60,028	53,577	44,118	30,337	24,046	19,663	15,491	8,554	3,801	2,622	409
Motor vehicle theft	16,229	9	1,701	3,696	2,756	2,513	2,047	1,311	889	628	436	153	53	33	4
Robbery	18,653	8	1,471	5,494	3,958	2,675	1,765	1,168	786	612	425	192	58	27	14
Stolen property offenses	21,025	9	1,320	4,268	3,951	3,632	2,804	1,760	1,281	918	628	255	110	72	17
Crimes against society	474,659	114	13,236	97,495	104,163	78,590	60,497	39,932	28,333	21,075	16,241	8,809	3,491	1,832	851
Drug/narcotic offenses	433,424	35	10,899	90,734	95,599	72,127	55,555	36,481	25,680	19,083	14,517	7,688	2,939	1,266	821
Gambling offenses	527		36	94	72	48	40	36	43	31	49	32	24	20	2
Pornography/obscene material	1,934	5	421	337	213	242	146	142	120	97	78	56	31	44	2
Prostitution offenses	8,080	0	12	487	1,397	1,469	1,208	980	810	596	504	313	156	147	1
Weapon law violations	30,694	74	1,868	5,843	6,882	4,704	3,548	2,293	1,680	1,268	1,093	720	341	355	25
Group B offenses*	1,596,061	789	41,424	201,473	287,439	253,390	214,688	159,944	129,414	111,050	95,195	56,443	26,090	18,384	338
Bad checks	7,686	0	10	250	740	1,055	1,262	1,138	1,008	824	582	370	211	231	5
Curfew/loitering/vagrancy violations	13,418	38	4,333	5,057	671	614	497	409	355	474	432	325	139	74	0
Disorderly conduct	115,437	294	11,869	17,813	20,257	14,984	11,953	9,266	7,933	7,513	6,571	3,979	1,745	1,244	16
Driving under the influence	306,977	3	108	19,141	61,610	50,425	40,887	31,596	27,910	24,508	22,655	14,832	7,557	5,665	80
Drunkenness	101,476	0	343	7,353	15,405	13,395	12,423	10,640	9,998	11,028	10,837	6,213	2,623	1,191	27
Family offenses, nonviolent	28,346	20	446	1,303	3,823	5,207	5,518	4,385	3,072	2,051	1,436	656	263	163	3
Liquor law violations	93,691	8	3,962	49,991	8,391	5,138	4,560	3,853	3,984	4,250	4,486	2,989	1,350	718	11
Peeping Tom	311	1	30	42	40	53	33	33	21	19	16	9	5	8	1
Trespass of real property	75,519	66	3,262	10,718	11,215	9,545	8,483	6,687	6,119	6,248	5,999	3,954	1,877	1,335	11
All other offenses	853,200	359	17,061	89,805	165,287	152,974	129,072	91,937	69,014	54,135	42,181	23,116	10,320	7,755	184

*In January 2011, the FBI's Uniform Crime Reporting Program discontinued the collection of arrest data for the category of runaways.

SOURCE: "Arrestees, Age by Arrest Offense Category, 2015," in "Tables with All Offenses," 2015 National Incident-Based Reporting System, U.S. Department of Justice, Federal Bureau of Investigation, Criminal Justice Information Services Division, 2016, https://ucr.fbi.gov/nibrs/2015/tables/data-tables (accessed January 9, 2017)

who engage in illegal or unacceptable social behavior) predict adolescents' hacking into social media accounts or accessing a website without authorization. Most studies note that juvenile computer- or cyber-criminals are only distinguished from youth who commit street crimes by their technological savvy and focus.

In 1998 the U.S. Secret Service filed the first criminal case against a juvenile for a computer crime. The unnamed hacker shut down an airport in Worcester, Massachusetts, for six hours in 1997. The airport was integrated into the Federal Aviation Administration traffic system by telephone lines. The perpetrator gained access to the communications system and disabled it by sending a series of computer commands that changed the data carried on the system. As a result, the airport could not function. (No accidents occurred during that time, however.) According to the DOJ, the juvenile pleaded guilty in return for two years' probation, a fine, and community service.

Juveniles have been caught hacking into school computer systems in an effort to change their grades and the grades of other students. Michael Birnbaum and Jenna Johnson report such an incident in Maryland in "Officials Can't Prove Who Changed Md. High-Schoolers' Grades" (WashingtonPost.com, March 9, 2010). The culprits (at least eight students) stole teachers' computer passwords using USB key loggers, and then used those passwords to change grades for several months before being detected. Although eight students were accused in the scheme, there was no way to prove exactly which students changed the grades.

In "Teenage Hacker 'Cosmo the God' Sentenced by California Court" (Wired.com, November 9, 2012), Mat Honan reports that in November 2012 a 15-year-old pleaded guilty in a California juvenile court to several felonies in exchange for probation, which includes terms that ban him from using the Internet until his 21st birthday. The charges against him included credit card fraud, identity theft, bomb threats, and online impersonation. The article "Teen Hackers: 10 Stories of Young Code-Crackers" (HuffingtonPost.com, July 18, 2012) recounts other instances of teens committing cybercrimes. In one instance an 18-year-old hacked into the computers of pop stars—including Mariah Carey (1970–), Ke$ha (1987–), Lady Gaga (1986–), Leona Lewis (1985–), and Justin Timberlake (1981–)—stole their unreleased tracks, and sold them online. The hacker was sentenced to 18 months in detention and treatment for Internet addiction. In 2011 a Greek teen was arrested for hacking into U.S. and other government websites. More than 100 fake credit cards were found in his home. In April 2012 a 15-year-old in Austria was arrested for hacking into more than 250 companies' computer systems.

In 2011 two 19-year-olds and two 21-year-olds in the United Kingdom were sentenced to a total of 15-and-a-half years in prison for running GhostMarket, a huge cyber-crime forum. In "Cyber Crime Teens Jailed in GhostMarket Bust" (ITPro.co.uk, March 3, 2011), Tom Brewster of IT Pro explains, "GhostMarket facilitated cyber criminals in various illicit acts, including data theft, credit card fraud, malware propagation and botnet activities. The forum also provided tips on how to avoid law enforcement and exchange details of vulnerable sites and servers."

In Q4 2012 AVG Community Powered Threat Report (2013, http://aa-download.avg.com/filedir/news/AVG _Community_Powered_Threat_Report_Q1_2012.pdf), Yuval Ben-Itzhak, the chief technology officer of AVG Technologies, cautions that preteens have also been implicated in cybercrimes targeting social networks, online gaming sites, and e-mail. He cites the example of an 11-year-old who developed code that enabled him to steal login information from online gamers.

In 2014 ninth graders in Winnipeg, Canada, hacked into the Bank of Montreal. In "Teens Hack ATM, Then Show Bank How Easily They Did It" (Consumerist.com, June 10, 2014), Chris Morran explains that the teens used an ATM operator's manual they found online to hack into the bank's ATM system. However, instead of using the access they had gained for illicit purposes, the teens told the bank how easily they had penetrated their system, in the hope that it would prompt the bank to intensify its security.

In 2016 a 16-year-old in the United Kingdom who, when he was just 14 years old, hacked multiple government networks and threatened U.S. airlines from his laptop, was fined and given two years of rehabilitation and supervision but no jail time. In "Teenager Who Hacked Governments Worldwide Is Spared Jail" (Telegraph.-co.uk, July 20, 2016), Martin Evans reports that the teen "caused chaos targeting Iraq's ministry of foreign affairs, the department of agriculture in Thailand and China's security ministry." He also launched a cyberattack of Florida's SeaWorld theme park and crashed computers in Japan. He was arrested after using Twitter to send bomb threats to U.S. airlines. In delivering his sentence the judge opined, "You didn't think of what truly happens in the real world if you do these things. I don't think there would be any positive outcome for you going into a youth detention centre. I think it would destroy you."

Illegal Drug Use

Various studies show that many violent offenders are substance abusers. For some people, drugs and alcohol may trigger violent behavior. Lloyd D. Johnston et al. of the Institute for Social Research find in *Monitoring the Future: 2015 Overview, Key Findings on Adolescent Drug Use* (February 2016, http://www.monitoringthe future.org/pubs/monographs/mtf-overview2015.pdf) that in 2015, 38.6% of 12th graders, 27.9% of 10th graders, and 14.8% of eighth graders had used an illicit drug in the

TABLE 7.3

Offenders' age by offense category, 2015

Offense category	Total offenders[a]	Adult	Juvenile[b]	Unknown
		Age category		
Total	4,607,928	3,445,659	464,873	697,396
Crimes against persons	1,265,077	1,044,980	147,869	72,228
Assault offenses	1,163,840	970,521	130,321	62,998
Homicide offenses	5,215	4,237	268	710
Human trafficking offenses	118	97	5	16
Kidnapping/abduction	17,662	15,518	690	1,454
Sex offenses	73,005	50,708	15,436	6,861
Sex offenses, nonforcible	5,237	3,899	1,149	189
Crimes against property	2,326,583	1,492,790	225,392	608,401
Arson	9,128	4,457	2,322	2,349
Bribery	426	403	12	11
Burglary/breaking & entering	263,671	144,314	24,107	95,250
Counterfeiting/forgery	66,108	53,696	1,239	11,173
Destruction/damage/ vandalism	404,547	237,950	56,438	110,159
Embezzlement	20,580	19,052	611	917
Extortion/blackmail	1,731	1,178	137	416
Fraud offenses	200,208	136,549	5,037	58,622
Larceny/theft offenses	1,105,594	732,977	106,266	266,351
Motor vehicle theft	104,057	57,199	10,584	36,274
Robbery	100,846	63,286	12,333	25,227
Stolen property offenses	49,687	41,729	6,306	1,652
Crimes against society	1,016,268	907,889	91,612	16,767
Drug/narcotic offenses	889,828	806,046	75,528	8,254
Gambling offenses	1,283	1,150	99	34
Pornography/obscene material	9,805	4,772	4,168	865
Prostitution offenses	13,326	13,014	155	157
Weapon law violations	102,026	82,907	11,662	7,457

[a]Offenders are counted once for each offense type to which they are connected. Neither the offender data nor the offense data for the 1,619,479 incidents reported with unknown offenders were used in constructing this table.
[b]For this table, a juvenile is an offender under the age of 18.

SOURCE: "Offenders, Age by Offense Category, 2015," in "Tables with All Offenses," *2015 National Incident-Based Reporting System*, U.S. Department of Justice, Federal Bureau of Investigation, Criminal Justice Information Services Division, 2016, https://ucr.fbi.gov/nibrs/2015/tables/data-tables (accessed January 9, 2017)

past year. Among 12th graders, the highest percentage (44.7%) reported having used marijuana/hashish; nearly two-thirds (64%) of 12th-grade students in the survey had used alcohol (not classed as an illicit drug by the study).

Other drugs gaining popularity among teens in the 21st century include so-called club drugs, such as MDMA (ecstasy), Rohypnol, gammahydroxybutyrate (GHB), and ketamine (Special K). Because each of these drugs is scheduled under the Controlled Substances Act (Title II of the Comprehensive Drug Abuse Prevention and Control Act of 1970), they are illegal and their use constitutes a criminal offense. The FBI reports that of 889,828 known drug/narcotic offenders in 2015, 75,528 (8.5%) were aged 18 years or younger. (See Table 7.3.)

JUVENILE VICTIMS OF CRIME

Between 1993 and 2015 the rate of violent victimizations decreased in most age categories, but between 2014 and 2015 it did not decrease among youth aged 12 to 17 years. In *Criminal Victimization, 2015* (October 2016, https://www.bjs.gov/content/pub/pdf/cv15.pdf), Jennifer L. Truman and Rachel E. Morgan explain that the FBI's 2015 UCR program found a 4% increase in the number of serious violent crimes compared with 2014, whereas the BJS's NCVS did not show a statistically significant change in the number of serious violent victimizations during this same period. This discrepancy is attributed to the fact that the two programs consider a similar, but not identical list of offenses and analyze their data differently. For example, the UCR excludes simple assault and sexual assault, which are included in the NCVS.

Truman and Morgan report that NCVS data indicate that the violent victimization rate for those aged 12 to 17 years was 31.3 per 1,000, the highest rate of any age group. (See Table 7.4.) The rate of serious violent criminal victimization among 12- to 17-year-olds, which includes rape or sexual assault, robbery, and aggravated assault, decreased from 8.8 per 1,000 in 2014 to 7.8 per 1,000 in 2015.

People aged 18 to 24 years had the second-highest rate of violent criminal victimization in 2015, at 25.1 per 1,000 people. (See Table 7.4.) Their serious violent crime victimization rate of 10.7 was the highest for any age group that year. In 2015, 18- to 24-year-olds were almost twice as likely as 50- to 64-year-olds to be victims of violent crime.

Becoming a victim of crime can have serious consequences—outcomes that the victim neither asks for nor deserves. Victims rarely expect to be victimized and seldom know where to turn for help. They may end up in the hospital to be treated and released, or may be confined to bed for days, weeks, or longer. Injuries may be temporary, or permanent and forever change victims' lives. Victims may lose money or property, limbs, senses, or even their lives. In many cases they lose their confidence, self-esteem, and feelings of security.

Niclas Olofsson et al. note in "Long-Term Health Consequences of Violence Exposure in Adolescence: A 26-Year Prospective Study" (*BMC Public Health*, vol. 12, no. 411, June 7, 2012) that one of the reasons that violent victimization in adolescence leads to long-term health consequences is because the teen years are when important personal and psychological resources that shape thinking and decision making develop. The researchers suggest that because exposure to violence disturbs and potentially harms normal psychological development, it may be more harmful during adolescence than later in life.

Olofsson et al. followed men and women over the course of more than 20 years, questioning them about their childhood, family relationships, life events, living conditions, health history, and working conditions, as

TABLE 7.4

Rates of violent victimization, by selected characteristics of victim, 2014 and 2015

Victim demographic characteristic	Violent crime[a]		Serious violent crime[b]	
	2014[c]	2015	2014[c]	2015
Total	20.1	8.6	7.7	6.8
Sex				
Male	21.1	15.9[!]	8.3	5.4
Female	19.1	21.1	7.0	8.1
Race/Hispanic origin				
White[d]	20.3	17.4	7.0	6.0
Black[d]	22.5	22.6	10.1	8.4
Hispanic	16.2	16.8	8.3	7.1
Other[d,e]	23.0	25.7	7.7	10.4
Age				
12–17	30.1	31.3	8.8	7.8
18–24	26.8	25.1	13.6	10.7
25–34	28.5	21.8	8.6	9.3
35–49	21.6	22.6	8.9	7.8
50–64	17.9	14.2	7.0	5.7
65 or older	3.1	5.2	1.3	1.5
Marital status				
Never married	27.9	26.2	10.7	9.4
Married	12.4	9.9	4.0	3.5
Widowed	8.7	8.5	2.9	2.9
Divorced	30.3	35.3	14.2	13.0
Separated	52.8	39.5	27.7	20.6
Household income[f]				
$9,999 or less	39.7	39.2	18.7	17.7
$10,000–$14,999	36.0	27.7	16.8	12.0
$15,000–$24,999	25.3	25.9	8.4	8.2
$25,000–$34,999	19.7	16.3	8.3	5.5
$35,000–$49,999	19.0	20.5	8.1	7.1
$50,000–$74,999	16.4	16.3	5.4	5.9
$75,000 or more	15.1	12.8	4.7	4.5

[a]Includes rape or sexual assault, robbery, aggravated assault, and simple assault. Excludes homicide because the National Crime Victimization Survey (NCVS) is based on interviews with victims and therefore cannot measure murder.
[b]In the NCVS, serious violent crime includes rape or sexual assault, robbery, and aggravated assault.
[c]Comparison year.
[d]Excludes persons of Hispanic or Latino origin.
[e]Includes American Indian and Alaska Natives; Asian, Native Hawaiian, and other Pacific Islanders; and persons of two or more races.
[f]Household income was imputed for 2014 and 2015.
Note: Victimization rates are per 1,000 persons age 12 or older.

SOURCE: Jennifer L. Truman and Rachel E. Morgan, "Table 7. Rate of Violent Victimization, by Victim Demographic Characteristics, 2014 and 2015," in *Criminal Victimization, 2015*, U.S. Department of Justice, Office of Justice Programs, Bureau of Justice Statistics, October 2016, https://www.bjs.gov/content/pub/pdf/cv15.pdf (accessed January 10, 2017)

well as behavioral, psychosocial, and other factors. When compared with people who were not victimized as adolescents, young women exposed to violence in late adolescence had increased rates of serious illness and bad self-reported health. The researchers did not find this relationship in males and report that "the magnitude, nature and health impact of violence differ greatly for young men and women." This may be because of sex differences in how the brain develops, or it may be that adolescent females are more fragile psychologically or experience violence differently than do males.

In "Do Coping Mechanisms Affect the Quality of Life in Adolescents Who Have Experienced Trauma?" (*Virginia Commonwealth University*, 2014, http://scholarscompass.vcu.edu/cgi/viewcontent.cgi?article=1064&context=uresposters), Tess Davis et al. analyzed data from more than 350 adolescents aged nine to 16 years and find that victimization predicts future life satisfaction. Specifically, adolescents who experience more victimization will later experience lower life satisfaction. Furthermore, in "Violent Victimization across the Life Course Moving a 'Victim Careers' Agenda Forward" (*Criminal Justice and Behavior*, vol. 41, no. 5, May 2014), Marie Skubak Tillyer finds that violent victimization in adolescence is related to subsequent risk in adulthood. Adults who report early and persistent violent victimization in their youth appear particularly vulnerable to subsequent victimization.

In the aftermath of crime, when victims most need support and comfort, there is often no one available who understands. Parents or spouses may be dealing with their own feelings of guilt and anger for being unable to protect their loved ones. Friends may withdraw, not knowing how to respond. As a result, victims may lose their sense of self-esteem and no longer trust other people. These effects of violent victimization can be particularly devastating when the victim is a young person.

Child Abuse and Neglect

It is impossible to determine how many children suffer abuse. Estimates of the number of cases only include those reported to public authorities or rely on the results of surveys in which participants may deny or play down abuse. For these reasons, estimates of child abuse are generally considered low. The Administration on Children, Youth, and Families (ACYF) is the primary source of national information on abused and neglected children that has been reported to state child protective services (CPS) agencies.

According to the ACYF, in *Child Maltreatment 2014* (2016, https://www.acf.hhs.gov/sites/default/files/cb/cm2014.pdf), in federal fiscal year (FY) 2014 there were an estimated 3.6 million referrals involving 6.6 million children alleged to have been abused or neglected. Approximately 2.2 million reports involving 3.2 million children were responded to by a CPS agency, and about 702,000 children were found to be victims of child maltreatment. Reports most often came from professional sources, such as the legal system (18.1%), educators (17.7%), and social service employees (11%). Reports also were made by nonprofessionals, such as friends, relatives, and neighbors of the alleged victims (18.6%); unclassified and unknown sources made 18.7% of reports.

The ACYF states that in federal FY 2014, 75% of reported victims were neglected, 17% were physically abused, and some experienced both types of maltreatment. The largest group of victims were abused by one or both parents (91.6%). Parental abuse is probably the most devastating of all abuse because child victims are often highly dependent on their parents and may have nowhere to turn for help. The ACYF reports that 13% of victims were abused by people other than their parents, and the largest categories in this group were male relatives and male partners of parents.

The most tragic result of child maltreatment is death. The ACYF indicates that in 2014 an estimated 1,546 children died as a result of abuse or neglect. Children in the youngest age groups were the most likely to die of maltreatment; more than two-thirds (70.7%) of the children who died were younger than three years old. Nearly 80% of child fatalities involved at least one parent.

Missing Children

During the 1980s, following several high-profile abductions and tragedies, the media focused public attention on the problem of missing children. Citizens became concerned and demanded action to address what appeared to be a national crisis. Congress passed the Missing Children's Assistance Act of 1984. The legislation mandated the Office of Juvenile Justice and Delinquency Prevention (OJJDP) to conduct national incidence studies to determine the number of juveniles who were "victims of abduction by strangers" and the number of children who were victims of "parental kidnapping." The result was the National Incidence Studies of Missing, Abducted, Runaway, and Thrownaway Children (NISMART), the first of which was conducted in 1988, with the results published in 1990. The second and most recent NISMART (NISMART-2) was conducted mainly in 1999, with many of the data published in a series of reports from 2002 through 2008. A third NISMART was commissioned by the DOJ's Office of Justice Programs, Office of Juvenile Justice and Delinquency Prevention in 2010 and will measure the number of kidnappings by strangers and the prevalence of familial abductions; lost, injured, or otherwise missing children; runaway children as well as thrownaway children (i.e., those who are turned out of the home by parents or caregivers).

The Missing Children's Assistance Act has been amended several times, most recently in 2013 by the E. Clay Shaw, Jr. Missing Children's Assistance Reauthorization Act (P.L. 113-38). This authorization, which expires at the end of FY 2018, requires more frequent (every three years) studies on missing and sexually exploited children. The act also creates a national resource center for missing and exploited children. The National Center for Missing and Exploited Children (NCMEC, http://www.ncmec.org), a private, nonprofit organization, was founded in 1984. The center operates the 24-hour hotline 1-800-THE-LOST. It provides state and local governments and private agencies with information, reports data on missing and exploited children to the DOJ annually, helps to train and assist law enforcement agencies, tracks patterns of attempted child abductions, operates a cyber tip line for reports of Internet-related child sexual exploitation, and disseminates information on Internet safety and the prevention of child abduction and sexual exploitation.

FAMILY ABDUCTIONS. According to Adrienne L. Fernandes-Alcantara of the Congressional Research Service, in *Missing and Exploited Children: Background, Policies, and Issues* (April 29, 2015, https://fas.org/sgp/crs/misc/RL34050.pdf), the second NISMART found that family abductions, "the taking or keeping of a child by a family member in violation of a custody order, a decree, or other legitimate custodial rights, where the taking or keeping involved some element of concealment, flight, or intent to deprive a lawful custodian indefinitely of custodial privileges," made up 9% of the caretaker missing children population (those children whose whereabouts were unknown to their caretakers) and 7% of the reported missing children population (those missing children whose caretakers sought the assistance of authorities to locate them).

Fernandes-Alcantara notes that in FY 2014 NCMEC case managers were involved with 11,800 cases of child abduction, and although the majority of cases (83%) were considered endangered runaways, victims of family abduction were the next largest group.

In *The Crime of Family Abduction* (May 2010, https://www.ncjrs.gov/pdffiles1/ojjdp/229933.pdf), the OJJDP emphasizes the harm that is done to the 200,000 children who are the victims of family abduction annually. Although the OJJDP stresses the physical dangers of family abduction to children, it states that "most often, however, the worst damage is imperceptible to the eye, occurring deep within the child, leaving traces that may last a lifetime." The concealment of the child, deprivation of contact with other family members, and the physical flight are all traumatic and have a lasting impact. Other damaging aspects of family abduction include being made to fear discovery, being given a new name and identity, not being allowed to grieve the loss of those left behind, being told to lie about the past, coercion and emotional abuse by the abductor, being kept out of school, and being told lies about the searching parent.

According to the FBI, in "Parental Kidnappings" (https://www.fbi.gov/wanted/parental-kidnappings), as of March 2017 there were 25 individuals "most wanted" for parental kidnappings. Many of these parents were involved in custody disputes prior to the abductions of which they were accused. Some were believed to have taken their children and fled to another country.

NONFAMILY ABDUCTIONS. Although far fewer children are abducted by strangers than by family members, the consequences are often far worse. Violence, the use of force or weapons, sexual assault, and murder are more prevalent in nonfamily abductions. Fernandes-Alcantara reports that the NISMART-2 found that nonfamily abduction accounted for 3% of caretaker missing children and 2% of reported missing children. She observes that the stereotypical kidnapping, in which a stranger or acquaintance holds the child for ransom or kills the child, is one type of nonfamily abduction. Fernandes-Alcantara explains that widespread media coverage about kidnapping cases, such as those involving Adam Walsh (1974–1981) in 1981, Polly Klaas (1981–1993) in 1993, and Elizabeth Smart (1987–) in 2002, may create the mistaken belief that kidnapping is common, when in fact it is a relatively rare occurrence. Nonetheless, children who are not recovered immediately are at increased risk of being harmed. Research reveals that the first three hours following abduction constitute the critical window of time for recovery of the child. More than 75% of abducted children who are killed are dead within this critical period.

In a widely publicized case, 14-year-old Smart was taken from her bedroom in Salt Lake City, Utah, in June 2002 by Brian David Mitchell (1953–). Mitchell succeeded in keeping Smart concealed for nine months. In March 2003 Smart was spotted with Mitchell and Mitchell's wife, Wanda Barzee (1945–), on a Salt Lake City street. Mitchell and Barzee were arrested. During the five-week trial, Smart described daily sexual assaults and other abuses. Barzee pleaded guilty to kidnapping and unlawful transportation of a minor across state lines in 2009 and was sentenced to 15 years in prison. In December 2010 Mitchell was found guilty of the same charges. In May 2011 Mitchell was sentenced to life in federal prison.

Another dramatic and widely publicized kidnapping case was the story of the 2009 release of Jaycee Lee Dugard (1980–), who was kidnapped in 1991 by Phillip Garrido (1951–) and his wife, Nancy. Dugard was held for 18 years, during which time she gave birth to two children conceived after being raped by her kidnapper. Phillip Garrido was sentenced in 2011 to a prison term of 431 years. Nancy Garrido (1955–) received a sentence of 36 years to life. In July 2010 the state of California agreed to pay Dugard a $20 million settlement. State officials admitted that many mistakes were made by the parole agents responsible for monitoring Phillip Garrido, a convicted rapist, during the time Dugard was held captive. Dugard wrote the book *A Stolen Life: A Memoir* (2012) about her life in captivity.

Yet another horrific abduction case occurred in Cleveland, Ohio. Ariel Castro (1960–2013) kidnapped two girls and a young woman between 2002 and 2004 and held them captive in his home. One of the victims, Amanda Berry, who was 17 when she was abducted, gave birth to a child fathered by Castro in 2006. On May 6, 2013, she and her six-year-old daughter escaped from the house and contacted authorities, which resulted in the release of the other two young women and the arrest of Castro. Castro was sentenced to life in prison and committed suicide just one month into his sentence.

RUNAWAYS AND THROWNAWAYS. In *Runaway/ Thrownaway Children: National Estimates and Characteristics* (October 2002, http://www.missingkids.com/ en_US/documents/nismart2_runaway.pdf), Heather Hammer, David Finkelhor, and Andrea J. Sedlak state that runaways are children who meet at least one of the following criteria:

- A child who leaves home without permission and stays away overnight
- A child 14 years old or younger (or older and mentally incompetent) who is away from home chooses not to come home when expected to and stays away overnight
- A child 15 years old or older who is away from home chooses not to come home and stays away two nights

During the 1970s the term *throwaways* or *thrownaways* was given by researchers to juveniles who were made to leave home or were abandoned. A thrownaway child meets one of the following criteria:

- A child is asked or told to leave home by a parent or other household adult, no adequate alternative care is arranged for the child by a household adult, and the child is out of the household overnight
- A child who is away from home is prevented from returning home by a parent or other household adult, no adequate alternative care is arranged for the child by a household adult, and the child is out of the household overnight

The number of runaways and thrownaways is difficult to estimate because the children's status is oftentimes concealed by either the runaways themselves or the families of thrownaways. Fernandes-Alcantara observes that the categorization of runaway or thrownaway frequently depends on whether the episode is described by the children (who tend to describe themselves as thrownaway) or their caretakers, who tend to describe the children as runaways. As a result, the OJJDP combines its estimates of runaways and thrownaways.

Hammer, Finkelhor, and Sedlak state in *Runaway/ Thrownaway Children* that 1.7 million youths had a runaway/thrownaway episode in 1999. Of these youth, 1.2 million were considered "potentially endangered." The most common reasons for endangerment were that the child was:

- Afraid of abuse upon return (21%) or had been physically or sexually abused at home in the year before the episode

- Substance dependent (19%)

- 13 years old or younger (18%)

- In the company of someone known to be abusing drugs (18%)

- Using hard drugs (17%)

Most runaway/thrownaway youth (68%) were aged 15 years or older, and half were female. Most runaways (77%) were gone for less than one week, and more than 99% returned home. An estimated 38,600 of the runaways were at risk of sexual endangerment (assault, attempted assault, or prostitution) while away from home.

In "Runaway and Throwaway Youth: Time for Policy Changes and Public Responsibility" (*Journal of Applied Research on Children: Informing Policy for Children at Risk*, vol. 2, no. 1, March 15, 2011), Ira Colby of the University of Houston writes that runaway and thrownaway youth are at increased risk for:

- High-risk behaviors, including engaging in unprotected sex, having multiple sex partners, and injection drug use

- Survival sex—exchanging sex for food, clothing, and shelter

- Dealing drugs to meet basic needs

- Anxiety and depression, suicide, poor health and nutrition, and low self-esteem

- Problems attending school because they lack necessary documentation such as immunization and medical records and proof of residence, and/or do not have transportation to and from school

Murder Victims

According to the BJS, homicide rates for all age groups have been declining since the mid-1990s. Although violent crime has diminished, it still plays a significant role as a cause of death for youth. The CDC indicates in *Key Injury and Violence Data* (2017, https://www.cdc.gov/injury/wisqars/overview/key_data.html) that three-quarters of all deaths among young people result from injuries and violence. In 2015 homicide was the third-leading cause of death among young people aged one to four years and 15 to 24 years and the fourth-leading cause of death among those aged five to nine years and 10 to 14 years and was responsible for 5,400 deaths. (See Table 7.5.)

The FBI's UCR data confirm that murder victims are disproportionately young people. Out of 13,455 murder victims in 2015, 1,093 victims were under age 18, including 282 victims who were 13 to 16 years old and 260 who were aged one to four years. (See Table 7.6.) The number

TABLE 7.5

Five leading causes of death, by age group, 2015

Rank	<1	1–4	5–9	10–14	15–24
			Age groups		
1	Congenital anomalies 4,825	Unintentional injury 1,235	Unintentional injury 755	Unintentional injury 763	Unintentional injury 12,514
2	Short gestation 4,084	Congenital anomalies 435	Malignant neoplasms 437	Malignant neoplasms 428	Suicide 5,491
3	SIDS 1,568	Homicide 369	Congenital anomalies 181	Suicide 409	Homicide 4,733
4	Maternal pregnancy comp. 1,522	Malignant neoplasms 354	Homicide 140	Homicide 158	Malignant neoplasms 1,469
5	Unintentional injury 1,291	Heart disease 147	Heart disease 85	Congenital anomalies 156	Heart disease 997

SIDS = Sudden Infant Death Syndrome

SOURCE: "5 Leading Causes of Death, United States 2015, All Races, Both Sexes," in *WISQARS: Leading Causes of Death Reports, National and Regional, 1999–2015*, Centers for Disease Control and Prevention, National Center for Injury Prevention and Control, 2016, https://webappa.cdc.gov/sasweb/ncipc/leadcaus10_us.html (accessed January 10, 2017)

of young murder victims more than doubled to 2,624 when looking at all victims under age 22.

The FBI reports in *Crime in the United States, 2015* that African Americans were disproportionately victims of homicide in 2015. More African Americans (7,039) than whites (5,854) were murdered in 2015, although white people far outnumber African Americans in the general population. Of the 1,093 victims under age 18, 504 victims were white (46.1% of victims in that age group) and 544 victims (49.8%) were African American. Of the 2,624 victims under the age of 22 years, 954 were white (36.4% of victims in that age group) and 1,598 (60.9%) were African American. Homicide has been the leading cause of death for African American teenagers for many years.

VICTIM-OFFENDER RELATIONSHIP. The OJJDP in its *Statistical Briefing Book* (2016, https://www.ojjdp.gov/ojstatbb/victims/qa02302.asp?qaDate=2014) reports that the most frequent killers of children under the age of six years were their parents or family members, whereas parents were less likely to be involved in the murder of teens aged 15 to 17 years. Between 1980 and 2014 two-thirds (68%) of homicide victims under age six were murdered by a family member, compared with 54% of victims aged six to 11 years, 21% of victims aged 12 to 14 years, and 7% of victims aged 15 to 17 years. In contrast, the proportion of murders perpetrated by an acquaintance or a stranger increased with age. Twenty-nine percent of victims under age five had been killed by

TABLE 7.6

Murder victims by age and weapon, 2015

Age	Total murder victims	Firearms	Knives or cutting instruments	Blunt objects (clubs, hammers, etc.)	Personal weapons (hands, fists, feet, etc.)[a]	Poison	Explosives	Fire	Narcotics	Strangulation	Asphyxiation	Other weapon or weapon not stated[b]
												Weapons
Total	**13,455**	**9,616**	**1,544**	**437**	**624**	**7**	**1**	**82**	**70**	**96**	**120**	**858**
Percent distribution[c]	100.0	71.5	11.5	3.2	4.6	0.1	0.0	0.6	0.5	0.7	0.9	6.4
Under 18[d]	1,093	553	76	42	205	2	0	16	13	9	42	135
Under 22[d]	2,624	2,011	195	43	150	2	0	18	16	11	29	149
18 and over[d]	12,227	9,014	1,460	388	404	5	1	61	53	85	77	679
Infant (under 1)	168	8	5	15	77	1	0	3	2	3	17	37
1 to 4	260	42	9	20	107	1	0	3	5	2	15	56
5 to 8	91	42	10	2	8	0	0	2	3	2	6	16
9 to 12	56	30	8	2	3	0	0	6	0	0	3	4
13 to 16	282	235	21	2	5	1	0	1	2	1	1	14
17 to 19	996	854	72	7	17	1	0	4	5	3	1	32
20 to 24	2,431	2,060	211	18	25	0	0	6	10	9	8	84
25 to 29	2,071	1,704	187	27	39	2	0	6	15	7	13	73
30 to 34	1,647	1,308	164	34	38	2	0	4	4	10	5	78
35 to 39	1,263	938	164	32	39	0	0	5	4	6	5	70
40 to 44	925	679	107	24	27	1	0	4	7	8	6	62
45 to 49	781	499	121	41	34	1	0	7	2	11	7	58
50 to 54	737	399	156	48	50	0	0	7	4	6	10	57
55 to 59	580	293	107	58	47	0	0	4	1	8	4	58
60 to 64	360	174	68	34	34	0	1	6	1	5	3	34
65 to 69	235	113	57	17	16	0	0	0	0	3	3	26
70 to 74	159	70	27	13	14	0	0	2	0	4	5	24
75 and over	279	119	43	36	29	0	0	7	1	6	7	31
Unknown	134	49	7	7	15	0	0	5	4	2	1	44

[a]Pushed is included in personal weapons.
[b]Includes drowning.
[c]Because of rounding, the percentages may not add to 100.0.
[d]Does not include unknown ages.

SOURCE: "Expanded Homicide Data Table 9. Murder Victims by Age, by Weapon, 2015," in *Crime in the United States, 2015*, U.S. Department of Justice, Federal Bureau of Investigation, 2016, https://ucr.fbi.gov/crime-in-the-u.s/2015/crime-in-the-u.s.-2015/tables/expanded_homicide_data_table_9_murder_victims_by_age_by_weapon_2015.xls (accessed January 10, 2017)

an acquaintance, compared with 65% of 15- to 17-year-olds; only 3% of the youngest children had been killed by strangers, compared with 27% of 15- to 17-year-old victims. Among all victims aged 17 years and younger, a greater proportion of male victims (50%) than female victims (39%) were killed by acquaintances, and a higher proportion of male victims (18%) than female victims (9%) were killed by strangers.

WEAPONS USED IN ASSAULT AND MURDER OF JUVE-NILES. In "Hospitalizations Due to Firearm Injuries in Children and Adolescents" (*Pediatrics*, vol. 133, no. 2, February 2014), John M. Leventhal, Julie R. Gaither, and Robert Sege report that in the United States, about 20 children per day are injured by gunshot wounds seriously enough to require hospitalization, and more than 6% die as a result of their injuries.

The FBI reports in *Crime in the United States, 2015* that firearms were used in many murders of juveniles and young adults in 2015. Of the 1,093 murder victims under the age of 18 years, 553 (51%) were killed with firearms. (See Table 7.6.) Of the 2,624 murder victims under the age of 22 years, 2,011 (77%) were killed with firearms. A lower proportion of the youngest murder victims were killed by firearms, but that proportion rose with age. The most firearms-related murders were in the 20- to 24-year-old age group (2,060 deaths). However, the greatest percentage of firearms-related murders was among those aged 17 to 19 years (854 out of 996 murders, or 86%). After firearms, the weapons most frequently used to kill juveniles were personal weapons (hands, feet, and fists), especially among the youngest children, and knives.

Rape

Official statistics on rape are incomplete because the crime often goes unreported. The BJS estimates that only about one-third of the cases of completed or attempted rape are ever reported to police; other organizations estimate that the percentage of reported rapes is even lower. Because its data are collected through interviews, the BJS recognizes underreporting in its statistics. Acquaintance rape is far more common than stranger rape. Most experts conclude that in 80% to 85% of all rape cases, the victim knows the rapist.

The UCR defines rape as "penetration, no matter how slight, of the vagina or anus with any body part or object, or oral penetration by a sex organ of another person, without the consent of the victim." Rape is a crime of violence in which the victim may suffer serious physical injury and long-term psychological pain. According to the FBI, in *Crime in the United States, 2015*, there were 90,185 reported cases of rape in 2015, an increase of 6.3% from the year before.

Rape and sexual assault victims are disproportionately young. In "Sexual Violence: Facts at a Glance" (2012, https://www.cdc.gov/ViolencePrevention/pdf/SV-DataSheet-a.pdf), the CDC reports that 12.3% of female rape victims and 27.8% of male rape victims were first raped when they were aged 10 years or younger. More than a quarter (29.9%) of female rape victims were first raped between the ages of 11 and 17, 42.2% were first raped before age 18, and 37.4% were first raped between the ages of 18 and 24.

In "Rape and Sexual Assault Victimization among College-Age Females, 1995–2013" (December 2014, https://www.bjs.gov/content/pub/pdf/rsavcaf9513.pdf), Sofi Sinozich and Lynn Langton of the BJS report that from 1995 to 2013 females aged 18 to 24 years had the highest rate of rape and sexual assault victimization of any age group. The researchers find that in about 80% of cases the offender was known to the victim, and in about one out of 10 victimizations the offender had a weapon. They also note that most victims, whether students or nonstudents, did not report the rape or sexual assault to the police, and fewer than one in five received assistance from a victim services agency.

Serious Violent Victimization

In "America's Children in Brief: Key National Indicators of Well-Being, 2016" (2016, https://www.childstats.gov/americaschildren/phys4.asp), the Federal Interagency Forum on Child and Family Statistics notes that in 2014 the rates at which non-Hispanic white, non-Hispanic African American, and Hispanic youth aged 12 to 17 years were victims of serious violent crimes were comparable. For all teens aged 12 to 17 years, the rate of serious violent victimization dramatically decreased from the early 1990s through the early 2000s and has declined more slowly in the first decades of the 21st century. In 1993 teens aged 12 to 17 years experienced 40 serious violent crimes per 1,000 youth, compared with 8 crimes per 1,000 teens in 2014. (See Figure 7.1.)

Resources for Young Crime Victims

The National Center for Victims of Crimes (2017, http://victimsofcrime.org/help-for-crime-victims) provides services to help crime victims, including a national help line, 1-855-4VICTIM (1-855-484-2846), and online chat (Chat.VictimConnect.org), as well as web-based information and service referrals at VictimConnect.org. Other sites include the National Domestic Violence Hotline program Love Is Respect (http://www.loveisrespect.org) and Jennifer Ann's Group (http://jenniferann.org), which aim to prevent teen dating violence, and Childhelp's (https://www.childhelp.org) National Child Abuse Hotline (1-800-4-A-Child), which has served more than 10 million children with prevention, intervention, and treatment programs. The National Criminal Justice Reference Service (NCJRS, https://www.ncjrs.gov/faithbased/related.html) offers a variety of community- and faith-based resources for crime victims.

FIGURE 7.1

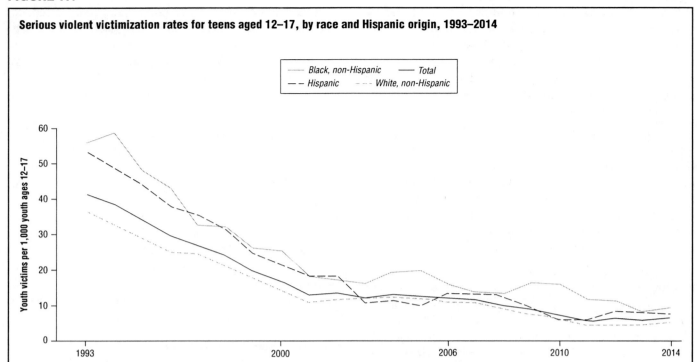

Serious violent victimization rates for teens aged 12–17, by race and Hispanic origin, 1993–2014

SOURCE: "Figure 15. Serious Violent Victimization Rates for Youth Ages 12–17 by Race and Hispanic Origin, 1993–2014," in *America's Children in Brief: Key National Indicators of Well-Being, 2016*, Federal Interagency Forum on Child and Family Statistics, 2016, https://www.childstats.gov/americaschildren/phys4.asp (accessed January 2, 2017)

CHAPTER 8

VIOLENCE AND GANGS

THE SCOPE OF THE GANG PROBLEM

Gangs have a long history in the United States, dating back to the 1800s. The United States became a self-styled melting pot during the 19th century as people of diverse ethnicities and religions entered the country. Some immigrants joined gangs to help them gain a group identity, defend themselves against other groups, and establish a unified presence. Although people feared street gangs of the 19th century, the gangs of the 21st century pose a greater threat to public safety than in years past.

Most criminal activities of the street gangs of the early 20th century involved delinquent acts or petty crimes, such as brawls with rival gangs. As the 20th century progressed, however, gangs became involved in more serious crimes. By the late 20th century, law enforcement officials had come to regard gang members in general as serious criminals who engaged in the illegal trafficking of drugs or weapons and used intimidation tactics and violence to pursue their goals. Respondents to the National Youth Gang Survey (NYGS) emphasized that a gang was defined by involvement in group criminal activity along with some degree of definition of a group as a separate entity, such as having a name, displaying distinct colors or symbols, or engaging in activities to protect the group's so-called territory. Law enforcement officers note that during the 1980s and 1990s more and more gang members began to support themselves through dealing drugs, such as crack cocaine and heroin. Many were said to have easy access to high-powered weapons. In addition, the proliferation of gangs during the late 20th century meant that groups moved beyond city boundaries into suburban and rural areas as well. At about the same time, youth violence surged.

Researchers noted various reasons for the growth of gangs during the end of the 20th century. According to Finn-Aage Esbensen of the University of Nebraska, Omaha, in *Preventing Adolescent Gang Involvement*

(September 2000, https://www.ncjrs.gov/pdffiles1/ojjdp/182210.pdf), "American society witnessed a reemergence of youth gang activity and media interest in this phenomenon in the 1980's and 1990's. 'Colors,' 'Boyz n the Hood,' other Hollywood productions, and MTV brought Los Angeles gang life to suburban and rural America." Glamorous media portrayals may have further enticed youth to become involved in gangs.

In an effort to track the growth and activities of gangs, the Office of Juvenile Justice and Delinquency Prevention's (OJJDP) National Youth Gang Center (now the National Gang Center [NGC]) began conducting the NYGS in 1996. The NGC reports in "National Youth Gang Survey Analysis" (2017, https://www.nationalgang center.gov/Survey-Analysis#SurveySampleAndMethodology) that for purposes of the survey, researchers annually query police and sheriff's departments serving cities, suburbs, and counties. Survey participants provide information on youth gangs within their jurisdiction. Motorcycle gangs, prison gangs, adult gangs, and hate or ideology-based groups are not included in the sample.

Statistics about gang membership show the growth of gangs during the early to mid-1990s. In *National Youth Gang Survey Analysis* (2017, https://www.nationalgang center.gov/Survey-Analysis/Prevalence-of-Gang-Problems), the NGC finds that after a decline between 1996 and 2001, gang activity increased between 2001 and 2005, and thereafter it remained relatively unchanged.

At first, gangs were big-city problems, but they soon spread to smaller areas. Arlen Egley Jr., James C. Howell, and Meena Harris of the OJJDP find in the fact sheet "Highlights of the 2012 National Youth Gang Survey" (December 2014, https://www.ojjdp.gov/pubs/248025.pdf) that in 2012 there were 30,790 gangs and 850,000 gang members in 3,100 jurisdictions throughout the United States. Not unexpectedly, law enforcement agencies in larger cities reported more gang activity and serious gang crime.

According to the National Gang Intelligence Center (NGIC), in *2015 National Gang Report* (2016, https://www.fbi.gov/file-repository/national-gang-report-2015.pdf/view), neighborhood-based gangs threaten many communities, encouraging violence, drug distribution, and crimes, such as robbery. About half of survey respondents said street gang–related crime had increased over the past two years, whereas an additional 36% reported no change in crime rates.

Street gangs are linked to crime in elementary, middle, and high schools and on some college campuses. Gangs recruit new members in schools, and many public schools are hotbeds of gang activity such as assaults, robberies, threats, and intimidation, as well as drug and weapons offenses. Gangs generally recruit from middle schools, although some gangs recruit students as early as the first grade. The NGIC reports that gang members use social media and messaging platforms such as Snapchat, Kik, and WhatsApp to communicate and reports that members of a Virginia gang recruited middle school students using Kik.

Gang presence on college campuses is increasing as more gang members head to college to escape gang life, participate in college athletic programs, or acquire skills their gang needs. A 2012 survey at a Tennessee university found that about 10% of students were active gang members, and about 10% of campus crime was attributed to suspected gang members. In 2013 three suspected gang members were arrested in connection with the shooting death of rival gang members near Santa Monica College in California. Reportedly, one of the victims attended the college.

New York City police have succeeded in reducing gang violence. In "Drop in Gang Violence Drove New York City Shootings below 1,000 in 2016" (NYTimes.com, January 3, 2017), Benjamin Mueller and Al Baker report that gang-related shootings fell from 560 in 2015 to 412 in 2016, and gang-related killings dropped from 129 to 70 during the same period. Police department spokesman Stephen P. Davis explains, "precision policing targets those people who are responsible for the violence, which in a significant amount of cases are gangs. By going after the gang members, arresting them, we recognize the resultant reduction in violence."

YOUTH GANG ACTIVITIES

Researchers, law enforcement agencies, and community groups devote time to learning more about gangs and the types of characteristics they share. They scrutinize gang slang, graffiti, hand signs, colors, and initiations, among other characteristics. The goal is to learn more about how gangs communicate and interact, both internally and externally. If educators, law enforcement officials, and other concerned adults can recognize the signs that young people may be involved in gangs, they will be better able to intervene.

Paul Boxer of Rutgers University points out in "Youth Gangs and Adolescent Development: New Findings, New Challenges, and New Directions: Introduction to the Special Section" (*Journal of Research on Adolescence*, vol. 24, no. 2, June 2014) that youth gang activity is "more entrenched and more widespread than in years past." He observes that youth gangs can exert positive and protective influences such as support, safety, and companionship, but more often increase adolescents' risk for violent victimization. Gangs use clothing, graffiti, symbols, slang, and other signals to establish and reinforce gang membership. Some of these signals are described in this section.

Various gangs have created their own slang language. Although some terms are used in gangs throughout the country, others are only used regionally and within certain gangs. Several terms originated with the infamous Bloods and Crips gangs of Los Angeles, California, who have been adversaries for many years. Examples include "banging" (involved in gang activities), "colors" (clothing of a particular color, such as jackets, shoes, or bandanas, worn by gang members to identify themselves as part of the gang), "O.G." ("original gangster," meaning a gang member who has killed someone or a founding member or leader of a gang), "tagging" (marking a territory with graffiti), and "turf" (territory).

Graffiti

The most common type of graffiti is that of personal musings—thoughts written down quickly in public places, such as restrooms and phone booths. Sometimes humorous, this type of graffiti might be of a sexual nature or might include memorable quotes. Tagging is another type of graffiti. A tag is a signature, or moniker, that may incorporate the artist's physical features or symbolize his or her personality. Tags are usually found on exterior building walls in urban areas. They may also appear on mass transit systems (buses and trains), freeway overpasses, and other public spaces. Mural-type graffiti is known as piecing or bombing. The piece usually contains elaborate depictions or a montage of images. Often, slogans appear within the piece. Whereas tags can be done quickly, piecing may take several hours to complete and require many cans of spray paint in a variety of colors.

Gangs use graffiti for many purposes: to communicate with other gang members or as a newsletter. Tags or monikers may be used to show a gang's hierarchy. Pieces may memorialize a dead gang member or pay tribute to the crimes committed by gang members. Some pieces may enumerate rules in the gang's society, whereas others may advertise a gang's presence in the neighborhood. Gang graffiti may also serve as a threatening message to rival gangs, as if to say, "Stay away from our turf." In the 21st century graffiti is considered vandalism and a public nuisance and is punishable by law in the United States.

Hand Signs

Hand signs are a way of communicating concepts or ideas without using words. However, only those individuals who are familiar with the gesture's meaning are able to understand the message being conveyed. The rise of gang hand signs began in the Los Angeles area during the 1950s. Since that time many gangs have developed hand signs for use between members of the group. Gang members "throw" or "flash" hand signs as a way of communicating among themselves, such as to send secret messages to other members within the group. For example, placing a clenched fist over the heart means "I'll die for you."

According to the NGIC, in *QuickGuide to Gangs* (April 2009, http://www.communitycorrections.org/images/publi cations/QuickGuidetoGangs.pdf), each gang usually has a hand sign that symbolizes affiliation with the gang. For example, the Los Angeles Bloods use the sign B (creating a circle with the thumb and index finger, with the other fingers raised) to signify membership in the gang. Crips use a sign that represents the letter C. Although this enables gang members to recognize other members or affiliates, it can also be used against them. A gang might use gestures created by a rival gang in an act called false flagging. When this occurs, a gang member will flash a rival gang's hand sign as a way to infiltrate the opposing gang or to lure an unsuspecting adversary into a bad situation.

Flying the Colors

The idea of wearing different colors to identify opposing sides is not new. For example, during wartime opposing armies use different colors to symbolize their cause or to protect their territory. Flags, uniforms, and the like are made in the color chosen to represent the nation or army at war. By donning the color of the army, soldiers are identified as being on one side or the other, and the enemy can be spotted more easily. During the American Revolution (1775–1783) most of the British forces wore red uniforms; thus, they were called the Redcoats. To distinguish themselves from the British, the American colonists chose uniforms of blue.

This is also true of gangs. In *QuickGuide to Gangs*, the NGIC notes that gangs use color to distinguish themselves from rival gangs and to protect their territory. Gang members often show support for the gang by wearing so-called uniforms. Wearing clothes in the gang's colors, such as bandanas, shoes, jackets, jewelry, and other articles of clothing, shows a person's membership in one gang over another. For example, two of the largest gangs in Los Angeles are the Bloods and the Crips. The Bloods use red, and the Crips use blue. These colors are a way to symbolize the gang's unity, power, and pride.

Dave Collins, however, reports in "Gangs Aren't Wearing Colors Anymore" (Associated Press, September 16, 2014) that to avoid detection by law enforcement many gangs no longer fly their colors, flaunt distinctive tattoos, or use hand signs. Instead, gang members (especially those involved in white-collar crime and activities on the Internet) use electronic communications and technology to stay in touch and to track law enforcement efforts to monitor them.

Technology

In the *2015 National Gang Report*, the NGIC notes that the social media platforms used most often by gang members are Facebook, YouTube, Instagram, and Twitter. The NGIC indicates that technology plays an important role in gang communication and the recruitment of gang members. Gangs use smartphones and global positioning systems to communicate, monitor law enforcement and rivals, and expose informants. Websites and social media platforms are used to intimidate other gangs as well as to recruit new members.

CHARACTERISTICS OF GANG MEMBERS

Based on reports by law enforcement agencies, most gang members are male; however, female involvement in gangs is on the rise in the 21st century. In fact, the NGIC notes in *2015 National Gang Report* that prison-based gangs rely on female members to operate outside of the confines of prison.

The NGIC observes that females are assuming active roles in gangs, such as "serving as soldiers and co-conspirators, assisting with drug transactions, acting as decoys, initiating fights, providing stash houses for drugs and fugitive members, acquiring weapons and weapons permits, recruiting other females for membership and prostitution, working as prostitutes, and acting as leaders while their significant other is incarcerated."

In "Improving Understanding of and Responsiveness to Gang-Involved Girls" (*National Gang Center Newsletter*, Fall 2016, http://www.nccdglobal.org/sites/default/files/content/ngc-newsletter-2016-fall.pdf), Angie M. Wolf, Estivaliz Castro, and Caroline Glesmann of the National Council on Crime and Delinquency present the results of interviews with 114 girls and young women aged 14 to 25 years in gangs in California. Nearly half (44%) of the interviewees were Hispanic or Latino, 36% were African American, 14% were mixed race, 3% were Native American, 2% were Pacific Islander, and 1% were white. About one-quarter identified as lesbian, gay, bisexual, or questioning, and 40% were pregnant or parents at the time of the interview.

The researchers find that nearly three-quarters (71%) had been arrested at some point, about half (49%) had been on probation, and the same proportion had been in detention. More than 90% had at least one family member who had been arrested, in jail or in prison, and 86% had at least one family member or close friend involved in a gang.

Although most young women said they did not have a specific role in the gang, some described their role as "being loyal," "doing what you're told," or "being a fighter," which included training other female gang members or opposing females from rival gangs.

Reasons for Joining a Gang

Why juveniles, youths, and even adults participate in gangs is the subject of much research. Published studies include those by Phelan A. Wyrick and James C. Howell in "Strategic Risk-Based Response to Youth Gangs" (*Juvenile Justice*, vol. 9, no. 1, September 2004); Pamela Lachman, Caterina G. Roman, and Meagan Cahill in "Assessing Youth Motivations for Joining a Peer Group as Risk Factors for Delinquent and Gang Behavior" (*Youth Violence and Youth Justice*, October 17, 2012); and Jane L. Wood in "Understanding Gang Membership: The Significance of Group Processes" (*Group Process and Intergroup Relations*, vol. 17, no. 6, November 2014). The reasons for gang participation vary greatly among gang members, but there are a few basic motives. Some of the most common reasons to join a gang are:

- Feeling marginalized by society and seeking a commonality with others in similar situations

- Wanting power and respect

- Having friends involved in gangs and wanting to be a part of that

- Desiring a sense of belonging when that is not available through a traditional family setting

- Seeking safety and/or protection from bullies, rival gangs, family members, or others

- Having power in numbers

- Ending poverty and joblessness by turning to criminal activities, such as stealing and drug trafficking

- Needing to feel a sense of purpose

- Having trouble or a disinterest in school

- Living in neighborhoods or communities where other troubled youth roam the streets

- Adding organization and structure to one's life

- Having feelings of low self-esteem that are diminished through encouragement from other gang members

In "Why American Boys Join Street Gangs" (*International Journal of Sociology and Anthropology*, vol. 5, no. 9, December 2013), Stanley S. Taylor of California State University, Sacramento, looks at the criteria that make children good candidates for gang membership. Taylor reviewed the relevant literature on gangs and conducted face-to-face interviews with people, some of whom were teachers, who have had close, regular interaction with gang members. Others were Los Angeles area gang members themselves and knew firsthand about gang socialization techniques and methods.

Taylor indicates that among African American and Hispanic youth who join gangs, most join between the ages of 11 and 15 years. Among the gang members interviewed, he finds a clear progression from anxiety, fear, and disturbed irrational behaviors in their families in early childhood to oppositional defiance; angry or disruptive behavior toward family and other authority figures before 10 years of age; conduct disorder issues (behavior that violates the rights of others or basic social rules) by 11 to 16 years of age; and sociopathic behavior (acting without morals and capable of violence) from 17 years of age onward.

Taylor's literature review reveals that children in single-parent mother-headed households have higher rates of gang involvement, as do those who have little contact with their father. Not unexpectedly, children with gang members in their family are also at increased risk for gang membership. The interviews confirm that children's frustration and anxiety stemming from their family life can develop into the antisocial behavior that is valued and rewarded in gangs. Taylor concludes that this study suggests a strong relationship between children's home life, their frustrations, and gang membership.

Wolf, Castro, and Glesmann find that many girls and young women join gangs because their families, friends, and romantic partners are gang members. Some of the female gang members interviewed said they felt they did not have a choice about being in a gang or being labeled as gang members.

Recruitment and Initiation

Gang recruiters offer prospective members a chance to be a part of something—to gain a sense of belonging that might be lacking in their life. The gang attracts and recruits new members to increase its power. In turn, some juveniles see this power in their school or neighborhood and may feel pressured into joining a gang. Gang members may threaten juveniles into joining by offering protection from bullies or rival gangs. Others may be eager to join a gang, thinking it is cool and exciting to be part of a clique that engages in criminal activity.

In response to gang recruitment activities, some states and localities have changed their laws to make any kind of gang recruitment, even if it does not involve criminal behavior, illegal. For example, the NGC (2015, https://www.nationalgangcenter.gov/legislation/indiana)

reports that effective July 1, 2014, Indiana legislation made illegal "solicitation, recruitment, enticement, or intimidation" of anyone under 18 years of age, as well as such activities within 1,000 feet (308 m) of school property. As of 2017, gang recruitment was illegal in at least 20 states.

As is common in some social clubs, many prospective gang inductees must undergo an initiation to show the gang that they are worthy enough to be accepted into the group. Initiates generally must endure an initiation rite that is similar to severe hazing. In rare instances a new member may be "blessed in" (not having to prove his or her worth) because a brother or a sister is already a member of the gang. In "The Right to Belong: Individual Motives and Youth Gang Initiation Rites" (*Deviant Behavior*, June 2016), Karine Descormiers and Raymond R. Corrado describe three kinds of initiations youth gang members may undergo: the prospective member is asked to commit one or more nonviolent crimes; the prospective member is beaten by gang members to show that he or she can take the beating and fight back if permitted; and the prospective member must inflict violence or perform a violent criminal act such as robbery.

Studies show that in many cases adolescents may refuse to join a gang or leave it without fear of reprisal, even though gangs try to maintain the illusion that leaving is impossible. Eryn Nicole O'Neal et al. explain in "Girls, Gangs, and Getting Out: Gender Differences and Similarities in Leaving the Gang" (*Youth Violence and Juvenile Justice*, vol. 14, no. 1, 2016) that although some males and females report "pull motivations for disengagement (i.e., external to the gang) and active or hostile methods for leaving (i.e., getting 'jumped out')," the most common exit strategies were passive ones such as moving out of the area and being allowed out by the gang. Family helped many former members to disengage from gangs. After leaving gangs, females were more concerned about attacks on their families and themselves, whereas males were more concerned about being treated like a gang member by police after they had relinquished their gang membership.

Indicators of Gang Involvement

Many groups have compiled lists to aid parents, educators, and others looking for signs that a juvenile has joined a gang. Examples can be found in Wyrick and Howell's "Strategic Risk-Based Response to Youth Gangs" and in the U.S. Department of Justice's "A Parent's Quick Reference Card: Recognizing and Preventing Gang Involvement" (July 2005, https://www.justice.gov/sites/default/files/usao-sdfl/legacy/2012/12/31/Parents QuickReference.pdf). Although a youth may present several warning signs that might indicate he or she is in a gang, these signs are not foolproof; that is, the youth may actually not be in a gang or even be a so-called wannabe or gonnabe (at-risk youth). Nonetheless, the more signs

that a youth displays, the more likely it is that he or she is headed for gang involvement. The following are some potential warning signs:

- Experiences a sudden drop in school grades
- Lacks interest in school and other activities that were once important
- Becomes truant (skips school)
- Comes home late
- Acts more outwardly aggressive or outright defiant
- Develops a new circle of friends who seem more rough and tough
- Behaves more secretively and is less forthcoming
- Changes clothing style; begins wearing some colors exclusively or wears clothes in a unique way consistently (such as rolling up pant legs)
- Exhibits more antisocial tendencies and becomes withdrawn or uninterested in family activities
- Suddenly acquires costly material possessions (such as jewelry or electronics equipment) or large amounts of cash, and the source of the funds cannot be explained
- Starts using a new nickname (or street name)
- Becomes fascinated with weapons, particularly guns
- Has new cuts and bruises indicating evidence of being in a fight and is unable to provide a reasonable explanation
- Sports new unusual tattoos
- Writes gang graffiti on notebooks, schoolbooks, and posters
- Develops an increased interest in gangsta rap music
- Hides a stash of spray paint, permanent markers, and other graffiti supplies
- Has encounters with law enforcement
- Shows dependency on drugs and/or alcohol

THE SPREAD OF GANGS

In *2015 National Gang Report*, the NGIC states that Hispanic gangs that originated in the southwestern United States pose a significant threat to the region, operating along the nearly 2,000 miles (3,200 km) of border between the United States and Mexico. Figure 8.1 shows the criminal activities gangs engage in across the border.

Outlaw motorcycle gangs (OMGs) are among the most violent gangs, engaging in crimes such as assault, robbery, and homicide. Although the percentage of OMGs is relatively low, they are viewed as extremely problematic, and a significant threat to the communities where they operate. The NGIC reports that in recent years, OMG members have been employed in white-

FIGURE 8.1

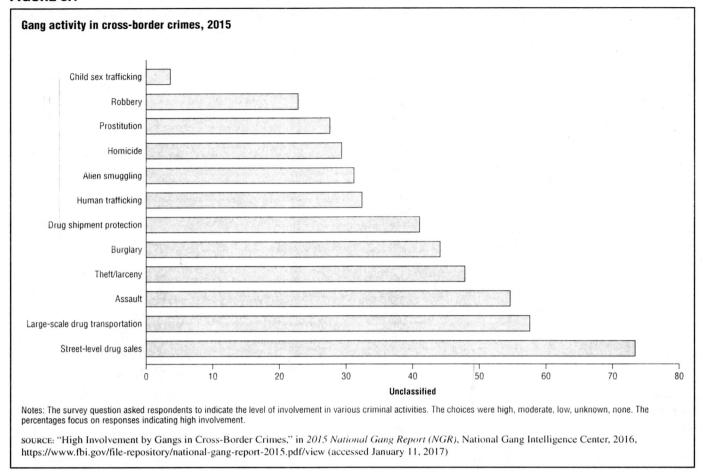

Gang activity in cross-border crimes, 2015

Notes: The survey question asked respondents to indicate the level of involvement in various criminal activities. The choices were high, moderate, low, unknown, none. The percentages focus on responses indicating high involvement.

SOURCE: "High Involvement by Gangs in Cross-Border Crimes," in *2015 National Gang Report (NGR)*, National Gang Intelligence Center, 2016, https://www.fbi.gov/file-repository/national-gang-report-2015.pdf/view (accessed January 11, 2017)

collar professions and as business owners, operating retail venues such as motorcycle repair shops and tattoo parlors. Some of these businesses may be used as fronts to enable criminal activity.

GANGS IN NATIVE AMERICAN COMMUNITIES

Native American communities are not exempt from gang problems. These gangs are primarily composed of youth and engage in less criminal activity than other types of gangs. Transnational criminal organizations transport cocaine, marijuana, and methamphetamine north and south through the region with the assistance of these youth and other gangs.

To learn more about Native American gangs, Adrienne Freng et al. conducted a survey of high school students in a western reservation community and reported their findings in "The New American Gang? Gangs in Indian Country" (*Journal of Contemporary Criminal Justice*, vol. 28, no. 4, November 2012). The researchers observe that Native American gangs were large, with many containing more than 30 members. Their members tended to be primarily between 12 and 24 years of age, with most under the age of 18 years. Native American gangs generally participated in less violence than other gangs.

Freng et al. find that more than a quarter (27%) of the students reported that they were currently or had been gang members. The majority of students that identified as being in a gang were male (60%). More than three-quarters (79%) joined a gang before the age of 13 years. Just 16% of gang members surveyed came from intact two-parent families, and two-thirds (67%) of gang members reported that a family member belonged to a gang. Interestingly, about one-third (35%) of those not in a gang also reported gang members in their family.

Native American gang members said they joined a gang for "fun" (36%), to gain respect (36%), because a family member was in a gang (32%), because a friend was in a gang (24%), for protection (24%), or for money (16%). As expected, gang members were significantly more involved in delinquency than nonmembers. Gang members were more likely to be arrested (48%) and more involved in burglary (28%) than nonmembers. About one-third (32%) of gang members admitted committing assault compared with only 11% of nonmembers. Nearly half (48%) of gang members said they carried a concealed weapon.

In *Voices of Native Youth Report: Volume IV* (2014, https://assets.aspeninstitute.org/content/uploads/files/content/upload/Voices%20Report%20Vol%20%20IV_2015.pdf), the Center for Native American Youth at the Aspen Institute confirms that gang activity is a problem in many Native American tribal and urban communities and explains that some attribute the rise of gang activity in tribal nation communities to the lack of youth programming available in the communities. The center reports, "Youth expressed concerns about gang activity off-reservation transferring to the reservation. Without positive activities and safe environments, like after-school programs offered in evenings and on weekends, at-risk youth are more likely to turn to gangs as an outlet for their frustrations and source for a sense of a belonging."

GANGS IN SCHOOLS

The presence of street gangs is a serious concern in U.S. schools. These gangs are often involved in illegal activities, such as drugs and weapons trafficking. Gang presence in schools often leads to fear among students who are not affiliated with gangs and may encourage them to join a gang for protection. In schools with significant gang presence, the level of violence is frequently higher than in schools with less gang presence.

Anlan Zhang, Lauren Musu-Gillette, and Barbara A. Oudekerk address in *Indicators of School Crime and Safety: 2015* (May 2016, https://www.bjs.gov/content/pub/pdf/iscs15.pdf) the issue of student reports of street gangs in schools. In 2013, 13% of public school students in grades nine to 12 said there were gangs in their school, compared with just 2% of private school students.

Urban school students were the most likely to report the presence of street gangs at their school. Nearly one in five (18.3%) of urban school students said gangs were present at their school in 2013. (See Figure 8.2.) Suburban school students (10.8%) and rural students (6.8%) were much less likely to report gang activities.

Zhang, Musu-Gillette, and Oudekerk note that African American and Hispanic students were more likely than white or Asian American students to report that gangs were present at their school in 2013. One in five Hispanic students (20.1%) and 18.6% of African American students reported gangs at their school. (See Figure 8.3.) In contrast, 7.5% of white students and 9.4% of Asian American students reported the presence of gangs at their school.

Indicators of Gang Presence at School

Michelle Arciaga, Wayne Sakamoto, and Errika Fearbry Jones assert in *Responding to Gangs in the School Setting* (November 2010, https://www.nationalgangcenter.gov/Content/Documents/Bulletin-5.pdf) that school staff and administrators may not recognize gang activity. The researchers advise schools to assess the impact of gangs by monitoring crime and law enforcement data, collecting data about gang-related incidents and activity in and around their school, and exploring student and staff perceptions of gang activity.

FIGURE 8.2

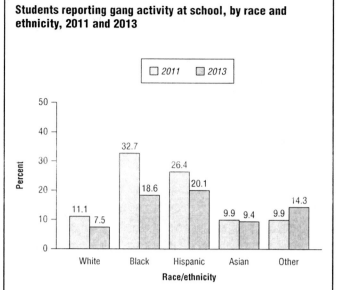

Students reporting gang activity at school, by race and ethnicity, 2011 and 2013

Note: Race categories exclude persons of Hispanic ethnicity. "Other" includes American Indians/Alaska Natives, Pacific Islanders, and persons of two or more races. All gangs, whether or not they are involved in violent or illegal activity, are included. "At school" includes in the school building, on school property, on a school bus, and going to and from school.

SOURCE: Anlan Zhang, Lauren Musu-Gillette, and Barbara A. Oudekerk, "Figure 8.2. Percentage of Students Ages 12–18 Who Reported That Gangs Were Present at School during the School Year, By Race/Ethnicity: 2011 and 2013," in *Indicators of School Crime and Safety: 2015*, U.S. Department of Education, National Center for Education Statistics, and U.S. Department of Justice, Bureau of Justice Statistics, May 2016, https://www.bjs.gov/content/pub/pdf/iscs15.pdf (accessed January 11, 2017)

They also recommend using an assessment guide such as *A Guide to Assessing Your Community's Youth Gang Problem* (May 2009, https://www.nationalgangcenter.gov/Content/Documents/Assessment-Guide/Assessment-Guide.pdf) by the OJJDP. The guide stresses the importance of assessing the gang-related problems by analyzing different types of data including:

- Community Demographic Data: General information about the community and its residents to provide a context for the assessment

- Law Enforcement Data: The type and extent of gang activity and crime and the characteristics of local gangs

- School Data: Information about the school environment and culture and characteristics of school students who are involved in and/or at risk of involvement in gangs as well as the perceptions of teachers and other school personnel

- Community Perceptions Data: Information about how the community views and experiences the gang problem, including community members, parents, community leaders, students, and gang members themselves

FIGURE 8.3

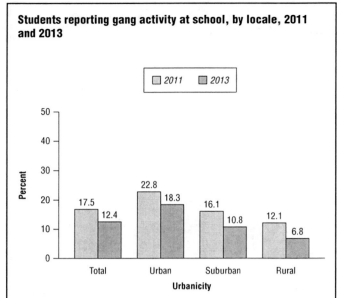

Students reporting gang activity at school, by locale, 2011 and 2013

□ 2011   ▩ 2013

Note: Urbanicity refers to the Standard Metropolitan Statistical Area (MSA) status of the respondent's household as defined in 2000 by the U.S. Census Bureau. Categories include "central city of an MSA (urban)," "in MSA but not in central city (suburban)," and "not MSA (rural)." All gangs, whether or not they are involved in violent or illegal activity, are included. "At school" includes in the school building, on school property, on a school bus, and going to and from school.

SOURCE: Anlan Zhang, Lauren Musu-Gillette, and Barbara A. Oudekerk, "Figure 8.1. Percentage of Students Ages 12–18 Who Reported That Gangs Were Present at School during the School Year, by Urbanicity: 2011 and 2013," in *Indicators of School Crime and Safety: 2015*, U.S. Department of Education, National Center for Education Statistics, and U.S. Department of Justice, Bureau of Justice Statistics, May 2016, https://www.bjs.gov/content/pub/pdf/iscs15.pdf (accessed January 11, 2017)

- Community Resources Data: Past and current responses to gang problems, including access to and availability of services to prevent gang activity or intervene to curtail it

Gangs and Drugs at School

Research has demonstrated the relationship between drug availability and gang presence at school. For example, in "The Impact of Gangs on Communities" (*NYGC Bulletin*, August 2006, https://www.nationalgangcenter .gov/Content/Documents/Impact-of-Gangs-on-Communities .pdf), James C. Howell asserts that "there is a strong correlation between gang presence in schools and both guns in schools and availability of drugs in school." Students who report that any drugs are readily available at school are much more likely to report gangs at their school than those who say that no drugs are available at their school. Still, the exact nature of this relationship remains unclear. Is the availability of drugs because of the gang activity, or is the presence of gangs part of an underlying problem that contributes to the availability of drugs? Zhang, Musu-Gillette, and Oudekerk note that more than one in five (22%) high school students reported that drugs were available to them on school

property in 2013, down from about 26% in 2011. (See Figure 8.4.)

Gang Criminality at School

The presence of gangs in school is related to criminal activity. According to Howell, "Where they have a substantial presence, youth gangs are linked with serious delinquency problems in elementary and secondary schools." The National Crime Victimization Survey (administered by the Bureau of Justice Statistics) and other studies find that higher percentages of students report knowing a student who brought a gun to school when there is gang presence in the school than when gangs were not present. Furthermore, gang presence at a school is related to seeing a student with a gun at school—more students say they have seen a student with a gun in school when gangs are present than when gangs are not present.

Howell also asserts that gangs contribute substantially to victimizations at school. It is believed that some students join gangs to avoid persecution by gang members. For them, gang membership serves as a form of protection from other students who may threaten them or wish them harm.

GANG CRIME AND VIOLENCE

There is an established association between gang membership and violent delinquency. In "The Impact of Gang Formation on Local Patterns of Crime" (*Journal of Research in Crime and Delinquency*, vol. 44, no. 2, May 2007), George Tita and Greg Ridgeway acknowledge that gang members commit more crimes and more serious crimes than do nonmembers, but they also examine whether the emergence of gangs has an impact on the crime rate. They argue that gangs typically form in areas that have higher crime than other areas, but once gangs form, they attract or generate even higher levels of crime. In "Estimating the Effect of Gang Membership on Nonviolent and Violent Delinquency: A Counterfactual Analysis" (*Aggressive Behavior*, vol. 36, no. 6, November–December 2006), J. C. Barnes, Kevin M. Beaver, and J. Mitchell Miller find that gang membership predicts involvement in violent delinquency and report that "gang members are more likely to be involved in violent activities up to 5 years after joining the gang."

Homicides and Violent Crimes

The impact and severity of gang activity in an area is often measured by the numbers of gang-related homicides. The term *gang-motivated homicides* refers to those murders that further the interests of a gang, whereas *gang-related homicides* generally refers to murders where a gang member is either a perpetrator or the victim. Most localities use this broader definition, rather

FIGURE 8.4

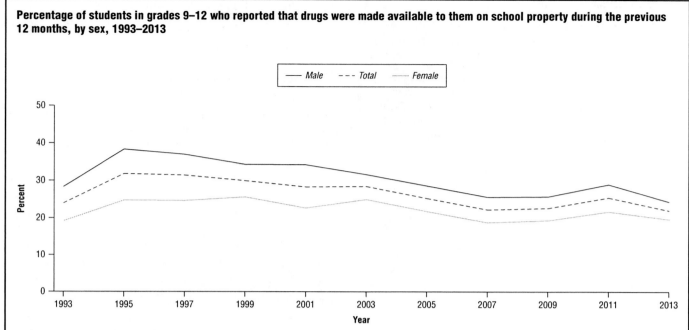

Percentage of students in grades 9–12 who reported that drugs were made available to them on school property during the previous 12 months, by sex, 1993–2013

Note: "On school property" was not defined for survey respondents.

SOURCE: Anlan Zhang, Lauren Musu-Gillette, and Barbara A. Oudekerk, "Figure 9.1. Percentage of Students in Grades 9–12 Who Reported That Illegal Drugs Were Made Available to Them on School Property during the Previous 12 Months, by Sex: Selected Years, 1993 through 2013," in *Indicators of School Crime and Safety: 2015*, U.S. Department of Education, National Center for Education Statistics, and U.S. Department of Justice, Bureau of Justice Statistics, May 2016, https://www.bjs.gov/content/pub/pdf/iscs15.pdf (accessed January 11, 2017)

than the motive-based definition, when classifying a homicide as gang related.

Nearly half of respondents to the National Youth Gang Survey reported an increase in nonlethal gang-related violent crime from 2011 to 2012. The total number of gang-related homicides reported by NYGS respondents averaged about 2,000 per year from 2007 to 2012. Although the number of gang-related homicides decreased 2% from 2010 to 2011, it increased 28% from 2011 to 2012 in cities with populations over 100,000.

CONSEQUENCES OF BEING IN A GANG

Gang membership can be dangerous. Besides living a life with the potential for more violence and crime than the average youth would experience, there are many other consequences. Researchers find that joining a gang in adolescence has consequences in adulthood beyond criminal behavior, even after a person leaves the gang. For example, Amanda B. Gilman, Karl G. Hill, and J. David Hawkins of the University of Washington, Seattle, describe in "Long-Term Consequences of Adolescent Gang Membership for Adult Functioning" (*American Journal of Public Health*, vol. 104, no. 5, May 2014) some of the common consequences. These include "higher rates of self-reported crime, receipt of illegal income, incarceration, drug abuse or dependence, poor general health, and welfare receipt and lower rates of high school graduation."

Gilman, Hill, and Hawkins note that when compared with their age peers who did not join gangs, youth who joined gangs were half as likely to graduate from high school, nearly three times more likely as adults to commit a crime, more than three times more likely to receive income from illegal sources, and more than twice as likely to have been incarcerated during the previous year. Former gang members were also nearly three times more likely to have drug-abuse issues and were about twice as likely to say they were in poor health or receiving public assistance.

GANG PREVENTION STRATEGIES

The OJJDP operates Gang Reduction Programs in certain high-risk neighborhoods. These programs use the OJJDP's Comprehensive Gang Model, which is described in *Comprehensive Gang Prevention, Intervention, and Suppression Model* (2017, https://www.national gangcenter.gov/SPT/Programs/53). This model has been extensively researched and proven effective in combating gang activity in many states.

The model consists of five key strategies:

- Community mobilization: involvement of local citizens, including former gang-involved youth, community groups, agencies, and coordination of programs and staff functions within and across agencies

- Opportunities provision: development of a variety of specific education, training, and employment programs targeting gang-involved youth

- Social intervention: involving youth-serving agencies, schools, grassroots groups, faith-based organizations, police, and other juvenile/criminal justice organizations in "reaching out" to gang-involved youth and their families, and linking them with the conventional world and needed services

- Suppression: formal and informal social control procedures, including close supervision and monitoring of gang-involved youth by agencies of the juvenile/criminal justice system and also by community-based agencies, schools, and grassroots groups

- Organizational change and development: development and implementation of policies and procedures that result in the most effective use of available and potential resources, within and across agencies, to better address the gang problem

Gang Resistance Education and Training (GREAT) is another example of a federal program that helps combat youth gangs. GREAT (2015, https://www.great-online.org/GREAT-Home) trains law enforcement officers to go into classrooms and teach elementary- and middle-school students how to avoid delinquent behavior and violence. There are also private organizations such as National School Safety and Security Services that help schools develop gang prevention, intervention, and enforcement strategies.

Gang Prevention through Targeted Outreach (https://www.ojjdp.gov/pubs/gun_violence/sect08-k.html) is a program operated by the Boys and Girls Clubs of America that attempts to recruit youth aged six to 18 years at risk of gang involvement into their community's Boys and Girls Club, where they can learn skills to help them avoid gang membership and succeed in life.

Gang Free Inc. (http://www.gangfreeinc.org) is a nonprofit organization that targets at-risk children and teens and provides programs and services aimed at helping them and their families resist joining gangs. Besides gang awareness and prevention education programs, Gang Free offers a school-based gang prevention curriculum for children in second, fourth, and sixth grades, a court-approved parent and teen education program, graffiti pre-

vention and abatement education programs, and after-school and youth job training and development programs.

In *It's about Time: Prevention and Intervention Services for Gang-Affiliated Girls* (March 2012, http://www.nccdglobal.org/sites/default/files/publication_pdf/focus-its-about-time.pdf), Angela Wolf and Livier Gutierrez of the National Council on Crime and Delinquency note that although increasing numbers of girls are involved in gangs, most prevention and intervention services are not designed for them. The researchers assert that girls in gangs need services that address sexual abuse as well as special support when they try to leave a gang, especially if pregnancy is the reason they are choosing to leave. They also stress that girls in gangs and those at risk of joining gangs need programs that help them develop life skills and provide mentorship and peer support. Wolf and Gutierrez cite several programs, including the Los Angeles–based Girls & Gangs, as providing the gender-specific services that female gang members need.

Anthony A. Braga, David M. Hureau, and Andrew V. Papachristos evaluate in "Deterring Gang-Involved Gun Violence: Measuring the Impact of Boston's Operation Ceasefire on Street Gang Behavior" (*Journal of Quantitative Criminology*, vol. 30, no. 1, March 2014) Boston's novel approach to preventing youth violence. During the 1990s the approach known as Operation Ceasefire "focused enforcement and social service resources on a small number of gang-involved offenders at the heart of the city's youth violence problem." The researchers compare the gangs treated with the Operation Ceasefire approach to those untreated and find the Ceasefire intervention was "associated with statistically significant reductions in gun violence."

The extent to which gang prevention programs are effective varies. In "Promises Kept? A Meta-analysis of Gang Membership Prevention Programs" (*Journal of Criminological Research, Policy and Practice*, vol. 2, no. 2, 2016), Jennifer S. Wong et al. report that their review of six studies evaluating the effectiveness of gang prevention programs finds "a significant, positive effect of gang prevention programs at reducing gang membership." The researchers caution, however, that this finding was based largely on the results of a single study, and they observe that "There is a critical need in the field of gang control for rigorous evaluation of prevention strategies."

CHAPTER 9
CRIME AND VIOLENCE IN THE SCHOOLS

School is supposed to be a safe haven where young people can go to learn the basics of mathematics, literature, science, and other subjects without fearing for their safety, feeling intimidated, or being harassed. Although school administrators and teachers work to create and maintain safe and secure schools, crime and violence have found their way into the hallways and classrooms and onto school grounds. Despite media attention to school shootings, fatal violence at schools is relatively low. Nonfatal crime, however, occurs in far greater numbers, sometimes even more frequently at school than away from school.

Safety is and will continue to be a concern at schools. A rash of school shootings and bomb threats that occurred during the 1990s, and that continued to occur in the 21st century, brought increasing attention to school safety issues and what must be done to protect students. Two horrific school shootings—Columbine High School in Littleton, Colorado, in April 1999 and Sandy Hook Elementary School in Newtown, Connecticut, in December 2012—have become icons of the worst school massacres in U.S. history. The Columbine High School shooting took the lives of 12 students and one teacher, and the Sandy Hook Elementary School shooting claimed the lives of 20 first graders and six adults. In 2016 there were 15 school shooting incidents in the United States.

Discussions about school safety that began after the shootings at Columbine High School and at the Virginia Polytechnic Institute and State University in 2007, in which a student killed 32 people and then himself, were reignited by the Newtown shooting. Various studies about school violence and crime were issued during the late 1990s and the first decade of the 21st century as researchers examined past trends and tried to predict patterns for the future. Researchers looked at how many children bring weapons to school, are injured in fights, are afraid to go to school, or are subjected to disciplinary actions. Educators,

school administrators, parents, and students themselves are striving to make schools safe places.

Many questions remain unanswered. Exactly how much crime and violence exist in U.S. schools in the 21st century? Has it increased or decreased in recent years? What effect did the Newtown shooting have on students and public opinion in general? Is there a danger that students, educators, and school officials will under-report school crime and violence to police? Will enhanced security such as upgraded intercom systems, emergency preparedness drills, metal detectors, and the presence of uniformed security guards in schools prevent future violence? Should teachers be armed or trained in self-defense? Who should pay for intensified security measures in schools?

VIOLENT DEATHS AT SCHOOL

During the 2012–13 school year there were 53 school-associated violent deaths in elementary and secondary schools, including 41 homicides, 11 suicides, and 1 death caused by legal intervention (caused by police and other people with legal authority to use deadly force) of students, staff, and other school personnel. (See Table 9.1.)

Anlan Zhang, Lauren Musu-Gillette, and Barbara A. Oudekerk state in *Indicators of School Crime and Safety: 2015* (May 2016, https://www.bjs.gov/content/pub/pdf/iscs15.pdf) that of the 53 violent school-associated deaths that occurred during the 2012–13 school year, 31 homicides, 6 suicides, and 1 legal intervention death were of students aged five to 18 years. Between July 1, 1992, and June 30, 2013, 963 school-associated violent deaths occurred across the United States, including 493 homicides of school-age children.

Despite the understandable fear that is generated by the media coverage of such events, the probability of being killed at school is very low. The percentage of

TABLE 9.1

Number of school-associated violent deaths, school years 1992–93 to 2012–13

Year	Total	School-associated violent deaths[a] of all persons (includes students, staff, and other nonstudents)				Homicides of youth ages 5–18		Suicides of youth ages 5–18	
		Homicides	Suicides	Legal interventions	Unintentional firearm-related deaths	Homicides at school[b]	Total homicides	Suicides at school[b]	Total suicides[c]
1992–1993	57	47	10	0	0	34	2,721	6	1,680
1993–1994	48	38	10	0	0	29	2,932	7	1,723
1994–1995	48	39	8	0	1	28	2,696	7	1,767
1995–1996	53	46	6	1	0	32	2,545	6	1,725
1996–1997	48	45	2	1	0	28	2,221	1	1,633
1997–1998	57	47	9	1	0	34	2,100	6	1,626
1998–1999	47	38	6	2	1	33	1,777	4	1,597
1999–2000	37[d]	26[d]	11[d]	0[d]	0[d]	14[d]	1,567	8[d]	1,415
2000–2001	34[d]	26[d]	7[d]	1[d]	0[d]	14[d]	1,509	6[d]	1,493
2001–2002	36[d]	27[d]	8[d]	1[d]	0[d]	16[d]	1,498	5[d]	1,400
2002–2003	36[d]	25[d]	11[d]	0[d]	0[d]	18[d]	1,553	10[d]	1,331
2003–2004	45[d]	37[d]	7[d]	1[d]	0[d]	23[d]	1,474	5[d]	1,285
2004–2005	52[d]	40[d]	10[d]	2[d]	0[d]	22[d]	1,554	8[d]	1,471
2005–2006	44[d]	37[d]	6[d]	1[d]	0[d]	21[d]	1,697	3[d]	1,408
2006–2007	63[d]	48[d]	13[d]	2[d]	0[d]	32[d]	1,801	9[d]	1,296
2007–2008	48[d]	39[d]	7[d]	2[d]	0[d]	21[d]	1,744	5[d]	1,231
2008–2009	44[d]	29[d]	15[d]	0[d]	0[d]	18[d]	1,605	7[d]	1,344
2009–2010	35[d]	27[d]	5[d]	3[d]	0[d]	19[d]	1,410	2[d]	1,467
2010–2011	32[d]	26[d]	6[d]	0[d]	0[d]	11[d]	1,339	3[d]	1,456
2011–2012	45[d]	26[d]	14[d]	5[d]	0[d]	15[d]	1,201	5[d]	1,568
2012–2013	53[d]	41[d]	11[d]	1[d]	0[d]	31[d]	1,186	6[d]	1,590

[a]A school-associated violent death is defined as "a homicide, suicide, or legal intervention (involving a law enforcement officer), in which the fatal injury occurred on the campus of a functioning elementary or secondary school in the United States," while the victim was on the way to or from regular sessions at school, or while the victim was attending or traveling to or from an official school-sponsored event.

[b]"At school" includes on school property, on the way to or from regular sessions at school, and while attending or traveling to or from a school-sponsored event.

[c]Total youth suicides are reported for calendar years 1992 through 2012 (instead of school years 1992–93 through 2012–13).

[d]Data from 1999–2000 onward are subject to change until interviews with school and law enforcement officials have been completed. The details learned during the interviews can occasionally change the classification of a case.

Note: Unless otherwise noted, data are reported for the school year, defined as July 1 through June 30. Some data have been revised from previously published figures.

SOURCE: Anlan Zhang, Lauren Musu-Gillette, and Barbara A. Oudekerk, "Table 1.1. School-Associated Violent Deaths of All Persons, Homicides and Suicides of Youth Ages 5–18 at School, and Total Homicides and Suicides of Youth Ages 5–18, by Type of Violent Death: 1992–93 to 2012–13," in *Indicators of School Crime and Safety: 2015*, U.S. Department of Education, National Center for Education Statistics, and U.S. Department of Justice, Bureau of Justice Statistics, May 2016, https://www.bjs.gov/content/pub/pdf/iscs15.pdf (accessed January 11, 2017)

youth homicides occurring at school was less than 3% between 1992 and 2013; the percentage of youth suicides occurring at school was less than 1% during this period. Nevertheless, Americans were shocked by the high-profile rash of school shootings, and some were afraid to send their children to school. The shootings at Sandy Hook Elementary School and Columbine High School, in particular, weighed heavily on the minds of many students and parents.

Columbine High School

The tragedy occurred on April 20, 1999, as senior Eric Harris (1981–1999) and his friend and classmate Dylan Klebold (1982–1999) arrived at Columbine High School in Littleton, a suburb of Denver, Colorado. Carrying two large duffel bags, they walked to the school cafeteria. Each of the bags contained a 20-pound (9.1-kg) propane bomb, set to detonate at exactly 11:17 a.m. Harris and Klebold looked for an inconspicuous place to leave their bomb-concealing bags among the hundreds of other backpacks and bags there. After choosing a spot, Harris and Klebold returned to the parking lot to wait for the bombs to detonate; however, the bombs failed to explode.

Part of their plan aimed to divert the Littleton Fire Department, the Jefferson County Sheriff's Office, and other emergency personnel away from the high school as the pair stormed the school. To achieve this, they had planted pipe bombs 3 miles (4.8 km) southwest of the high school that were set to explode and start grass fires. As the explosions began, Harris and Klebold prepared to reenter the school. Dressed in black trench coats, Harris and Klebold concealed 9-millimeter semiautomatic weapons from view. They opened fire toward the doors of the school, killing 17-year-old Rachel Scott.

After entering the school, they roamed the halls, library, and cafeteria, killing 12 other victims, including a teacher, before finally killing themselves. They also injured 23 other students physically and many others emotionally. The details of the event are outlined in *The Columbine High School Shootings: Jefferson County Sheriff Department's Investigation Report* (May 15, 2000) by the Jefferson County Sheriff's Department.

Investigations after the Columbine shooting focused on incidents in the boys' past that might have indicated the potential for such violent behavior. Among the people most surprised by the shooting were Klebold's family. Tom Klebold, Dylan's father, told investigators that his son never showed any interest in guns. The Klebolds told authorities that Dylan had been accepted at the University of Arizona and had planned to study computer science. Klebold's friends and teachers described him as a nice, normal teenager. Authorities learned, however, that Klebold and Harris were often harassed and bullied by other students. Much discussion of this fact was reported by the media, which prompted various research organizations to investigate the effects of bullying on juveniles. Some speculated that ridicule from other students prompted Harris and Klebold to seek revenge.

Sandy Hook Elementary School

On the morning of December 14, 2012, 20-year-old Adam Lanza (1992–2012) fatally shot his mother at their home in Newtown. He then drove to Sandy Hook Elementary School where, using an assault weapon, he shot and killed 20 children and six adults, including the school principal and psychologist, before committing suicide. It was the second-deadliest incident at a U.S elementary school.

Lanza was described as a troubled, isolated young man who played violent video games. Law enforcement officials speculate that Lanza may have been trying to murder more people than Anders Behring Breivik (1979–), a Norwegian man who killed 77 people in several attacks in Oslo, Norway, on July 22, 2011. Investigators also found evidence that Lanza chose Sandy Hook Elementary School because he believed it was an easy target with a high concentration of people.

The tragedy galvanized organizations seeking more stringent gun control, including banning the sale of assault weapons and intensifying background checks on gun buyers. In his State of the Union address in February 2013 (https://obamawhitehouse.archives.gov/blog/2013/02/13/president-obamas-2013-state-union), President Barack Obama (1961–) called on Congress to pass new gun control laws, declaring, "Because in the two months since Newtown, more than a thousand birthdays, graduations, anniversaries have been stolen from our lives by a bullet from a gun."

In "Senate Rejects 4 Gun Proposals Inspired by Orlando Attack" (NPR.org, June 20, 2015), Richard Gonzales, Don Gonyea, and Ailsa Chang report that even after multiple school shootings and other mass shootings such as the June 12, 2016, mass shooting in an Orlando, Florida, nightclub, no gun control measures offered by Democrats or Republicans advanced to become federal law. Gonzales, Gonyea, and Chang note that the National Rifle Association (NRA) objects to any measures to control gun sales. NRA executive director Wayne LaPierre is quoted as saying such measures are like "trying to stop a freight train with a piece of Kleenex."

State measures, however, were passed in the wake of the Sandy Hook shooting. In "Appeals Court Affirms State Gun Control Laws Passed after Sandy Hook Shooting" (NPR.org, October 19, 2015), Laura Wagner reports that state laws banning certain semiautomatic weapons and high-capacity magazines were passed in New York and Connecticut. The laws were challenged by gun rights advocates, but a federal appeals court upheld the laws, asserting that they do not violate the Second Amendment.

School Shootings in 2016

In 2016 there were school shootings in 12 states—Alabama, Arizona, California, Indiana, Massachusetts, Michigan, Ohio, Pennsylvania, South Carolina, Texas, Utah, and Wisconsin. School-related shootings that year claimed nine lives and injured 26 people.

Federal Bureau of Investigation Examines School Shooters

School shooting incidents prompted the Federal Bureau of Investigation (FBI) to research this phenomenon. In *The School Shooter: A Threat Assessment Perspective* (September 2000, https://www.fbi.gov/file-repository/stats-services-publications-school-shooter-school-shooter/view), Mary Ellen O'Toole of the FBI asserts that the profile of a school shooter cannot be determined, nor is it possible to create a checklist of the warning signs that indicate the next juvenile who will bring lethal violence to school.

O'Toole assesses "the totality of the circumstances" known about a student in four areas: the student's personality, family dynamics, school dynamics, and social dynamics. She states, "If an act of violence occurs at a school, the school becomes the scene of the crime. As in any violent crime, it is necessary to understand what it is about the school which might have influenced the student's decision to offend there rather than someplace else."

According to O'Toole, the FBI considers the following factors to make this determination:

- The student's attachment to school—the student appears to be detached from school, including other students, teachers, and school activities.

- Tolerance for disrespectful behavior—the school does little to prevent or punish disrespectful behavior between individual students or groups of students.

- Inequitable discipline—discipline is inequitably (unfairly) applied (or is perceived as inequitably applied) by students and/or staff.

- Inflexible culture—the school's culture is static, unyielding, and insensitive to changes in society and the changing needs of newer students and staff.

- Pecking order among students—certain groups of students are officially or unofficially given more prestige and respect than others.

- Code of silence—few students feel they can safely tell teachers or administrators if they are concerned about another student's behavior or attitudes. Little trust exists between students and staff.

- Unsupervised computer access—access to computers and the Internet is unsupervised and unmonitored. Students are able to use the school's computers to play violent computer games or to explore inappropriate websites, such as those that promote violent hate groups or give instructions for making a bomb.

Despite the factors that might indicate a school will be more likely to be the site of a deadly incident, O'Toole reemphasizes in "School Shootings: What You Should Know" (October 6, 2006, https://archives.fbi.gov/archives/news/stories/2006/october/school_shoot100606) that there may be nothing that can be done to prevent a violent incident from occurring. Nevertheless, she advises that school personnel should pay attention to students' moods and behaviors and take all threats seriously.

In "Research Quality and Psychological Theory in Publications on School Shooters with Multiple Victims— A Systematic Review of the Literature" (*Cogent Psychology* vol. 3, no. 1, 2016), Pål Grøndahl and Stål Bjørkly found 10 studies that used varying methods including interviews with the perpetrators themselves and reviews of their medical records and produced conflicting characterizations of school shooters. Although the studies' authors attempted to find commonalities between the perpetrators, a wide range of profiles emerged and Grøndahl and Bjørkly conclude that these studies fail to explain school shootings or why these young people become extremely violent. The researchers explain, "there exists no substantial scientific base for assuming that valid risk factors or profiles can be identified to predict or prevent any event with a base rate as extremely low as multiple school shootings actually have," and advise focusing on school violence in general instead of shooters, asserting, "There are good reasons to believe that this research will generate findings that are relevant to develop efficient violence prevention strategies to mitigate school violence."

COLLEGE CAMPUS SHOOTINGS AND VIOLENCE. In "These Are All the College Campus Shootings in 2015" (Time.com, October 9, 2015), Josh Sanburn reports that 23 shootings claimed 20 lives and injured 23 people on college campuses in 2015. The October 1, 2015, shooting at Umpqua Community College in Roseburg, Oregon, in which the gunman and nine others died was the worst such occurrence in 2015.

There were 10 incidents of gun or mass violence on college campuses in 2016. For example, on June 1, 2016, an associate professor and a Ph.D. student he had taught at the University of California, Los Angeles, were killed in a murder-suicide. In a violent attack at Ohio State University in November, a knife-wielding student injured 11 people before he was shot and killed by a security officer.

In "Aiming at Students: The College Gun Violence Epidemic" (Citizens Crime Commission of New York City, October 2016, http://www.nycrimecommission.org/pdfs/CCC-Aiming-At-Students-College-Shootings-Oct2016.pdf), Ashley Cannon reports that the Crime Commission scrutinized 190 incidents at 142 colleges that occurred from fall 2001 through August 2016 in which at least one person was intentionally shot (excluding the shooter). The commission finds that the number of shootings and casualties increased dramatically. During this period, six states—Tennessee (14), California (14), Virginia (13), Georgia (13), North Carolina (11), and Florida (11)—suffered more than 10 incidents on or near college campuses.

SECURITY AND DISCIPLINE

After the Columbine shooting, U.S. schools began implementing security measures to try to prevent future violent incidents. For example, during the 2013–14 school year, Zhang, Musu-Gillette, and Oudekerk report, 93% of public schools controlled access to school buildings during school hours, 74% used security cameras to monitor the school, and 68% required faculty and staff to wear badges or photo IDs.

Security measures differed by school level. Zhang, Musu-Gillette, and Oudekerk state that during the 2013–14 school year some security measures were used more frequently in middle or high schools than in elementary schools. Drug tests, security cameras, random sweeps for contraband, metal detector checks, strict dress codes, and drug-sniffing dogs were much more likely to be used in high schools than in earlier grades. Fewer high schools than middle schools and primary schools controlled access to buildings during school hours, and more primary and middle schools required students to wear uniforms than did high schools.

Efforts to decrease crime and violence in schools have produced favorable results. Zhang, Musu-Gillette, and Oudekerk find that thefts at school declined from 114 per 1,000 students in 1992 to 14 per 1,000 students in 2014, and violent victimizations at school among students aged 12 to 18 years decreased from 68 per 1,000 students in 1992 to 19 per 1,000 students in 2014, down from 37 per 1,000 in 2013.

Disciplinary Problems and Actions

Schools contend with a wide range of disciplinary problems that can affect the safety and positive educational experience of students and staff alike. These include bullying, gang activities, verbal abuse of teachers, disrespectful acts against teachers, widespread disorder in the classroom, cult or extremist group activities, and racial tension. For public schools, according to Zhang, Musu-Gillette, and Oudekerk, the proportions of public and private schools as well as urban and suburban schools experiencing problems with student bullying at least once a week during the 2013–14 school year were comparable, at slightly more than 20%.

There were 1.3 million reported discipline problems at public schools in 2013–14, which included alcohol, drugs, violence, or weapons possession. More than three-quarters (78%) of discipline incidents involved violence with or without injury, 15% were drug-related, 2% were alcohol-related, and 5% were for weapons possession.

One of the ways that schools attempt to deal with safety issues is to take serious disciplinary action (suspensions of five days or more, expulsions, and transfers to specialized schools) against students who commit crimes and violent acts. Zhang, Musu-Gillette, and Oudekerk note that during the 2011–12 school year 3.4 million students received in-school suspensions, and 3.2 million received out-of-school suspensions. Less than 1% of students were referred to law enforcement, expelled, or were subject to corporal punishment or school-related arrests.

NONFATAL CRIMES

Between 1992 and 2014 the rate of nonfatal crimes against students between the ages of 12 and 18 years at school (in the building, on school property, and en route to and from school) generally declined. (See Figure 9.1.) National Crime Victimization Survey data show that although thefts often occur more frequently at school than they do away from school, the reverse is true of serious violent crimes such as sexual assault, rape, aggravated assault, and robbery. In 2014, 850,100 crimes were committed against students at school or 33 victimizations per 1,000 students at school.

Physical Fights, Avoidance, and Fear

According to Laura Kann et al. of the Centers for Disease Control and Prevention, in "Youth Risk Behavior Surveillance—United States, 2015" (*Morbidity and Mortality Weekly Report*, vol. 65, no. 6, June 10, 2016), in 2015, 22.6% of high school students nationwide reported being in one or more physical fights anywhere (not necessarily at school) during the previous 12 months; however, just 7.8% of students fought on school property in 2015. Male students (10.3%) were twice as likely as female students (5%) to engage in fights on

school property, and non-Hispanic African American male students (15.4%) and Hispanic male students (10.7%) were more likely than non-Hispanic white male students (8%) to report this behavior. The incidence of fighting on school grounds decreased with advancing age.

In 2015, 6% of female high school students and 5% of male students said they did not go to school because they felt unsafe at school or on their way to or from school. A greater percentage of Hispanic (7.6%) and non-Hispanic African American students (6.8%) than non-Hispanic white students (4.2%) did not go to school because they feared for their safety.

Weapons in School

Violence at school makes students feel vulnerable and intimidated. Sometimes it prompts them to carry a weapon to school for self-protection. The Gun-Free Schools Act of 1994 required states to pass laws forcing school districts to expel any student who brings a firearm to school. Zhang, Musu-Gillette, and Oudekerk indicate that in 2013, 7% of high school students reported they had carried a weapon (a gun, knife, or club) on school property in the last 30 days. The percentage of students who reported carrying a weapon on school property decreased from 12% in 1993 to 5% in 2013. The number of disciplinary actions taken for illegal weapon possession fell from 1,900 in 2006 to 1,400 in 2013.

The reasons students are carrying fewer weapons to school include enhanced security measures at school, such as metal detectors, locker searches, and stricter punishment of students found with weapons in school. Many schools have adopted zero-tolerance rules that call for the immediate expulsion of students found with weapons.

SHOULD TEACHERS CARRY WEAPONS IN SCHOOL? About 20 states have laws that permit adults to carry licensed guns into schools. John Eligon, however, reports in "A State Backs Guns in Class for Teachers" (NY Times.com, March 9, 2013) that South Dakota "became the first state in the nation to enact a law explicitly authorizing school employees to carry guns on the job." It remains to be seen how many teachers will begin carrying guns as a result of this legislation and if it will have an impact on school safety.

In "This Town Is Encouraging Teachers to Carry Guns: Here's Their Reasoning" (HuffingtonPost.com, February 5, 2016), Sebastian Murdock reports that 5% of teachers in a rural Oklahoma public school district are carrying guns to school. Besides having a concealed carry permit, teachers who carry guns must have undergone a psychiatric evaluation, been granted a certificate from Oklahoma's Council on Law Enforcement Education and Training, and take a shooting course three times a year.

FIGURE 9.1

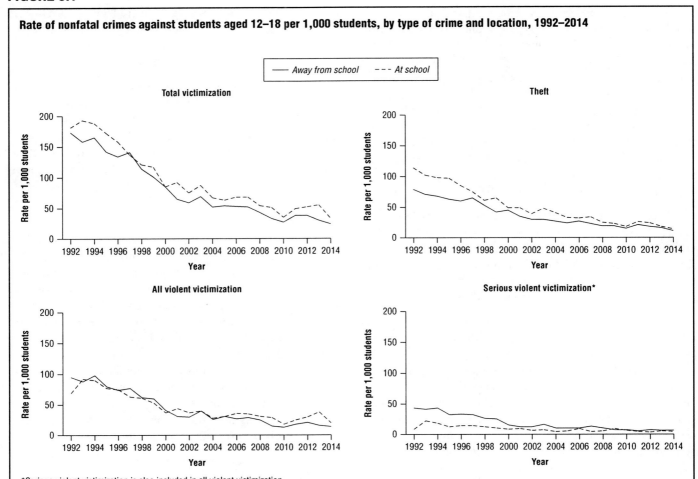

Rate of nonfatal crimes against students aged 12–18 per 1,000 students, by type of crime and location, 1992–2014

Legend: —— Away from school   - - - At school

Total victimization

Theft

All violent victimization

Serious violent victimization*

*Serious violent victimization is also included in all violent victimization.
Note: Due to methodological changes, use caution when comparing 2006 estimates to other years. "Serious violent victimization" includes the crimes of rape, sexual assault, robbery, and aggravated assault. "All violent victimization" includes serious violent crimes as well as simple assault. "Theft" includes attempted and completed purse-snatching, completed pickpocketing, and all attempted and completed thefts, with the exception of motor vehicle thefts. Theft does not include robbery, which involves the threat or use of force and is classified as a violent crime. "Total victimization" includes theft and violent crimes. "At school" includes inside the school building, on school property, or on the way to or from school. Although Indicators 2 and 3 present information on similar topics, Indicator 2 is based solely on data collected in National Crime Victimization Survey (NCVS), whereas Indicator 3 is based on data collected in the School Crime Supplement (SCS) to the NCVS as well as demographic data collected in the NCVS. Indicator 2 uses data from all students ages 12–18 who responded to the NCVS, while Indicator 3 uses data from all students ages 12–18 who responded to both the NCVS and the SCS. The population size for students ages 12–18 was 25,773,800 in 2014. Detail may not sum to totals due to rounding. Estimates may vary from previously published reports.

SOURCE: Anlan Zhang, Lauren Musu-Gillette, and Barbara A. Oudekerk, "Figure 2.1. Number of Nonfatal Victimizations against Students Ages 12–18 and Rate of Victimization per 1,000 Students, by Type of Victimization, Location, and Year: 1992 through 2014," in *Indicators of School Crime and Safety: 2015*, U.S. Department of Education, National Center for Education Statistics, and U.S. Department of Justice, Bureau of Justice Statistics, May 2016, https://www.bjs.gov/content/pub/pdf/iscs15.pdf (accessed January 11, 2017)

In April 2016 California's Kingsburg school board voted to permit school personnel to carry guns on school grounds. In "California School District Votes to Allow Teachers to Carry Guns in the Classroom" (Salon.com, April 13, 2016), Sophia Tesfaye reports that as many as five staff members are allowed to carry guns on each campus, and they are permitted to bring them into classrooms.

Advocates for teachers bringing guns to school point out that Utah law has permitted guns on public school grounds for more than a decade, and there have been no fatal school shootings during that period. Opponents assert that guns in schools are more likely to accidentally result in harm than to offer protection.

WEAPON USE ON SCHOOL PROPERTY. According to Zhang, Musu-Gillette, and Oudekerk, the percentage of students who reported being threatened with or injured by a weapon while on school property remained fairly steady between 1993 and 2013. Approximately 7% of students in grades nine to 12 reported being threatened with or injured by a weapon on school property within the previous 12 months in 2013. This figure was comparable with that of 1993, when 7.3% of students reported being threatened with or injured by a weapon, and less than the highest figure during this period, 9.2% in 2003.

Male students received considerably more weapons threats and injuries in all the years surveyed between 1993 and 2013 than did female students. Among students from different ethnic and racial backgrounds, the group with the highest victimization rate—Pacific Islanders—saw a decrease from 24.8% in 2001 to 8.7% in 2013. In 2013 the group with the highest victimization rate was Native Americans/Alaskan Natives (18.5%).

BULLIES AND BULLYING

Most people can recall individuals or a group of children at school being identified as bullies. This type of behavior is not new to schools. Bullies harass those they know will not fight back. Bullying includes pushing students against lockers and taking their lunch money or other personal possessions; humiliating others and causing extreme embarrassment; shoving others out of their way; threatening violence or setting up derogatory websites; sending threatening or insulting text messages; disrupting class; and making threatening gestures, even toward teachers.

In *Bullying in Schools* (May 2009, http://digital commons.unl.edu/usjusticematls/6/), Rana Sampson indicates that bullying has two key components: repeated harmful acts and an imbalance of power between the victim and the perpetrator. Bullying behaviors include physical, verbal, and psychological attacks, such as assault, intimidation, spreading of rumors, destruction of property, theft, and name-calling. Sexual harassment, hazing, ostracism based on sexual orientation, taunting, and teasing also constitute bullying.

According to Kann et al., in 2015 more than 20% of students said they had been bullied on school property in the past 12 months—15.8% of male students and 24.8% of female students. (See Table 9.2.) Non-Hispanic

African American students (13.2%) and Hispanic students (16.5%) reported less bullying than did non-Hispanic white students (23.5%). Nearly one in six (15.3%) students reported that they had been electronically bullied—via e-mail, chat rooms, instant messaging, websites, or texting. Female students (21.7%) were more than twice as likely as male students (9.7%) to report having been electronically bullied.

According to Sameer Hinduja and Justin W. Patchin of the Cyberbullying Research Center, in *State Cyberbullying Laws: A Brief Review of State Cyberbullying Laws and Policies* (January 2016, http://cyberbullying .org/Bullying-and-Cyberbullying-Laws.pdf), all 50 states and the District of Columbia had antibullying laws in 2017. Although only 23 state laws included cyberbullying, 48 states had laws that prohibited electronic harassment as part of the statute. As of March 2017, no federal antibullying law had been passed.

Characteristics of Bullies

According to the American Academy of Child and Adolescent Psychiatry, in "Facts for Families: Bullying" (March 2011, http://www.aacap.org/AACAP/Families _and_Youth/Facts_for_Families/Facts_for_Families_Pages /Bullying_80.aspx), about half of all children are bullied at some point during their life, and 10% endure ongoing bullying. Boys are more likely to use physical abuse. Girls typically use verbal tactics.

Bullies look for situations in which they can gain power over someone else through intimidation and threats. Sometimes they work alone, and other times they work in groups. Some bullies surround themselves with

TABLE 9.2

Percentage of high school students who were electronically bullied and who were bullied at school, by sex, race and ethnicity, and grade, 2015

Category	Electronically bullied			Bullied on school property		
	Female	Male	Total	Female	Male	Total
	%	%	%	%	%	%
Race/ethnicity						
White*	26.0	10.8	18.4	29.1	18.1	23.5
Black*	11.9	5.6	8.6	15.1	11.2	13.2
Hispanic	16.7	8.1	12.4	19.3	13.7	16.5
Grade						
9	22.7	11.0	16.5	29.0	18.3	23.4
10	23.2	9.9	16.6	25.5	16.1	20.8
11	21.4	8.4	14.7	24.2	16.4	20.3
12	19.5	9.2	14.3	19.8	12.1	15.9
Total	**21.7**	**9.7**	**15.3**	**24.8**	**15.8**	**20.2**

*Non-Hispanic.
Note: Bullying includes being bullied through e-mail, chat rooms, instant messaging, Web sites, or texting, occurring during the 12 months before the survey.

SOURCE: Adapted from Laura Kann et al., "Table 17. Percentage of High School Students Who Were Electronically Bullied, and Were Bullied on School Property, by Sex, Race/Ethnicity, and Grade—United States, Youth Risk Behavior Survey, 2015," in "Youth Risk Behavior Surveillance—United States, 2015," *Morbidity and Mortality Weekly Report*, vol. 65, no. 6, June 10, 2016, https://www.cdc.gov/healthyyouth/data/yrbs/pdf/2015/ss6506_updated.pdf (accessed January 3, 2017)

weaker kids who act as henchmen. Bullies seek out situations to harass others in places such as playgrounds and school hallways that are not supervised by adults. In this way, there are no adult witnesses to either stop the act or report it to school authorities.

Research suggests that bullies tend to be aggressive, slightly below average in intelligence, and underperformers in school. They may be popular with their peers but lack empathy for their victims. Individual risk factors include being raised in dysfunctional families and living in households with low socioeconomic status.

In "Are Youth Psychopathic Traits Related to Bullying? Meta-analyses on Callous-Unemotional Traits, Narcissism, and Impulsivity" (*Child Psychiatry & Human Development*, 2016) Mitch van Geel et al. reviewed more than 20 studies that considered the relationship between bullying and specific characteristics: callous-unemotional (CU) traits (disregard for others, lack of empathy and guilt), narcissism (extreme selfishness and deep need for admiration), and impulsivity (acting suddenly without thinking or considering the consequences of one's actions). Geel et al. find significant relationships between these traits and bullying. They explain, "Children and adolescents scoring high on CU traits are less sensitive to the fear and suffering of others, and are more likely to expect positive outcomes of aggression which may explain a stronger inclination to bully others." Those who are narcissistic may bully others to gain a sense of power or to gain acceptance from peers. Children who are unusually impulsive may bully more because they act without thinking and do not consider long-term consequences such as punishment by teachers or school administrators.

Victims of Bullies

The victims of bullies tend to be smaller and weaker than other children, relatively passive, and socially awkward. Children with few friends are at greater risk than those with many friends. It is important to note that any student can become a victim of bullying and that the fault lies with the bully, not with the victim.

Victims of bullying may suffer from psychological and physical distress. They tend to be absent from school more than other children and have difficulty concentrating on schoolwork. Victimization can lead to depression and low self-esteem. Victims suffer from anxiety and insomnia and contemplate suicide more than other children. In "Mediating Role of Psychological Adjustment between Peer Victimization and Social Adjustment in Adolescence" (*Frontiers in Psychology*, no. 7, 2016), Eva M. Romera, Olga Gómez-Ortiz, and Rosario Ortega-Ruiz observe that as many as 30% of all children are bullied and that victims often suffer intentional and repeated abuse by peers that exert a greater control over them, which leads them to believe they are incapable of

changing the situation. Adolescents who are bullied suffer more social anxiety, lower self-esteem, and less ability to establish healthy peer relationships than their peers who are not bullied. The researchers conclude, "Victimized adolescents tend to have a poor perception of themselves which makes them feel incapable of engaging in positive relationships with others and fearful of social situations. These negative effects lead them to withdraw from and forsake rewarding and satisfying relationships, thus preventing them from learning the social skills required to achieve a balanced development."

Multiple studies, such as Farah Williams and Dewey G. Cornell's "Student Willingness to Seek Help for Threats of Violence in Middle School" (*Journal of School Violence*, vol. 5, no. 4, December 2006) and Lauren P. Ashbaugh and Dewey G. Cornell's "Sexual Harassment and Bullying Behaviors in Sixth-Graders" (*Journal of School Violence*, vol. 7, no. 2, February 2008), find that girls are more likely than boys to report and seek help for bullying.

Cyberbullying

Qing Li, Peter K. Smith, and Donna Cross report in "Research into Cyberbullying" (*Cyberbullying in the Global Playground: Research from International Perspectives*, 2012) that widespread use of the Internet and cell phones among students has enabled cyberbullying, also called digital or electronic bullying. Instead of abusing their victims at school, on the playground, or en route to and from school, bullies are able to taunt their victims day and night via current technology. Cyberbullying can take various forms, ranging from flaming (sending angry, rude, or vulgar insults) to harassing (repeatedly sending offensive messages) to cyberstalking (harassment that is intimidating or includes threats of harm). Victims may receive hateful and hurtful instant messages, e-mails, and text messages on their cell phones. Cyberbullies can also remain anonymous, if they so choose.

Some students have become the victims of hate-filled websites that discuss why the bullies and their friends do not like a certain individual. Visitors to such sites can add their insults and gossip as well. In some instances visitors have rallied to the defense of the victim and slammed the bully. Through the use of camera phones, bullies can take sensitive photos of students in locker rooms and bathrooms and while being intimidated. Then the bullies circulate the pictures via e-mail, text/digital image messaging, or on websites. Researchers point out that electronic bullying can be done anywhere and does not require the bully to have any in-person contact, especially eye contact, with the victim.

In the fact sheet "Summary of Our Research (2004–2016)" (November 26, 2016, http://cyberbullying.org/summary-of-our-cyberbullying-research), Justin W. Patchin and Sameer Hinduja of the Cyberbullying Research Center estimate that 27.9% of children have been cyberbullied at some point during their lifetime, and 15.8% students admit to perpetrating cyberbullying themselves.

In one highly publicized case, 13-year-old Megan Meier committed suicide after she was cyberbullied through the social networking website Myspace. She befriended a boy named Josh Evans through the site. The Josh Evans Myspace account, however, had been created by a group of people headed by Lori Drew, the mother of a former friend of Meier's. "Josh Evans" sent Meier increasingly hurtful messages and posted bulletins about her. In October 2006 Meier hanged herself in her bedroom. In May 2008 a federal grand jury indicted Drew on one count of conspiracy and three counts of accessing protected computers without authorization to obtain information to inflict emotional distress. Drew was convicted in November 2008 of three misdemeanors but acquitted of felony conspiracy charges. Hinduja and Patchin report in "Bullying, Cyberbullying, and Suicide" (*Archives of Suicide Research*, vol. 14, no. 3, July 2010) that middle school students who experience bullying or cyberbullying are more likely to have suicidal thoughts or attempt suicide than are other students.

Another instance of cyberbullying prompted the suicide of Tyler Clementi, an 18-year-old freshman at Rutgers University in New Jersey. Clementi took his life in September 2010, just three days after he realized that his roommate, Dharun Ravi, and a classmate, Molly Wei, had used a webcam to record video of an embrace between Clementi and another man; Ravi then gossiped about the recording via Twitter and tried to set up another viewing, which, although greatly rumored to have happened, never occurred. Clementi's death ignited an international outcry against bullying, especially cyberbullying. Although he was not convicted of a hate crime, which would have carried a harsher sentence, Ravi was found guilty of bias intimidation, invasion of privacy, hindering apprehension, and tampering with evidence; in May 2012 he was sentenced to 30 days in jail. In November 2010 New Jersey passed an "Anti-bullying Bill of Rights," and it was signed into law in January 2011.

SEXTING AND CYBERBULLYING. In "Youth Sexting: Prevalence Rates, Driving Motivations, and the Deterrent Effect of Legal Consequences" (*Sexuality Research and Social Policy*, vol. 11, no. 3, September 2014), Heidi Strohmaier, Megan Murphy, and David DeMatteo explain that sexting (sending sexually explicit images via cell phone) is commonplace. The researchers report that nearly 30% of college undergraduates admit to having sent sexually explicit images as teens, and 61% were unaware that sending nude photos could be considered child pornography. The researchers conclude that sexting may be the new normal in terms of teens' sexual behavior.

Although such images are generally sent in the context of a dating relationship, recipients can easily distribute the images to others, which can have severe consequences. In the fact sheet "Sexting: A Brief Guide for Educators and Parents" (2010, http://cyberbullying.org/sexting-a-brief-guide-for-educators-and-parents-2), Hinduja and Patchin report the case of Jesse Logan, an 18-year-old girl who sent nude pictures of herself to her boyfriend. When they broke up, he forwarded the pictures to his friends. Her classmates taunted her, and two months later she committed suicide. Thirteen-year-old Hope Witsell sent a topless picture of herself to a boy she liked. After the image was forwarded to others, she endured vicious name-calling for weeks before she killed herself.

Because sexting is a relatively new phenomenon, many states do not have laws that specifically prohibit it, but in most states it can be punished under existing laws that govern child pornography. In all states possession of a sexually explicit image of a minor is a crime, and teens who text nude images of themselves to other teens could be charged with three crimes: promoting, distributing, and possessing child pornography. As of July 2015, just 20 states had instituted sexting laws, and they varied widely. For example, Hinduja and Patchin note in "State Sexting Laws: A Brief Review of State Sexting Laws and Policies" (July 2015, http://www.cyberbullying.us/state-sexting-laws.pdf) that Connecticut law distinguishes between the age of the sender and the recipient, punishing teens aged 13 to 15 years who send pictures of themselves and those aged 13 to 17 years who receive the images. Louisiana bars anyone under the age of 17 years from sending or keeping explicit photographs and punishes offenders with fines, probation, or jail time.

DOES THE PUNISHMENT FIT THE CRIME? In some states teens who sext may face felony charges, which can land them in state prison and require them to register as a sex offender for the rest of their life. In "Attitudes toward Juvenile Sex Offender Legislation: The Influence of Case-Specific Information" (*Journal of Child Sexual Abuse*, vol. 25, no. 4, July 9, 2016), Julia Campregher and Elizabeth L. Jeglic report the results of their study of attitudes about adolescent sex offender legislation. They assert that noncontact juvenile sexting cases "do not warrant incarceration, registration, or notification" and that these harsh punishments are not strongly supported by the public.

Prevention Programs

Many U.S. schools have implemented antibullying programs aimed at increasing awareness of the problem. Antibullying efforts are geared toward not only bullies but also the students and teachers who do not do enough to stop it. Some victims claim there are teachers who allow bullying to occur and even encourage it. Others say they are afraid to tell teachers because the educators will ignore it and tell the victims to toughen up. Still others are ashamed that they cannot stop the bullies, so they retreat into themselves and do not seek the help they need to stop the aggression.

One successful antibullying program, the Olweus Bullying Prevention Program (2017, http://www.clemson.edu/olweus), teaches students, parents, and school staff to work together to address the issue. By discussing bullying and its effects, people learn the consequences of bullying on individuals and on the school environment. Rules and plans are developed and enforced. The Office of Juvenile Justice and Delinquency Prevention notes that the Olweus program is successful in elementary and middle schools. In "Pilot Test of StandUp, an Online School-Based Bullying Prevention Program" (*Children & Schools*, vol. 38, no. 2, April 2016), Jane Timmons-Mitchell et al. acknowledge that the Olweus Bullying Prevention Program is the most widely implemented school-based program but observe that one of its drawbacks is the time necessary to implement it. Timmons-Mitchell et al. evaluated StandUp, an online program, consisting of three sessions, that aimed to improve students' relationship skills and decrease bullying and victimization. A pilot study with high school students finds participants displayed an increase in use of healthy relationship skills along with reduced likelihood of perpetrating and experiencing bullying, and of passively standing by while others are bullied.

HAZING

Like bullying, hazing involves humiliating people into doing something that they would not do normally. In some instances the hazing act is silly and harmless. In the early 21st century, however, parents and educators have become concerned that hazings are becoming more aggressive and violent. Hazings, which often occur as initiations to a school or social club, are considered a "rite of passage" to some, just "horseplay" to others, and degrading and devastating to many victims. Some athletic teams claim that hazing aims to toughen up younger players and help them bond with the team. Unlike bullying, however, hazing is often done with the consent of its victims. For example, by succumbing to peer pressure and wanting to be part of the group or clique, many students allow themselves to be subjected to humiliating acts that they do not report.

Hazings, however, can go too far, and the victims can be seriously harmed or even killed. Hazings usually involve older students (veterans) initiating young classmates (newcomers) into the club. The situation can quickly turn violent when older students gang up on the younger ones, who have no idea what has been planned or what to expect. Researchers note that students will do things in a mob situation that they would never do on their own.

Several brutal hazings made the news in 2016. For example, Juliet Macur reports in "Something Is Missing in High School Hazing Stories: Adults" (NYTimes.com, March 14, 2016) that in March 2016 three high school seniors in Pennsylvania were charged with crimes related to an assault in their football team's locker room. Macur recounted other incidents including charges against four high school wrestlers in Oklahoma accused of raping two other wrestlers, one of whom was just 12 years old, in a school bus returning from a tournament. Macur wants adults such as teachers, coaches, and others to be held accountable. She suggests, "Require them to be present in, or at least within earshot of, the locker room and to ride on team buses. Force them to realize that it's their job to keep their athletes safe. Otherwise, they won't have a job. Parents, too, have to be vigilant about what their children are up to; they shouldn't just hand them over to coaches with blind trust."

In "FAMU Settles Hazing Lawsuit Spawned by Death of Drum Major Robert Champion" (OrlandoSentinel.com, September 18, 2015), Stephen Hudak reports that the family of Florida A&M University drum major Robert Champion, who was 26 years old when he died as a result of hazing, received a settlement of $1.1 million from the university and an apology. The hazing required Champion to force his way from the front of a parked bus to the back, while band members punched, kicked, and clubbed him with drum mallets and an orange traffic cone. The medical examiner determined that Champion died as a result of internal bleeding from the injuries his bandmates inflicted.

NO CHILD LEFT BEHIND ACT: PERSISTENTLY DANGEROUS SCHOOLS

The No Child Left Behind Act (NCLB; described in Chapter 6) was passed by Congress in 2001 and signed into law by President George W. Bush (1946–) in January 2002. The NCLB calls upon states to make schools safer. According to the U.S. Department of Education, in "Questions and Answers on No Child Left Behind" (November 17, 2004, https://www2.ed.gov/nclb/freedom/safety/creating.html):

> Under Title IV of ESEA as reauthorized by the No Child Left Behind Act, states are required to establish a uniform management and reporting system to collect information on school safety and drug use among young people. The states must include incident reports by school officials and anonymous student and teacher surveys in the data they collect. This information is to be publicly reported so that parents, school officials and others who are interested have information about any violence and drug use at their schools. They can then assess the problems at their schools and work toward finding solutions. Continual monitoring and reports will track progress over time.

To hold schools accountable for ensuring student safety, the NCLB requires states to identify persistently dangerous schools. States must permit students to have public school choice if their school consistently falls into this category. In addition, student victims of violent crime are allowed public school choice even if their schools are not considered persistently dangerous.

Underreporting of Violence and Crime at School

National School Safety and Security Services, a private consulting firm, notes in "School Crime Reporting and Underreporting" (2017, http://www.schoolsecurity .org/trends/school-crime-reporting-and-underreporting/) that the unsafe school requirement of the NCLB concerns educators, parents, and police. Some believe schools are hesitant to report crimes so that they will not be labeled as persistently dangerous. They suggest that because being designated as unsafe causes schools to lose enrollment and jeopardizes funding, schools may underreport crimes to maintain a clean rating.

According to Zhang, Musu-Gillette, and Oudekerk, many crimes—even violent crimes—that are committed at school are not reported to the police. During the 2009–10 school year an estimated 85% of public schools experienced one or more crimes, but only about 60% reported these crimes to the police.

Proportionally, public schools were more likely to report seriously violent incidents to the police, presumably because of the gravity of such offenses. Nevertheless, even some serious violent crimes were not reported. Zhang, Musu-Gillette, and Oudekerk indicate that during the 2013–14 school year, 74% of public schools experienced one or more serious violent crimes, and only 40% reported at least one serious violent crime to the police.

CRITICISM OF "PERSISTENTLY DANGEROUS SCHOOLS": GEORGIA'S EXAMPLE. Some critics argue that the NCLB provisions that require states to define the phrase "persistently dangerous schools" allows them to underestimate the security concerns at some schools. For example, the Georgia Department of Education defines persistently dangerous schools in "Unsafe School Choice Option" (2017, http:// public.doe.k12.ga.us/AYP/Pages/USCO.aspx). To meet the criteria, a school must experience the following conditions for three consecutive years:

> At least 1 student is found by official tribunal action to have violated a school rule related to a violent criminal offense (including aggravated battery, aggravated child molestation, aggravated sexual battery, aggravated sodomy, armed robbery, arson, kidnapping, murder, rape, & voluntary manslaughter) either on campus or at a school-sanctioned event;

> At least 2% of the student body or 10 students, whichever is greater, have been found to have violated school rules related to other identified criminal offenses, including non-felony drugs, felony drugs, felony weapons, terroristic threats;

> Any combination of [the above].

The Georgia Department of Education reports that "No Georgia school has met the persistently dangerous school criteria pursuant to State Board Rule 160-4-8-.16 since 2005." In July 2016, however, the state declared a Muscogee County special education center as an unsafe and unhealthful environment. In "State Declares Muscogee County Special-Education Center Unsafe, Unhealthy" (Ledger-Enquirer .com, July 31, 2016), Robin Trimarchi reports that complaints included the fact that the facility was dirty and had air conditioners that functioned only sporadically.

CHAPTER 10
CRIME PREVENTION AND PUNISHMENT

Although preventing violence before it happens is desirable, questions persist about the effectiveness of the strategies that are employed to do so. For example, the school environment would seem to be an ideal place to implement violence prevention programs. Hyoun-Kyoung Park-Higgerson et al. evaluate school-based violence prevention programs and report their results in "The Evaluation of School-Based Violence Prevention Programs: A Meta-analysis" (*Journal of School Health*, vol. 78, no. 9, September 2008). The researchers examined 26 school-based programs designed to reduce aggressive and violent behaviors in school-age children. Five program characteristics were considered: whether they were theory-based, whether the program was used with all children or just some, whether the program used multiple approaches, traits shared by the target population, and the type of instructor. Only one program strategy (focusing on a single approach) had any effect on reducing violence, and that effect was moderate. Using multiple approaches, beginning antiviolence education at young ages, and using theory-based approaches—all considered desirable in the theoretical literature—were found to have no effect on violence reduction.

Nevertheless, Park-Higgerson et al. do not suggest that youth violence prevention programs cannot be effective; rather, they argue that more work needs to be done to identify effective interventions to prevent violence. In the 21st century there are many responses to youth violence. Prevention efforts range from laws that hold parents responsible, to community efforts to educate youth, to curfews, to police suppression, and to antigang programs. Reactive efforts range from allowing juveniles to be tried as adults for certain crimes to increased punishments. A range of responses to youth violence is discussed in this chapter.

Reporting the results of a study to determine how many children and youth have been exposed to violence prevention programs, David Finkelhor et al. find in "Youth Exposure to Violence Prevention Programs in a National Sample" (*Child Abuse and Neglect*, vol. 38, no. 4, April 2014) that nationally about two-thirds (65%) of children aged five to 17 years had ever been exposed to such programs. The majority (71%) of program participants said the programs were helpful, and younger participants aged five to nine years had lower rates of victimization and perpetration than their age peers without exposure to violence prevention programs.

CRIME PREVENTION

Over the years, politicians, law enforcement officials, teachers, parents, and other concerned citizens have considered strategies to decrease youth violence and crime, from holding parents responsible for their children's crimes to conducting after-school programs aimed at preventing violence. A variety of prevention, intervention, and suppression programs have been implemented, and efforts are under way to determine the effectiveness of these programs. The following sections discuss laws as well as a range of prevention programs, including community prevention programs, law enforcement prevention strategies, and school-based prevention programs.

Laws Enacted to Prevent Juvenile Crime

HOLDING PARENTS RESPONSIBLE. Nearly every state has some sort of parental responsibility law that holds parents or guardians responsible for property damage, personal injury, theft, shoplifting, and vandalism resulting from the intentional or willful acts of their children. In addition, child welfare laws include actions against those who contribute to the delinquency of a minor. By the 1990s, in response to rising juvenile crime rates, communities and states passed tougher laws about parental responsibility. In "What Are the Main Sections of the Parent Liability Child's Act" (2014, https://www.enotes.com/homework-help/what-main-sections-parent-liability

-childs-act-466307), the *Encyclopedia of Everyday Law* notes that some states hold parents of delinquent youth criminally liable. However, other less-stringent parental responsibility laws are more common. State laws vary. Some require parents to pay court costs for their children who have been adjudicated as delinquent. Others require parents to pay the costs of caring for, treating, or detaining delinquent children or to pay restitution to victims of their children's crimes.

California, Massachusetts, Minnesota, and the District of Columbia hold adults criminally responsible for storing a loaded firearm in a place that allows minors access to it. According to Sejal H. Patel, in "Kids and Gun Safety" (April 10, 2014, http://apps.americanbar.org/litigation/committees/childrights/content/articles/spring2014-0414-kids-gun-safety.html), five other states hold adults criminally liable if minors gain access to a firearm because the adults stored it carelessly. In most states that hold adults liable for storing a loaded firearm within the reach of minors, it is a misdemeanor offense, but in some it may be a felony. Many states hold adults liable if a minor uses the firearm obtained this way to harm someone.

Critics of parental liability suggest that victims are just looking for someone to blame. They assert that U.S. law usually holds people responsible for crimes only if they actively participate in the commission of such acts. They believe that if standard rules of law are practiced, the prosecutor should have to prove that the parents intended to participate in a crime to be found guilty. Eve M. Brank, Edie Greene, and Katherine Hochevar note in "Holding Parents Responsible: Is Vicarious Responsibility the Public's Answer to Juvenile Crime?" (*Psychology, Public Policy and Law*, vol. 17, no. 4, October 2011) that although cities and states have enacted laws to penalize parents for their children's actions, public support for these measures varies and is influenced by the age of the child, the nature of the offense, and the behavior of the parents. The researchers find considerable public support for parental responsibility in addition to the responsibility of the child but less support when parents alone are blamed for a child's offense. Parents are more likely to be held responsible for the acts of a younger child than an older teen because the public believes parents exert less influence and control over adolescents. Brank, Greene, and Hochevar also find that mothers are more likely than fathers to assign parents responsibility, and parents are more likely than nonparents to hold other parents responsible.

According to Brank, Greene, and Hochevar, parents are more likely to be viewed as responsible for acts of commission rather than acts of omission. For example, the public would view parents who gave a child hazardous materials such as fireworks more responsible than parents who left the potentially hazardous materials in a place where a child could gain access to them. The public assigns more responsibility to juveniles who commit more serious offenses. The researchers also determine that juveniles themselves do not feel their parents are responsible for their delinquent behaviors.

In "Young Adulthood as a Transitional Legal Category: Science, Social Change and Justice Policy" (*Fordham Law Review*, vol. 85, 2016), law professors Elizabeth S. Scott, Richard J. Bonnie, and Laurence Steinberg explain that the trend of viewing juvenile offenders as less deserving of harsh punishment than their adult counterparts has influenced sentencing reform for youth. It also has inspired policy makers to focus on the impact of juvenile justice settings and programs on crime reduction. Scott, Bonnie, and Steinberg observe that some policy makers feel that these considerations should extend to young adults since biological and psychological development continues into the early 20s. The likelihood that involvement in criminal activity results from psychological and social immaturity raises the question of "whether the presumption of reduced culpability and greater potential for reform should be applied to young adult offenders as well as juveniles." Scott, Bonnie, and Steinberg favor classifying young adult offenders as a separate category, asserting that "young adults are not fully mature and are more likely to reform than are older offenders. Also like juveniles, young adult offenders are in a critical period in which programs targeted to their developmental needs may powerfully influence their future lives in a positive direction."

CURFEWS. To "break the cycle" of youth violence and crime, lawmakers in more than 1,000 jurisdictions have enacted curfews in various cities, towns, and rural areas across the country. Most curfew laws restrict juveniles to their home or property between the hours of 11 p.m. and 6 a.m. weekdays but allow juveniles to stay out a little later on weekends. Exceptions are made for youth who need to travel to and from school, attend church events, or go to work at different times. Other exceptions include family emergencies or situations when juveniles are accompanied by their parents.

Although many people believe curfews are important in the effort to deter youth crime, critics of curfew ordinances argue that such laws violate the constitutional rights of children and their parents. They contend that the First, Fourth, Ninth, and 14th Amendment rights of people are endangered by curfew laws, especially the rights of free speech and association, privacy, and equal protection. Opponents also assert that no studies have proven curfew laws to be effective. David B. Wilson et al. report the results of a review of 12 studies that looked at the impact of curfews on youth criminal behavior and victimization in "Juvenile Curfew Effects on Criminal Behavior and Victimization: A Systematic Review" (*Campbell Systematic Reviews*, no. 3, 2016). The researchers find that although curfews have some intuitive appeal (keeping youth at home during the late night and early morning hours could prevent them from committing crimes or becoming victims of crimes), the best available evidence indicates that they are ineffective at reducing crime and victimization.

Community Prevention and Intervention Programs

Community prevention programs aim to keep youth, particularly at-risk youth, from engaging in criminal behavior, joining gangs, or otherwise ending up in prison or jail. Intervention programs are designed to remove youth from gangs, criminal activities, and patterns of reckless behavior that would ultimately put them in prison or jail. Such programs typically include helping the individual build self-esteem, confidence, and socialization skills while offering education, recreation, and job skills assistance. Many prevention and intervention programs have been successful in redirecting the activities of delinquent and at-risk youth. Those that succeed offer a safe place to hang out, make new friends, and learn life skills.

THE CHICAGO AREA PROJECT. Chicago, Illinois, experienced extensive gang activity throughout the 20th century. In an effort to deal with the gangs on the city's streets, the Chicago Area Project (CAP), the nation's first community-based delinquency prevention program, was founded in 1934. Developed by the sociologist Clifford R. Shaw (1895–1957), the program worked with delinquent youth in the poverty-stricken areas of Chicago. Project staff sought to prevent youth from joining gangs and ultimately committing crimes.

CAP advocates believed that neighborhoods and communities in Chicago needed improvement. According to CAP, in "About Chicago Area Project" (2017, http://www .chicagoareaproject.org/about-us), "The agency believes that residents must be empowered through the development of community organizations so that they can act together to improve neighborhood conditions, hold institutions serving the community accountable, reduce antisocial behavior by young people, protect them from inappropriate institutionalization, and provide them with positive models for personal development." The organization emphasizes that juvenile delinquency in low-income areas is a product of social disadvantages, not a flaw of the individual child or of individuals from certain ethnic or racial backgrounds. By 2017 CAP had grown to include more than 40 affiliates and special projects.

BOYS AND GIRLS CLUBS OF AMERICA. A variety of programs to help youth are offered by the Boys and Girls Clubs of America. The organization explains in the fact sheet "Boys and Girls Clubs of America: At a Glance" (2016, http://www.bgca.org/Documents/At-A-Glance-Fact -Sheet_2016.pdf) that in 2016 it worked with nearly 4 million children throughout the United States, Puerto Rico, the Virgin Islands, and U.S. military bases in the United States and abroad. Operating more than 4,200 club facilities, the group had 58,000 trained, full-time staff and 270,000 program volunteers.

Law Enforcement Strategies

OFFICE OF JUVENILE JUSTICE AND DELINQUENCY PREVENTION'S COMPREHENSIVE GANG MODEL. The Office of Juvenile Justice and Delinquency Prevention (OJJDP) advocates the use of the Comprehensive Gang Model that was developed by Irving A. Spergel (1924–2010) to combat gangs. The model consists of five strategies, which are described in Chapter 8. The following sections present examples of programs that are consistent with the goals, objectives, and strategies of the Comprehensive Gang Model.

SUPPRESSION PROGRAMS. Suppression is a tactic used by law enforcement agencies throughout the country and usually involves a show of force, such as saturating an area with uniformed police officers. The idea is to demonstrate to criminals that they are being watched and that criminal activities will not be tolerated. Suppression techniques also include sweeps, where officers converge on an area, rounding up youth and adult offenders. Some suppression programs have proven to be effective. Suppression programs have been tested in various cities, including Los Angeles, Chicago, and Houston.

For example, in Houston the Mayor's Anti-Gang Office (2017, http://www.houstontx.gov/antigang/programs.html) offers prevention, suppression, and intervention programs and services. Working with the Houston Police Department, the office focuses on areas with high gang activity by providing a visible presence in an effort to lessen gang violence and crime. Initiatives aim to target, arrest, and incarcerate gang members who are involved in criminal activities. Meanwhile, the office works with communities, neighborhoods, service organizations, and schools to provide supportive services to at-risk youth, including counseling, job training, conflict resolution, and recreation programs. The Mayor's Anti-Gang Office has also provided gang awareness training to individuals, including educators, law enforcement personnel, probation officers, and members of the public since 1994.

NEW YORK CITY JUVENILE INTERVENTION PROGRAM. In "To Stem Juvenile Robberies, Police Trail Youths before the Crime" (NYTimes.com, March 3, 2013), Wendy Ruderman reports on the Juvenile Robbery Intervention Program (J-RIP), an approach the New York City Police Department created to prevent juveniles from engaging in crime and joining gangs. The J-RIP identifies youth who have already had a brush with the law and are likely to get into trouble again, and police apply intensive surveillance and intervention techniques. They keep track of the teens, monitoring their social networking sites, visiting them at home and at school, and establishing relationships with their families. A key tactic is to isolate the at-risk teens from the peers with whom they might commit crimes. Chief Joanne Jaffe explains that J-RIP teens know "we are going to learn about every bad friend you have. And you're going to get alienated from those friends because we are going to be all over you."

Despite its promise, the J-RIP failed to achieve its objectives. In "Report Finds Juvenile Program Failed to Reduce Robberies, but Police Are Expanding It" (NYTimes.com, January 4, 2016), J. David Goodman reports that a November 2014 internal Police Department report found that the program did not stop robberies nor did it change the likelihood that offenders would commit robberies again. Goodman explains that even though it did not reduce crime, the police department is expanding the program because it "fosters in minority communities, a goal that has grown in importance for the Police Department as it seeks to enhance its image after a series of national protests over police practices."

SCHOOL RESOURCE OFFICERS. The School Resource Officer (SRO) program is intended to improve relations between youth and police. The project was designed to prevent and intercept the commission of youth crime and violence, and it gives students and police officers the chance to get to know one another. In some metropolitan areas children grow up with contempt for or fear of police. The SRO program works to eliminate these concerns as well as to educate students about the law and provide one-on-one mentoring.

Under the program, a police officer is assigned to a school as an SRO. The officer works to prevent crime, violence, and substance abuse; makes arrests if necessary during the commission of crimes; counsels students; and conducts classes about law enforcement and school safety. The program calls this the triad concept (police officer, educator, and counselor). To participate as an SRO, candidates must complete a specialized training program. The SRO program is credited with helping reduce youth crime in schools and communities.

Founded in 1991, the National Association of School Resource Officers (2017, https://nasro.org) has a national membership of over 3,000 police officers. The association holds annual conferences and provides workshops for the SROs that focus on various procedures, techniques, and prevention measures.

School-Based Prevention Programs

STUDENTS AGAINST VIOLENCE EVERYWHERE. After the high school student Alex Orange was shot and killed in Charlotte, North Carolina, while trying to stop a fight in 1989, his classmates at West Charlotte High School decided to organize the group Students against Violence

Everywhere (SAVE). SAVE (2017, http://nationalsave.org/wp-content/uploads/2016/12/SAVE-2016-2017-Press-Kit-FINAL.pdf) has grown far beyond Orange's high school; in 2017 it had more than 240,000 student members. The group is active in elementary, middle, and high schools across the United States. Members have their own "colors": orange for Alex Orange and purple for peace and nonviolence.

The group focuses on violence prevention and helping students gain life skills, knowledge, and an understanding of the consequences of violence and crime. SAVE helps members overcome negative peer-pressure situations through the development of positive peer interactions. It also plans safe activities, including cosponsorship of the annual National Youth Violence Prevention Week in late March or early April, during which participants spend each day focused on one aspect of violence prevention. For example, the first day seeks to "promote respect and tolerance," and other days focus on anger management, conflict resolution, school and community safety, and unity.

BIG BROTHERS BIG SISTERS IN SCHOOL. The Big Brothers Big Sisters program has been serving children for more than 100 years. The organization provides one-on-one mentoring services to young people (aged five to 18 years) throughout the United States. Big Brothers Big Sisters seeks to help youth perform better at school, stay clear of drugs and alcohol, improve their relationships with others, and avoid engaging in crime and violence. Under the classic program, a child is paired with an adult who spends time with him or her several times each month on outings, which can include sports, recreation, visits to museums or parks, and other activities. Through the experience, the "Bigs" help the "Littles" develop life skills, confidence, and self-esteem.

Big Brothers Big Sisters also has programs for school children. Through the group's outreach program, volunteers visit schools weekly to provide one-on-one mentoring to students needing help. In addition, high school students gain experience mentoring elementary school children through the High School Bigs program. While helping older students develop skills working with children, the project helps younger children bond with teens closer to their own age and see that they, too, can grow up to lead productive lives. In *Targeting Investments in Children: Fighting Poverty When Resources Are Limited* (2010), Phillip B. Levine and David J. Zimmerman describe the program as "impressive" and find that children in the program have improved academic outcomes.

PUNISHMENT

Juvenile Justice

The OJJDP (April 29, 2016, https://www.ojjdp.gov/ojstatbb/structure_process/qa04106.asp?qaDate=2015&text=) explains that juvenile court generally has original jurisdiction in cases involving youth who are under the age of 18 years when the crime was committed, when the youth was arrested, or when the offender was referred to the court. In 2015, 46 states and the District of Columbia had extended jurisdiction, which means that if the court deems that it is in the interests of the juvenile and the public, juvenile courts in these states may retain jurisdiction over juvenile offenders past the age at which original juvenile court jurisdiction ends. For example, California, Montana, Oregon, and Wisconsin extend juvenile court jurisdiction to age 24. Extended jurisdiction may, however, be limited by legislation to specific crimes or certain juveniles, enabling prosecutors to decide whether to try an offender as a juvenile or an adult.

The OJJDP (April 29, 2016, https://www.ojjdp.gov/ojstatbb/structure_process/qa04102.asp?qaDate=2015) further explains that the youngest age at which a juvenile can be transferred to criminal court for trial as an adult

also varies by state. In 2015, 33 states and the District of Columbia had no minimum age requirement for transferring juveniles to criminal court for trial as adults. In North Carolina, children as young as age six may be tried as adults, and in Connecticut, Maryland, Massachusetts, New York, and North Dakota, children age seven and older may be tried as adults.

DOES IT WORK? The Federal Bureau of Investigation (FBI) notes in *Crime in the United States, 2015* (2016, https://ucr.fbi.gov/crime-in-the-u.s/2015/crime-in-the-u.s.-2015/tables/table-32) that between 2006 and 2015 the number of juveniles arrested for murder and nonnegligent manslaughter fell 34.4%. (See Table 10.1.) Based on these results, some public officials believe that efforts to reduce crime through adult sentencing are working. However, many experts attribute the decrease in the number of juveniles arrested for murder and nonnegligent manslaughter to expanded after-school crime prevention programs,

TABLE 10.1

Ten-year arrest trends, 2006–15

[9,581 agencies; 2015 estimated population 199,921,204; 2006 estimated population 186,371,331]

| | Number of persons arrested | | | | | | | | |
| | Total all ages | | | Under 18 years of age | | | 18 years of age and over | | |
Offense charged	2006	2015	Percent change	2006	2015	Percent change	2006	2015	Percent change
Total[a]	8,676,456	6,739,363	−22.3	1,280,195	578,538	−54.8	7,396,261	6,160,825	−16.7
Murder and nonnegligent manslaughter	7,104	6,201	−12.7	642	421	−34.4	6,462	5,780	−10.6
Rape[b]	14,120	13,945	—	2,111	2,239	—	12,009	11,706	—
Robbery	68,437	54,003	−21.1	18,201	9,753	−46.4	50,236	44,250	−11.9
Aggravated assault	271,740	231,828	−14.7	35,984	17,717	−50.8	235,756	214,111	−9.2
Burglary	188,122	136,465	−27.5	51,953	22,056	−57.5	136,169	114,409	−16.0
Larceny-theft	679,290	753,665	+10.9	180,623	101,898	−43.6	498,667	651,767	+30.7
Motor vehicle theft	72,650	46,463	−36.0	17,651	7,547	−57.2	54,999	38,916	−29.2
Arson	10,445	5,737	−45.1	5,223	1,811	−65.3	5,222	3,926	−24.8
Violent crime[c]	361,401	305,977	−15.3	56,938	30,130	−47.1	304,463	275,847	−9.4
Property crime[c]	950,507	942,330	−0.9	255,450	133,312	−47.8	695,057	809,018	+16.4
Other assaults	792,178	678,537	−14.3	152,396	83,689	−45.1	639,782	594,848	−7.0
Forgery and counterfeiting	68,319	34,911	−48.9	2,288	632	−72.4	66,031	34,279	−48.1
Fraud	181,863	86,484	−52.4	5,090	2,776	−45.5	176,773	83,708	−52.6
Embezzlement	13,008	9,923	−23.7	949	391	−58.8	12,059	9,532	−21.0
Stolen property; buying, receiving, possessing	79,077	57,918	−26.8	14,032	6,600	−53.0	65,045	51,318	−21.1
Vandalism	189,867	124,058	−34.7	76,202	27,793	−63.5	113,665	96,265	−15.3
Weapons; carrying, possessing, etc.	114,104	86,443	−24.2	27,707	11,614	−58.1	86,397	74,829	−13.4
Prostitution and commercialized vice	33,402	17,663	−47.1	733	269	−63.3	32,669	17,394	−46.8
Sex offenses (except rape and prostitution)	50,656	32,356	−36.1	9,948	5,643	−43.3	40,708	26,713	−34.4
Drug abuse violations	1,078,156	928,122	−13.9	113,132	63,035	−44.3	965,024	865,087	−10.4
Gambling	2,807	1,657	−41.0	292	133	−54.5	2,515	1,524	−39.4
Offenses against the family and children	79,568	58,377	−26.6	3,348	2,208	−34.1	76,220	56,169	−26.3
Driving under the influence	925,818	675,960	−27.0	12,947	4,294	−66.8	912,871	671,666	−26.4
Liquor laws	408,511	174,230	−57.3	94,729	29,530	−68.8	313,782	144,700	−53.9
Drunkenness	368,271	251,424	−31.7	11,093	3,528	−68.2	357,178	247,896	−30.6
Disorderly conduct	422,187	240,723	−43.0	129,948	45,659	−64.9	292,239	195,064	−33.3
Vagrancy	18,106	15,017	−17.1	3,475	598	−82.8	14,631	14,419	−1.4
All other offenses (except traffic)	2,477,981	1,997,799	−19.4	248,829	107,250	−56.9	2,229,152	1,890,549	−15.2
Suspicion	1,125	480	−57.3	203	127	−37.4	922	353	−61.7
Curfew and loitering law violations	60,669	19,454	−67.9	60,669	19,454	−67.9	—	—	—

[a]Does not include suspicion.

[b]The 2006 rape figures are based on the legacy definition, and the 2015 rape figures are aggregate totals based on both the legacy and revised Uniform Crime Reporting definitions. For this reason, a percent change is not provided.

[c]Violent crimes are offenses of murder and nonnegligent manslaughter, rape, robbery, and aggravated assault. Property crimes are offenses of burglary, larceny-theft, motor vehicle theft, and arson.

SOURCE: "Table 32. Ten-Year Arrest Trends: Totals, 2006–2015," in *Crime in the United States, 2015*, U.S. Department of Justice, Federal Bureau of Investigation, 2016, https://ucr.fbi.gov/crime-in-the-u.s/2015/crime-in-the-u.s.-2015/tables/table-32 (accessed January 16, 2017)

the decline of crack cocaine and violent gangs, and law enforcement efforts to confiscate illegal guns in major urban areas.

Franklin E. Zimring and Stephen Rushin ask in "Did Changes in Juvenile Sanctions Reduce Juvenile Crime Rates? A Natural Experiment" (*Ohio State Journal of Criminal Law*, vol. 11, no. 1, October 2013) whether statutes enacted by 47 states between 1992 and 1997 that made the juvenile justice system more punitive were responsible for the decrease in juvenile homicides between 1993 and 2010. They determine that these changes were not responsible for the reduction in crime because the same decrease was observed in young people aged 18 to 24 years who were unaffected by transferring more juveniles to adult court where they received harsher sentences. Zimring and Rushin conclude, "If harsh juvenile legislation does little to deter future juvenile offenders, states may be wise to reconsider their use of limited criminal justice resources to incarcerate certain juvenile offenders for lengthy, adult sentences. While proponents of these laws might defend their existence on the basis of retribution, their usefulness as a deterrent is highly questionable."

Juvenile Arrests

Between 2006 and 2015 the number of juveniles arrested for all crimes dropped 54.8%; during this same period the number of adults arrested declined 22.3%. (See Table 10.1.) Arrests of juveniles for some offenses declined dramatically. For example, arrests of juveniles for forgery and counterfeiting dropped 72.4%; for drunkenness, dropped 68.2%; for driving under the influence, dropped 66.8%; for arson, dropped 65.3%; for motor vehicle theft, dropped 57.2%; and for aggravated assault, dropped 50.8%.

The FBI reports that 6.7 million arrests were made nationwide in 2015, a decrease of 22.3% from 2006. (See Table 10.1.) In 2015, 9% of all people arrested were juveniles, and 91% were adults. Adults were most often arrested for drug abuse violations (865,087 arrests), whereas juveniles were most often arrested for property crime (133,312). The FBI reports in *Crime in the United States, 2015* that in 2015 juveniles under age 18 represented 14.3% of property crime arrests and 10.2% of violent crime arrests.

ARRESTS AMONG SPECIFIC AGE GROUPS. In *Crime in the United States, 2015*, the FBI reports arrest-rate statistics for specific age groups: under the age of 15 years, under the age of 18 years, under the age of 21 years, and under the age of 25 years. Whereas 8.5% of all arrests were of juveniles in 2015, 34.2% of all people arrested were under the age of 25 years, indicating that crime is often perpetrated by young adults, rather than by juveniles. (See Table 10.2.) Table 10.2 shows which crimes are more likely to be committed by juveniles than by young adults.

A high percentage does not necessarily indicate a high number of arrests in a category. Instead, it means the age group was responsible for a high percentage of arrests within that category. For example, 76,172 people under the age of 18 years were arrested on drug abuse violations in 2015, which was 6.7% of the total arrests in that category. (See Table 10.2.) For comparison, 32,145 people under the age of 18 years were arrested for vandalism. Although the number of vandalism offenses was far less than the number of drug abuse violations for those under the age of 18 years, it represented 21.8% of the total arrests for vandalism. Tracking these percentages helps law enforcement personnel identify trends in juvenile crime.

Another offense with consistently high arrest percentages in each of the four age groups was arson. (See Table 10.2.) Nearly half (48.7%) of arrests for arson were of young adults under the age of 25 years. Of the 6,802 arrests for arson in 2015, 18.3% were of youth under the age of 15 years, 30.6% were of juveniles under the age of 18 years, and 38.6% were of people under the age of 21 years.

Other categories with high arrest percentages for those under the age of 15 years include vandalism (8.5%); sex offenses, except forcible rape and prostitution (8.1%); disorderly conduct (7.1%); and rape (6.3%). (See Table 10.2.) The under 15 age group also scored high in curfew and loitering law violations. More than a quarter (29.1%) of all arrests for curfew violations were of people under the age of 15 years, and all arrests for curfew violations and loitering law violations were of youth under the age of 18 years.

Despite the overall decrease in arrests of juveniles, delinquency cases handled by juvenile courts nationwide more than doubled between 1960 (1,100 cases per day) and 2013 (2,900 cases per day) as reported by Sarah Hockenberry and Charles Puzzanchera of the National Center for Juvenile Justice in *Juvenile Court Statistics 2013* (July 2014, https://www.ojjdp.gov/ojstatbb/njcda/pdf/jcs2013.pdf). Between 1985 and 2013 the number of public order offenses increased 40%, and the number of drug law violation cases increased 83%. During the same period property offense cases decreased 48%. (See Figure 10.1.)

ARRESTS BY SEX. Between 2006 and 2015, young males were arrested in far greater numbers than young females. However, juvenile female arrest rates grew proportionately in relation to the arrests of young males, particularly in violent crime. In 2006 females under the age of 18 years represented 29% (357,696 out of a total of 1,280,195 juvenile arrests) of the juveniles arrested. (See Table 10.3.) By 2015 the percentage of juvenile arrests that was female increased slightly to 30% (173,213 out of a total of 578,538 juvenile arrests). Although arrests of both young males and young females

TABLE 10.2

Arrests of persons under the ages of 15, 18, 21, and 25 years, 2015

[12,706 agencies; 2015 estimated population 246,947,242]

Offense charged	Total all ages	Number of persons arrested				Percent of total all ages			
		Under 15	Under 18	Under 21	Under 25	Under 15	Under 18	Under 21	Under 25
Total	8,305,919	197,123	709,333	1,583,565	2,841,957	2.4	8.5	19.1	34.2
Murder and nonnegligent manslaughter	8,533	52	605	1,994	3,803	0.6	7.1	23.4	44.6
Rape[a]	17,504	1,098	2,745	4,913	7,171	6.3	15.7	28.1	41.0
Robbery	73,230	2,752	14,176	27,741	40,903	3.8	19.4	37.9	55.9
Aggravated assault	288,815	7,134	21,993	45,628	88,067	2.5	7.6	15.8	30.5
Burglary	166,609	8,172	27,473	50,121	75,448	4.9	16.5	30.1	45.3
Larceny-theft	900,077	33,010	120,967	231,426	357,163	3.7	13.4	25.7	39.7
Motor vehicle theft	59,831	2,417	11,169	18,899	27,817	4.0	18.7	31.6	46.5
Arson	6,802	1,245	2,083	2,625	3,311	18.3	30.6	38.6	48.7
Violent crime[b]	388,082	11,036	39,519	80,276	139,944	2.8	10.2	20.7	36.1
Property crime[b]	1,133,319	44,844	161,692	303,071	463,739	4.0	14.3	26.7	40.9
Other assaults	831,684	38,402	100,980	164,460	279,526	4.6	12.1	19.8	33.6
Forgery and counterfeiting	42,681	98	791	5,220	11,874	0.2	1.9	12.2	27.8
Fraud	102,339	670	3,474	11,746	25,807	0.7	3.4	11.5	25.2
Embezzlement	12,247	27	450	2,467	4,760	0.2	3.7	20.1	38.9
Stolen property; buying, receiving, possessing	68,341	1,762	7,990	16,630	27,809	2.6	11.7	24.3	40.7
Vandalism	147,191	12,440	32,145	50,145	72,952	8.5	21.8	34.1	49.6
Weapons; carrying, possessing, etc.	111,316	4,610	14,779	29,449	49,971	4.1	13.3	26.5	44.9
Prostitution and commercialized vice	31,534	51	442	3,832	9,799	0.2	1.4	12.2	31.1
Sex offenses (except rape and prostitution)	39,393	3,180	6,699	10,319	14,424	8.1	17.0	26.2	36.6
Drug abuse violations	1,144,021	12,103	76,172	243,199	451,132	1.1	6.7	21.3	39.4
Gambling	3,607	45	357	884	1,394	1.2	9.9	24.5	38.6
Offenses against the family and children	72,418	990	2,628	5,732	13,580	1.4	3.6	7.9	18.8
Driving under the influence	833,833	120	5,064	52,259	191,793	c	0.6	6.3	23.0
Liquor laws	204,665	3,489	33,155	125,262	139,800	1.7	16.2	61.2	68.3
Drunkenness	314,856	538	4,243	24,196	67,536	0.2	1.3	7.7	21.4
Disorderly conduct	298,253	21,190	55,102	83,257	127,307	7.1	18.5	27.9	42.7
Vagrancy	19,414	212	825	2,129	4,041	1.1	4.2	11.0	20.8
All other offenses (except traffic)	2,471,772	31,398	128,770	334,865	710,455	1.3	5.2	13.5	28.7
Suspicion	1,045	51	148	259	406	4.9	14.2	24.8	38.9
Curfew and loitering law violations	33,908	9,867	33,908	33,908	33,908	29.1	100.0	100.0	100.0

[a]The rape figures in this table are aggregate totals of the data submitted based on both the legacy and revised Uniform Crime Reporting definitions.
[b]Violent crimes are offenses of murder and nonnegligent manslaughter, rape, robbery, and aggravated assault. Property crimes are offenses of burglary, larceny-theft, motor vehicle theft, and arson.
[c]Less than one-tenth of 1 percent.

SOURCE: "Table 41. Arrests: Persons under 15, 18, 21, and 25 Years of Age, 2015," in *Crime in the United States, 2015*, U.S. Department of Justice, Federal Bureau of Investigation, 2016, https://ucr.fbi.gov/crime-in-the-u.s/2015/crime-in-the-u.s.-2015/tables/table-41 (accessed January 16, 2017)

decreased between 2006 and 2015, arrests of females decreased less. Overall, arrests of males under the age of 18 years decreased 56.1% over the decade, whereas arrests of females under the age of 18 years decreased 51.6%. The difference could also be seen in some crime categories. For example, between 2006 and 2015 juvenile male arrests for aggravated assault dropped 52.2%, whereas juvenile female arrests dropped 46.1%.

Juvenile males and females engage in many of the same types of crimes. For example, the crimes most frequently committed by both male and female juveniles were property crimes; in 2015 males under the age of 18 years were arrested 87,184 times, and females in the same age group were arrested 46,128 times. (See Table 10.3.)

Offenses with high arrest rates of both juvenile males and females include larceny-theft, drug abuse violations, other assaults, and disorderly conduct. Young males were arrested 60,365 times on larceny-theft charges, and young females were arrested 41,533 times for that offense in 2015. (See Table 10.3.) Drug abuse violations accounted for the arrests of 49,170 young males and 13,865 young females, other assaults resulted in arrests of 52,882 young males and 30,807 young females, and disorderly conduct resulted in arrests of 29,356 young males and 16,303 young females.

ARRESTS BY RACE. African Americans are disproportionately arrested in the United States. The U.S. Census Bureau (2017, https://www.census.gov/quickfacts/table/PST045216/00) estimates that in 2015 the U.S. population was 61.6% non-Hispanic white, 13.3% non-Hispanic African American, 5.5% Asian American, and 1.2% Native American or Alaskan Native. Hispanics, who can be of any race, represented 17.6% of the total population. In *Crime in the United States, 2015*, the FBI notes that more than two-thirds (69.7%) of all arrested individuals in 2015 were white (Hispanic or non-Hispanic), 26.6% were African American, and the remaining 3.5% were other races.

FIGURE 10.1

Delinquency cases, by offense category, 1960 and 2013, and delinquency caseloads for selected offenses, 1985–2013

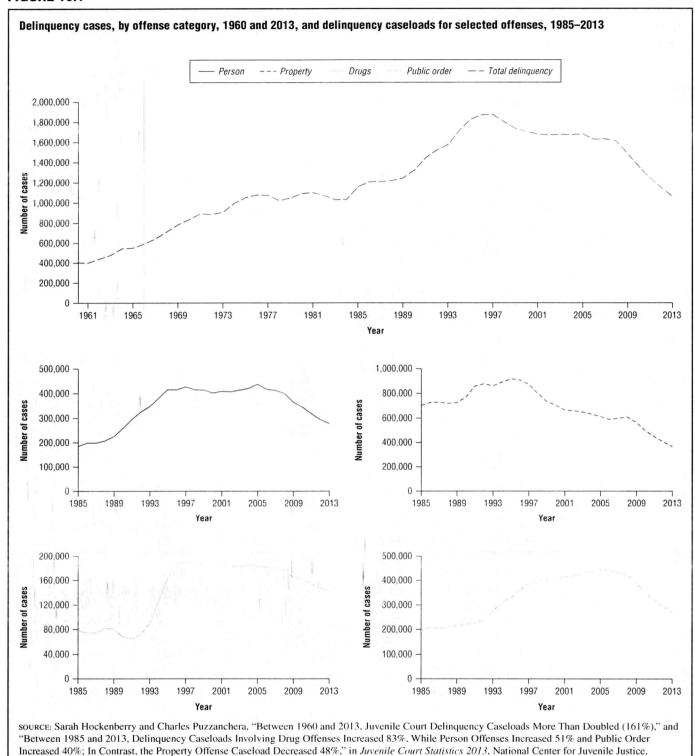

SOURCE: Sarah Hockenberry and Charles Puzzanchera, "Between 1960 and 2013, Juvenile Court Delinquency Caseloads More Than Doubled (161%)," and "Between 1985 and 2013, Delinquency Caseloads Involving Drug Offenses Increased 83%, While Person Offenses Increased 51% and Public Order Increased 40%; In Contrast, the Property Offense Caseload Decreased 48%," in *Juvenile Court Statistics 2013*, National Center for Juvenile Justice, July 2015, https://www.ojjdp.gov/ojstatbb/njcda/pdf/jcs2013.pdf (accessed January 16, 2017)

Arrested juveniles exhibited a similar racial distribution in 2015; 62.9% were white (Hispanic or non-Hispanic), 33.9% were African American, 22.8% were Hispanic, 1.7% were Native American or Alaskan Native, 1.1% were Asian American, and 0.4% were native Hawaiian or Pacific Islander. (See Table 10.4.) Among juveniles, a particularly high proportion of those arrested for driving under the influence (88.7%), violation of liquor laws (87.8%), drunkenness (83%), drug abuse violation (75%), arson (73.4%), vandalism (70.2%), and suspicion (68.8%) were white. A particularly high proportion of those arrested for gambling (75.2%), robbery (68.6%), prostitution and

TABLE 10.3

Ten-year arrest trends by sex, 2006–15

[9,581 agencies; 2015 estimated population 199,921,204; 2006 estimated population 186,371,331]

| | Male | | | | | | Female | | | | | |
| | Total | | | Under 18 | | | Total | | | Under 18 | | |
Offense charged	2006	2015	Percent change	2006	2015	Percent change	2006	2015	Percent change	2006	2015	Percent change
Total[a]	6,605,457	4,913,199	−25.6	922,499	405,325	−56.1	2,070,999	1,826,164	−11.8	357,696	173,213	−51.6
Murder and nonnegligent manslaughter	6,292	5,463	−13.2	612	394	−35.6	812	738	−9.1	30	27	−10.0
Rape[b]	13,932	13,536	—	2,071	2,154	—	188	409	—	40	85	—
Robbery	60,460	46,060	−23.8	16,413	8,658	−47.2	7,977	7,943	−0.4	1,788	1,095	−38.8
Aggravated assault	216,482	179,138	−17.3	27,741	13,273	−52.2	55,258	52,690	−4.6	8,243	4,444	−46.1
Burglary	159,767	110,416	−30.9	45,896	19,254	−58.0	28,355	26,049	−8.1	6,057	2,802	−53.7
Larceny-theft	418,187	424,952	+1.6	106,506	60,365	−43.3	261,103	328,713	+25.9	74,117	41,533	+44.0
Motor vehicle theft	59,234	36,177	−38.9	14,361	6,029	−58.0	13,416	10,286	−23.3	3,290	1,518	−53.9
Arson	8,738	4,633	−47.0	4,538	1,536	−66.2	1,707	1,104	−35.3	685	275	−59.9
Violent crime[c]	297,166	244,197	−17.8	46,837	24,479	−47.7	64,235	61,780	−3.8	10,101	5,651	−44.1
Property crime[c]	645,926	576,178	−10.8	171,301	87,184	−49.1	304,581	366,152	−20.2	84,149	46,128	+45.2
Other assaults	592,204	486,355	−17.9	101,366	52,882	−47.8	199,974	192,182	−3.9	51,030	30,807	−39.6
Forgery and counterfeiting	41,028	22,493	−45.2	1,513	470	−68.9	27,291	12,418	−54.5	775	162	−79.1
Fraud	99,184	52,967	−46.6	3,297	1,811	−45.1	82,679	33,517	−59.5	1,793	965	−46.2
Embezzlement	6,101	4,850	−20.5	517	220	−57.4	6,907	5,073	−26.6	432	171	−60.4
Stolen property; buying, receiving, possessing	63,904	45,331	−29.1	11,930	5,514	−53.8	15,173	12,587	−17.0	2,102	1,086	−48.3
Vandalism	158,590	97,844	−38.3	66,281	23,174	−65.0	31,277	26,214	−16.2	9,921	4,619	−53.4
Weapons; carrying, possessing, etc.	105,054	78,496	−25.3	25,051	10,331	−58.8	9,050	7,947	−12.2	2,656	1,283	−51.7
Prostitution and commercialized vice	11,754	7,103	−39.6	182	85	−53.3	21,648	10,560	−51.2	551	184	−66.6
Sex offenses (except rape and prostitution)	47,168	29,862	−36.7	9,029	4,914	−45.6	3,488	2,494	−28.5	919	729	−20.7
Drug abuse violations	865,257	715,904	−17.3	93,508	49,170	−47.4	212,899	212,218	−0.3	19,624	13,865	−29.3
Gambling	2,366	1,272	−46.2	279	121	−56.6	441	385	−12.7	13	12	−7.7
Offenses against the family and children	60,217	41,552	−31.0	2,070	1,379	−33.4	19,351	16,825	−13.1	1,278	829	−35.1
Driving under the influence	738,512	5,08,633	−31.1	9,943	3,251	−67.3	187,306	167,327	−10.7	3,004	1,043	−65.3
Liquor laws	294,825	123,435	−58.1	60,064	17,707	−70.5	113,686	50,795	−55.3	34,665	11,823	−65.9
Drunkenness	310,500	202,628	−34.7	8,281	2,503	−69.8	57,771	48,796	−15.5	2,812	1,025	−63.5
Disorderly conduct	308,923	171,960	−44.3	87,098	29,356	−66.3	113,264	68,763	−39.3	42,850	16,303	−62.0
Vagrancy	13,876	11,847	−14.6	2,390	457	−80.9	4,230	3,170	−25.1	1,085	141	−87.0
All other offenses (except traffic)	1,902,249	1,477,329	−22.3	180,909	77,354	−57.2	575,732	520,470	−9.6	67,920	29,896	−56.0
Suspicion	869	384	−55.8	157	95	−39.5	256	96	−62.5	46	32	−30.4
Curfew and loitering law violations	40,653	12,963	−68.1	40,653	12,963	−68.1	20,016	6,491	−67.6	20,016	6,491	−67.6

[a]Does not include suspicion.

[b]The 2006 rape figures are based on the legacy definition, and the 2015 rape figures are aggregate totals based on both the legacy and revised Uniform Crime Reporting definitions. For this reason, a percent change is not provided.

[c]Violent crimes are offenses of murder and nonnegligent manslaughter, rape, robbery, and aggravated assault. Property crimes are offenses of burglary, larceny-theft, motor vehicle theft, and arson.

SOURCE: "Table 33. Ten-Year Arrest Trends by Sex, 2006–2015," in *Crime in the United States, 2015*, U.S. Department of Justice, Federal Bureau of Investigation, 2016, https://ucr.fbi.gov/crime-in-the-u.s/2015/crime-in-the-u.s.-2015/tables/table-33 (accessed January 16, 2017)

commercialized vice (60.4%), murder and nonnegligent manslaughter (60.1%), and buying, receiving, or possessing stolen property (54.4%) were African American. The highest arrest rates of youth of Hispanic origin were for drunkenness (41%), vagrancy (36%), weapons offenses (31.2%), drug abuse violations (29%), and motor vehicle theft (26.4%).

DISPOSITION OF JUVENILES ARRESTED. Ann L. Pastore and Kathleen Maguire report in *Sourcebook of Criminal Justice Statistics* (2003, http://www.albany.edu/sourcebook/pdf/t4262004.pdf) that during the 1970s a change occurred in the disposition of arrested juveniles. Statistics for 1972 show that 50.8% of arrested minors were referred to juvenile court, 45% were handled within the police department and then released, and 1.3% were referred to criminal or adult court. In other words, almost half of all arrested juveniles were not formally charged with offenses in either juvenile or criminal court. Between 1972 and 2000, however, those referred to juvenile court increased to 70.8%, whereas those handled internally and then released dropped to 20.3%. The percentage of juvenile cases referred to criminal or adult court rose to 7%. In 2015, 58.8% of juveniles arrested were referred to juvenile court, 25.5% were released after being handled internally within the department, and 7.9% were referred to criminal or adult court. (See Table 10.5.)

Juveniles in Custody

According to the OJJDP (2017, https://www.ojjdp.gov/ojstatbb/glossary.html), *committed* juveniles include

TABLE 10.4

Arrests of juveniles by race, 2015

[12,692 agencies; 2015 estimated population 246,920,373]

	Arrests under 18 — Race						Percent distribution[a]						Arrests under 18 — Ethnicity			Percent distribution[a]		
Offense charged	Total	White	Black or African American	American Indian or Alaska Native	Asian	Native Hawaiian or other Pacific Islander	Total	White	Black or African American	American Indian or Alaska Native	Asian	Native Hawaiian or other Pacific Islander	Total[b]	Hispanic or Latino	Not Hispanic or Latino	Total	Hispanic or Latino	Not Hispanic or Latino
Total	**702,957**	**442,364**	**238,542**	**11,999**	**7,392**	**2,660**	**100.0**	**62.9**	**33.9**	**1.7**	**1.1**	**0.4**	**545,870**	**124,563**	**421,307**	**100.0**	**22.8**	**77.2**
Murder and nonnegligent manslaughter	601	234	361	5	1	0	100.0	38.9	60.1	0.8	0.2	0.0	463	118	345	100.0	25.5	74.5
Rape[c]	2,715	1,802	835	42	26	10	100.0	66.4	30.8	1.5	1.0	0.4	1,975	397	1,578	100.0	20.1	79.9
Robbery	14,142	4,190	9,702	60	100	90	100.0	29.6	68.6	0.4	0.7	0.6	11,733	2,520	9,213	100.0	21.5	78.5
Aggravated assault	21,865	12,180	9,061	333	222	69	100.0	55.7	41.4	1.5	1.0	0.3	17,845	4,597	13,248	100.0	25.8	74.2
Burglary	27,344	15,287	11,373	344	262	78	100.0	55.9	41.6	1.3	1.0	0.3	22,536	5,688	16,848	100.0	25.2	74.8
Larceny-theft	119,712	72,434	43,232	1,751	1,815	480	100.0	60.5	36.1	1.5	1.5	0.4	92,529	19,125	73,404	100.0	20.7	79.3
Motor vehicle theft	11,111	5,535	5,296	176	71	33	100.0	49.8	47.7	1.6	0.6	0.3	8,056	2,124	5,932	100.0	26.4	73.6
Arson	2,067	1,517	469	58	17	6	100.0	73.4	22.7	2.8	0.8	0.3	1,701	326	1,375	100.0	19.2	80.8
Violent crime[d]	39,323	18,406	19,959	440	349	169	100.0	46.8	50.8	1.1	0.9	0.4	32,016	7,632	24,384	100.0	23.8	76.2
Property crime[d]	160,234	94,773	60,370	2,329	2,165	597	100.0	59.1	37.7	1.5	1.4	0.4	124,822	27,263	97,559	100.0	21.8	78.2
Other assaults	100,264	58,646	39,133	1,332	772	381	100.0	58.5	39.0	1.3	0.8	0.4	78,816	16,974	61,842	100.0	21.5	78.5
Forgery and counterfeiting	786	481	291	6	6	2	100.0	61.2	37.0	0.8	0.8	0.3	644	147	497	100.0	22.8	77.2
Fraud	3,425	1,730	1,583	60	47	5	100.0	50.5	46.2	1.8	1.4	0.1	2,710	364	2,346	100.0	13.4	86.6
Embezzlement	443	256	175	5	6	1	100.0	57.8	39.5	1.1	1.4	0.2	368	65	303	100.0	17.7	82.3
Stolen property; buying, receiving, possessing	7,941	3,442	4,322	72	88	17	100.0	43.3	54.4	0.9	1.1	0.2	6,370	1,341	5,029	100.0	21.1	78.9
Vandalism	31,840	22,359	8,562	508	308	103	100.0	70.2	26.9	1.6	1.0	0.3	26,635	5,890	20,745	100.0	22.1	77.9
Weapons; carrying, possessing, etc.	14,687	8,308	5,994	135	215	35	100.0	56.6	40.8	0.9	1.5	0.2	11,500	3,589	7,911	100.0	31.2	68.8
Prostitution and commercialized vice	442	162	267	2	6	5	100.0	36.7	60.4	0.5	1.4	1.1	377	53	324	100.0	14.1	85.9
Sex offenses (except rape and prostitution)	6,632	4,739	1,697	73	83	40	100.0	71.5	25.6	1.1	1.3	0.6	4,949	1,179	3,770	100.0	23.8	76.2
Drug abuse violations	75,461	56,617	16,419	1,347	836	242	100.0	75.0	21.8	1.8	1.1	0.3	60,323	17,506	42,817	100.0	29.0	71.0
Gambling	355	77	267	6	5	0	100.0	21.7	75.2	1.7	1.4	0.0	208	34	174	100.0	16.3	83.7
Offenses against the family and children	2,597	1,656	784	135	22	0	100.0	63.8	30.2	5.2	0.8	0.0	1,769	314	1,455	100.0	17.8	82.2
Driving under the influence	4,993	4,430	295	177	73	18	100.0	88.7	5.9	3.5	1.5	0.4	3,861	928	2,933	100.0	24.0	76.0
Liquor laws	32,663	28,684	2,184	1,326	386	83	100.0	87.8	6.7	4.1	1.2	0.3	25,066	4,114	20,952	100.0	16.4	83.6
Drunkenness	4,209	3,495	386	271	47	10	100.0	83.0	9.2	6.4	1.1	0.2	3,943	1,618	2,325	100.0	41.0	59.0
Disorderly conduct	54,686	30,061	23,100	1,058	367	100	100.0	55.0	42.2	1.9	0.7	0.2	37,696	6,793	30,903	100.0	18.0	82.0
Vagrancy	820	472	313	26	9	0	100.0	57.6	38.2	3.2	1.1	0.0	573	209	364	100.0	36.5	63.5
All other offenses (except traffic)	127,312	85,689	37,354	2,284	1,250	735	100.0	67.3	29.3	1.8	1.0	0.6	94,047	22,576	71,471	100.0	24.0	76.0
Suspicion	144	99	34	11	0	0	100.0	68.8	23.6	7.6	0.0	0.0	52	4	48	100.0	7.7	92.3
Curfew and loitering law violations	33,700	17,782	15,053	396	352	117	100.0	52.8	44.7	1.2	1.0	0.3	29,125	5,970	23,155	100.0	20.5	79.5

TABLE 10.4

Arrests of juveniles by race, 2015 [CONTINUED]

[12,692 agencies; 2015 estimated population 246,920,373]

^aBecause of rounding, the percentages may not add to 100.0.
^bThe ethnicity totals are representative of those agencies that provided ethnicity breakdowns. Not all agencies provide ethnicity data; therefore, the race and ethnicity totals will not equal.
^cThe rape figures in this table are aggregate totals of the data submitted based on both the legacy and revised Uniform Crime Reporting definitions.
^dViolent crimes are offenses of murder and nonnegligent manslaughter, rape, robbery, and aggravated assault. Property crimes are offenses of burglary, larceny-theft, motor vehicle theft, and arson.

SOURCE: "Table 43B. Arrests by Race and Ethnicity, 2015," in *Crime in the United States, 2015,* U.S. Department of Justice, Federal Bureau of Investigation, 2016, https://ucr.fbi.gov/crime-in-the-u.s/2015/crime-in-the-u.s.-2015/tables/table-43 (accessed January 16, 2017)

TABLE 10.5

Police disposition of juvenile offenders taken into custody, 2015

[2015 estimated population]

Population group		Total[a]	Handled within department and released	Referred to juvenile court jurisdiction	Referred to welfare agency	Referred to other police agency	Referred to criminal or adult court	Number of agencies	2015 estimated population
Total agencies:	Number	130,210	33,148	76,596	4,107	6,084	10,275	4,692	110,559,392
	Percent[b]	100.0	25.5	58.8	3.2	4.7	7.9		
Total cities	Number	106,536	29,760	59,600	3,682	5,675	7,819	3,532	76,914,669
	Percent[b]	100.0	27.9	55.9	3.5	5.3	7.3		
Group I (250,000 and over)	Number	27,659	15,151	11,438	15	185	870	30	19,848,382
	Percent[b]	100.0	54.8	41.4	0.1	0.7	3.1		
Group II (100,000 to 249,999)	Number	7,105	969	5,472	0	16	648	81	11,925,121
	Percent[b]	100.0	13.6	77.0	0	0.2	9.1		
Group III (50,000 to 99,999)	Number	14,543	2,237	11,921	33	55	297	218	15,181,383
	Percent[b]	100.0	15.4	82.0	0.2	0.4	2.0		
Group IV (25,000 to 49,999)	Number	16,489	3,403	7,919	1,345	1,780	2,042	326	11,189,383
	Percent[b]	100.0	20.6	48.0	8.2	10.8	12.4		
Group V (10,000 to 24,999)	Number	16,494	2,153	12,077	357	585	1,322	696	11,204,123
	Percent[b]	100.0	13.1	73.2	2.2	3.5	8.0		
Group VI (under 10,000)	Number	24,246	5,847	10,773	1,932	3,054	2,640	2,181	7,566,277
	Percent[b]	100.0	24.1	44.4	8.0	12.6	10.9		
Metropolitan counties	Number	7,148	936	5,183	211	269	549	492	6,397,513
	Percent[b]	100.0	13.1	72.5	3.0	3.8	7.7		
Nonmetropolitan counties	Number	16,526	2,452	11,813	214	140	1,907	668	27,247,210
	Percent[b]	100.0	14.8	71.5	1.3	0.8	11.5		
Suburban area[c]	Number	56,828	8,700	37,020	2,321	3,261	5,526	3,163	61,000,503
	Percent[b]	100.0	15.3	65.1	4.1	5.7	9.7		

[a]Includes all offenses except traffic and neglect cases.
[b]Because of rounding, the percentages may not add to 100.0.
[c]Suburban areas include law enforcement agencies in cities with less than 50,000 inhabitants and county law enforcement agencies that are within a metropolitan statistical area. Suburban areas exclude all metropolitan agencies associated with a principal city. The agencies associated with suburban areas also appear in other groups within this table.

SOURCE: "Table 68. Police Disposition: Juvenile Offenders Taken into Custody, 2015," in *Crime in the United States, 2015*, U.S. Department of Justice, Federal Bureau of Investigation, 2016, https://ucr.fbi.gov/crime-in-the-u.s/2015/crime-in-the-u.s.-2015/tables/table-68 (accessed January 16, 2017)

those who are placed in the facility as part of a court-ordered disposition; *detained* juveniles include those who are held awaiting a court hearing, adjudication, disposition, or placement elsewhere; and *diversion* juveniles include those in the facility who are part of a diversion agreement.

DETENTION. According to Hockenberry and Puzzanchera, approximately 21% of juveniles are put in detention as their cases are processed in juvenile court. Detention may be used if the juvenile is judged to be a threat to the community, will be at risk if returned to the community, or may not appear at an upcoming hearing if released. The researchers report that the proportion of delinquency cases involving detention increased from 19% in 1985 to 21% in 2013. However, between 1985 and 2013, the use of detention decreased for public order offense cases (from 26% to 24%) and for drug law violation cases (from 21% to 14%), but increased for person offense cases (from 23% to 26%), and was basically unchanged for property offense cases (from 16% to 17%).

Hockenberry and Puzzanchera indicate that although African Americans made up 35% of the overall delinquency caseload in 2013, they made up 42% of those detained. Cases involving African American youth were more likely to be detained than those involving white youth for all offenses.

RESIDENTIAL PLACEMENT. Youths sentenced under the jurisdiction of juvenile courts could be generally confined in residential placement facilities. In "Juveniles in Residential Placement, 2013" (May 2016, https://www.ojjdp.gov/pubs/249507.pdf), Hockenberry reports that in 2013, 54,148 juvenile offenders were confined in public and private juvenile correctional, detention, and shelter facilities. Public facilities housed more than twice as many juvenile offenders (36,830) than did private facilities (17,318).

The OJJDP divides juvenile crimes into delinquency offenses and status offenses. Delinquency offenses are acts that are illegal regardless of the age of the perpetrator. Status offenses are acts that are illegal only for minors, such as truancy and running away. Eighty-six percent of juveniles in residential placement in 2013 were delinquents. One-third of juveniles in residential placement (19,922 offenders) were held for offenses against people (homicide, sexual assault, robbery, aggravated or simple assault, or other person offenses), whereas just 4% (2,524 offenders) were held for status offenses.

TABLE 10.6

Number of inmates in local jails, by characteristics, midyear 2000 and 2005–14

Characteristic	2000	2005	2006	2007	2008	2009	2010	2011[a]	2012[a]	2013[a]	2014[a, i]
Total[b]	621,149	747,529	765,819	780,174	785,533	767,434	748,728	735,601	744,524	731,208	744,592
Sex											
Male	550,162	652,958	666,819	679,654	685,862	673,728	656,360	642,300	645,900	628,900	635,500
Female	70,987	94,571	99,000	100,520	99,670	93,706	92,368	93,300	98,600	102,400	109,100
Adult	613,534	740,770	759,717	773,341	777,829	760,216	741,168	729,700	739,100	726,600	740,400
Male	543,120	646,807	661,164	673,346	678,657	667,039	649,284	636,900	640,900	624,700	631,600
Female	70,414	93,963	98,552	99,995	99,172	93,176	91,884	92,800	98,100	101,900	108,800
Juvenile[c]	7,615	6,759	6,102	6,833	7,703	7,218	7,560	5,900	5,400	4,600	4,200
Held as adult[d]	6,126	5,750	4,835	5,649	6,410	5,846	5,647	4,600	4,600	3,500	3,700
Held as juvenile	1,489	1,009	1,268	1,184	1,294	1,373	1,912	1,400	900	1,100	500
Race/Hispanic origin[e]											
White[f]	260,500	331,000	336,500	338,200	333,300	326,400	331,600	329,400	341,100	344,900	352,800
Black/African American[f]	256,300	290,500	295,900	301,700	308,000	300,500	283,200	276,400	274,600	261,500	263,800
Hispanic/Latino	94,100	111,900	119,200	125,500	128,500	124,000	118,100	113,900	112,700	107,900	110,600
American Indian/ Alaska Native[f, g]	5,500	7,600	8,400	8,600	9,000	9,400	9,900	9,400	9,300	10,200	10,400
Asian/Native Hawaiian/ other Pacific Islander[f, g]	4,700	5,400	5,100	5,300	5,500	5,400	5,100	5,300	5,400	5,100	6,000
Two or more races[f]	i	1,000	700	800	1,300	1,800	800	1,200	1,500	1,600	1,000
Conviction status[e, h]											
Convicted	271,300	284,400	290,000	296,700	291,200	290,100	291,300	289,600	293,100	278,000	277,100
Unconvicted	349,800	463,200	475,800	483,500	494,200	477,300	457,400	446,000	451,400	453,200	467,500

[a]Data for 2011–2014 are adjusted for nonresponse and rounded to the nearest 100.
[b]Midyear count is the number of inmates held on the last weekday in June.
[c]Persons age 17 or younger at midyear.
[d]Includes juveniles who were tried or awaiting trial as adults.
[e]Data adjusted for nonresponse and rounded to the nearest 100.
[f]Excludes persons of Hispanic or Latino origin.
[g]Previous reports combined American Indians and Alaska Natives and Asians, Native Hawaiians, and other Pacific Islanders into an Other race category.
[h]Includes juveniles who were tried or awaiting trial as adults.
[i]Not collected.
[j]Comparison year for each characteristic.
Note: Detail may not sum to total because of rounding.

SOURCE: Todd D. Minton and Zhen Zeng, "Table 2. Number of Inmates in Local Jails, by Characteristics, Midyear 2000 and 2005–2014," in "Jail Inmates at Midyear 2014," *Bulletin*, U.S. Department of Justice Office of Justice Programs, Bureau of Justice Statistics, June 2015, https://www.bjs.gov/content/pub/pdf/jim14.pdf (accessed March 21, 2017)

DEMOGRAPHICS OF THOSE IN RESIDENTIAL PLACEMENT. Hockenberry observes that in 2013 the majority of juveniles in residential placement were male (86%). Of the males in confinement, 38% had committed offenses against people, and 24% had committed property offenses. Females were less likely to have committed person offenses (31%) and property offenses (19%) than were males. Females (11%) were substantially more likely to be held for status offenses than were males (4%).

Hockenberry also reports that in 2013, minority youth were overrepresented in residential placements— 40% of juvenile offenders in residential placement were African American, 23% were Hispanic, 2% were Native American, and 1% were Asian American. In contrast, 32% of juveniles in custody were white.

Incarcerated Juveniles

In *Jail Inmates at Midyear 2014—Statistical Tables* (August 12, 2014, https://www.bjs.gov/content/pub/pdf/jim13st.pdf), Todd D. Minton and Zhen Zeng of the Bureau of Justice Statistics report that 4,200 youth aged 17 years or younger were held in local jails in 2014— 3,700 as adults and 500 as juveniles. (See Table 10.6.)

Liz Ryan of the Campaign for Youth Justice reports in "Youth in the Adult Criminal Justice System" (*Cardoza Law Review*, vol. 35, February 18, 2014) that about 200,000 youth are prosecuted every year and that the overwhelming majority of youth in the adult courts are not there for serious violent crimes. Ryan observes that every day an estimated 7,500 youth are being held pretrial in adult jails, where they are at high risk for assault, abuse, and even death. Federal protections to protect youth from the dangers of adult jails do not apply to youth who are prosecuted as adults. The vast majority of states have statutes that require or allow youth prosecuted as adults to be placed in adult jails without federal protections.

Furthermore, Ryan observes that the juvenile court judge, who is best able to analyze the youth's case and make an informed decision, does not have the authority to decide whether a youth should be prosecuted in adult court. Ryan notes that minority youth are disproportionately represented among those youth transferred to the adult corrections system and generally receive harsher treatment in that system than white youth. Moreover, much research confirms that these practices do not promote public safety. On the contrary, Ryan asserts, "every study conducted on this issue shows that sending youth to the adult criminal justice system increases the likelihood that they will reoffend."

IMPRISONING ADULTS AND JUVENILES TOGETHER. In "Introducing the Issue" (*Future of Children*, vol. 18, no. 2, Fall 2008), Laurence Steinberg of Temple University observes that beginning in the 1990s U.S. society experienced a "moral panic" about juvenile crime that fueled "get tough on crime" policies that treated many juvenile offenders as adults. This included imprisoning juveniles with adults, despite the known risks associated with incarcerating them together. Among the chief concerns is that housing youth with hardened adult prisoners will likely cause youth offenders to become more violent, tougher, and repeat offenders. Instead of rehabilitation and education, such juveniles will be subjected to more physical and sexual abuse and violence, increasing their likelihood of showing violent tendencies when returning to society.

Steinberg contends that at the end of the first decade of the 21st century get-tough policies softened "as politicians and the public [came] to regret the high economic costs and ineffectiveness of the punitive reforms and the harshness of the sanctions." Elizabeth S. Scott and Laurence Steinberg find in "Adolescent Development and the Regulation of Youth Crime" (*Future of Children*, vol. 18, no. 2, Fall 2008) that by 2008 the justice system was once again recognizing that age and maturity should be taken into account when calculating punishment for crimes. The researchers suggest that most juveniles who commit crimes are "adolescence-limited" offenders who will mature out of their criminal tendencies; however, contact with a harsh, adult corrections system can push juveniles into adult criminality. Instead, Scott and Steinberg indicate that successful programs "seek to provide young offenders with supportive social contexts and authoritative adult figures and to help them acquire the skills necessary to change problem behavior and attain psychosocial maturity."

In "You're an Adult Now: Youth in Adult Criminal Justice Systems" (December 2011, http://static.nicic.gov/Library/025555.pdf), Jason Ziedenberg, a consultant to the National Institute of Corrections, notes that some states and localities have developed novel ways to manage youth when they have been charged, convicted, and committed to the adult corrections system. These initiatives aim to "improve public safety, contain costs, successfully rehabilitate youth and help them transition to adulthood." Examples include:

- Separating wards by age, which helps keep them safe and enables provision of age-appropriate education and rehabilitation services

- Initially committing youth with adult convictions to the juvenile corrections system for assessment of whether their needs may be better met in the juvenile corrections system

- Designating specific units where youth who are on community supervision for an adult offense receive age-appropriate services and supervision

According to the Pew Charitable Trusts, in *Public Opinion on Juvenile Justice in America* (December 11, 2014, http://www.pewtrusts.org/en/research-and-analysis/issue-briefs/2014/12/public-opinion-on-juvenile-justice-in-america), U.S. voters distinguish juvenile offenders from adult offenders and support programs to prevent juveniles from reoffending. They also support sending fewer less-serious juvenile offenders to corrections facilities and using some of the resulting savings to strengthen the probation system and other alternatives to incarceration. For example, most believe the juvenile justice system should be involved exclusively with serious offenses, and status offenses such as running away from home should be addressed by families, schools, and social service agencies.

Improving Care for Juvenile Offenders

In *Core Principles for Reducing Recidivism and Improving Other Outcomes for Youth in the Juvenile Justice System* (2014, https://csgjusticecenter.org), Elizabeth Seigle, Nastassia Walsh, and Josh Weber examine the status of state and local juvenile justice systems' policies and practices, evaluate progress made to improve them, and recommend additional actions to strengthen them. The researchers observe that recidivism (relapse into criminal activity) rates remain high for most juvenile justice systems and that graduation and employment rates for youth released from system supervision remain low. They also point out that minority youth receive harsher treatment and are less likely to receive needed services and community support than their white peers.

Seigle, Walsh, and Weber provide recommendations to improve the state and local juvenile justice systems, including:

- Ending the use of programs and practices that do not reduce recidivism, such as large overcrowded juvenile corrections facilities and curfew laws

- Supporting and funding programs and services that have demonstrated effectiveness in reducing reoffending

- Minimizing juvenile justice system supervision and services for youth who are at a low risk of reoffending

- Addressing juvenile justice system bias and the disparate treatment of minority youth

- Making collaborative efforts that involve the juvenile justice system and other youth service providers to address the needs of at-risk youth

- Minimizing the use of confinement for youth who are likely to reoffend and arranging programs and services for them

- Identifying the causes of a youth's delinquent behavior as well as the need for mental health and substance use treatment, and addressing them with appropriate interventions

- Involving families and other adults to support youth in juvenile justice system proceedings, planning, and decisions

- Holding youth responsible for their actions in ways that repair the harm done, such as community service or monetary or some other form of restitution

In "Motivating Compliance: Juvenile Probation Officer Strategies and Skills" (*Journal of Offender Rehabilitation*, vol. 56, no. 1, 2017), Katherine Schwartz et al. point out that reoffending by youth on probation can lead to more serious involvement in the justice system. Schwartz et al. observe that juvenile probation officers (JPOs) have a key role in preventing youths' involvement in the justice system and have considerable impact on conditions of probation via their recommendations to the court. By motivating juveniles on probation to comply with court orders JPOs can improve how youth fare in the justice system. Schwartz et al. conclude, "Given the unique role of JPOs to effect behavior change within the system, our findings should encourage efforts to determine whether improving JPO competence in motivational interviewing skills improves youth probationer outcomes."

Children and the Death Penalty

Until 2005 convicted criminals could face the death penalty for crimes they committed as juveniles. In *The Juvenile Death Penalty Today: Death Sentences and Executions for Juvenile Crimes, January 1, 1973–February 28, 2005* (October 7, 2005, http://www.deathpenaltyinfo.org/files/pdf/juvdeathstreib.pdf), Victor L. Streib of Ohio Northern University reports that between 1973 and 2005, 22 offenders were executed for crimes they committed when they were younger than age 18. Historically, the U.S. Supreme Court restricted the application of the death penalty for crimes committed by juveniles. In *Eddings v. Oklahoma* (455 U.S. 104 [1982]), the court reversed the death sentence of a 16-year-old who had been tried as an adult, observing that a juvenile's mental and emotional development should be considered as a mitigating factor,

given that adolescents are less able to weigh the long-term consequences of their actions than are adults.

Later Supreme Court rulings continued to limit the application of the death penalty for crimes committed by juveniles. In the 1988 case *Thompson v. Oklahoma* (487 U.S. 815), the court deemed a death sentence for an offender who had been 15 years old at the time of the murder to be cruel and unusual punishment, concluding that it could not be applied to offenders who were younger than 16 years old. Just one year later, however, in *Stanford v. Kentucky* (492 U.S. 361 [1989]), the court determined that the death penalty for offenders aged 16 to 17 years at the time of their crime was not cruel and unusual punishment.

The court reconsidered this issue in 2005 in *Roper v. Simmons* (543 U.S. 551). By a vote of 5–4, the court rejected the death sentence of Christopher Simmons, concluding that the "Eighth and 14th Amendments forbid imposition of the death penalty on offenders who were under the age of 18 when their crimes were committed." Although few states applied death penalty provisions to juveniles at the time of this decision, legislation in 20 states permitted juveniles to be sentenced to death.

In 2003, 16-year-old Terrance Jamar Graham tried to rob a restaurant. He was charged as an adult for armed burglary with assault and battery, a first-degree felony that is punishable by life in prison. Six months later, he was arrested again for home invasion robbery. Graham denied involvement in the crime but conceded that he had violated his plea agreement. In 2006 Graham was sentenced to life in prison, and because Florida abolished parole, it became a sentence without parole. In May 2010 the Supreme Court ruled in *Graham v. Florida* (No. 08-7412) that life imprisonment-without-parole sentences could no longer be imposed on juveniles convicted of non-homicide offenses. In February 2012 Graham was resentenced to 25 years by the judge who first tried the case.

In June 2012 the Supreme Court issued a landmark decision in *Miller v. Alabama* (567 U.S. ___ [2012]) and *Jackson v. Hobbs* (No. 10-9647), ruling that mandatory life-without-parole sentences for children aged 17 years or younger convicted of homicide are unconstitutional. The ruling affected hundreds of youth who received sentences that did not consider their age at sentencing. The court did not ban all juvenile life-without-parole sentences but wrote that requiring sentencers to consider "children's diminished culpability, and heightened capacity for change" should make such sentences "uncommon."

In July 2013 Wyoming enacted a law that abolished life-without-parole sentences for juveniles and provided that youth sentenced to life imprisonment for an offense committed before the age of 18 years are eligible for parole after serving 25 years. The law also authorizes the governor to commute a life sentence imposed on a juvenile to a term of years.

In March 2015 the U.S. Supreme Court agreed to hear an appeal from Henry Montgomery, who was 17 years old when he was sentenced to life in prison for murdering a police officer in 1963. The court considered whether its *Miller* ruling could be applied retroactively to convicts who were sentenced before 2012, when *Miller* was decided. On January 25, 2016, the U.S. Supreme Court reversed the judgment of the Supreme Court of Louisiana, holding that *Miller v. Alabama* ruling ensures that under the Constitution, mandatory life sentences without parole should not apply to juveniles convicted of murder.

IMPORTANT NAMES
AND ADDRESSES

Advocates for Youth
2000 M St. NW, Ste. 750
Washington, DC 20036
(202) 419-3420
FAX: (202) 419-1448
URL: http://www.advocatesforyouth.org/

American Academy of Child and Adolescent Psychiatry
3615 Wisconsin Ave. NW
Washington, DC 20016-3007
(202) 966-7300
FAX: (202) 464-0131
URL: http://www.aacap.org/

Boys and Girls Clubs of America
1275 Peachtree St. NE
Atlanta, GA 30309-3506
(404) 487-5700
E-mail: info@bgca.org
URL: https://www.bgca.org/

Center for Law and Social Policy
1200 18th St. NW, Ste. 200
Washington, DC 20036
(202) 906-8000
FAX: (202) 842-2885
URL: http://www.clasp.org/

Child Care Aware of America
1515 N. Courthouse Rd., Second Floor
Arlington, VA 22201
1-800-424-2246
URL: http://childcareaware.org/

Child Trends
7315 Wisconsin Ave., Ste. 1200W
Bethesda, MD 20814
(240) 223-9200
URL: https://www.childtrends.org/

Children's Defense Fund
25 E St. NW
Washington, DC 20001
1-800-233-1200
E-mail: cdfinfo@childrensdefense.org
URL: http://www.childrensdefense.org/

College Board
250 Vesey St.
New York, NY 10281
(212) 713-8000
URL: https://www.collegeboard.org/

Cyberbullying Research Center
URL: http://cyberbullying.org/

Feeding America
35 E. Wacker Dr., Ste. 2000
Chicago, IL 60601
1-800-771-2303
FAX: (312) 263-5626
URL: http://www.feedingamerica.org/

Gangfree.org
PO Box 408
San Pedro, CA 90733
1-888-293-9323
FAX: (310) 519-8730
E-mail: contact@gangfree.org
URL: http://www.gangfree.org/

Guttmacher Institute
125 Maiden Ln., Seventh Floor
New York, NY 10038
(212) 248-1111
1-800-355-0244
FAX: (212) 248-1951
URL: http://www.guttmacher.org/

Kaiser Family Foundation
2400 Sand Hill Rd.
Menlo Park, CA 94025
(650) 854-9400
FAX: (650) 854-4800
URL: http://www.kff.org/

Monitoring the Future
Survey Research Center Director's Office
University of Michigan
PO Box 1248
Ann Arbor, MI 48106-1248
(734) 764-8365
E-mail: mtfinformation@umich.edu
URL: http://monitoringthefuture.org/

National Association of School Resource Officers
2020 Valleydale Rd., Ste. 207A
Hoover, AL 35244
(205) 739-6060
1-888-316-2776
FAX: (205) 536-9255
URL: https://nasro.org/

National Campaign to Prevent Teen and Unplanned Pregnancy
1776 Massachusetts Ave. NW, Ste. 200
Washington, DC 20036
(202) 478-8500
FAX: (202) 478-8588
URL: http://thenationalcampaign.org/

National Center for Children in Poverty
215 W. 125th St., Third Floor
New York, NY 10027
(646) 284-9600
FAX: (646) 284-9623
E-mail: info@nccp.org
URL: http://www.nccp.org/

National Center for Missing and Exploited Children
Charles B. Wang International
Children's Bldg.
699 Prince St.
Alexandria, VA 22314-3175
(703) 224-2150
1-800-843-5678
FAX: (703) 224-2122
URL: http://www.missingkids.com/

National Center for Victims of Crime
2000 M St. NW, Ste. 480
Washington, DC 20036
(202) 467-8700
FAX: (202) 467-8701
URL: http://www.victimsofcrime.org/

National Crime Prevention Council
2614 Chapel Lake Dr., Ste. B
Gambrills, MD 21054
(443) 292-4565
URL: http://www.ncpc.org/

National Gang Center
Institute for Intergovernmental Research
PO Box 12729
Tallahassee, FL 32317
(850) 385-0600
1-800-446-0912
FAX: (850) 386-5356

E-mail: information@nationalgangcenter.gov
URL: https://www.nationalgangcenter.gov/

**National Institute on
Drug Abuse**
Office of Science Policy and
Communications
Public Information and Liaison Branch
6001 Executive Blvd.
Rm. 5213, MSC 9561
Bethesda, MD 20892
(301) 443-1124
URL: https://www.drugabuse.gov/

**Office of Juvenile
Justice and Delinquency
Prevention**
810 Seventh St. NW
Washington, DC 20531
(202) 307-5911
URL: https://www.ojjdp.gov/

Urban Institute
2100 M St. NW
Washington, DC 20037
(202) 833-7200
URL: http://www.urban.org/

RESOURCES

The U.S. Census Bureau publishes numerous reports and statistics on children and youth in the United States, including *Methodology and Assumptions for the 2014 National Projections* (December 2014), *Families and Living Arrangements, Historical Time Series: House-holds* (2016), *Coresident Grandparents and Their Grandchildren: 2012* (Renee R. Ellis and Tavia Simmons, October 2014), *Income and Poverty in the United States: 2015* (Bernadette D. Proctor, Jessica L. Semega, and Melissa A. Kollar, September 2016), *Health Insurance Coverage in the United States: 2015* (Jessica C. Barnett and Marina S. Vornovitsky, September 2016), and *Custodial Mothers and Fathers and Their Child Support: 2013* (Timothy S. Grall, January 2016). The Census Bureau also provides information on national and state population projections by age, race, Hispanic origin, and sex.

The Federal Interagency Forum on Child and Family Statistics, in *America's Children in Brief: Key National Indicators of Well-Being, 2016* (2016), offers invaluable data on many aspects of the health and well-being of children and young adults.

The Centers for Disease Control and Prevention (CDC) published *National Vital Statistics Rapid Release: Quarterly Provisional Estimates* (Lauren M. Rossen et al., November 2016), "Births: Final Data for 2014" (Brady E. Hamilton et al., December 2015), and *Teen Birth Rates for Urban and Rural Areas in the United States, 2007–2015* (Brady E. Hamilton et al., November 2016), and issues the *Morbidity and Mortality Weekly Report*, which focuses on diseases and deaths. The "CDC's National Surveillance Data (1997–2015)" (October 2016) details elevated blood lead levels in children aged five years and younger. The CDC's "Youth Risk Behavior Surveillance—United States, 2015" (Laura Kann et al., June 2016) is a key source of survey information on risk behaviors among U.S. high school students. The CDC is also a leading source of HIV/AIDS statistics with its annual *HIV Surveillance Report* and *Sexual Risk Behavior: HIV, STD, & Teen Pregnancy Prevention* (July 2016). The National Center for Health Statistics published *Health, United States, 2015* (May 2016), which provides data on many health conditions, birth rates, fertility rates, and life expectancy.

The U.S. Conference of Mayors discusses the problem of homelessness in *Hunger and Homelessness Survey: A Status Report on Hunger and Homelessness in America's Cities* (December 2016). *Child Maltreatment 2014* (2016) by the Administration on Children, Youth, and Families counts cases of child abuse that were reported to state child protective agencies. The Administration for Children and Families provided data on child support collections.

The U.S. Bureau of Labor Statistics provides data on employment and unemployment in "The Employment Situation: November 2016" (March 2017), "Employment Characteristics of Families—2015" (April 2016), and "Characteristics of Minimum Wage Workers: 2015" (April 2016).

The U.S. Department of Agriculture published *Characteristics of Supplemental Nutrition Assistance Program Households: Fiscal Year 2014* (Kelsey Farson Gray and Shivani Kochhar, December 2015) and *Household Food Security in the United States in 2015* (Alisha Coleman-Jensen et al., September 2016), and provided statistics on the national school lunch program. The Feeding America report "Child Hunger Facts" (2017) offers information on children living in food insecure households.

The National Center for Education Statistics (NCES), which is part of the U.S. Department of Education, published *Primary Early Care and Education Arrangements and Achievement at Kindergarten Entry* (Amy Rathbun and Anlan Zhang, June 2016) and *The Condition of Education 2016* (Grace Kena et al., May 2016), which provides important statistics on education in the United States. The NCES collaborated with the Bureau of Justice Statistics to publish *Indicators of School Crime and Safety: 2015* (Anlan Zhang, Lauren Musu-Gillette, and Barbara A. Oudekerk, May 2016).

The Bureau of Justice Statistics provides other important information on juvenile crime and victimization in *Criminal Victimization, 2015* (Jennifer L. Truman and Lynn Langton, October 2016) and *Rape and Sexual Assault Victimization among College-Age Females, 1995–2013* (Sofi Sinozich and Lynn Langton, December 2014). The Federal Bureau of Investigation's *Crime in the United States, 2015* (September 2016) also covers crime and victimization.

The Office of Juvenile Justice and Delinquency Prevention (OJJDP) of the U.S. Department of Justice was a valuable resource of information about youth violence, crime, and gangs in the United States. Various sources of the OJJDP provided important data that helped in the compilation of this book, including *Statistical Briefing Book* (2016), *Juvenile Offenders and Victims: 2014 National Report* (Melissa Sickmund and Charles Puzzanchera, December 2014), and *The Crime of Family Abduction* (May 2010). The annual reports of the National Youth Gang Survey, which are prepared by the OJJDP, and the annual National Gang Threat Assessments, which are issued by the National Gang Intelligence Center, were also helpful.

The Pew Research Center provides information and analysis about teen birth rates in "Why Is the Teen Birth Rate Falling?" (Eileen Patten and Gretchen Livingston, April 2016) and presents public opinion about juvenile offenders in *Public Opinion on Juvenile Justice in America* (December 2014). The Guttmacher Institute provided information on state sex education and abortion policies in its fact sheets. Child Care Aware of America provided information on the cost of child care in all 50 states.

INDEX

children living in single-parent families, 8–9

dropout rates, 97

foster care, children in, 11

health insurance coverage for children, 52

HIV/AIDS, children/teens with, 58

homicide victims, 113

infant mortality rate for, 67

juvenile homicide offenders, 105

nonfatal crimes at school and, 131

overweight/obesity among children, 59–60

poverty rate among, 24

reading scores of, 91

romantic/sexual relationships among teens, 78

teens, unemployment among, 32

youth in detention, 150

After Years of Labor Market Pain, 2015 Finally Gave Millennial Workers Reasons for Optimism (Frothingham & West), 32–33

Afterschool Alliance, 39

"Afterschool Essentials: Research and Polling" (Afterschool Alliance), 39

After-school programs, 21st CCLC, 39–40

Age

of adopted children, 13

arrestee's age, by offense category, 107*t*

arrests of persons under ages of 15, 18, 21, 25 years, 145*t*

birth rates by age of mother, 5(*f*1.4)

child care for school-aged children, 38–40

childhood/adulthood, definitions of, 1

of children, effect on family expenditures, 22–23

of children joining gangs, 120

death, five leading causes of, by age group, 113*t*

death, percentage distribution of 10 leading causes of, by age group, 71*f*

of homicide victims, 113

of juvenile homicide offenders, 105

of juvenile offenders, 104, 106

murder victims by age/weapon, 114*t*

obesity, children aged 6–17 who were obese, by sex, age, race/Hispanic origin, 61(*t*4.7)

offenders' age by offense category, 109*t*

poverty, percentage of population living in by, 27*f*

poverty rates by, 26*f*

prosecution of juveniles and, 143

of rape victims, 115

of runaways/thrownaways, 113

violent victimization trends and, 109

weapons used in assault/murder of juveniles and, 115

Aggravated assault

juvenile offenders, 106

victimization rate for, 109

Aid to Families with Dependent Children (AFDC), 27

AIDS. *See* Acquired immunodeficiency syndrome

"Aiming at Students: The College Gun Violence Epidemic" (Cannon), 130

Alabama, 87

Alabama, Miller v., 153, 154

Alcohol

effects on driving, 71, 72*f*

high school students drinking/using drugs before last sexual intercourse, 80*t*

high school students who ever used alcohol/marijuana and tried either before age 13, by sex, race/ethnicity, grade, 66(*t*4.12)

school discipline problems, 131

sexual activity among teens and, 79

use by children/adolescents, 64, 66

Allergic reactions, vaccine, 48

American Academy of Child and Adolescent Psychiatry, 133

American Academy of Pediatrics (AAP)

on sexual content in media, 79

on SIDS, 68

American Association of Community Colleges, 101

American Lung Association, 64

American Opportunity Tax Credit, 101–102

American Psychological Association (APA), 85–86

American Public Welfare Association, 11

American Recovery and Reinvestment Act (ARRA)

Race to the Top Fund, 92

SNAP maximum allotments of, 28

"American Teens' Sources of Sexual Health Education" (Guttmacher Institute), 87

America's Children in Brief: Key National Indicators of Well-Being, 2016 (Federal Interagency Forum on Child and Family Statistics)

on asthma, 60

on child care for school-aged children, 38–39

on family households, 6–7

on immunizations, 48

on population of children in U.S., 1, 2–3

on poverty rate for children, 8

on violent victimization of children, 115

America's Families and Living Arrangements (U.S. Census Bureau)

on children with stay-at-home parents, 7

on one- and two-parent families, 8

Anaphylactic shock, 48

Anencephaly, 47

Anophthalmia/microphthalmia, 47

Anorexia nervosa, 63–64

Anotia/microtia, 47

AOUM (abstinence-only-until-marriage) program, 87

APA (American Psychological Association), 85–86

"Appeals Court Affirms State Gun Control Laws Passed after Sandy Hook Shooting" (Wagner), 129

Arciaga, Michelle, 123

"Are Sexual Media Exposure, Parental Restrictions on Media Use and Co-viewing TV and DVDs with Parents and Friends Associated with Teenagers' Early Sexual Behaviour?" (Parkes et al.), 79

"Are Youth Psychopathic Traits Related to Bullying? Meta-analyses on Callous-Unemotional Traits, Narcissism, and Impulsivity" (van Geel et al.), 134

ARRA. *See* American Recovery and Reinvestment Act

Arrests

arrest trends, ten-year, 143*t*

arrest trends, ten-year, by sex, 147*t*

arrestee's age, by offense category, 107*t*

of juvenile offenders, 106

juvenile, trends in, 104

of juveniles, 144–147

of juveniles by race, 148*t*–149*t*

of persons under ages of 15, 18, 21, 25 years, 145*t*

Arson, juvenile arrests for, 144

Ashbaugh, Lauren P., 134

Asian Americans

birth trends, projected, 2

foster care, children in, 11

health insurance coverage for children, 52

HIV/AIDS, children/teens with, 58

juvenile homicide offenders, 105

reading scores of, 91

"Asking the Right Questions to Ascertain Early Childhood Secondhand Smoke Exposures" (Myers et al.), 57

"Assessing Youth Motivations for Joining a Peer Group as Risk Factors for Delinquent and Gang Behavior" (Lachman, Roman, & Cahill), 120

Associated Press, 48

"Association between Social Media Use and Depression among U.S. Young Adults" (Lin et al.), 73

"Associations between Life Contexts and Early Sexual Initiation among Young Women in France" (Jovic et al.), 77

Asthma

among children, 60

secondhand smoke and, 57

Attention-deficit/hyperactivity disorder (ADHD)

among children/adolescents, 64

diagnostic criteria, prevalence, treatment, timeline of, 65*f*

"Attitudes toward Juvenile Sex Offender Legislation: The Influence of Case-Specific Information" (Campregher & Jeglic), 135

Autism, MMR vaccine and, 48
"Awkward or Amazing: Gender and Age Trends in First Intercourse Experiences" (Walsh et al.), 78

B

Baby boomers, 96
Bachelor's degree
    number earned, 102
    percentage of persons aged 25–29 who completed bachelor's or higher degree, 90f
    percentage of young people who earned, 89
Baker, Al, 118
Balanced Budget Act, 52
Bank of Montreal, 108
Bar/bat mitzvah ceremonies, 1
Barnes, J. C., 124
Barnett, Jessica C., 49, 52
Barzee, Wanda, 112
Beaver, Kevin M., 124
Behavior
    disciplinary problems at schools, 131
    of homeless youth, 56
    school shooters and, 129
Ben-Itzhak, Yuval, 108
Berry, Amanda, 112
Betts, Julian R., 92
"Beyond an 'Either-Or' Approach to Home- and Center-Based Child Care: Comparing Children and Families Who Combine Care Types with Those Who Use Just One" (Gordon et al.), 42
"Beyond Correlations: Usefulness of High School GPA and Test Scores in Making College Admissions Decisions" (Sawyer), 100
Big Brothers Big Sisters program, 142
Bill & Melinda Gates Foundation, 90
Birnbaum, Michael, 108
Birth control
    condom/birth control pills, use among high school students by sex/race/ethnicity/grade, 82t
    pills, use of among teens, 81
Birth defects, 47–48
Birth rates
    by age of mother, 5(f1.4)
    birth trends, projected, 1–3
    births/birth rates for unmarried/married women, 10t
    calculation of, 1
    decline of, 3–4
    school enrollment rate and, 96
    for teens aged 15–17 by race/Hispanic origin, 6f
Births
    teen birth rates, urban/rural counties, 84f
    to unmarried women, rise in, 8
"Births: Final Data for 2014" (Hamilton et al.), 8

Bjørkly, Stål, 130
BJS. *See* U.S. Bureau of Justice Statistics
Blais, Martin, 78
Block grants, 43–44
Bloods, Los Angeles, 119
BLS. *See* U.S. Bureau of Labor Statistics
Body mass index (BMI)
    eating disorders and, 63
    measurement of obesity, 59
Boislard, Marie-Aude P.
    on effects of sexual activity on younger teens, 80–81
    on teens' first sexual experience, attitudes towards, 78
Bombs
    Columbine High School shooting and, 128
    threats at schools, 127
Bonnie, Richard J., 140
Boxer, Paul, 118
Boys. *See* Males
Boys and Girls Clubs of America, 141
"Boys and Girls Clubs of America: At a Glance" (Boys and Girls Club of America), 141
Braga, Anthony A., 126
Brank, Eve M., 140
Branum, Amy M., 83
Breckenridge, Ross A., 69
Breivik, Anders Behring, 129
Brewster, Tom, 108
Brown, Emma, 100
Brown, Jeffrey, 100–101
Bulimia nervosa, 63–64
Bullying
    bullies, characteristics of, 133–134
    cyberbullying, 134–135
    of Eric Harris/Dylan Klebold, 129
    high school students who were electronically bullied and who were bullied at school, by sex, race/ethnicity, grade, 133t
    prevention programs, 135–136
    at school, trends in, 131
    at schools, 132–136
    victims of, 134
    youth suicide and, 72
"Bullying, Cyberbullying, and Suicide" (Hinduja & Patchin), 135
Bullying in Schools (Sampson), 133
Burchinal, Margaret, 43
Burglary, 106
Buse, Kent, 86
Bush, George W.
    Individuals with Disabilities Education Improvement Act, 98
    No Child Left Behind Act, 136
Bush, Jeb, 91

C

Cahill, Meagan, 120
California
    Dugard, Jaycee Lee, kidnapping, 112
    gun carrying by school personnel in, 132
    gun safety law of, 140
"California School District Votes to Allow Teachers to Carry Guns in the Classroom" (Tesfaye), 132
Callous-unemotional (CU) traits, 134
Campaign for Youth Justice, 151–152
Campregher, Julia, 135
Cannon, Ashley, 130
CAP (Chicago Area Project), 141
Caring for Our Children: National Health and Safety Performance Standards; Guidelines for Early Care and Education (National Resource Center for Health and Safety in Child Care and Early Education), 42
Carr, Jillian B., 86
Castro, Ariel, 112
Castro, Estivaliz, 119–120
Cato Institute, 91
CCAA. *See* Child Care Aware of America
CCDBG (Child Care and Development Block Grant), 43
CCSS. *See* Common Core state standards
CDC. *See* Centers for Disease Control and Prevention
"CDC's National Surveillance Data (1997–2015)" (CDC), 57
Cell phones, cyberbullying with, 134–135
Center for American Progress, 91
Center for Law and Social Policy, 44
Center for Native American Youth, 122–123
Center-based care
    percentage of children aged 3–6 in, by child and family characteristics/region, 41t
    percentage of children receiving, 40
Centers for Disease Control and Prevention (CDC)
    on ADHD, 64
    on asthma, 60
    on birth defects, 47
    on deaths among young people, cases of, 113
    on e-cigarettes, 64
    on HIV/AIDS in children/teens, 58–59
    on immunizations, 48–49
    on lead poisoning, 56–57
    LGBT Youth Resources (website), 86
    on motor vehicle crashes, 71
    on physical fights at schools, 131
    on risk factors for youth violence, 104
    on sexual experience among teen girls, 79–80
    on SIDS, 67–68
    on STIs among young people, 82–83

depression, youth aged 12–17 who had at least one major depressive episode in past year by age, sex, race/Hispanic origin, poverty status, 75(t4.21)

drug/alcohol use by, 64, 66

eating disorders and, 63–64

e-cigarette advertising sources that affect youth, 68f

e-cigarette use among youth, advertising spending and, 69f

exercise by, 59–60

GPA, future earnings and, 102

having sexual intercourse/sexual intercourse for first time before age 13, by sex/race/ethnicity/grade, 78t

illegal drug use by, 108–109

nonfatal crimes against students aged 12–18 per 1,000 students, rate of, by type of crime/location, 132f

nonfatal crimes at school, 131–133

not using pregnancy prevention method-drinking/using drugs before last sexual intercourse, 80t

physical/sexual dating violence among, by sex/race/ethnicity/grade, 81t

school-based violence prevention programs, 142

suicide, students who attempted, whose suicide attempt resulted in injury that required medical treatment, by sex, race/ethnicity, grade, 74(t4.19)

suicide, students who seriously considered attempting, made suicide plan, by sex, race/ethnicity, grade, 74(t4.18)

violent deaths at school, 127–130

who attended physical education classes on one or more days per week, by sex, grade, race/ethnicity, 62(t4.10)

who bought cigarettes in store or gas station, by sex, race/ethnicity, grade, 66(t4.13)

who currently used tobacco, by sex, race/ethnicity, grade, 67(t4.15)

who did not participate in at least 60 minutes of physical activity on at least 1 day/students who were physically active at least 60 minutes/day on 5 or more days, by sex, race/ethnicity, grade, 62(t4.9)

who ever smoked cigarettes, students who smoked cigarette before age 13, by sex, race/ethnicity, grade, 67(t4.14)

who ever used alcohol/marijuana, tried either before age 13, by sex, race/ethnicity, grade, 66(t4.12)

who ever used electronic vapor products, current users by sex, race/ethnicity, grade, 69t

who felt sad or hopeless, by sex, race/ethnicity, grade, 75(t4.20)

who were electronically bullied/who were bullied at school, by sex, race/ethnicity, grade, 133t

who were overweight/obese, by sex/race/ethnicity/grade, 61(t4.8)

Higher education. See College

"Highlights of the 2012 National Youth Gang Survey" (Egley, Howell, & Harris), 117–118

Hildebrand, Mikaela, 86

Hill, Holly A., 48

Hill, Karl G., 125

Hinduja, Sameer
  on bullying at school, 133
  on cyberbullying, 134–135

Hispanics
  arrests of juveniles, numbers of, 145–147
  birth trends, projected, 2
  bullying at school and, 133
  children, poverty among, 24
  children living in single-parent families, 9
  dropout rates, 97
  foster care, children in, 11
  health insurance coverage for children, 52
  Hispanic gangs, spread of, 121
  Hispanic origin, employed teens/young adults 16–24 by, 32t
  Hispanic origin, median income by, 22t
  HIV/AIDS, children/teens with, 58
  juvenile homicide offenders, 105
  nonfatal crimes at school and, 131
  overweight/obesity among children, 59–60
  reading scores of, 91

HIV. See Human immunodeficiency virus

HIV Surveillance Report, 2014 (CDC), 58–59

Hobbs, Frank, 4, 6

Hobbs, Jackson v., 153

Hochevar, Katherine, 140

Hockenberry, Sarah
  on juvenile public order/drug/property offense cases, 144
  on juveniles in detention, 150
  on youth in residential placement, 150–151

"Holding Parents Responsible: Is Vicarious Responsibility the Public's Answer to Juvenile Crime?" (Brank, Greene, & Hochevar), 140

Homelessness
  among children, 53, 56
  school attendance by, 98–99

Homeschool Legal Defense Association, 99

Homeschooled children, 99

Homicide
  gang related, 124–125
  juvenile homicide offenders, 105
  murder offenders by age, sex, race/ethnicity, 105t
  murder victims by age/weapon, 114t
  nonfamily abductions and, 112

school-associated violent deaths, number of, 128t

victims of, 113, 115

violent deaths at school, 127–130

Homma, Yuko, 80

Homosexuality
  education on, state mandated, 87
  among teens, 85–86

Honan, Mat, 108

"Hospitalizations Due to Firearm Injuries in Children and Adolescents" (Leventhal, Gaither, & Sege), 115

Household Food Security in the United States in 2015 (Coleman-Jensen), 56

Households
  children under 18 who live with their mother only, percentage of, 1960–2016, 8f
  children with stay-at-home parents, 7–8
  effects on children's inclination to gang membership, 120
  family groups, 2016, 9t
  family/household size, 4, 6
  living arrangements of children, 1960 to 2016, 7f
  nonfamily households, increase in, 6–7
  one- and two-parent families, 8
  single-parent families, 8–9
  SNAP maximum monthly allotment by numbers in household, 28t
  types of, median income by, 22t

Housing
  lack of affordable housing as cause of homelessness, 56
  lead paint and, 57

Houston, Texas, 141

Houston Police Department, 141

How America Pays for College 2016 (Sallie Mae), 101

How Has Labor Force Participation among Young Moms and Dads Changed? A Comparison of Two Cohorts (Dey), 35–37

Howell, James C.
  on gang involvement, indicators of, 121
  on gang members, distribution of in U.S., 117–118
  on gangs, drugs/guns/crime at school and, 124
  on gangs, reasons for joining, 120

Hoxby, Caroline, 100–101

HPV. See Human papillomavirus

Hudak, Stephen, 136

HuffingtonPost.com, 108

Human immunodeficiency virus (HIV)
  children/teens with, 58–59
  school education about, 87

Human papillomavirus (HPV)
  among teens, 83
  vaccine, adolescents who received, 48
  vaccine, teens and, 58

on involuntary sexual activity among teens, 80
on physical fights at schools, 131
on physical/sexual violence by boyfriend/girlfriend among teens, 81
on sexual activity among teens, 77
on suicide, 71–73
on use of contraceptives among teens, 81
Kasich, John, 91
Keeping Informed about School Vouchers: A Review of Major Developments and Research (Usher & Kober), 92
Kena, Grace
The Condition of Education 2016, 89
on private school enrollment, 96–97
on public school enrollment, 96
on testing for student performance assessment, 91
Kentucky, Stanford v., 153
Ketamine (Special K), 109
Key Injury and Violence Data (CDC), 113
Kidnapping
family abductions, 111
Missing Children's Assistance Act, 111
nonfamily abductions, 112
"Kids and Gun Safety" (Patel), 140
Klaas, Polly, 112
Klebold, Dylan, 128–129
Klebold, Tom, 129
Kober, Nancy, 92
Kochhar, Shivani, 28
Kollar, Melissa A.
on household income, post–Great Recession, 21
on poverty rate among children, 23
Kreager, Derek A., 77

L

Labor force
weeks men spent out of, by race/parental status, 37*f*
weeks new mothers spent out of, in year following birth of first child, by presence of father in household/race, 37(*t*3.3)
weeks spent out of after birth of first child, by education/sex, 37(*t*3.2)
weeks women spent out of, by race/parental status, 36*f*
working mothers, 35–38
See also Employment
Lachman, Pamela, 120
Lancet, 48
Langton, Lynn, 115
Language, gang, 118
Lanza, Adam, 129
LaPierre, Wayne, 129
Larceny-theft, 106
Larson, Kandyce, 63
Larsson, Margareta, 80

Latchkey kids, 39
"Latest Research Shows School Meals Improve Food Security, Dietary Intake, and Weight Outcomes, Says Food Research & Action Center" (Food Research and Action Center), 29
Lauen, Douglas Lee, 89–90
Lavery, Lesley E., 90
Law enforcement
crime prevention strategies of, 141–142
laws for juvenile crime prevention, 139–141
police disposition of juvenile offenders taken into custody, 150*t*
Layton, Lyndsey, 100
LBW (low birth weight), 83
Lead poisoning, 56–57
Lecesne, James, 86
Legal intervention, 127
Legislation and international treaties
Adoption and Safe Families Act, 10
Affordable Care Act, 35, 52–53
American Recovery and Reinvestment Act, 28, 92
Balanced Budget Act, 52
Child Support Recovery Act, delinquent noncustodial parents and, 30–31
Children's Health Insurance Program Reauthorization Act, 52
Consumer Product Safety Improvement Act, 57
E. Clay Shaw, Jr. Missing Children's Assistance Reauthorization Act, 111
Economic Opportunity Act, 95
Education of the Handicapped Act, 97–98
Elementary and Secondary Education Act, 39
Family and Medical Leave Act, 35, 44–45
Gun-Free Schools Act, 131
Individuals with Disabilities Education Act, 98
Individuals with Disabilities Education Improvement Act, 98
McKinney-Vento Homeless Assistance Act, 98–99
McKinney-Vento Homeless Education Assistance Improvements Act, 99
Missing Children's Assistance Act, 111
No Child Left Behind Act, 39–40, 89–92, 136–137
Personal Responsibility and Work Opportunity Reconciliation Act, 24, 31, 43
Pregnancy Discrimination Act, 35
Social Security Act, Title V, 86, 87
Lesbian, gay, bisexual, transgender (LGBT)
prejudice/discrimination against, 85–86
programs in support of, 86
sexual minority status as risk factor for suicide, 72–73

Leubsdorf, Ben, 7–8
Leventhal, John M., 115
Levine, Phillip B., 142
LGBT Youth Resources (website), 86
Li, Qing, 134
Licensing requirements, child care facilities, 42
Life imprisonment-without-parole, 153
Lin, Liu yi, 73
"Linking Childhood Sexual Abuse and Early Adolescent Risk Behavior: The Intervening Role of Internalizing and Externalizing Problems" (Jones et al.), 77
Living arrangements
of children, 1960 to 2016, 7*f*
children under 18 who live with their mother only, percentage of, 1960–2016, 8*f*
family groups, 2016, 9*t*
foster care/adoption, 10–14
grandparents, 10
marital conflict/divorce, effect on children, 60, 62–63
nontraditional families, 9–10
single-parent families, 8–9
of young adults, 15–17
Livingston, Gretchen, 4
Logan, Jesse, 135
Long, Bridget Terry, 100–101
"A Longitudinal Study of the Effects of Child-Reported Maternal Warmth on Cortisol Stress Response 15 Years after Parental Divorce" (Luecken et al.), 63
"Long-Term Consequences of Adolescent Gang Membership for Adult Functioning" (Gilman, Hill, & Hawkins), 125
"Long-Term Health Consequences of Violence Exposure in Adolescence: A 26-Year Prospective Study" (Olofsson et al.), 109–110
"Long-Term Health Correlates of Timing of Sexual Debut: Results from a National U.S. Study" (Sandfort et al.), 77
Los Angeles Bloods, 119
Louisiana, sexting law of, 135
Love Is Respect, 115
Low birth weight (LBW), 83
Luecken, Linda J., 63
Lyles, Sylvia, 40

M

Macur, Juliet, 136
Maguire, Kathleen, 147
Makenzius, Marlene, 80
"Male Involvement in Family Planning: The Estimated Influence of Improvements in Condom Use and Efficacy on Nonmarital Births among Teens and Young Adults" (Manlove et al.), 84–85

Program for International Student
Assessment (PISA), 91

Projections of Education Statistics to 2023
(NCES), 100

"Promises Kept? A Meta-analysis of Gang
Membership Prevention Programs"
(Wong et al.), 126

"Promoting Resilience for Children Who
Experience Family Homelessness:
Opportunities to Encourage
Developmental Competence" (Cutuli &
Herbers), 56

Property crime
robbery, burglary, larceny-theft, 106
trends in, 103

Puberty, 1

"The Public Charter Schools Dashboard"
(National Alliance for Public Charter
Schools), 92

Public health insurance, 52

*Public Opinion on Juvenile Justice in
America* (Pew Charitable Trusts), 152

Public school
cost of, 93–94
elementary/secondary school, 96–99
expenditures per pupil in public
elementary/secondary schools, 94t
No Child Left Behind Act and, 89–92
public school choice program, 92
public school enrollment, actual/
projected, 2003–04 through 2025–26,
96f
reporting of violence/crime at school,
137
students with disabilities and, 97–98
See also Education; Schools

Punishment. *See* Crime prevention/
punishment

Putnam-Hornstein, Emily, 83–84

Puzzanchera, Charles
on juvenile crime trends, 103–104
on juvenile public order/drug/property
offense cases, 144
on juveniles in detention, 150
on youth in residential placement,
150–151

Q

*Q4 2012 AVG Community Powered Threat
Report* (Ben-Itzhak), 108

"Quarterly Provisional Estimates for
Selected Birth Indicators, 2014—Quarter
2, 2016" (Rossen et al.), 1

"Questions and Answers on No Child Left
Behind" (U.S. Department of
Education), 136

QuickGuide to Gangs (NGIC), 119

"QuickStats: Death Rates for Motor Vehicle
Traffic Injury, Suicide, and Homicide
among Children and Adolescents Aged
10–14 Years—United States,
1999–2014" (Curtin et al.), 71

R

Race/ethnicity
adolescents aged 13–17 vaccinated for
selected diseases by poverty status,
race/Hispanic origin, 50t–51t
of adopted children, 13
AIDS in children younger than 13 years
of age, diagnoses of, by year of
diagnosis, race/Hispanic origin, 59t
arrests of juveniles by, 148t–149t
asthma among children and, 60
birth rates for teens aged 15–17 by, 6f
birth trends, projected, 2–3
bullying at school and, 133
child care, differences by, 40–41
children aged 0–17, percentage of, by
race/Hispanic origin, 5(f1.3)
of children in foster care, 11
of children living in single-parent
families, 8–9
children living with grandparents and,
10
of children served by Head Start, 96
death rates among infants by race/
Hispanic origin of mother, 70t
dropout rates by, 97, 97f
employed teens/young adults 16–24 by,
32t
fertility rates, total, by race/Hispanic
origin, 3t
health insurance coverage for children
by, 52
HIV/AIDS, children/teens with, 58
of homicide victims, 113
hunger and, 56
infant mortality rate and, 67
juvenile arrests by, 145–147
of juvenile homicide offenders, 105
median income by, 22t
nonfatal crimes at school and, 131
obesity, children aged 6–17 who were
obese, by sex, age, race/Hispanic
origin, 61(t4.7)
obesity, high school students who were
overweight or obese, by sex, race/
ethnicity, grade, 61(t4.8)
overweight/obesity among children by,
59–60
population distribution by race/Hispanic
origin, 2014 and 2060, 4f
reading scores by, 91
serious violent victimization rates for
teens aged 12–17 by, 116f
teen birth rate and, 4
tobacco users by, 64
vaccination coverage among children
aged 19–35 months by race/ethnicity/
poverty level, 49t
of victims of serious violent
victimization, 115

Race to the Top Fund, 92–93

"Race to the Top Program: Executive
Summary" (U.S. Department of
Education), 92

Rajski, Peggy, 86

Rape
juvenile offenders, 106
victimization rate for, 109
victims of, 115

"Rape and Sexual Assault Victimization
among College-Age Females,
1995–2013" (Sinozich & Langton),
115

Rasmussen, Sonja A., 48

Rathbun, Amy, 40

Ravi, Dharun, 135

Ravitch, Diane, 91

Ray, Brian D., 99

Reading, 91

"Recent Recalls" (CPSC), 57

Recruitment, gang, 120–121

Regret, early sexual activity, 78

Regulation, child care facility, 42–43

Relationship
homicide victim-offender relationship,
113, 115
rape victim-offender relationship, 115

"The Relationship between Sexual Abuse
and Risky Sexual Behavior among
Adolescent Boys: A Meta-analysis"
(Homma et al.), 80

Religious schools, 96–97

"Report Finds Juvenile Program Failed to
Reduce Robberies, but Police Are
Expanding It" (Goodman), 142

Reporting, violence/crime at school, 137

Republican National Committee, 91

"Research Facts on Homeschooling"
(Ray), 99

"Research into Cyberbullying" (Li, Smith,
& Cross), 134

"Research Quality and Psychological
Theory in Publications on School
Shooters with Multiple Victims— A
Systematic Review of the Literature"
(Grøndahl & Bjørkly), 130

Residential placement, 150–151

Resources, young crime victims, 115

Responding to Gangs in the School Setting
(Arciaga, Sakamoto, & Jones), 123

Ridgeway, Greg, 124

"The Right to Belong: Individual Motives
and Youth Gang Initiation Rites"
(Descormiers & Corrado), 121

"Risk, Promotive, and Protective Factors in
Youth Offending: Results from the
Cambridge Study in Delinquent
Development" (Farrington, Ttofi, &
Piquero), 105

Risks
factors, youth violence/delinquency,
104–105
for runaways/thrownaways, 113

"Women, Infants and Children (WIC): Frequently Asked Questions about WIC" (FNS), 28

Wong, Jennifer S., 126

Wood, Jane L., 120

"Work-Life Earnings by Field of Degree and Occupation for People with a Bachelor's Degree: 2011" (Julian), 102

The World Factbook (CIA), 3–4

Wyrick, Phelan A.
  on gang involvement, indicators of, 121
  on gangs, reasons for joining, 120

X

Xuan, Ziming, 73

Y

"Young Adulthood as a Transitional Legal Category: Science, Social Change and Justice Policy" (Scott, Bonnie, & Steinberg), 140

Young adults
  crime prevention, 139–142
  justice system classification of, 140
  living arrangements of, 15–17

victimization rate for, 109

young adults living with their parents, 20*f*

"You're an Adult Now: Youth in Adult Criminal Justice Systems" (Ziedenberg), 152

Youth, definition of, 104

"Youth Exposure to Violence Prevention Programs in a National Sample" (Finkelhor et al.), 139

"Youth Gangs and Adolescent Development: New Findings, New Challenges, and New Directions: Introduction to the Special Section" (Boxer), 118

"Youth in the Adult Criminal Justice System" (Ryan), 151–152

"Youth Risk Behavior Surveillance— United States, 2015" (Kann et al.)
  on drugs/alcohol use among teens, 79
  on inactive lifestyles of children, 59
  on involuntary sexual activity among teens, 80
  on physical fights at schools, 131
  on physical/sexual violence by boyfriend/girlfriend among teens, 81
  on sexual activity among teens, 77

on use of contraceptives among teens, 81

"Youth Sexting: Prevalence Rates, Driving Motivations, and the Deterrent Effect of Legal Consequences" (Strohmaier, Murphy, & DeMatteo), 135

YouTube, 119

Z

Zahn, Margaret A., 104–105

Zeng, Zhen, 151

Zhang, Anlan
  on child care for preschoolers, 40
  on gang presence in schools, 123, 124
  on reporting of violence/crime at school, 137
  on school security/discipline, 130–131
  on violent deaths at school, 127
  on weapons in school, 131, 132–133

Ziedenberg, Jason, 152

Zika virus, 47–48

"Zika Virus and Birth Defects—Reviewing the Evidence for Causality" (Rasmussen et al.), 47–48

Zimmerman, David J., 142

Zimring, Franklin E., 144